H O W D Y

I JUST FINISHED DRAWING THE LAST PAGE FOR THIS BOOK, THE LAST SPOKEN WORD BEING 'TIT'. I THOUGHT I'D LEAVE WRITING THIS FOREWORD UNTIL THE VERY END, SO THAT AFTER COMPLETING THE EXTRA PAGES (SORRY, EXCLUSIVE PAGES), I'D HAVE SOME VERY POIGNANT THINGS TO SAY UPON GREETING YOU. NO OKAY, I JUST DIDN'T KNOW WHAT TO SAY. THIS BOOK COMPLETES THE BEAR SERIES, AND THE LAST THREE YEARS OF MY LIFE. IT'S BEEN AN INTENSIVE PERIOD, ISSUES TAKE A LONG TIME TO COMPLETE AS ANY COMIC TYPE WILL TELL YOU, BUT IT'S BEEN WORTH EVERY SECOND. I DIDN'T DO COMICS TO GET RICH, OR A TWO GRAND TV, I DID THEM BECAUSE OTHERWISE I'D HAVE VENTED THE THINGS IN MY HEAD BY SUMMONING UNEARTHLY SPIRITS AND JOYRIDING. DRAWING COMICS IS A VERY PERSONAL THING, IT CAN'T NOT BE. AND AS SUCH IT'S QUITE A SELFISH PURSUIT. I DID THIS CRAP TO KEEP ME AMUSED. THE FACT THAT ANYONE ELSE GOT A BUZZ OUT OF IT WAS MOST UNEXPECTED. ANYWAY, PLEASE ENJOY THIS SECOND BEAR COLLECTION. I'M WORKING ON A FEW OTHER THINGS, COMICS AND OTHERWISE, DETAILS OF WHICH CAN INVARIABLY BE FOUND ON THE LINKS BELOW IF YOU'RE INTERESTED. A CLAWING NEED TO DRAW MORE BEAR MAY ARISE IN THE FUTURE, I DON'T KNOW, BUT FOR NOW I'D LIKE TO LEAVE IT WHEN IT'S DOING WELL AND BE PROUD OF IT FOR THAT.
THANK YOU TO SLAVE LABOR FOR NOT ONLY LETTING ME DO STUPID STUFF, BUT ACTIVELY ENCOURAGING IT. THANKS ALSO TO MY FAMILY AND FRIENDS, WHO HAVE FINALLY HAD THEIR SUPPORT REWARDED WITH FREE BEAR TOYS. SO NO MORE BITCHING. THANK YOU TO EVAN, BARD, BENJAMIN, AARON AND JHONEN FOR THE FANTASTIC PAGES, NOT ONLY WAS IT REAL KIND THAT YOU AGREED TO IT, BUT IT MEANT I HAD 5 PAGES LESS WORK TO DO. EVERYONE'S A WINNER!! THANK YOU TO LISA FOR THE SPYING, AND RHIANNON FOR MAKING ME FIT IN MY OWN HEAD. THANK YOU TO THE STORES THAT SUPPORTED BEAR, AND POO TO THOSE THAT PREFER NOBBY SUPERHEROES. THANKS TO DEAN, NIGEL AND LISA AT ABSTRACT SPROCKET FOR THE UNNERVING ENTHUSIASM AND THE FREE GIRL!! HOORAY!! AND THANK YOU TO LIZI FOR HOLDING ME TOGETHER, WHO I LOVE LIKE A CRAZY ASSED BASTARD.

CHEERS THEN. SEE YOU SOON.
♡ JAMIE

Published by SLG Publishing

20 ANNIVERSARY

P.O. Box 26427
San Jose, CA 95159

Bear Volume Two: Demons
collects issues 6-10 of the
SLG Publishing series *Bear*.

www.slgpublishing.com
www.bearfoo.com

First Printing: May 2006

BOHDATE

come see the glories!! www.bohdate.com!! whoop diggy!!

C 02 0317894

D1512638

For. Lizi.

BEAR DEMONS

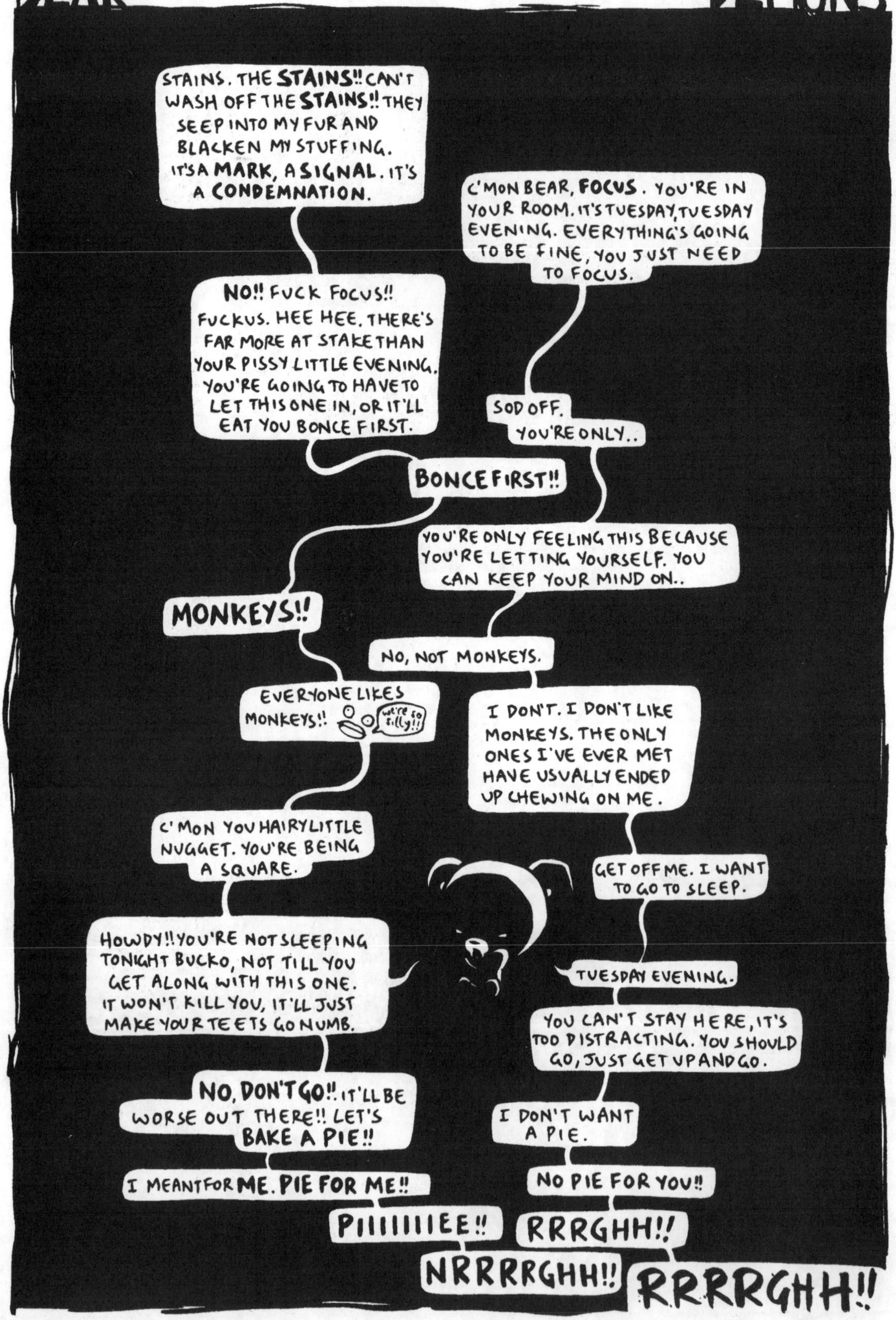
STAINS. THE STAINS!! CAN'T WASH OFF THE STAINS!! THEY SEEP INTO MY FUR AND BLACKEN MY STUFFING. IT'S A MARK, A SIGNAL. IT'S A CONDEMNATION.
C'MON BEAR, FOCUS. YOU'RE IN YOUR ROOM. IT'S TUESDAY, TUESDAY EVENING. EVERYTHING'S GOING TO BE FINE, YOU JUST NEED TO FOCUS.
NO!! FUCK FOCUS!! FUCKUS. HEE HEE. THERE'S FAR MORE AT STAKE THAN YOUR PISSY LITTLE EVENING. YOU'RE GOING TO HAVE TO LET THIS ONE IN, OR IT'LL EAT YOU BONCE FIRST.
SOD OFF. YOU'RE ONLY..
BONCE FIRST!!
YOU'RE ONLY FEELING THIS BECAUSE YOU'RE LETTING YOURSELF. YOU CAN KEEP YOUR MIND ON..
MONKEYS!!
NO, NOT MONKEYS.
EVERYONE LIKES MONKEYS!!
we're so silly!!
I DON'T. I DON'T LIKE MONKEYS. THE ONLY ONES I'VE EVER MET HAVE USUALLY ENDED UP CHEWING ON ME.
C'MON YOU HAIRY LITTLE NUGGET. YOU'RE BEING A SQUARE.
GET OFF ME. I WANT TO GO TO SLEEP.
HOWDY!! YOU'RE NOT SLEEPING TONIGHT BUCKO, NOT TILL YOU GET ALONG WITH THIS ONE. IT WON'T KILL YOU, IT'LL JUST MAKE YOUR TEETS GO NUMB.
TUESDAY EVENING.
YOU CAN'T STAY HERE, IT'S TOO DISTRACTING. YOU SHOULD GO, JUST GET UP AND GO.
NO, DON'T GO!! IT'LL BE WORSE OUT THERE!! LET'S BAKE A PIE!!
I DON'T WANT A PIE.
I MEANT FOR ME. PIE FOR ME!!
NO PIE FOR YOU!!
PIIIIIIIEE!!
RRRGHH!!
NRRRRGHH!!
RRRRGHH!!

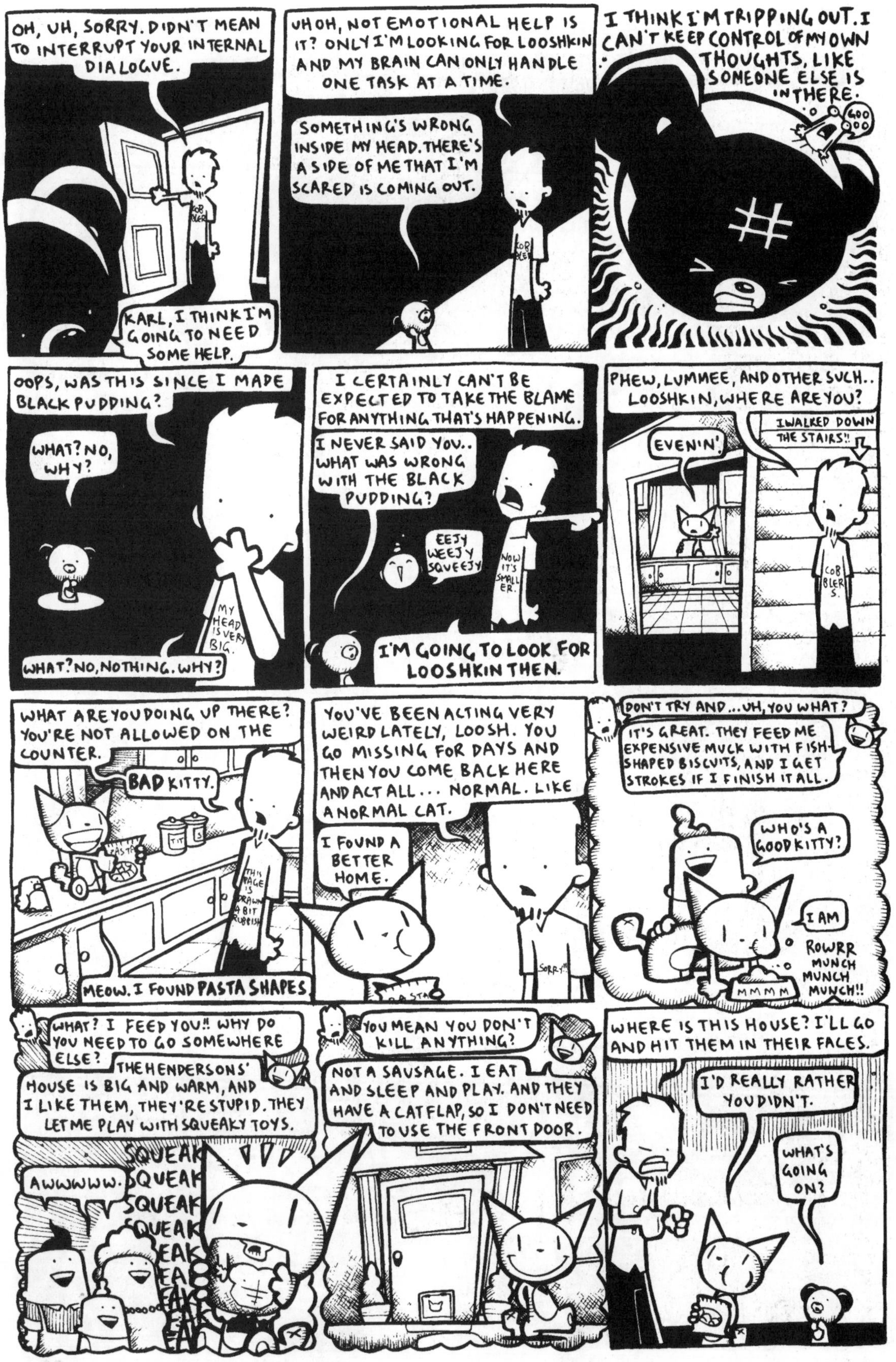

OH, UH, SORRY. DIDN'T MEAN TO INTERRUPT YOUR INTERNAL DIALOGUE.
KARL, I THINK I'M GOING TO NEED SOME HELP.
COB BLER
UH OH, NOT EMOTIONAL HELP IS IT? ONLY I'M LOOKING FOR LOOSHKIN AND MY BRAIN CAN ONLY HANDLE ONE TASK AT A TIME.
SOMETHING'S WRONG INSIDE MY HEAD. THERE'S A SIDE OF ME THAT I'M SCARED IS COMING OUT.
COB BLER
I THINK I'M TRIPPING OUT. I CAN'T KEEP CONTROL OF MY OWN THOUGHTS, LIKE SOMEONE ELSE IS IN THERE.
GOO
OOPS, WAS THIS SINCE I MADE BLACK PUDDING?
WHAT? NO, WHY?
MY HEAD IS VERY BIG.
WHAT? NO, NOTHING. WHY?
I CERTAINLY CAN'T BE EXPECTED TO TAKE THE BLAME FOR ANYTHING THAT'S HAPPENING.
I NEVER SAID YOU.. WHAT WAS WRONG WITH THE BLACK PUDDING?
EEJY WEEJY SQUEEJY
NOW IT'S SMALLER.
I'M GOING TO LOOK FOR LOOSHKIN THEN.
PHEW, LUMMEE, AND OTHER SUCH.. LOOSHKIN, WHERE ARE YOU?
EVENIN'.
I WALKED DOWN THE STAIRS!!
COB BLER S.
WHAT ARE YOU DOING UP THERE? YOU'RE NOT ALLOWED ON THE COUNTER.
BAD KITTY.
PASTA
TH
S
THIS PAGE IS DRAWN A BIT RUBBISH
MEOW. I FOUND PASTA SHAPES.
YOU'VE BEEN ACTING VERY WEIRD LATELY, LOOSH. YOU GO MISSING FOR DAYS AND THEN YOU COME BACK HERE AND ACT ALL... NORMAL. LIKE A NORMAL CAT.
I FOUND A BETTER HOME.
SORRY!!
PASTA
DON'T TRY AND... UH, YOU WHAT?
IT'S GREAT. THEY FEED ME EXPENSIVE MUCK WITH FISH-SHAPED BISCUITS, AND I GET STROKES IF I FINISH IT ALL.
WHO'S A GOOD KITTY?
I AM
ROWRR MUNCH MUNCH MUNCH!!
MMMM
WHAT? I FEED YOU!! WHY DO YOU NEED TO GO SOMEWHERE ELSE?
THE HENDERSONS' HOUSE IS BIG AND WARM, AND I LIKE THEM, THEY'RE STUPID. THEY LET ME PLAY WITH SQUEAKY TOYS.
SQUEAK SQUEAK SQUEAK SQUEAK
AWWWWW.
YOU MEAN YOU DON'T KILL ANYTHING?
NOT A SAUSAGE. I EAT AND SLEEP AND PLAY. AND THEY HAVE A CATFLAP, SO I DON'T NEED TO USE THE FRONT DOOR.
WHERE IS THIS HOUSE? I'LL GO AND HIT THEM IN THEIR FACES.
I'D REALLY RATHER YOU DIDN'T.
WHAT'S GOING ON?

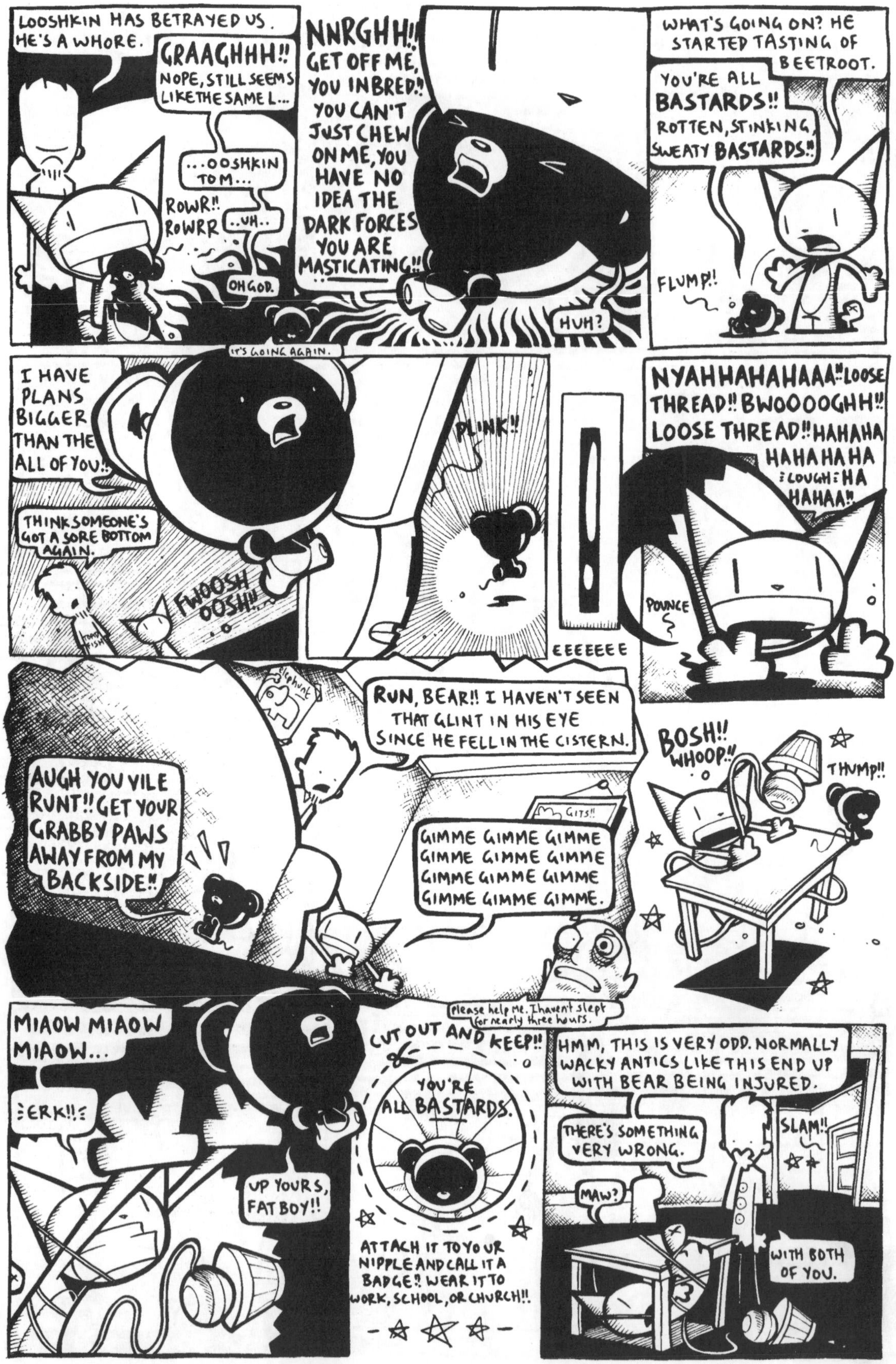
LOOSHKIN HAS BETRAYED US. HE'S A WHORE.
GRAAGHHH!! NOPE, STILL SEEMS LIKE THE SAME L...
...OOSHKIN TOM...
ROWR!! ROWRR
...UH...
OH GOD.
NNRGHH!! GET OFF ME, YOU INBRED!! YOU CAN'T JUST CHEW ON ME, YOU HAVE NO IDEA THE DARK FORCES YOU ARE MASTICATING!!
HUH?
WHAT'S GOING ON? HE STARTED TASTING OF BEETROOT.
YOU'RE ALL BASTARDS!! ROTTEN, STINKING, SWEATY BASTARDS!!
FLUMP!!
IT'S GOING AGAIN.
I HAVE PLANS BIGGER THAN THE ALL OF YOU!!
THINK SOMEONE'S GOT A SORE BOTTOM AGAIN.
FWOOSH OOSH!!
PLINK!!
EEEEEEE
NYAHHAHAHAAA!! LOOSE THREAD!! BWOOOOGHH!! LOOSE THREAD!! HAHAHA HAHAHAHA :COUGH: HA HAHAA!!
POUNCE
AUGH YOU VILE RUNT!! GET YOUR GRABBY PAWS AWAY FROM MY BACKSIDE!!
RUN, BEAR!! I HAVEN'T SEEN THAT GLINT IN HIS EYE SINCE HE FELL IN THE CISTERN.
GITS!!
GIMME GIMME GIMME GIMME GIMME GIMME GIMME GIMME GIMME GIMME GIMME GIMME.
Please help me. I haven't slept for nearly three hours.
BOSH!! WHOOP!!
THUMP!!
MIAOW MIAOW MIAOW...
:ERK!!:
UP YOURS, FAT BOY!!
CUT OUT AND KEEP!!
YOU'RE ALL BASTARDS.
ATTACH IT TO YOUR NIPPLE AND CALL IT A BADGE!! WEAR IT TO WORK, SCHOOL, OR CHURCH!!
HMM, THIS IS VERY ODD. NORMALLY WACKY ANTICS LIKE THIS END UP WITH BEAR BEING INJURED.
THERE'S SOMETHING VERY WRONG.
SLAM!!
MAW?
WITH BOTH OF YOU.

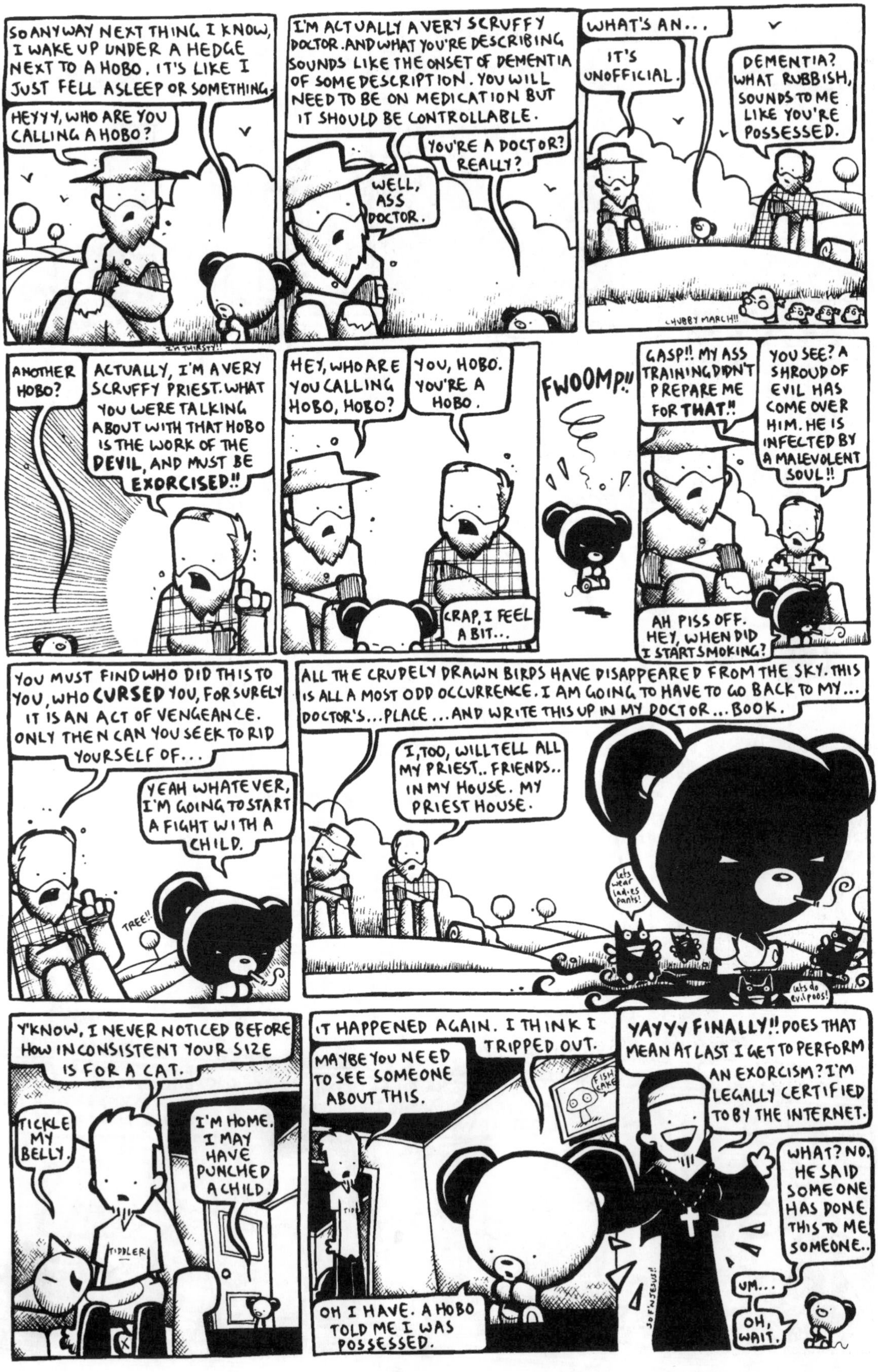

SO ANYWAY NEXT THING I KNOW, I WAKE UP UNDER A HEDGE NEXT TO A HOBO. IT'S LIKE I JUST FELL ASLEEP OR SOMETHING.
HEYYY, WHO ARE YOU CALLING A HOBO?
I'M ACTUALLY A VERY SCRUFFY DOCTOR. AND WHAT YOU'RE DESCRIBING SOUNDS LIKE THE ONSET OF DEMENTIA OF SOME DESCRIPTION. YOU WILL NEED TO BE ON MEDICATION BUT IT SHOULD BE CONTROLLABLE.
YOU'RE A DOCTOR? REALLY?
WELL, ASS DOCTOR.
WHAT'S AN...
IT'S UNOFFICIAL.
DEMENTIA? WHAT RUBBISH, SOUNDS TO ME LIKE YOU'RE POSSESSED.
CHUBBY MARCH!!
ANOTHER HOBO?
ACTUALLY, I'M A VERY SCRUFFY PRIEST. WHAT YOU WERE TALKING ABOUT WITH THAT HOBO IS THE WORK OF THE DEVIL, AND MUST BE EXORCISED!!
HEY, WHO ARE YOU CALLING HOBO, HOBO?
YOU, HOBO. YOU'RE A HOBO.
CRAP, I FEEL A BIT...
FWOOMP!!
GASP!! MY ASS TRAINING DIDN'T PREPARE ME FOR THAT!!
YOU SEE? A SHROUD OF EVIL HAS COME OVER HIM. HE IS INFECTED BY A MALEVOLENT SOUL!!
AH PISS OFF. HEY, WHEN DID I START SMOKING?
YOU MUST FIND WHO DID THIS TO YOU, WHO CURSED YOU, FOR SURELY IT IS AN ACT OF VENGEANCE. ONLY THEN CAN YOU SEEK TO RID YOURSELF OF...
YEAH WHATEVER, I'M GOING TO START A FIGHT WITH A CHILD.
TREE!!
ALL THE CRUDELY DRAWN BIRDS HAVE DISAPPEARED FROM THE SKY. THIS IS ALL A MOST ODD OCCURRENCE. I AM GOING TO HAVE TO GO BACK TO MY... DOCTOR'S... PLACE... AND WRITE THIS UP IN MY DOCTOR... BOOK.
I, TOO, WILL TELL ALL MY PRIEST.. FRIENDS.. IN MY HOUSE. MY PRIEST HOUSE.
lets wear ladies pants!
lets do evil poos!
Y'KNOW, I NEVER NOTICED BEFORE HOW INCONSISTENT YOUR SIZE IS FOR A CAT.
TICKLE MY BELLY.
I'M HOME. I MAY HAVE PUNCHED A CHILD.
TIDDLER
IT HAPPENED AGAIN. I THINK I TRIPPED OUT.
MAYBE YOU NEED TO SEE SOMEONE ABOUT THIS.
OH I HAVE. A HOBO TOLD ME I WAS POSSESSED.
FISH CAKE
YAYYY FINALLY!! DOES THAT MEAN AT LAST I GET TO PERFORM AN EXORCISM? I'M LEGALLY CERTIFIED TO BY THE INTERNET.
WHAT? NO. HE SAID SOMEONE HAS DONE THIS TO ME. SOMEONE..
UM...
OH, WAIT.

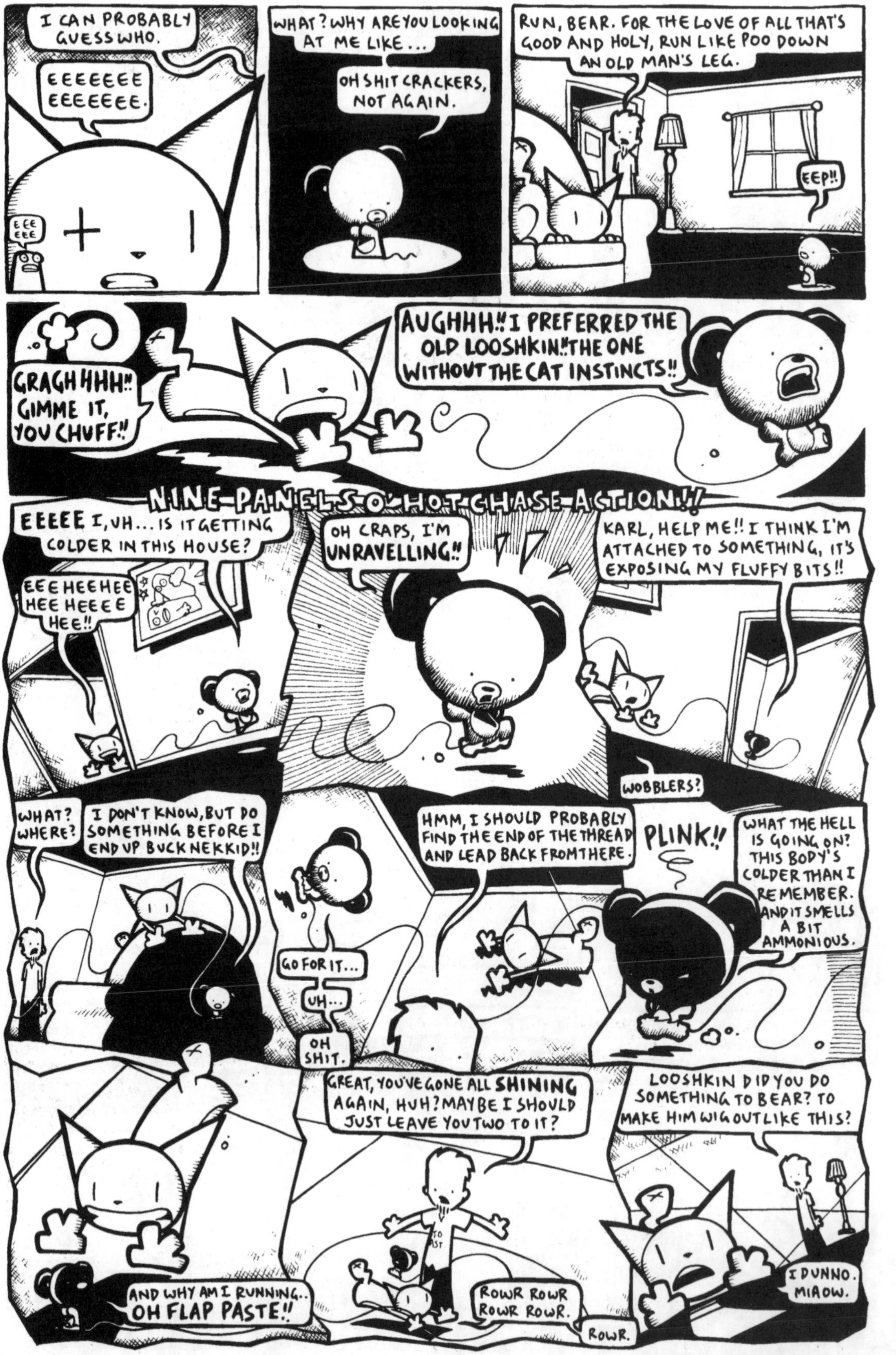
I CAN PROBABLY GUESS WHO.
EEEEEEE EEEEEEE.
EEE EEE
WHAT? WHY ARE YOU LOOKING AT ME LIKE...
OH SHIT CRACKERS, NOT AGAIN.
RUN, BEAR. FOR THE LOVE OF ALL THAT'S GOOD AND HOLY, RUN LIKE POO DOWN AN OLD MAN'S LEG.
EEP!!
GRAGHHHH!! GIMME IT, YOU CHUFF!!
AUGHHH!! I PREFERRED THE OLD LOOSHKIN!! THE ONE WITHOUT THE CAT INSTINCTS!!
NINE PANELS O' HOT CHASE ACTION!!
EEEEE I, UH... IS IT GETTING COLDER IN THIS HOUSE?
EEEHEEHEE HEE HEEEE HEE!!
OH CRAPS, I'M UNRAVELLING!!
KARL, HELP ME!! I THINK I'M ATTACHED TO SOMETHING, IT'S EXPOSING MY FLUFFY BITS!!
WOBBLERS?
WHAT? WHERE?
I DON'T KNOW, BUT DO SOMETHING BEFORE I END UP BUCK NEKKID!!
HMM, I SHOULD PROBABLY FIND THE END OF THE THREAD AND LEAD BACK FROM THERE.
GO FOR IT...
UH...
OH SHIT.
PLINK!!
WHAT THE HELL IS GOING ON? THIS BODY'S COLDER THAN I REMEMBER. AND IT SMELLS A BIT AMMONIOUS.
AND WHY AM I RUNNING.. OH FLAP PASTE!!
GREAT, YOU'VE GONE ALL SHINING AGAIN, HUH? MAYBE I SHOULD JUST LEAVE YOU TWO TO IT?
ROWR ROWR ROWR ROWR.
ROWR.
LOOSHKIN DID YOU DO SOMETHING TO BEAR? TO MAKE HIM WIG OUT LIKE THIS?
I DUNNO. MIAOW.

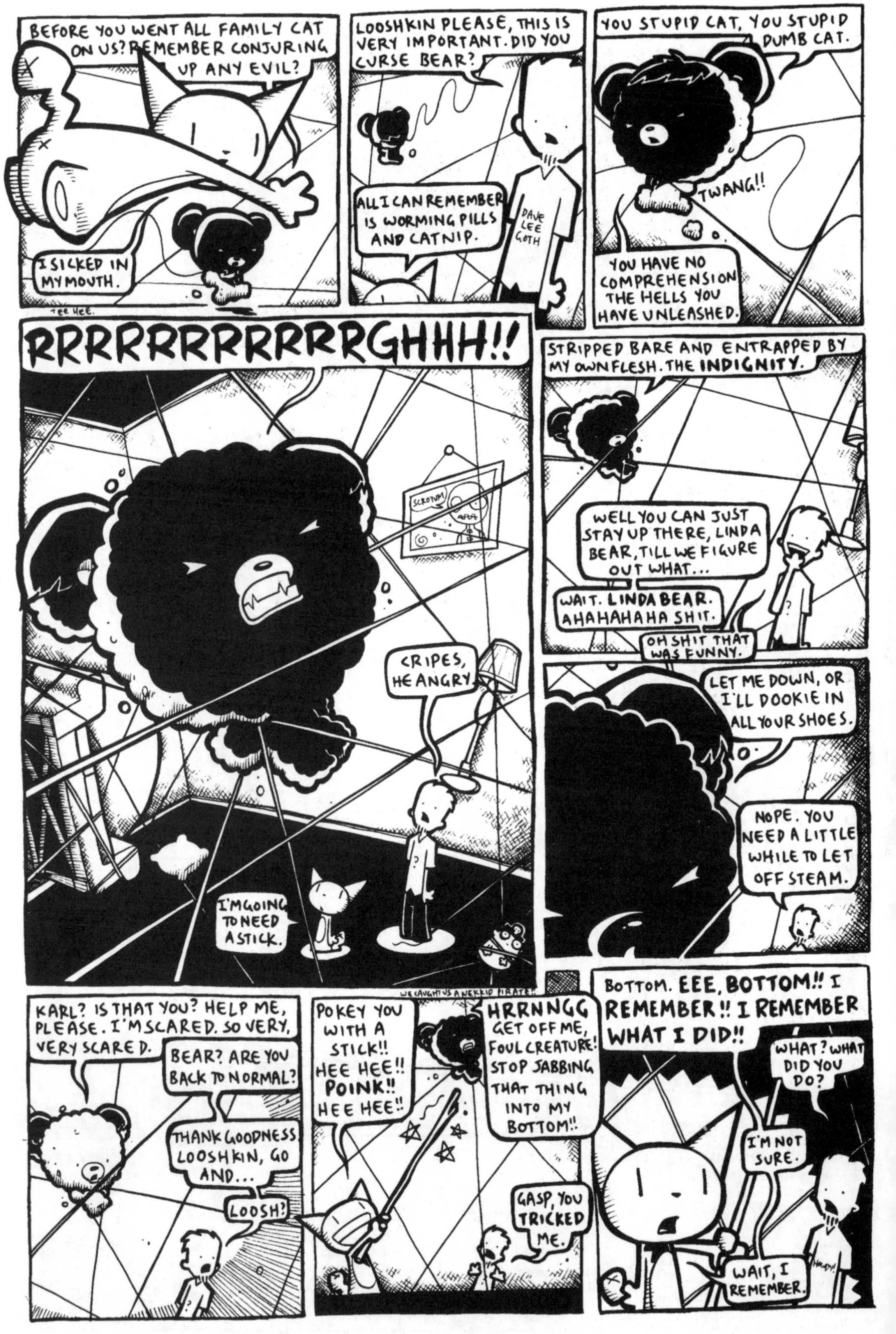

BEFORE YOU WENT ALL FAMILY CAT ON US? REMEMBER CONJURING UP ANY EVIL?
I SICKED IN MY MOUTH.
TEE HEE.
LOOSHKIN PLEASE, THIS IS VERY IMPORTANT. DID YOU CURSE BEAR?
ALL I CAN REMEMBER IS WORMING PILLS AND CATNIP.
DAVE LEE GOTH
YOU STUPID CAT, YOU STUPID DUMB CAT.
TWANG!!
YOU HAVE NO COMPREHENSION THE HELLS YOU HAVE UNLEASHED.
RRRRRRRRRRRGHHH!!
SCROTUM
CRIPES, HE ANGRY.
I'M GOING TO NEED A STICK.
WE CAUGHT US A NEKKID PIRATE!!
STRIPPED BARE AND ENTRAPPED BY MY OWN FLESH. THE INDIGNITY.
WELL YOU CAN JUST STAY UP THERE, LINDA BEAR, TILL WE FIGURE OUT WHAT...
WAIT. LINDA BEAR. AHAHAHAHA SHIT.
OH SHIT THAT WAS FUNNY.
LET ME DOWN, OR I'LL DOOKIE IN ALL YOUR SHOES.
NOPE. YOU NEED A LITTLE WHILE TO LET OFF STEAM.
KARL? IS THAT YOU? HELP ME, PLEASE. I'M SCARED. SO VERY, VERY SCARED.
BEAR? ARE YOU BACK TO NORMAL?
THANK GOODNESS. LOOSHKIN, GO AND...
LOOSH?
POKEY YOU WITH A STICK!! HEE HEE!! POINK!! HEE HEE!!
HRRNNGG GET OFF ME, FOUL CREATURE! STOP JABBING THAT THING INTO MY BOTTOM!!
GASP, YOU TRICKED ME.
BOTTOM. EEE, BOTTOM!! I REMEMBER!! I REMEMBER WHAT I DID!!
WHAT? WHAT DID YOU DO?
I'M NOT SURE.
WAIT, I REMEMBER.

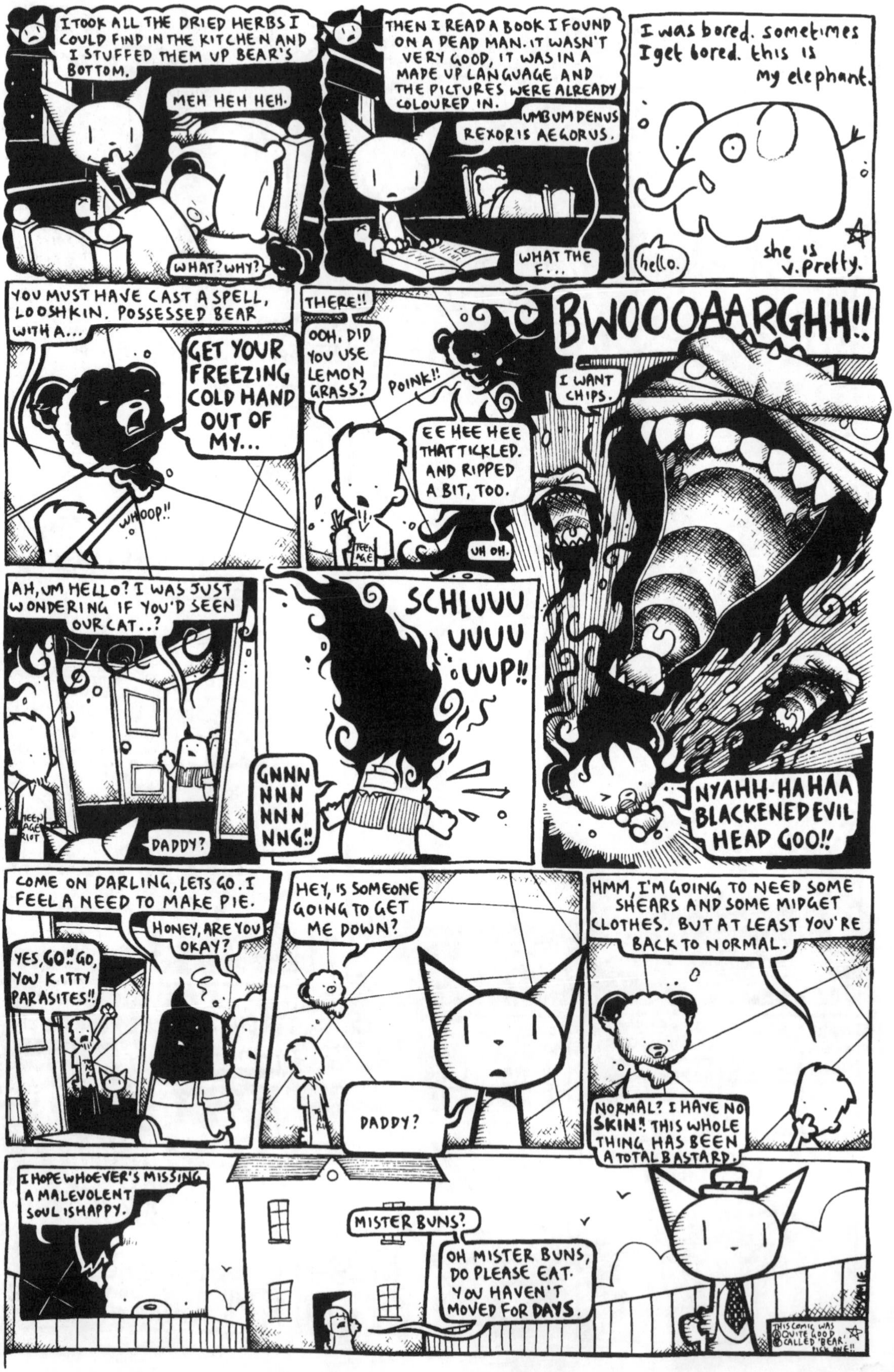
I TOOK ALL THE DRIED HERBS I COULD FIND IN THE KITCHEN AND I STUFFED THEM UP BEAR'S BOTTOM.
MEH HEH HEH.
WHAT? WHY?
THEN I READ A BOOK I FOUND ON A DEAD MAN. IT WASN'T VERY GOOD, IT WAS IN A MADE UP LANGUAGE AND THE PICTURES WERE ALREADY COLOURED IN.
UMBUM DENUS REXORIS AEGORUS.
WHAT THE F...
I was bored. sometimes I get bored. this is my elephant.
she is v. pretty.
hello.
YOU MUST HAVE CAST A SPELL, LOOSHKIN. POSSESSED BEAR WITH A...
GET YOUR FREEZING COLD HAND OUT OF MY...
WHOOP!!
THERE!!
OOH, DID YOU USE LEMON GRASS?
POINK!!
EE HEE HEE THAT TICKLED. AND RIPPED A BIT, TOO.
UH OH.
BWOOOAARGHH!!
I WANT CHIPS.
NYAHH-HAHAA BLACKENED EVIL HEAD GOO!!
AH, UM HELLO? I WAS JUST WONDERING IF YOU'D SEEN OUR CAT..?
DADDY?
SCHLUVU UUUU UUP!!
GNNN NNN NNN NNG!!
COME ON DARLING, LETS GO. I FEEL A NEED TO MAKE PIE.
HONEY, ARE YOU OKAY?
YES, GO!! GO, YOU KITTY PARASITES!!
HEY, IS SOMEONE GOING TO GET ME DOWN?
DADDY?
HMM, I'M GOING TO NEED SOME SHEARS AND SOME MIDGET CLOTHES. BUT AT LEAST YOU'RE BACK TO NORMAL.
NORMAL? I HAVE NO SKIN!! THIS WHOLE THING HAS BEEN A TOTAL BASTARD.
I HOPE WHOEVER'S MISSING A MALEVOLENT SOUL IS HAPPY.
MISTER BUNS?
OH MISTER BUNS, DO PLEASE EAT. YOU HAVEN'T MOVED FOR DAYS.
THIS COMIC WAS A QUITE GOOD B CALLED 'BEAR'. PICK ONE!!

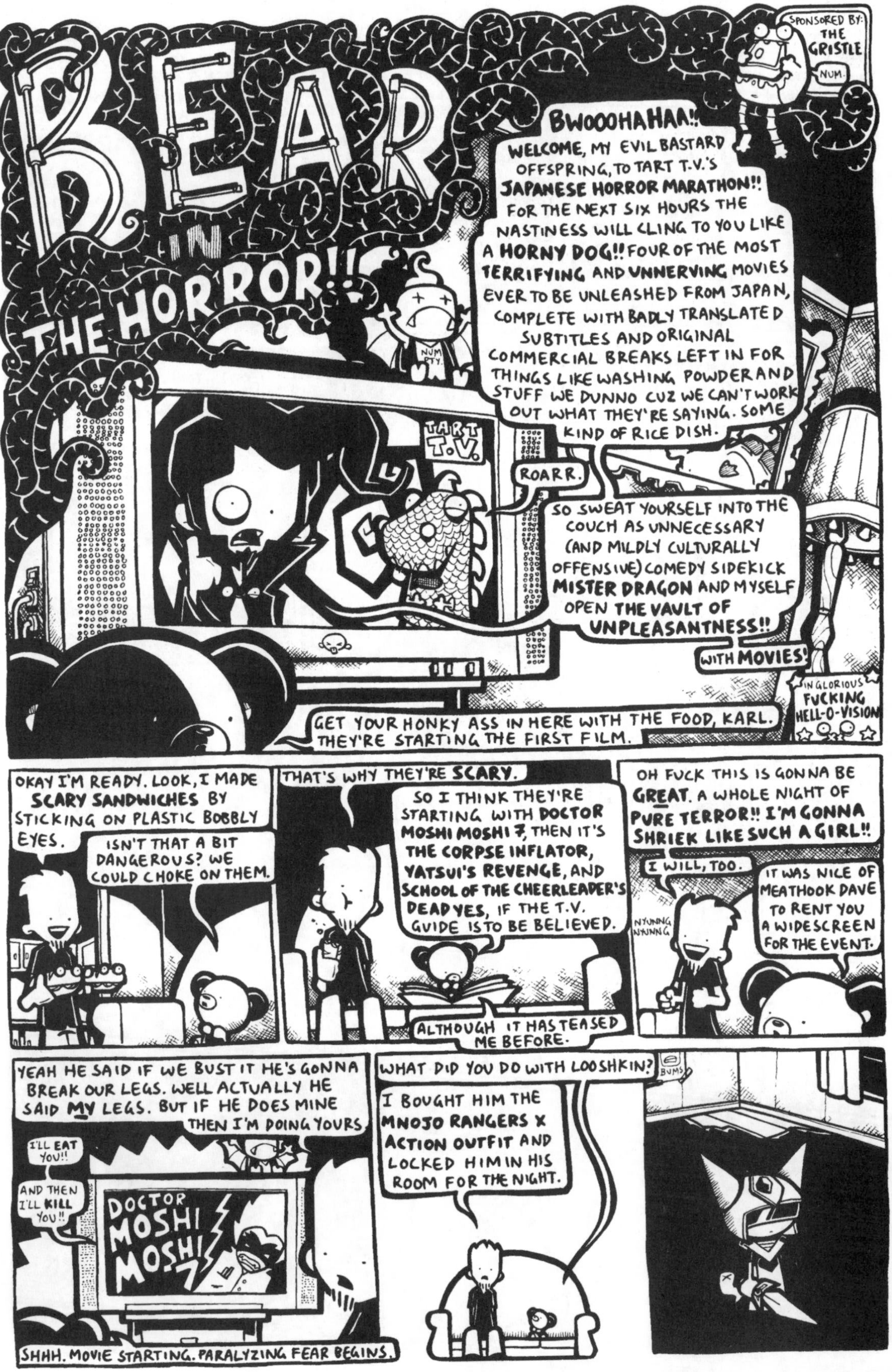
BEAR IN THE HORROR!!
SPONSORED BY: THE GRISTLE
NUM.
NUMPTY.
BWOOOHAHAA!! WELCOME, MY EVIL BASTARD OFFSPRING, TO TART T.V.'S JAPANESE HORROR MARATHON!! FOR THE NEXT SIX HOURS THE NASTINESS WILL CLING TO YOU LIKE A HORNY DOG!! FOUR OF THE MOST TERRIFYING AND UNNERVING MOVIES EVER TO BE UNLEASHED FROM JAPAN, COMPLETE WITH BADLY TRANSLATED SUBTITLES AND ORIGINAL COMMERCIAL BREAKS LEFT IN FOR THINGS LIKE WASHING POWDER AND STUFF WE DUNNO CUZ WE CAN'T WORK OUT WHAT THEY'RE SAYING. SOME KIND OF RICE DISH.
TART T.V.
ROARR.
SO SWEAT YOURSELF INTO THE COUCH AS UNNECESSARY (AND MILDLY CULTURALLY OFFENSIVE) COMEDY SIDEKICK MISTER DRAGON AND MYSELF OPEN THE VAULT OF UNPLEASANTNESS!!
WITH MOVIES!
IN GLORIOUS FUCKING HELL-O-VISION
GET YOUR HONKY ASS IN HERE WITH THE FOOD, KARL. THEY'RE STARTING THE FIRST FILM.
OKAY I'M READY. LOOK, I MADE SCARY SANDWICHES BY STICKING ON PLASTIC BOBBLY EYES.
ISN'T THAT A BIT DANGEROUS? WE COULD CHOKE ON THEM.
THAT'S WHY THEY'RE SCARY.
SO I THINK THEY'RE STARTING WITH DOCTOR MOSHI MOSHI 7, THEN IT'S THE CORPSE INFLATOR, YATSUI'S REVENGE, AND SCHOOL OF THE CHEERLEADER'S DEAD YES, IF THE T.V. GUIDE IS TO BE BELIEVED.
ALTHOUGH IT HAS TEASED ME BEFORE.
OH FUCK THIS IS GONNA BE GREAT. A WHOLE NIGHT OF PURE TERROR!! I'M GONNA SHRIEK LIKE SUCH A GIRL!!
I WILL, TOO.
NYUNNG NYUNNG
IT WAS NICE OF MEATHOOK DAVE TO RENT YOU A WIDESCREEN FOR THE EVENT.
YEAH HE SAID IF WE BUST IT HE'S GONNA BREAK OUR LEGS. WELL ACTUALLY HE SAID MY LEGS. BUT IF HE DOES MINE THEN I'M DOING YOURS.
I'LL EAT YOU!!
AND THEN I'LL KILL YOU!!
DOCTOR MOSHI MOSHI 7
SHHH. MOVIE STARTING. PARALYZING FEAR BEGINS.
WHAT DID YOU DO WITH LOOSHKIN?
I BOUGHT HIM THE MNOJO RANGERS X ACTION OUTFIT AND LOCKED HIM IN HIS ROOM FOR THE NIGHT.
BUMS

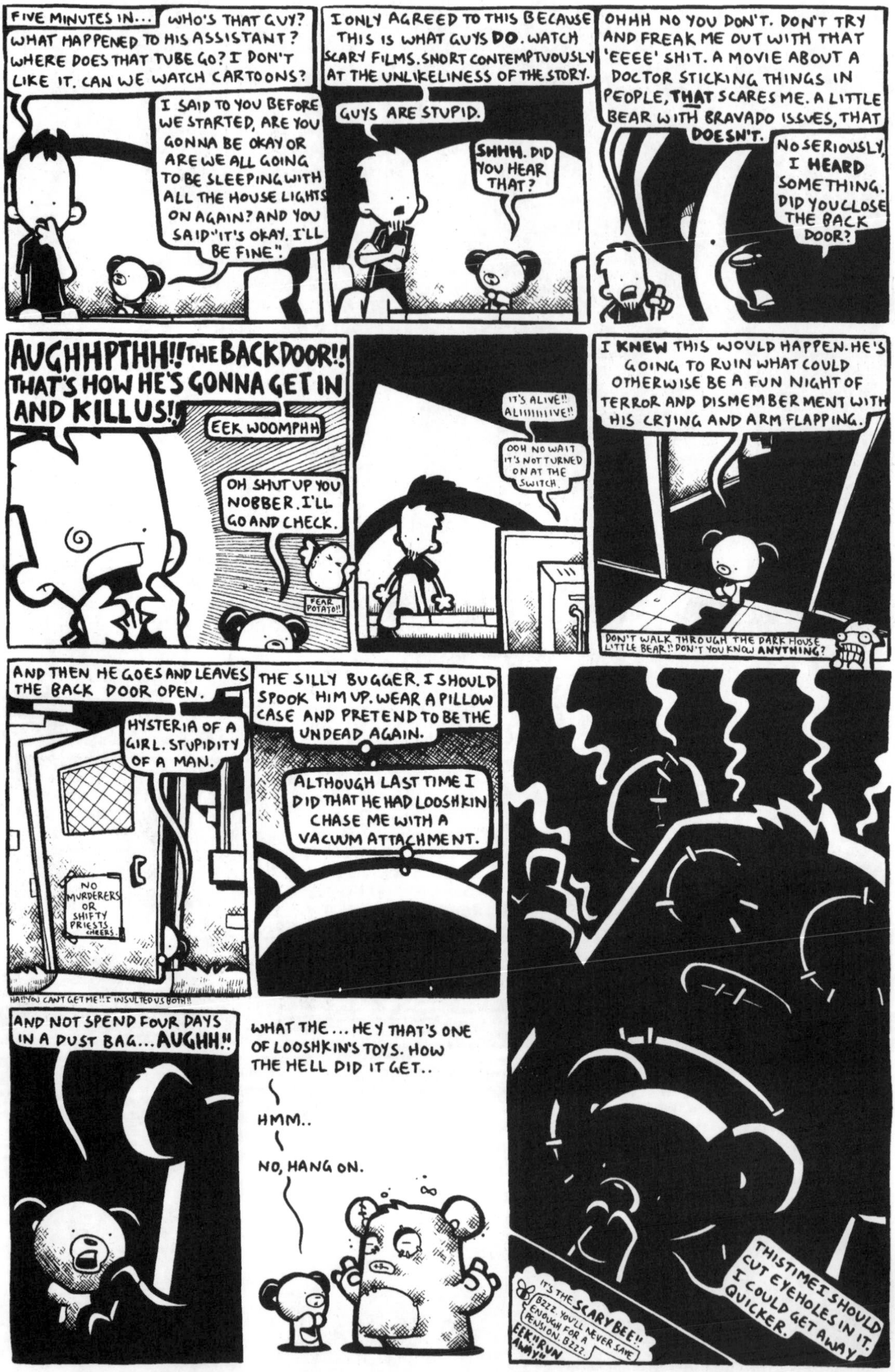
FIVE MINUTES IN...
WHO'S THAT GUY? WHAT HAPPENED TO HIS ASSISTANT? WHERE DOES THAT TUBE GO? I DON'T LIKE IT. CAN WE WATCH CARTOONS?
I SAID TO YOU BEFORE WE STARTED, ARE YOU GONNA BE OKAY OR ARE WE ALL GOING TO BE SLEEPING WITH ALL THE HOUSE LIGHTS ON AGAIN? AND YOU SAID "IT'S OKAY. I'LL BE FINE".
I ONLY AGREED TO THIS BECAUSE THIS IS WHAT GUYS DO. WATCH SCARY FILMS. SNORT CONTEMPTUOUSLY AT THE UNLIKELINESS OF THE STORY.
GUYS ARE STUPID.
SHHH. DID YOU HEAR THAT?
OHHH NO YOU DON'T. DON'T TRY AND FREAK ME OUT WITH THAT 'EEEE' SHIT. A MOVIE ABOUT A DOCTOR STICKING THINGS IN PEOPLE, THAT SCARES ME. A LITTLE BEAR WITH BRAVADO ISSUES, THAT DOESN'T.
NO SERIOUSLY, I HEARD SOMETHING. DID YOU CLOSE THE BACK DOOR?
AUGHHPTHH!! THE BACK DOOR!! THAT'S HOW HE'S GONNA GET IN AND KILL US!!
EEK WOOMPHH
OH SHUT UP YOU NOBBER. I'LL GO AND CHECK.
FEAR POTATO!!
IT'S ALIVE!! ALIIIIIIIIVE!!
OOH NO WAIT IT'S NOT TURNED ON AT THE SWITCH.
I KNEW THIS WOULD HAPPEN. HE'S GOING TO RUIN WHAT COULD OTHERWISE BE A FUN NIGHT OF TERROR AND DISMEMBERMENT WITH HIS CRYING AND ARM FLAPPING.
DON'T WALK THROUGH THE DARK HOUSE, LITTLE BEAR!! DON'T YOU KNOW ANYTHING?
AND THEN HE GOES AND LEAVES THE BACK DOOR OPEN.
HYSTERIA OF A GIRL. STUPIDITY OF A MAN.
NO MURDERERS OR SHIFTY PRIESTS. CHEERS.
HA!! YOU CAN'T GET ME!! I INSULTED US BOTH!!
THE SILLY BUGGER. I SHOULD SPOOK HIM UP. WEAR A PILLOW CASE AND PRETEND TO BE THE UNDEAD AGAIN.
ALTHOUGH LAST TIME I DID THAT HE HAD LOOSHKIN CHASE ME WITH A VACUUM ATTACHMENT.
AND NOT SPEND FOUR DAYS IN A DUST BAG...AUGHH!!
WHAT THE... HEY THAT'S ONE OF LOOSHKIN'S TOYS. HOW THE HELL DID IT GET..
HMM..
NO, HANG ON.
THIS TIME I SHOULD CUT EYEHOLES IN IT. I COULD GET AWAY QUICKER.
IT'S THE SCARY BEE!!
BZZZ. YOU'LL NEVER SAVE ENOUGH FOR A PENSION. BZZZ.
EEK!! RUN AWAY!!

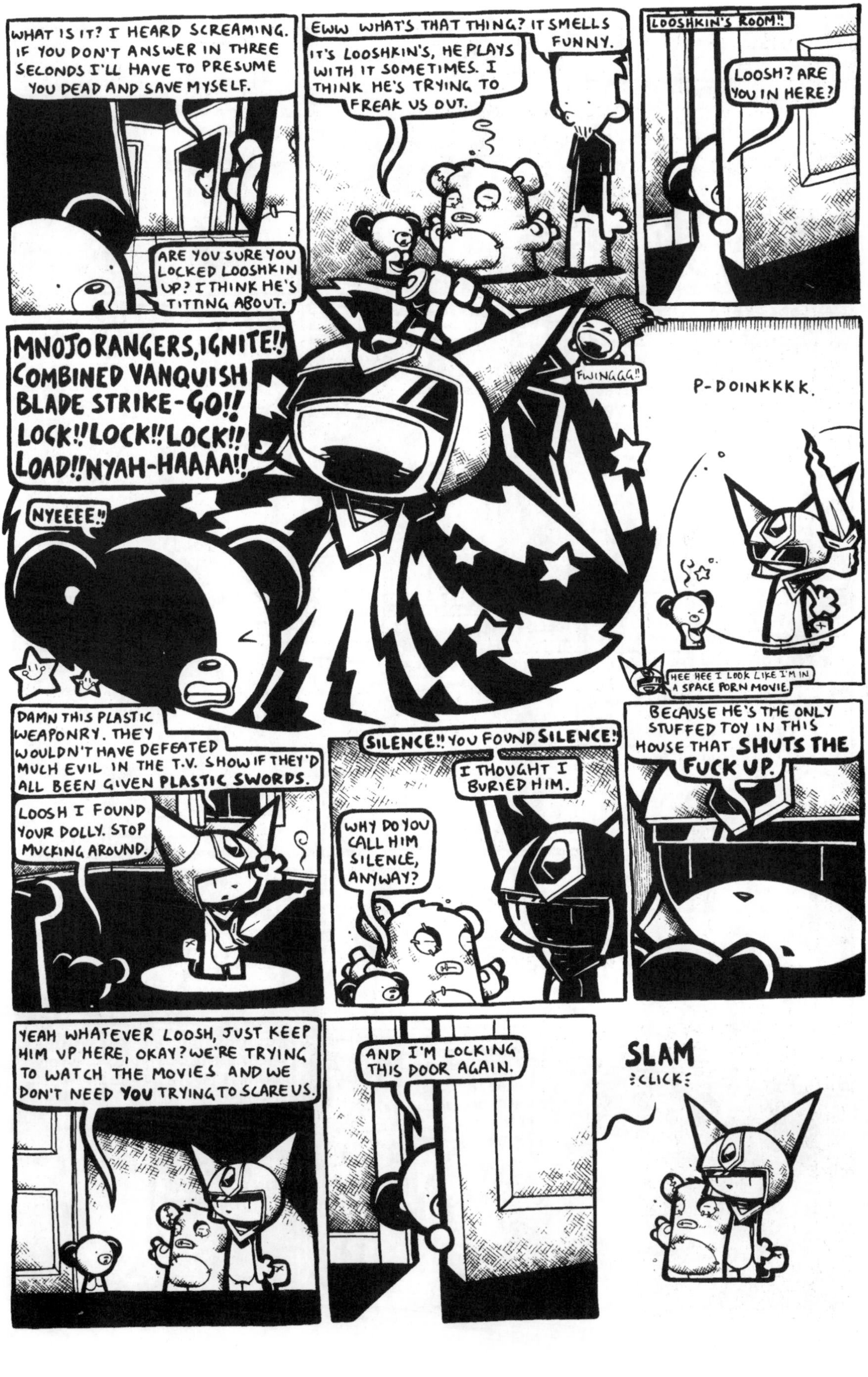
WHAT IS IT? I HEARD SCREAMING. IF YOU DON'T ANSWER IN THREE SECONDS I'LL HAVE TO PRESUME YOU DEAD AND SAVE MYSELF.
ARE YOU SURE YOU LOCKED LOOSHKIN UP? I THINK HE'S TITTING ABOUT.
EWW WHAT'S THAT THING? IT SMELLS FUNNY.
IT'S LOOSHKIN'S, HE PLAYS WITH IT SOMETIMES. I THINK HE'S TRYING TO FREAK US OUT.
LOOSHKIN'S ROOM!!
LOOSH? ARE YOU IN HERE?
MNOJO RANGERS, IGNITE!! COMBINED VANQUISH BLADE STRIKE-GO!! LOCK!! LOCK!! LOCK!! LOAD!! NYAH-HAAAA!!
FWINGGG!!
NYEEEE!!
P-DOINKKKK.
HEE HEE I LOOK LIKE I'M IN A SPACE PORN MOVIE.
DAMN THIS PLASTIC WEAPONRY. THEY WOULDN'T HAVE DEFEATED MUCH EVIL IN THE T.V. SHOW IF THEY'D ALL BEEN GIVEN PLASTIC SWORDS.
LOOSH I FOUND YOUR DOLLY. STOP MUCKING AROUND.
SILENCE!! YOU FOUND SILENCE!!
I THOUGHT I BURIED HIM.
WHY DO YOU CALL HIM SILENCE, ANYWAY?
BECAUSE HE'S THE ONLY STUFFED TOY IN THIS HOUSE THAT SHUTS THE FUCK UP.
YEAH WHATEVER LOOSH, JUST KEEP HIM UP HERE, OKAY? WE'RE TRYING TO WATCH THE MOVIES AND WE DON'T NEED YOU TRYING TO SCARE US.
AND I'M LOCKING THIS DOOR AGAIN.
SLAM
CLICK

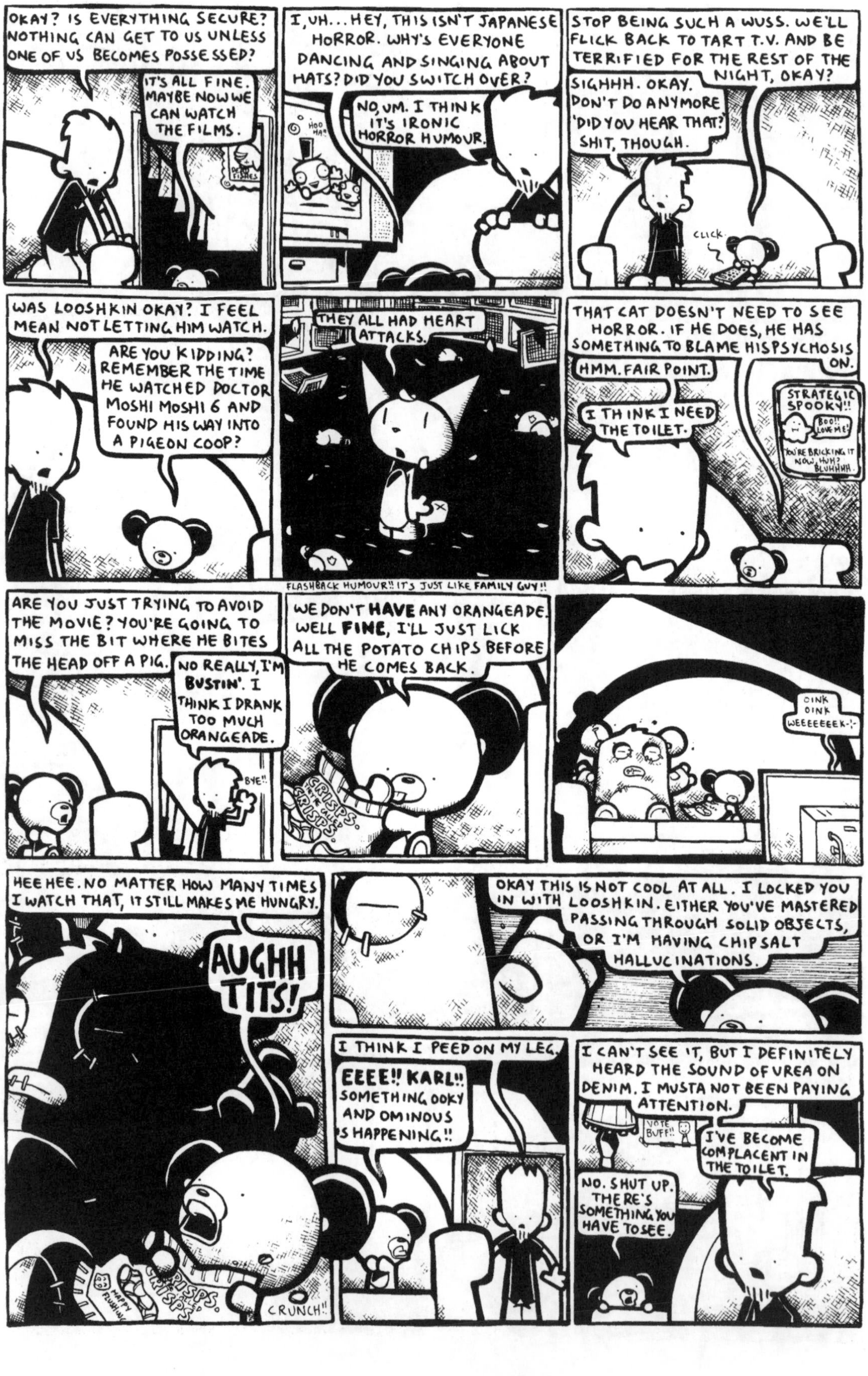
OKAY? IS EVERYTHING SECURE? NOTHING CAN GET TO US UNLESS ONE OF US BECOMES POSSESSED?
IT'S ALL FINE. MAYBE NOW WE CAN WATCH THE FILMS.
I, UH... HEY, THIS ISN'T JAPANESE HORROR. WHY'S EVERYONE DANCING AND SINGING ABOUT HATS? DID YOU SWITCH OVER?
NO, UM. I THINK IT'S IRONIC HORROR HUMOUR.
STOP BEING SUCH A WUSS. WE'LL FLICK BACK TO TART T.V. AND BE TERRIFIED FOR THE REST OF THE NIGHT, OKAY?
SIGHHH. OKAY. DON'T DO ANYMORE 'DID YOU HEAR THAT?' SHIT, THOUGH.
CLICK
WAS LOOSHKIN OKAY? I FEEL MEAN NOT LETTING HIM WATCH.
ARE YOU KIDDING? REMEMBER THE TIME HE WATCHED DOCTOR MOSHI MOSHI 6 AND FOUND HIS WAY INTO A PIGEON COOP?
THEY ALL HAD HEART ATTACKS.
THAT CAT DOESN'T NEED TO SEE HORROR. IF HE DOES, HE HAS SOMETHING TO BLAME HIS PSYCHOSIS ON.
HMM. FAIR POINT.
I THINK I NEED THE TOILET.
STRATEGIC SPOOKY!!
BOO!! LOVE ME!
YOU'RE BRICKING IT NOW, HUH? BLUHHHH.
FLASHBACK HUMOUR!! IT'S JUST LIKE FAMILY GUY!!
ARE YOU JUST TRYING TO AVOID THE MOVIE? YOU'RE GOING TO MISS THE BIT WHERE HE BITES THE HEAD OFF A PIG.
NO REALLY, I'M BUSTIN'. I THINK I DRANK TOO MUCH ORANGEADE.
BYE!!
WE DON'T HAVE ANY ORANGEADE. WELL FINE, I'LL JUST LICK ALL THE POTATO CHIPS BEFORE HE COMES BACK.
CRISPS
OINK OINK WEEEEEEEK-!-
HEE HEE. NO MATTER HOW MANY TIMES I WATCH THAT, IT STILL MAKES ME HUNGRY.
AUGHH TITS!
CRISPS.
CRUNCH!!
OKAY THIS IS NOT COOL AT ALL. I LOCKED YOU IN WITH LOOSHKIN. EITHER YOU'VE MASTERED PASSING THROUGH SOLID OBJECTS, OR I'M HAVING CHIP SALT HALLUCINATIONS.
I THINK I PEED ON MY LEG.
EEEE!! KARL!! SOMETHING OOKY AND OMINOUS IS HAPPENING!!
I CAN'T SEE IT, BUT I DEFINITELY HEARD THE SOUND OF UREA ON DENIM. I MUSTA NOT BEEN PAYING ATTENTION.
VOTE BUFF!!
I'VE BECOME COMPLACENT IN THE TOILET.
NO. SHUT UP. THERE'S SOMETHING YOU HAVE TO SEE.

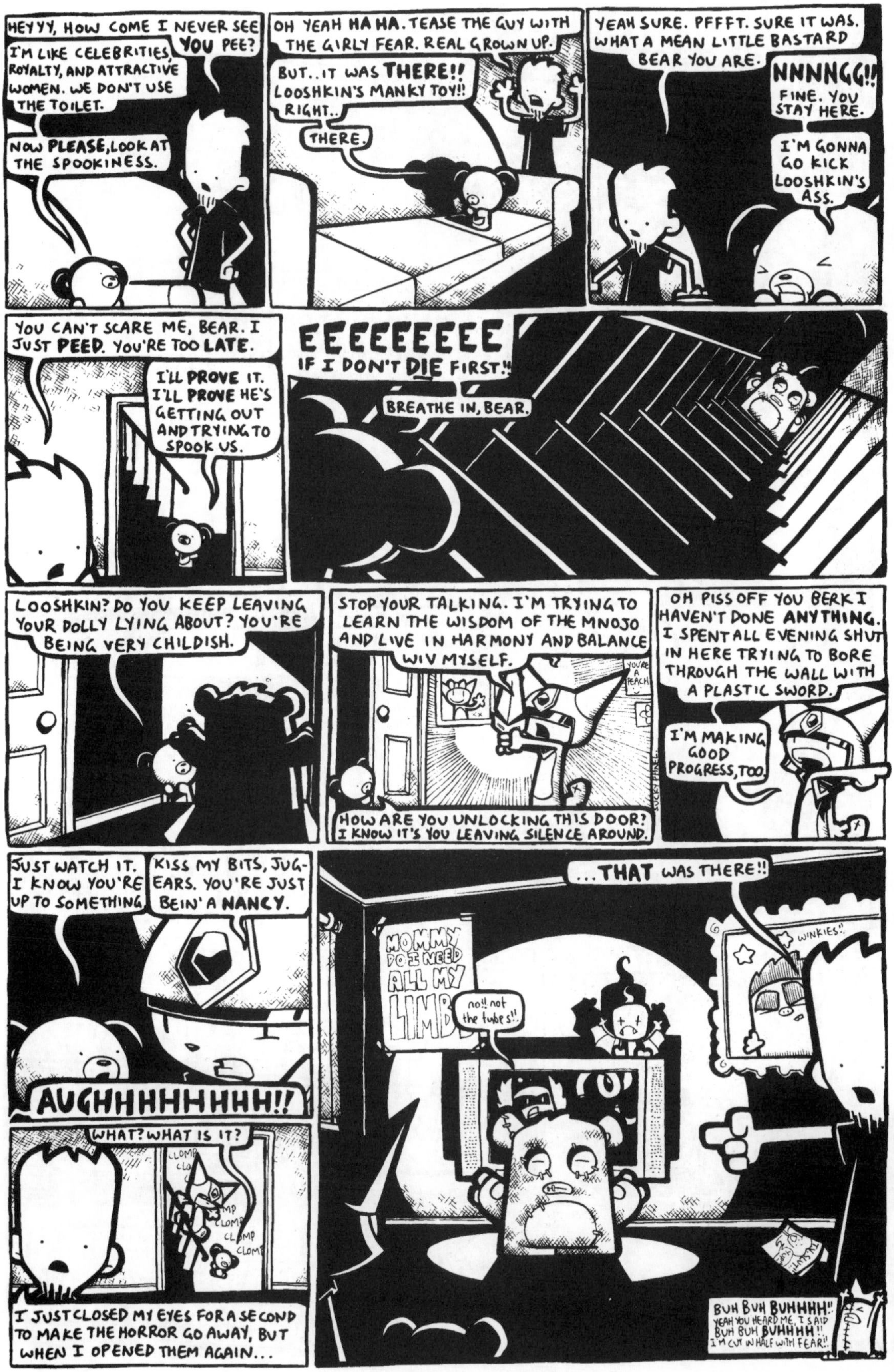
HEYYY, HOW COME I NEVER SEE YOU PEE?
I'M LIKE CELEBRITIES, ROYALTY, AND ATTRACTIVE WOMEN. WE DON'T USE THE TOILET.
NOW PLEASE, LOOK AT THE SPOOKINESS.
OH YEAH HA HA. TEASE THE GUY WITH THE GIRLY FEAR. REAL GROWN UP.
BUT.. IT WAS THERE!! LOOSHKIN'S MANKY TOY!! RIGHT..
THERE.
YEAH SURE. PFFFT. SURE IT WAS. WHAT A MEAN LITTLE BASTARD BEAR YOU ARE.
NNNNGG!! FINE. YOU STAY HERE.
I'M GONNA GO KICK LOOSHKIN'S ASS.
YOU CAN'T SCARE ME, BEAR. I JUST PEED. YOU'RE TOO LATE.
I'LL PROVE IT. I'LL PROVE HE'S GETTING OUT AND TRYING TO SPOOK US.
EEEEEEEEE IF I DON'T DIE FIRST!!
BREATHE IN, BEAR.
LOOSHKIN? DO YOU KEEP LEAVING YOUR DOLLY LYING ABOUT? YOU'RE BEING VERY CHILDISH.
STOP YOUR TALKING. I'M TRYING TO LEARN THE WISDOM OF THE MNOJO AND LIVE IN HARMONY AND BALANCE WIV MYSELF.
YOU'RE A PEACH
HOW ARE YOU UNLOCKING THIS DOOR? I KNOW IT'S YOU LEAVING SILENCE AROUND.
OH PISS OFF YOU BERK I HAVEN'T DONE ANYTHING. I SPENT ALL EVENING SHUT IN HERE TRYING TO BORE THROUGH THE WALL WITH A PLASTIC SWORD.
I'M MAKING GOOD PROGRESS, TOO.
JUST WATCH IT. I KNOW YOU'RE UP TO SOMETHING.
KISS MY BITS, JUG-EARS. YOU'RE JUST BEIN' A NANCY.
AUGHHHHHHHH!!
WHAT? WHAT IS IT?
CLOMP CLOMP CLOMP CLOMP CLOMP
I JUST CLOSED MY EYES FOR A SECOND TO MAKE THE HORROR GO AWAY, BUT WHEN I OPENED THEM AGAIN...
...THAT WAS THERE!!
MOMMY DO I NEED ALL MY LIMB
no!! not the tubes!!
WINKIES!!
BUH BUH BUHHHH!! YEAH YOU HEARD ME, I SAID BUH BUH BUHHHH!! I'M CUT IN HALF WITH FEAR!!

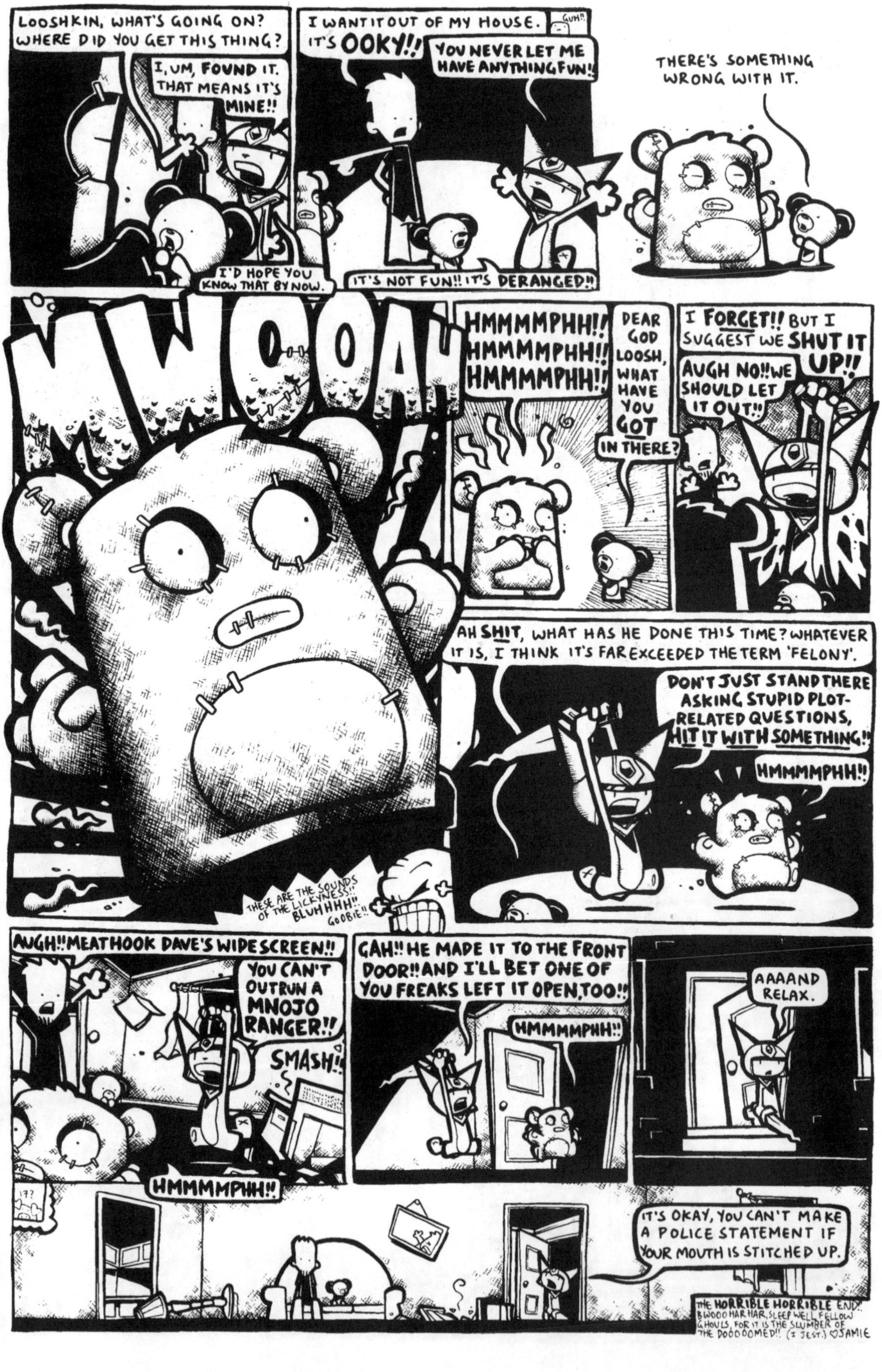

LOOSHKIN, WHAT'S GOING ON? WHERE DID YOU GET THIS THING?
I, UM, FOUND IT. THAT MEANS IT'S MINE!!
I'D HOPE YOU KNOW THAT BY NOW.
I WANT IT OUT OF MY HOUSE. IT'S OOKY!!
GUH!!
YOU NEVER LET ME HAVE ANYTHING FUN!!
IT'S NOT FUN!! IT'S DERANGED!!
THERE'S SOMETHING WRONG WITH IT.
MWOOAH
THESE ARE THE SOUNDS OF THE LICKYNESS!! BLUHHHH!! GOOBIE!!
HMMMMPHH!! HMMMMPHH!! HMMMMPHH!!
DEAR GOD LOOSH, WHAT HAVE YOU GOT IN THERE?
I FORGET!! BUT I SUGGEST WE SHUT IT UP!!
AUGH NO!! WE SHOULD LET IT OUT!!
AH SHIT, WHAT HAS HE DONE THIS TIME? WHATEVER IT IS, I THINK IT'S FAR EXCEEDED THE TERM 'FELONY'.
DON'T JUST STAND THERE ASKING STUPID PLOT-RELATED QUESTIONS, HIT IT WITH SOMETHING!!
HMMMMPHH!!
AUGH!! MEATHOOK DAVE'S WIDESCREEN!!
YOU CAN'T OUTRUN A MNOJO RANGER!!
SMASH!!
HMMMMPHH!!
GAH!! HE MADE IT TO THE FRONT DOOR!! AND I'LL BET ONE OF YOU FREAKS LEFT IT OPEN, TOO!!
HMMMMPHH!!
AAAAND RELAX.
IT'S OKAY, YOU CAN'T MAKE A POLICE STATEMENT IF YOUR MOUTH IS STITCHED UP.
THE HORRIBLE HORRIBLE END!! BWOOO HAR HAR, SLEEP WELL FELLOW GHOULS, FOR IT IS THE SLUMBER OF THE DOOOOOMED!! (I JEST.) ♡JAMIE

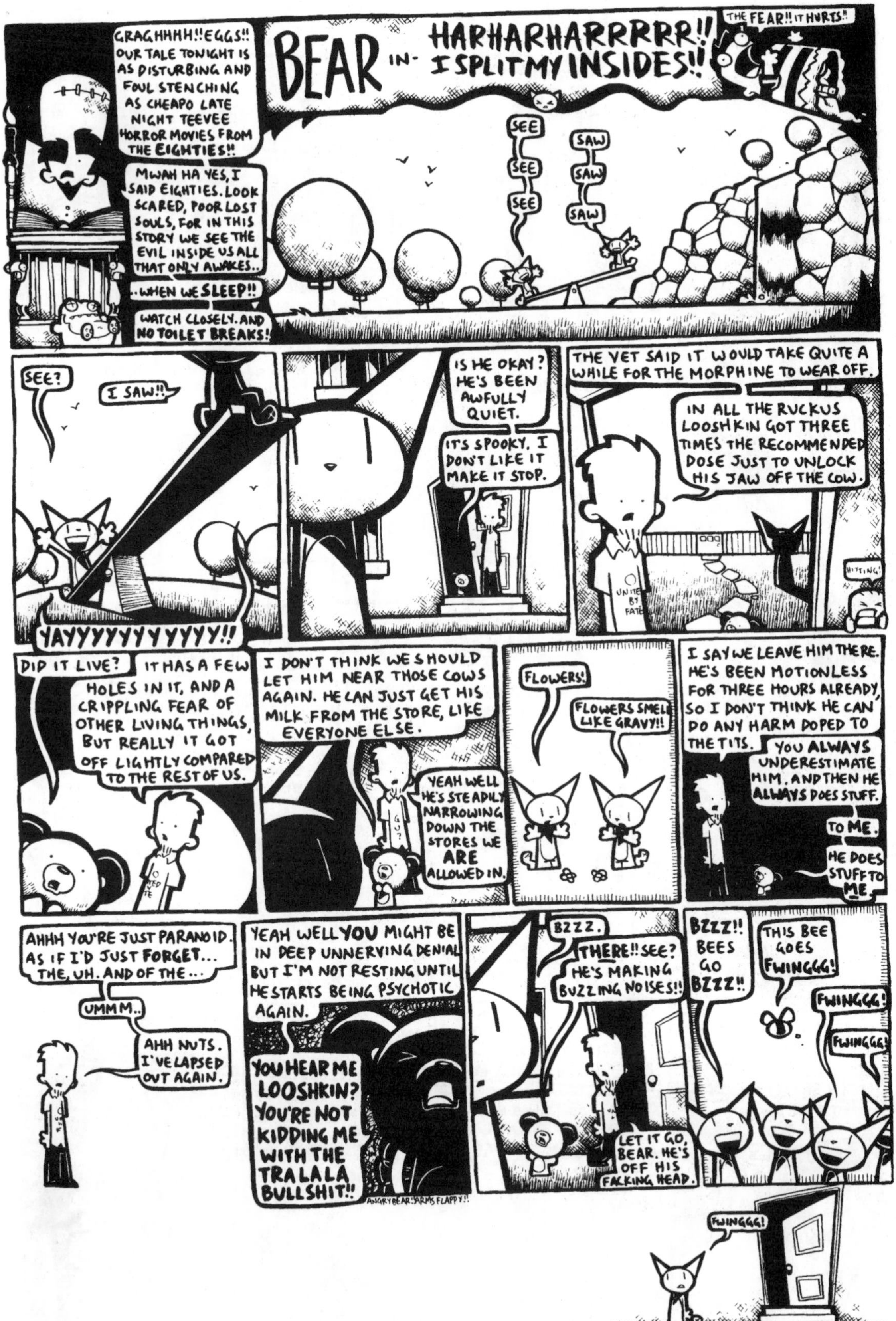

BEAR in- HARHARHARRRRR!! I SPLIT MY INSIDES!!
THE FEAR!! IT HURTS!!
GRAGHHHH!! EGGS!! OUR TALE TONIGHT IS AS DISTURBING AND FOUL STENCHING AS CHEAPO LATE NIGHT TEEVEE HORROR MOVIES FROM THE EIGHTIES!!
MWAH HA YES, I SAID EIGHTIES. LOOK SCARED, POOR LOST SOULS, FOR IN THIS STORY WE SEE THE EVIL INSIDE US ALL THAT ONLY AWAKES..
..WHEN WE SLEEP!!
WATCH CLOSELY. AND NO TOILET BREAKS!!
SEE SEE SEE
SAW SAW SAW
SEE?
I SAW!!
YAYYYYYYYYYYY!!
IS HE OKAY? HE'S BEEN AWFULLY QUIET.
IT'S SPOOKY. I DON'T LIKE IT MAKE IT STOP.
THE VET SAID IT WOULD TAKE QUITE A WHILE FOR THE MORPHINE TO WEAR OFF.
IN ALL THE RUCKUS LOOSHKIN GOT THREE TIMES THE RECOMMENDED DOSE JUST TO UNLOCK HIS JAW OFF THE COW.
UNITED BY FATE
HITTING!
DID IT LIVE?
IT HAS A FEW HOLES IN IT, AND A CRIPPLING FEAR OF OTHER LIVING THINGS, BUT REALLY IT GOT OFF LIGHTLY COMPARED TO THE REST OF US.
I DON'T THINK WE SHOULD LET HIM NEAR THOSE COWS AGAIN. HE CAN JUST GET HIS MILK FROM THE STORE, LIKE EVERYONE ELSE.
YEAH WELL HE'S STEADILY NARROWING DOWN THE STORES WE ARE ALLOWED IN.
FLOWERS!
FLOWERS SMELL LIKE GRAVY!!
I SAY WE LEAVE HIM THERE. HE'S BEEN MOTIONLESS FOR THREE HOURS ALREADY, SO I DON'T THINK HE CAN DO ANY HARM DOPED TO THE TITS.
YOU ALWAYS UNDERESTIMATE HIM, AND THEN HE ALWAYS DOES STUFF.
TO ME.
HE DOES STUFF TO ME.
AHHH YOU'RE JUST PARANOID. AS IF I'D JUST FORGET... THE, UH. AND OF THE...
UMMM..
AHH NUTS. I'VE LAPSED OUT AGAIN.
YEAH WELL YOU MIGHT BE IN DEEP UNNERVING DENIAL BUT I'M NOT RESTING UNTIL HE STARTS BEING PSYCHOTIC AGAIN.
YOU HEAR ME LOOSHKIN? YOU'RE NOT KIDDING ME WITH THE TRALALA BULLSHIT!!
ANGRY BEAR: ARMS FLAPPY!!
BZZZ.
THERE!! SEE? HE'S MAKING BUZZING NOISES!!
LET IT GO, BEAR. HE'S OFF HIS FACKING HEAD.
BZZZ!! BEES GO BZZZ!!
THIS BEE GOES FWINGGG!
FWINGGG!
FWINGGG!
FWINGGG!

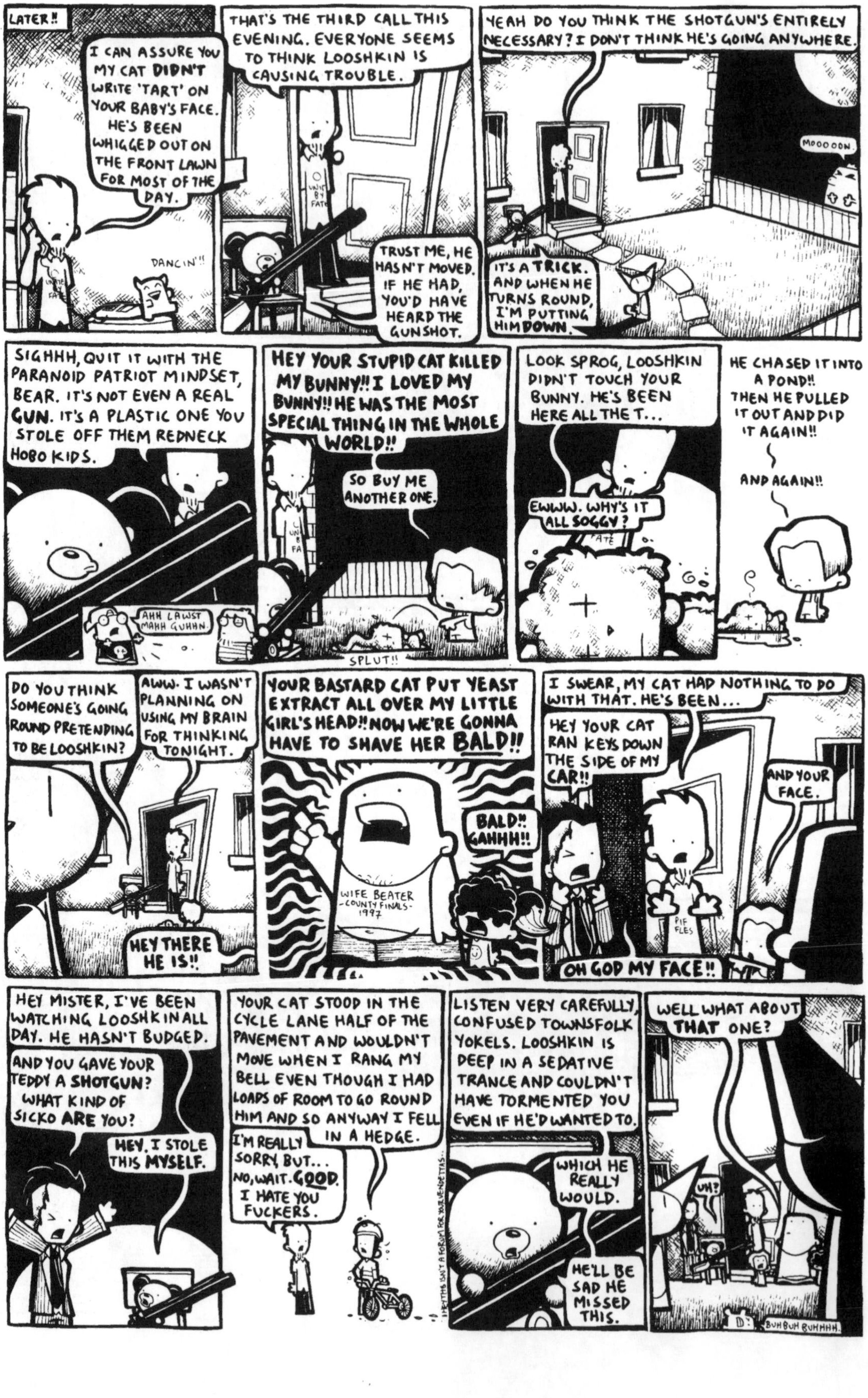

LATER!!
I CAN ASSURE YOU MY CAT DIDN'T WRITE 'TART' ON YOUR BABY'S FACE. HE'S BEEN WHIGGED OUT ON THE FRONT LAWN FOR MOST OF THE DAY.
DANCIN'!!
THAT'S THE THIRD CALL THIS EVENING. EVERYONE SEEMS TO THINK LOOSHKIN IS CAUSING TROUBLE.
TRUST ME, HE HASN'T MOVED. IF HE HAD, YOU'D HAVE HEARD THE GUNSHOT.
YEAH DO YOU THINK THE SHOTGUN'S ENTIRELY NECESSARY? I DON'T THINK HE'S GOING ANYWHERE.
MOOOOON.
IT'S A TRICK. AND WHEN HE TURNS ROUND, I'M PUTTING HIM DOWN.
SIGHHH, QUIT IT WITH THE PARANOID PATRIOT MINDSET, BEAR. IT'S NOT EVEN A REAL GUN. IT'S A PLASTIC ONE YOU STOLE OFF THEM REDNECK HOBO KIDS.
AHH LAWST MAHH GUHHN.
HEY YOUR STUPID CAT KILLED MY BUNNY!! I LOVED MY BUNNY!! HE WAS THE MOST SPECIAL THING IN THE WHOLE WORLD!!
SO BUY ME ANOTHER ONE.
SPLUT!!
LOOK SPROG, LOOSHKIN DIDN'T TOUCH YOUR BUNNY. HE'S BEEN HERE ALL THE T...
EWWW. WHY'S IT ALL SOGGY?
HE CHASED IT INTO A POND!! THEN HE PULLED IT OUT AND DID IT AGAIN!!
AND AGAIN!!
DO YOU THINK SOMEONE'S GOING ROUND PRETENDING TO BE LOOSHKIN?
AWW. I WASN'T PLANNING ON USING MY BRAIN FOR THINKING TONIGHT.
HEY THERE HE IS!!
YOUR BASTARD CAT PUT YEAST EXTRACT ALL OVER MY LITTLE GIRL'S HEAD!! NOW WE'RE GONNA HAVE TO SHAVE HER BALD!!
WIFE BEATER -COUNTY FINALS- 1997
BALD!! GAHHH!!
I SWEAR, MY CAT HAD NOTHING TO DO WITH THAT. HE'S BEEN...
HEY YOUR CAT RAN KEYS DOWN THE SIDE OF MY CAR!!
AND YOUR FACE.
OH GOD MY FACE!!
HEY MISTER, I'VE BEEN WATCHING LOOSHKIN ALL DAY. HE HASN'T BUDGED.
AND YOU GAVE YOUR TEDDY A SHOTGUN? WHAT KIND OF SICKO ARE YOU?
HEY, I STOLE THIS MYSELF.
YOUR CAT STOOD IN THE CYCLE LANE HALF OF THE PAVEMENT AND WOULDN'T MOVE WHEN I RANG MY BELL EVEN THOUGH I HAD LOADS OF ROOM TO GO ROUND HIM AND SO ANYWAY I FELL IN A HEDGE.
I'M REALLY SORRY, BUT... NO, WAIT. GOOD. I HATE YOU FUCKERS.
HEY THIS ISN'T A FORUM FOR YOUR VENDETTAS...
LISTEN VERY CAREFULLY, CONFUSED TOWNSFOLK YOKELS. LOOSHKIN IS DEEP IN A SEDATIVE TRANCE AND COULDN'T HAVE TORMENTED YOU EVEN IF HE'D WANTED TO.
WHICH HE REALLY WOULD.
HE'LL BE SAD HE MISSED THIS.
WELL WHAT ABOUT THAT ONE?
UH?
BUH BUH BUHHHH.

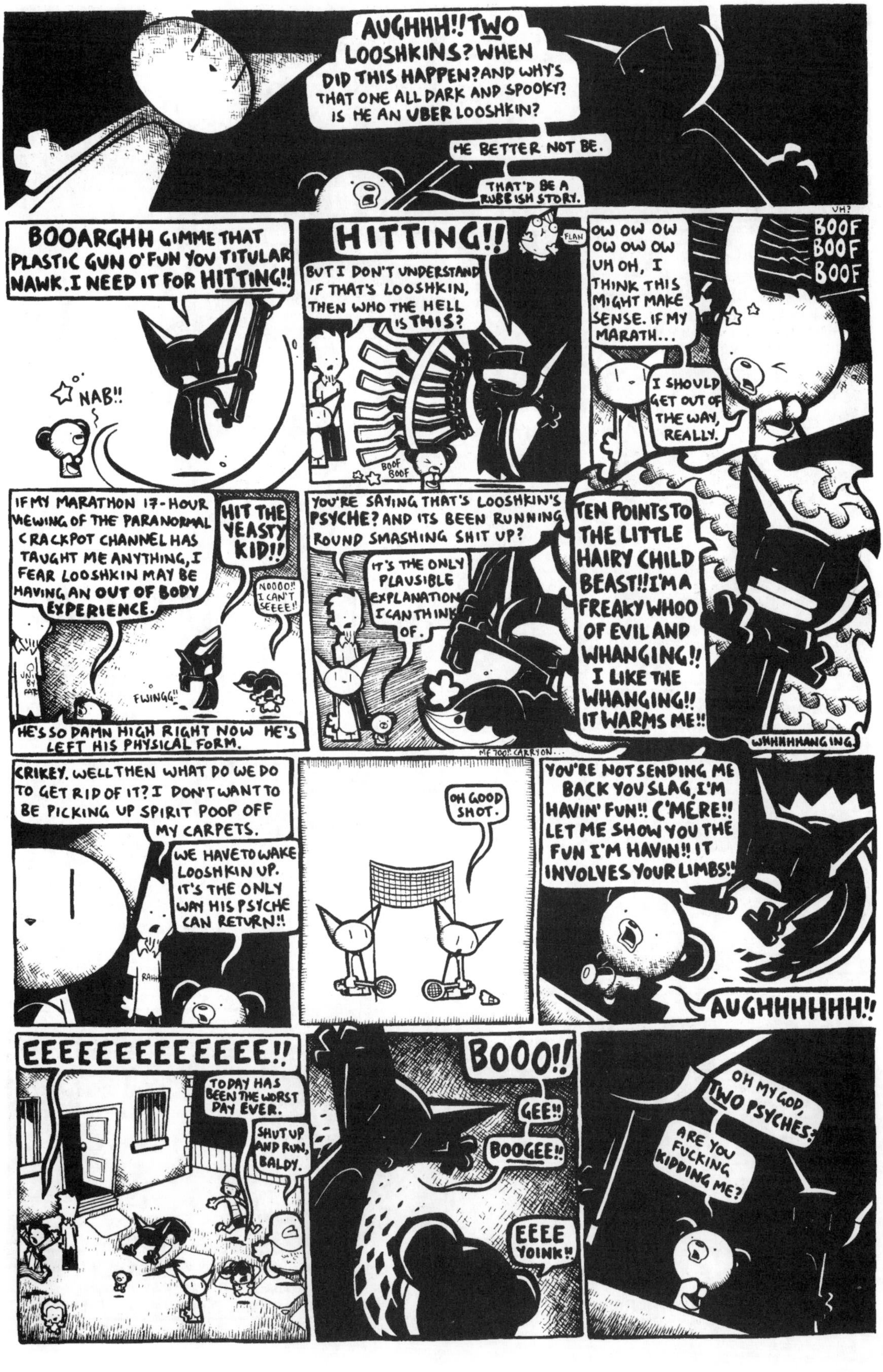
AUGHHH!! TWO LOOSHKINS? WHEN DID THIS HAPPEN? AND WHY'S THAT ONE ALL DARK AND SPOOKY? IS HE AN UBER LOOSHKIN?
HE BETTER NOT BE.
THAT'D BE A RUBBISH STORY.
BOOARGHH GIMME THAT PLASTIC GUN O' FUN YOU TITULAR NAWK. I NEED IT FOR HITTING!!
NAB!!
HITTING!!
FLAN
BUT I DON'T UNDERSTAND IF THAT'S LOOSHKIN, THEN WHO THE HELL IS THIS?
BOOF BOOF
UH?
BOOF BOOF BOOF
OW OW OW OW OW OW UH OH, I THINK THIS MIGHT MAKE SENSE. IF MY MARATH...
I SHOULD GET OUT OF THE WAY, REALLY.
IF MY MARATHON 17-HOUR VIEWING OF THE PARANORMAL CRACKPOT CHANNEL HAS TAUGHT ME ANYTHING, I FEAR LOOSHKIN MAY BE HAVING AN OUT OF BODY EXPERIENCE.
HIT THE YEASTY KID!!
NOOOO!! I CAN'T SEEEE!!
FWINGG!!
HE'S SO DAMN HIGH RIGHT NOW HE'S LEFT HIS PHYSICAL FORM.
YOU'RE SAYING THAT'S LOOSHKIN'S PSYCHE? AND ITS BEEN RUNNING ROUND SMASHING SHIT UP?
IT'S THE ONLY PLAUSIBLE EXPLANATION I CAN THINK OF.
ME TOO! CARRY ON...
TEN POINTS TO THE LITTLE HAIRY CHILD BEAST!! I'M A FREAKY WHOO OF EVIL AND WHANGING!! I LIKE THE WHANGING!! IT WARMS ME!!
WHHHHHANGING.
CRIKEY. WELL THEN WHAT DO WE DO TO GET RID OF IT? I DON'T WANT TO BE PICKING UP SPIRIT POOP OFF MY CARPETS.
WE HAVE TO WAKE LOOSHKIN UP. IT'S THE ONLY WAY HIS PSYCHE CAN RETURN!!
OH GOOD SHOT.
YOU'RE NOT SENDING ME BACK YOU SLAG, I'M HAVIN' FUN!! C'MERE!! LET ME SHOW YOU THE FUN I'M HAVIN!! IT INVOLVES YOUR LIMBS!!
AUGHHHHHH!!
EEEEEEEEEEEEE!!
TODAY HAS BEEN THE WORST DAY EVER.
SHUT UP AND RUN, BALDY.
BOOO!!
GEE!!
BOOGEE!!
EEEE YOINK!!
OH MY GOD, TWO PSYCHES?
ARE YOU FUCKING KIDDING ME?

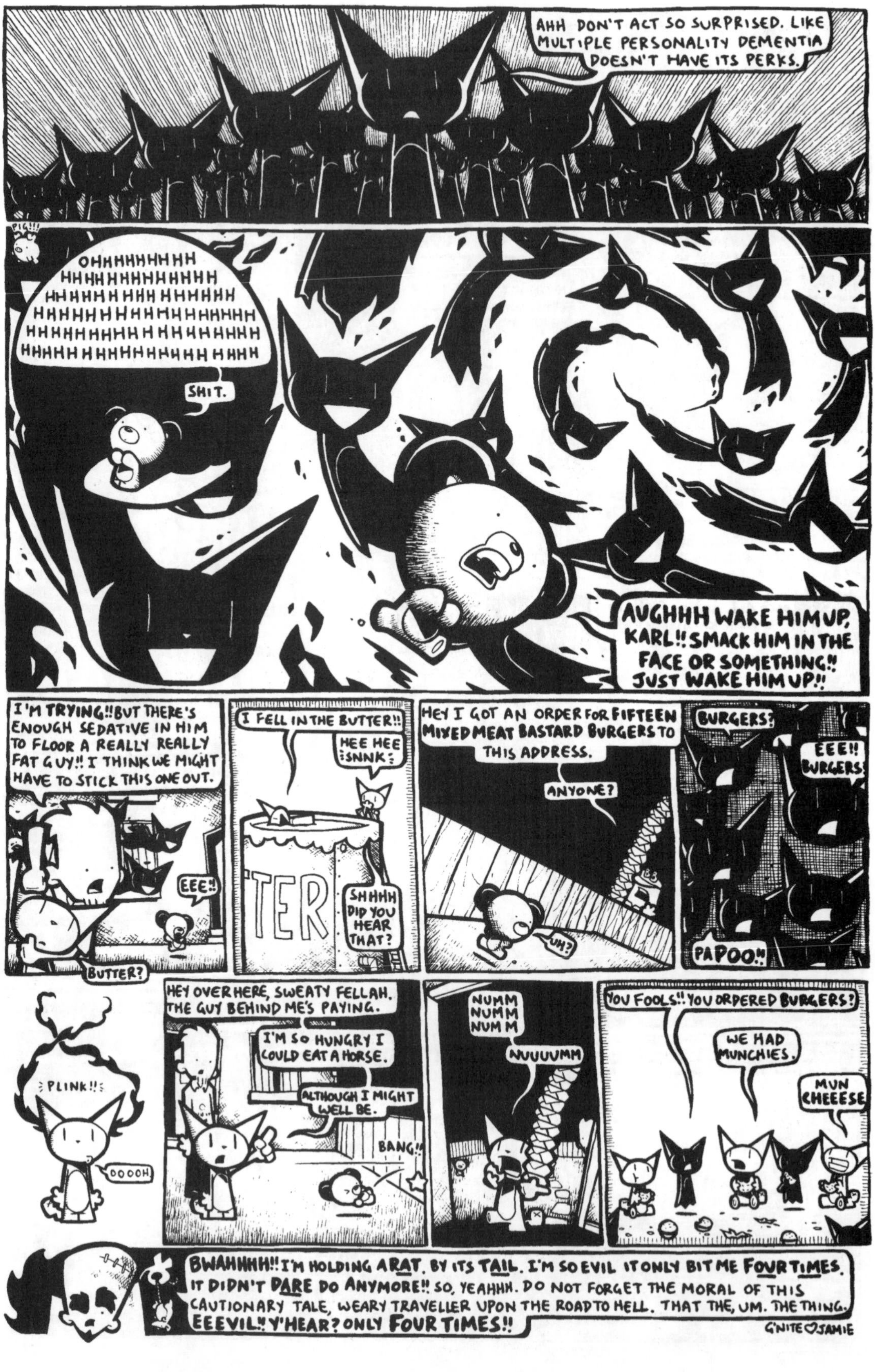
AHH DON'T ACT SO SURPRISED. LIKE MULTIPLE PERSONALITY DEMENTIA DOESN'T HAVE ITS PERKS.
OHHHHHHHHH HHHHHHHHHHHHH HHHHHH HHH HHHHHH HHHHHHHHHHHHHHHHH HHHHHHHHHH H HHHHHHH HHHHH HHHHHHHHHHH HHHH
SHIT.
AUGHHH WAKE HIM UP, KARL!! SMACK HIM IN THE FACE OR SOMETHING!! JUST WAKE HIM UP!!
I'M TRYING!! BUT THERE'S ENOUGH SEDATIVE IN HIM TO FLOOR A REALLY REALLY FAT GUY!! I THINK WE MIGHT HAVE TO STICK THIS ONE OUT.
EEE!!
BUTTER?
I FELL IN THE BUTTER!!
HEE HEE SNNK
TER
SHHHH DID YOU HEAR THAT?
HEY I GOT AN ORDER FOR FIFTEEN MIXED MEAT BASTARD BURGERS TO THIS ADDRESS.
ANYONE?
UH?
BURGERS?
EEE!! BURGERS!
PAPOO!!
PLINK!!
OOOOH.
HEY OVER HERE, SWEATY FELLAH. THE GUY BEHIND ME'S PAYING.
I'M SO HUNGRY I COULD EAT A HORSE.
ALTHOUGH I MIGHT WELL BE.
BANG!!
NUMM NUMM NUM M
NUUUUMM
YOU FOOLS!! YOU ORDERED BURGERS?
WE HAD MUNCHIES.
MUN CHEEESE
BWAHHHH!! I'M HOLDING A RAT. BY ITS TAIL. I'M SO EVIL IT ONLY BIT ME FOUR TIMES. IT DIDN'T DARE DO ANYMORE!! SO, YEAHHH. DO NOT FORGET THE MORAL OF THIS CAUTIONARY TALE, WEARY TRAVELLER UPON THE ROAD TO HELL. THAT THE, UM. THE THING. EEEVIL!! Y'HEAR? ONLY FOUR TIMES!!
G'NITE ♡ JAMIE

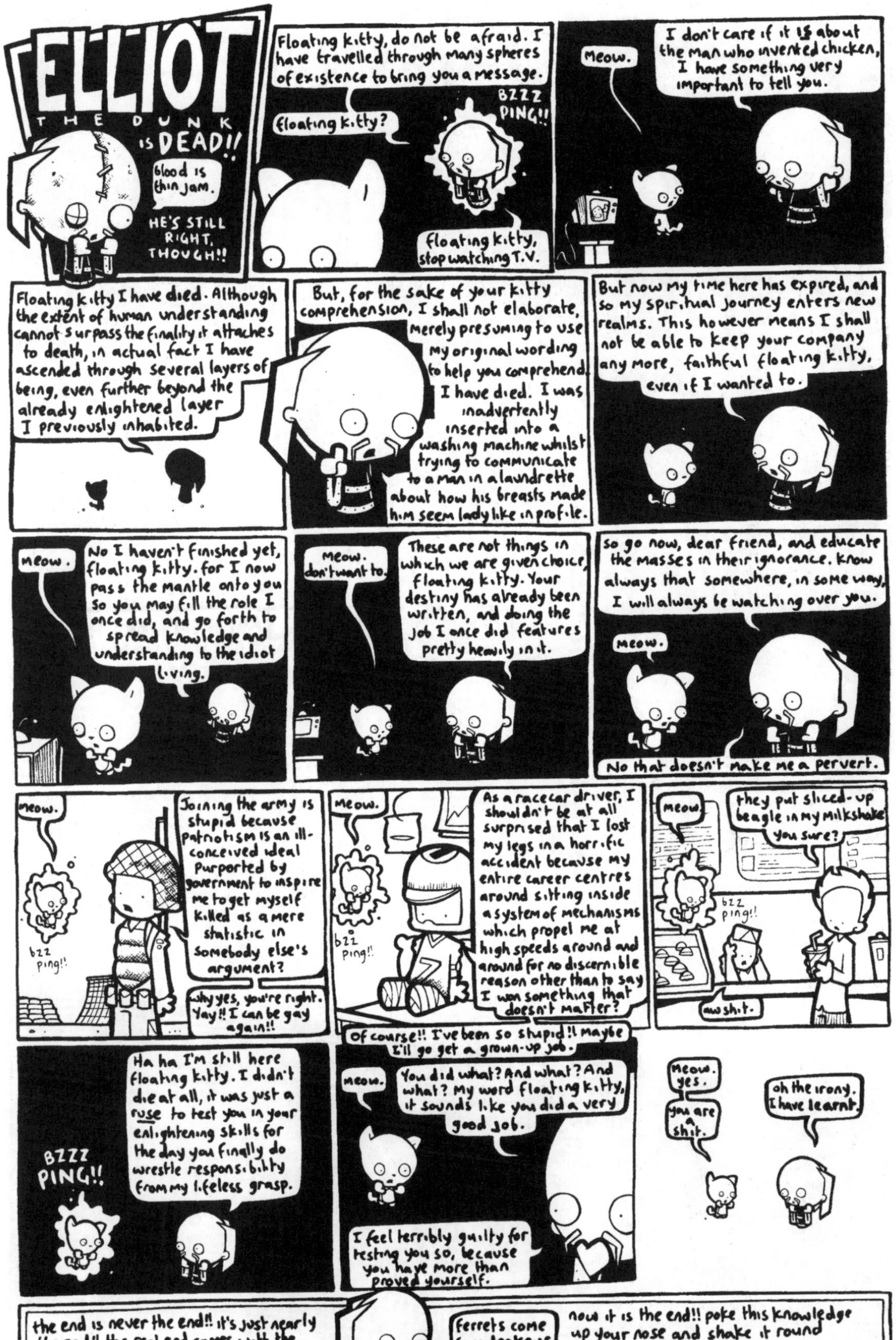
ELLIOT THE DUNK IS DEAD!!
blood is thin jam.
HE'S STILL RIGHT, THOUGH!!
Floating kitty, do not be afraid. I have travelled through many spheres of existence to bring you a message.
floating kitty?
BZZZ PING!!
floating kitty, stop watching T.V.
Meow.
I don't care if it IS about the man who invented chicken, I have something very important to tell you.
Floating kitty I have died. Although the extent of human understanding cannot surpass the finality it attaches to death, in actual fact I have ascended through several layers of being, even further beyond the already enlightened layer I previously inhabited.
But, for the sake of your kitty comprehension, I shall not elaborate, merely presuming to use my original wording to help you comprehend. I have died. I was inadvertently inserted into a washing machine whilst trying to communicate to a man in a laundrette about how his breasts made him seem lady like in profile.
But now my time here has expired, and so my spiritual journey enters new realms. This however means I shall not be able to keep your company any more, faithful floating kitty, even if I wanted to.
Meow.
No I haven't finished yet, floating kitty. for I now pass the mantle onto you so you may fill the role I once did, and go forth to spread knowledge and understanding to the idiot living.
Meow. don't want to.
These are not things in which we are given choice, floating kitty. Your destiny has already been written, and doing the job I once did features pretty heavily in it.
so go now, dear friend, and educate the masses in their ignorance. Know always that somewhere, in some way, I will always be watching over you.
Meow.
No that doesn't make me a pervert.
Meow.
Joining the army is stupid because patriotism is an ill-conceived ideal purported by government to inspire me to get myself killed as a mere statistic in somebody else's argument?
bzz ping!!
why yes, you're right. Yay!! I can be gay again!!
Meow.
As a racecar driver, I shouldn't be at all surprised that I lost my legs in a horrific accident because my entire career centres around sitting inside a system of mechanisms which propel me at high speeds around and around for no discernible reason other than to say I won something that doesn't matter?
bzz ping!!
Of course!! I've been so stupid!! Maybe I'll go get a grown-up job.
Meow.
they put sliced-up beagle in my milkshake? you sure?
bzz ping!!
aw shit.
Ha ha I'm still here floating kitty. I didn't die at all, it was just a ruse to test you in your enlightening skills for the day you finally do wrestle responsibility from my lifeless grasp.
BZZZ PING!!
Meow.
You did what? And what? And what? My word floating kitty, it sounds like you did a very good job.
I feel terribly guilty for testing you so, because you have more than proved yourself.
Meow. yes.
You are a shit.
oh the irony. I have learnt.
the end is never the end!! it's just nearly the end!! the real end comes with the learning of stuff!! stuff liiiike...
Ferrets come from donkeys.
now it is the end!! poke this knowledge up your nose and shake it round your head!! you flunky!!
JAMIE

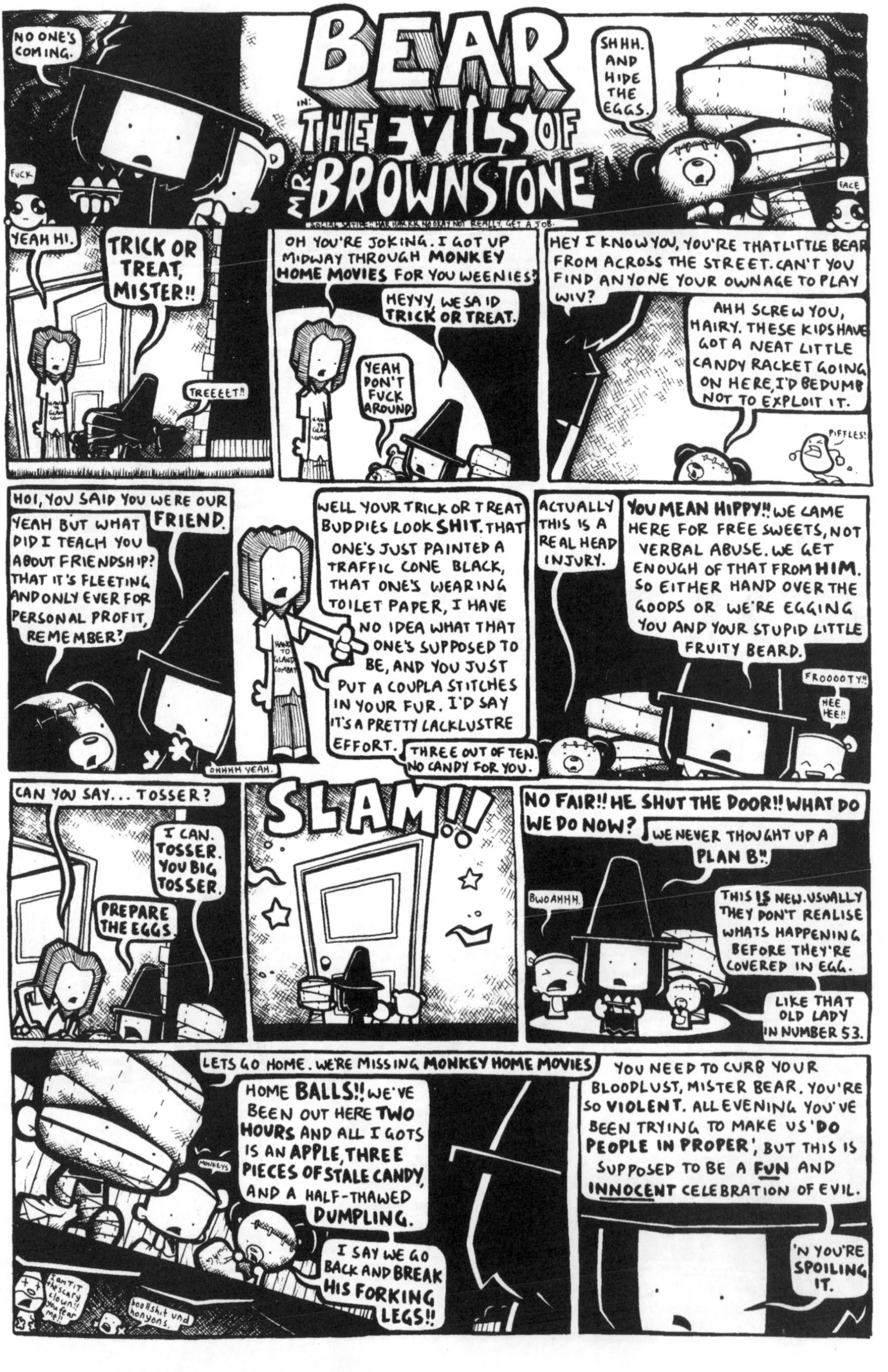
NO ONE'S COMING.
BEAR
IN: THE EVILS OF MR. BROWNSTONE
SHHH. AND HIDE THE EGGS.
FUCK
FACE
YEAH HI.
TRICK OR TREAT, MISTER!!
TREEEET!!
OH YOU'RE JOKING. I GOT UP MIDWAY THROUGH MONKEY HOME MOVIES FOR YOU WEENIES?
HEYYY, WE SAID TRICK OR TREAT.
YEAH DON'T FUCK AROUND.
HEY I KNOW YOU, YOU'RE THAT LITTLE BEAR FROM ACROSS THE STREET. CAN'T YOU FIND ANYONE YOUR OWN AGE TO PLAY WIV?
AHH SCREW YOU, HAIRY. THESE KIDS HAVE GOT A NEAT LITTLE CANDY RACKET GOING ON HERE, I'D BE DUMB NOT TO EXPLOIT IT.
PIFFLES!!
HOI, YOU SAID YOU WERE OUR FRIEND.
YEAH BUT WHAT DID I TEACH YOU ABOUT FRIENDSHIP? THAT IT'S FLEETING AND ONLY EVER FOR PERSONAL PROFIT, REMEMBER?
OHHHH YEAH.
WELL YOUR TRICK OR TREAT BUDDIES LOOK SHIT. THAT ONE'S JUST PAINTED A TRAFFIC CONE BLACK, THAT ONE'S WEARING TOILET PAPER, I HAVE NO IDEA WHAT THAT ONE'S SUPPOSED TO BE, AND YOU JUST PUT A COUPLA STITCHES IN YOUR FUR. I'D SAY IT'S A PRETTY LACKLUSTRE EFFORT.
THREE OUT OF TEN. NO CANDY FOR YOU.
ACTUALLY THIS IS A REAL HEAD INJURY.
YOU MEAN HIPPY!! WE CAME HERE FOR FREE SWEETS, NOT VERBAL ABUSE. WE GET ENOUGH OF THAT FROM HIM. SO EITHER HAND OVER THE GOODS OR WE'RE EGGING YOU AND YOUR STUPID LITTLE FRUITY BEARD.
FROOOOTY!!
HEE HEE!!
CAN YOU SAY... TOSSER?
I CAN. TOSSER. YOU BIG TOSSER.
PREPARE THE EGGS.
SLAM!!
NO FAIR!! HE SHUT THE DOOR!! WHAT DO WE DO NOW?
WE NEVER THOUGHT UP A PLAN B!!
BWOAHHH.
THIS IS NEW. USUALLY THEY DON'T REALISE WHATS HAPPENING BEFORE THEY'RE COVERED IN EGG.
LIKE THAT OLD LADY IN NUMBER 53.
LETS GO HOME. WE'RE MISSING MONKEY HOME MOVIES
MONKEYS
HOME BALLS!! WE'VE BEEN OUT HERE TWO HOURS AND ALL I GOTS IS AN APPLE, THREE PIECES OF STALE CANDY, AND A HALF-THAWED DUMPLING.
I SAY WE GO BACK AND BREAK HIS FORKING LEGS!!
I am TIT the scary clown!! you fear me!!
boollshit und honyons.
YOU NEED TO CURB YOUR BLOODLUST, MISTER BEAR. YOU'RE SO VIOLENT. ALL EVENING YOU'VE BEEN TRYING TO MAKE US 'DO PEOPLE IN PROPER', BUT THIS IS SUPPOSED TO BE A FUN AND INNOCENT CELEBRATION OF EVIL.
'N YOU'RE SPOILING IT.

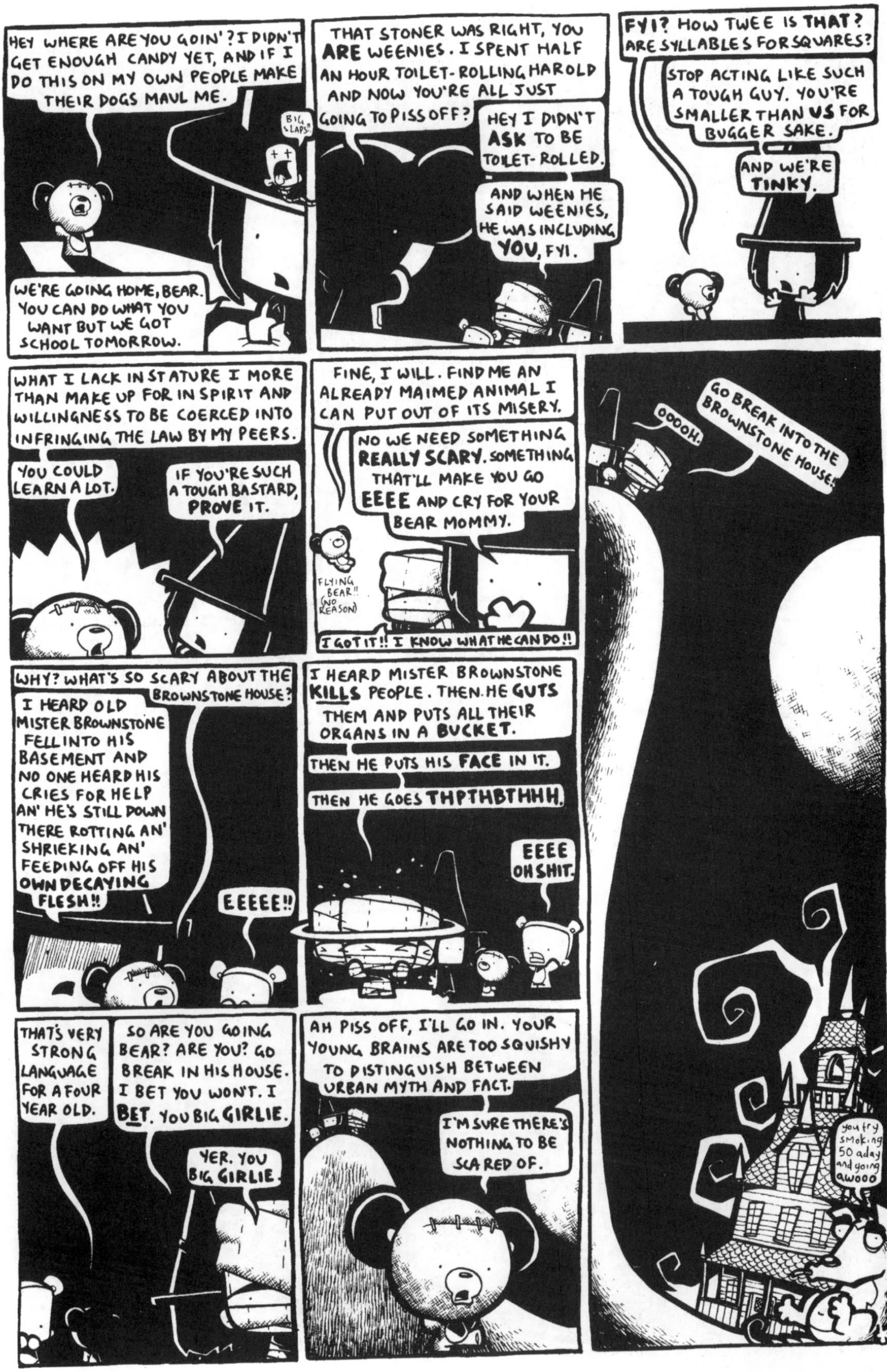

HEY WHERE ARE YOU GOIN'? I DIDN'T GET ENOUGH CANDY YET, AND IF I DO THIS ON MY OWN PEOPLE MAKE THEIR DOGS MAUL ME.
BIG SLAPS!!
WE'RE GOING HOME, BEAR. YOU CAN DO WHAT YOU WANT BUT WE GOT SCHOOL TOMORROW.
THAT STONER WAS RIGHT, YOU ARE WEENIES. I SPENT HALF AN HOUR TOILET-ROLLING HAROLD AND NOW YOU'RE ALL JUST GOING TO PISS OFF?
HEY I DIDN'T ASK TO BE TOILET-ROLLED.
AND WHEN HE SAID WEENIES, HE WAS INCLUDING YOU, FYI.
FYI? HOW TWEE IS THAT? ARE SYLLABLES FOR SQUARES?
STOP ACTING LIKE SUCH A TOUGH GUY. YOU'RE SMALLER THAN US FOR BUGGER SAKE.
AND WE'RE TINKY.
WHAT I LACK IN STATURE I MORE THAN MAKE UP FOR IN SPIRIT AND WILLINGNESS TO BE COERCED INTO INFRINGING THE LAW BY MY PEERS.
YOU COULD LEARN A LOT.
IF YOU'RE SUCH A TOUGH BASTARD, PROVE IT.
FINE, I WILL. FIND ME AN ALREADY MAIMED ANIMAL I CAN PUT OUT OF ITS MISERY.
NO WE NEED SOMETHING REALLY SCARY. SOMETHING THAT'LL MAKE YOU GO EEEE AND CRY FOR YOUR BEAR MOMMY.
FLYING BEAR!! (NO REASON)
I GOT IT!! I KNOW WHAT HE CAN DO!!
OOOOH.
GO BREAK INTO THE BROWNSTONE HOUSE!!
WHY? WHAT'S SO SCARY ABOUT THE BROWNSTONE HOUSE?
I HEARD OLD MISTER BROWNSTONE FELL INTO HIS BASEMENT AND NO ONE HEARD HIS CRIES FOR HELP AN' HE'S STILL DOWN THERE ROTTING AN' SHRIEKING AN' FEEDING OFF HIS OWN DECAYING FLESH!!
EEEEE!!
I HEARD MISTER BROWNSTONE KILLS PEOPLE. THEN HE GUTS THEM AND PUTS ALL THEIR ORGANS IN A BUCKET.
THEN HE PUTS HIS FACE IN IT.
THEN HE GOES THPTHBTHHH.
EEEE OH SHIT.
THAT'S VERY STRONG LANGUAGE FOR A FOUR YEAR OLD.
SO ARE YOU GOING BEAR? ARE YOU? GO BREAK IN HIS HOUSE. I BET YOU WON'T. I BET. YOU BIG GIRLIE.
YER. YOU BIG GIRLIE.
AH PISS OFF, I'LL GO IN. YOUR YOUNG BRAINS ARE TOO SQUISHY TO DISTINGUISH BETWEEN URBAN MYTH AND FACT.
I'M SURE THERE'S NOTHING TO BE SCARED OF.
you try smoking 50 aday and going awooo

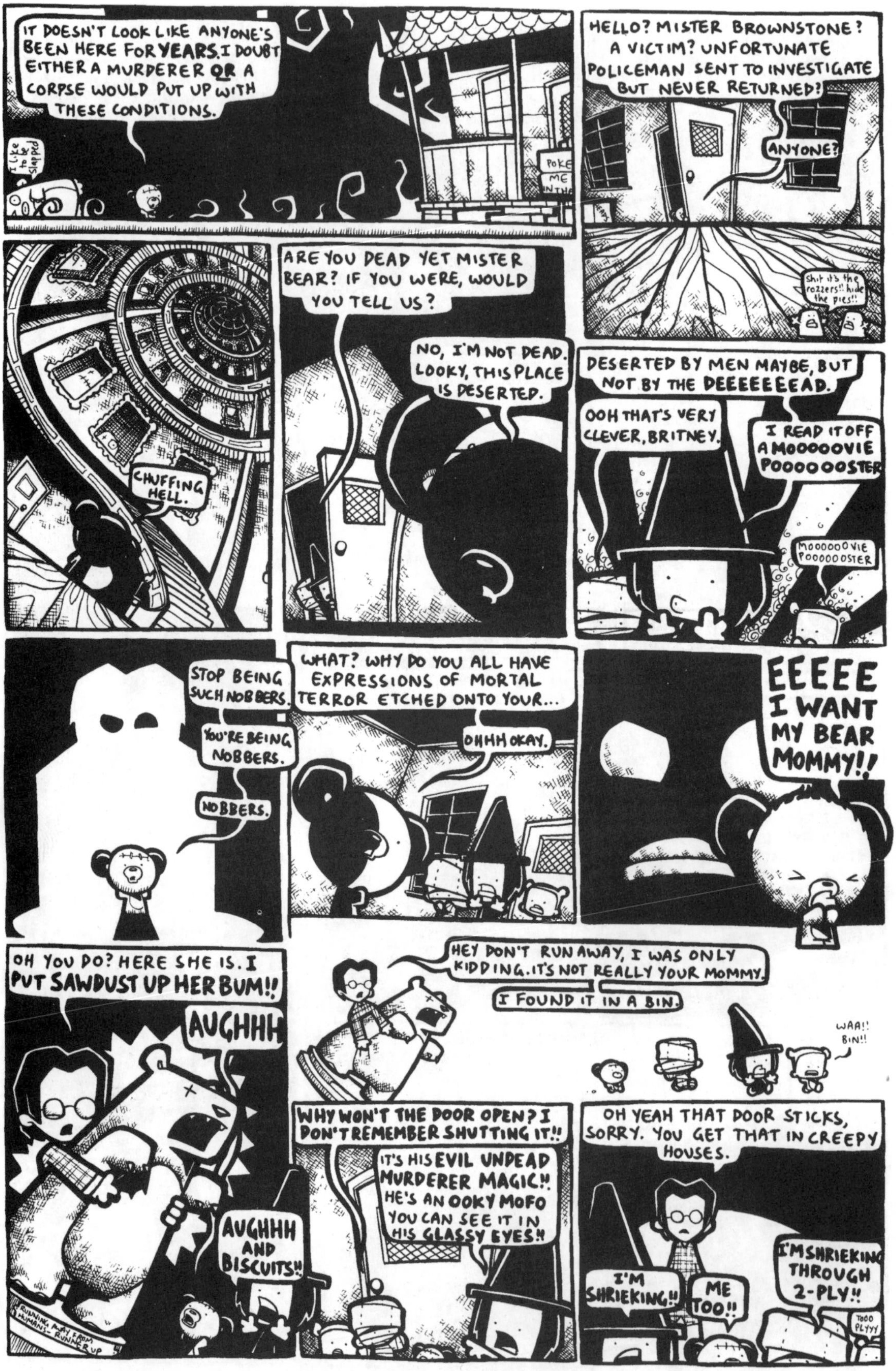
IT DOESN'T LOOK LIKE ANYONE'S BEEN HERE FOR YEARS. I DOUBT EITHER A MURDERER OR A CORPSE WOULD PUT UP WITH THESE CONDITIONS.
I like to be slapped
POKE ME IN THE
HELLO? MISTER BROWNSTONE? A VICTIM? UNFORTUNATE POLICEMAN SENT TO INVESTIGATE BUT NEVER RETURNED?
ANYONE?
Shit it's the rozzers!! hide the pies!!
CHUFFING HELL.
ARE YOU DEAD YET MISTER BEAR? IF YOU WERE, WOULD YOU TELL US?
NO, I'M NOT DEAD. LOOKY, THIS PLACE IS DESERTED.
DESERTED BY MEN MAYBE, BUT NOT BY THE DEEEEEEEAD.
OOH THAT'S VERY CLEVER, BRITNEY.
I READ IT OFF A MOOOOOVIE POOOOOOSTER
MOOOOOOVIE POOOOOOSTER
STOP BEING SUCH NOBBERS.
YOU'RE BEING NOBBERS.
NOBBERS.
WHAT? WHY DO YOU ALL HAVE EXPRESSIONS OF MORTAL TERROR ETCHED ONTO YOUR...
OHHH OKAY.
EEEEE I WANT MY BEAR MOMMY!!
OH YOU DO? HERE SHE IS. I PUT SAWDUST UP HER BUM!!
AUGHHH
AUGHHH AND BISCUITS!!
RUNNING AWAY FROM HUMANS - RUNNER UP
HEY DON'T RUN AWAY, I WAS ONLY KIDDING. IT'S NOT REALLY YOUR MOMMY.
I FOUND IT IN A BIN.
WAA!! BIN!!
WHY WON'T THE DOOR OPEN? I DON'T REMEMBER SHUTTING IT!!
IT'S HIS EVIL UNDEAD MURDERER MAGIC!! HE'S AN OOKY MOFO YOU CAN SEE IT IN HIS GLASSY EYES!!
OH YEAH THAT DOOR STICKS, SORRY. YOU GET THAT IN CREEPY HOUSES.
I'M SHRIEKING!!
ME TOO!!
I'M SHRIEKING THROUGH 2-PLY!!
TOOO PLYYY

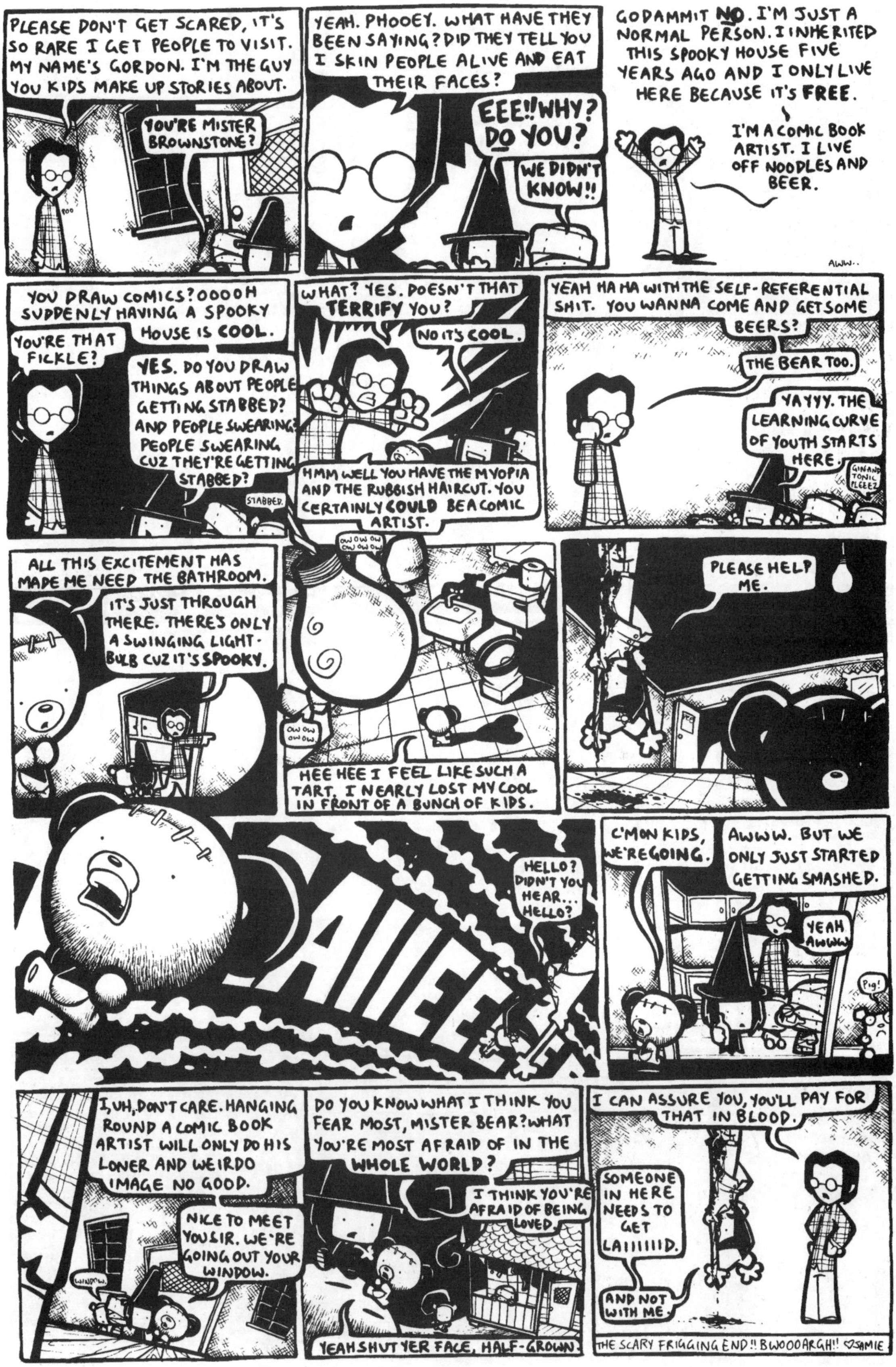

PLEASE DON'T GET SCARED, IT'S SO RARE I GET PEOPLE TO VISIT. MY NAME'S GORDON. I'M THE GUY YOU KIDS MAKE UP STORIES ABOUT.
YOU'RE MISTER BROWNSTONE?
YEAH. PHOOEY. WHAT HAVE THEY BEEN SAYING? DID THEY TELL YOU I SKIN PEOPLE ALIVE AND EAT THEIR FACES?
EEE!! WHY? DO YOU?
WE DIDN'T KNOW!!
GODAMMIT NO. I'M JUST A NORMAL PERSON. I INHERITED THIS SPOOKY HOUSE FIVE YEARS AGO AND I ONLY LIVE HERE BECAUSE IT'S FREE.
I'M A COMIC BOOK ARTIST. I LIVE OFF NOODLES AND BEER.
AWW..
YOU DRAW COMICS? OOOOH SUDDENLY HAVING A SPOOKY HOUSE IS COOL.
YOU'RE THAT FICKLE?
YES. DO YOU DRAW THINGS ABOUT PEOPLE GETTING STABBED? AND PEOPLE SWEARING? PEOPLE SWEARING CUZ THEY'RE GETTING STABBED?
STABBED.
WHAT? YES. DOESN'T THAT TERRIFY YOU?
NO IT'S COOL.
HMM WELL YOU HAVE THE MYOPIA AND THE RUBBISH HAIRCUT. YOU CERTAINLY COULD BE A COMIC ARTIST.
YEAH HA HA WITH THE SELF-REFERENTIAL SHIT. YOU WANNA COME AND GET SOME BEERS?
THE BEAR TOO.
YAYYY. THE LEARNING CURVE OF YOUTH STARTS HERE.
GIN AND TONIC PLEEEZ
ALL THIS EXCITEMENT HAS MADE ME NEED THE BATHROOM.
IT'S JUST THROUGH THERE. THERE'S ONLY A SWINGING LIGHT-BULB CUZ IT'S SPOOKY.
OW OW OW OW OW OW
OW OW OW OW
HEE HEE I FEEL LIKE SUCH A TART. I NEARLY LOST MY COOL IN FRONT OF A BUNCH OF KIDS.
PLEASE HELP ME.
AIIEEE
HELLO? DIDN'T YOU HEAR... HELLO?
C'MON KIDS, WE'RE GOING.
AWWW. BUT WE ONLY JUST STARTED GETTING SMASHED.
YEAH AWWW
Pig!
I, UH, DON'T CARE. HANGING ROUND A COMIC BOOK ARTIST WILL ONLY DO HIS LONER AND WEIRDO IMAGE NO GOOD.
NICE TO MEET YOU SIR. WE'RE GOING OUT YOUR WINDOW.
WINDOW.
DO YOU KNOW WHAT I THINK YOU FEAR MOST, MISTER BEAR? WHAT YOU'RE MOST AFRAID OF IN THE WHOLE WORLD?
I THINK YOU'RE AFRAID OF BEING LOVED.
YEAH SHUT YER FACE, HALF-GROWN.
I CAN ASSURE YOU, YOU'LL PAY FOR THAT IN BLOOD.
SOMEONE IN HERE NEEDS TO GET LAIIIIIID.
AND NOT WITH ME.
THE SCARY FRIGGING END!! BWOOOARGH!! ♡JAMIE

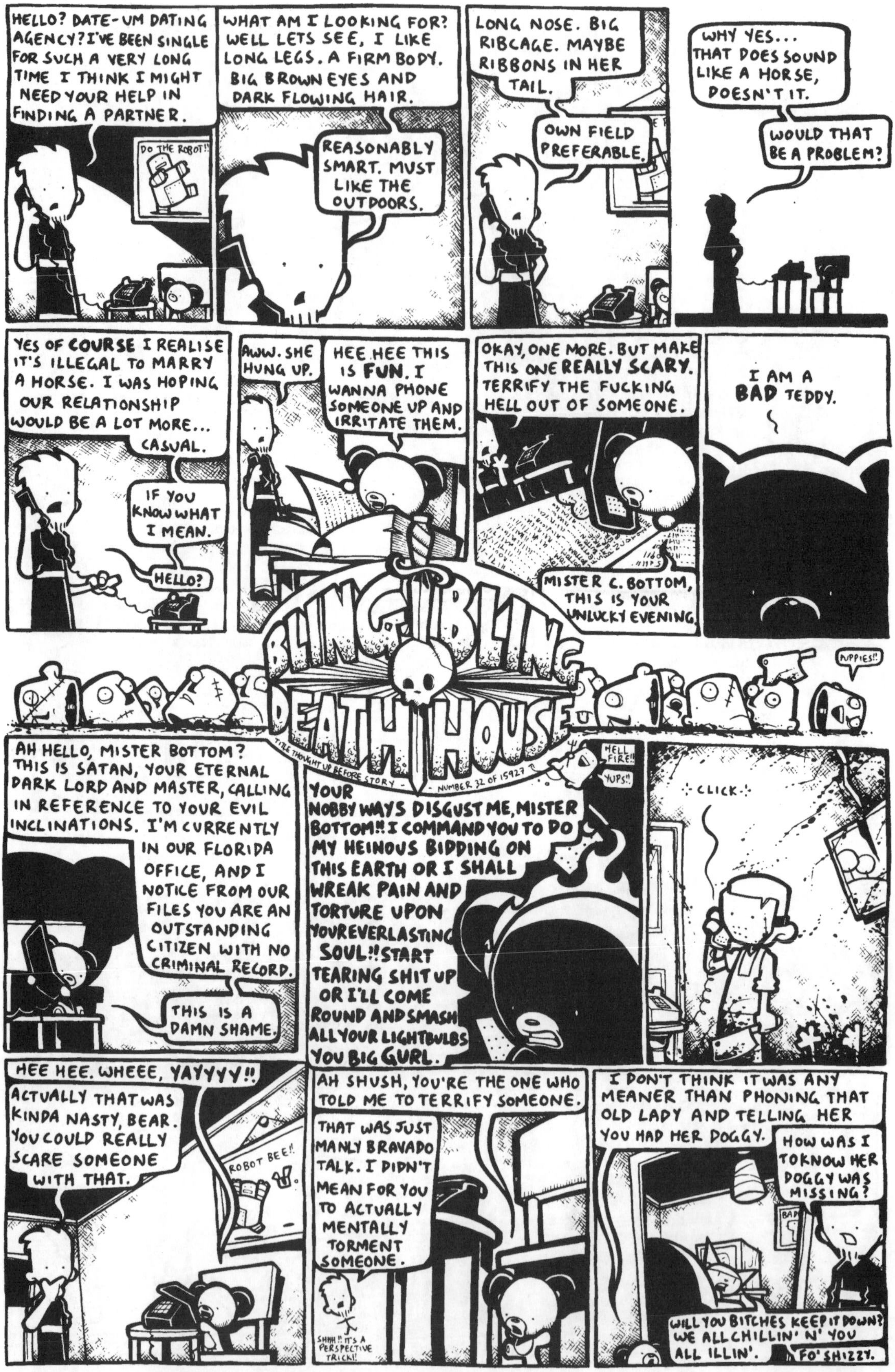

HELLO? DATE-UM DATING AGENCY? I'VE BEEN SINGLE FOR SUCH A VERY LONG TIME I THINK I MIGHT NEED YOUR HELP IN FINDING A PARTNER.
DO THE ROBOT!!
WHAT AM I LOOKING FOR? WELL LETS SEE, I LIKE LONG LEGS. A FIRM BODY. BIG BROWN EYES AND DARK FLOWING HAIR.
REASONABLY SMART. MUST LIKE THE OUTDOORS.
LONG NOSE. BIG RIBCAGE. MAYBE RIBBONS IN HER TAIL.
OWN FIELD PREFERABLE.
WHY YES... THAT DOES SOUND LIKE A HORSE, DOESN'T IT.
WOULD THAT BE A PROBLEM?
YES OF COURSE I REALISE IT'S ILLEGAL TO MARRY A HORSE. I WAS HOPING OUR RELATIONSHIP WOULD BE A LOT MORE... CASUAL.
IF YOU KNOW WHAT I MEAN.
HELLO?
AWW. SHE HUNG UP.
HEE HEE THIS IS FUN. I WANNA PHONE SOMEONE UP AND IRRITATE THEM.
OKAY, ONE MORE. BUT MAKE THIS ONE REALLY SCARY. TERRIFY THE FUCKING HELL OUT OF SOMEONE.
MISTER C. BOTTOM, THIS IS YOUR UNLUCKY EVENING.
I AM A BAD TEDDY.
BLING BLING DEATH HOUSE
TITLE THOUGHT UP BEFORE STORY - NUMBER 32 OF 15927
PUPPIES!!
HELL FIRE!!
YUPS!!
AH HELLO, MISTER BOTTOM? THIS IS SATAN, YOUR ETERNAL DARK LORD AND MASTER, CALLING IN REFERENCE TO YOUR EVIL INCLINATIONS. I'M CURRENTLY IN OUR FLORIDA OFFICE, AND I NOTICE FROM OUR FILES YOU ARE AN OUTSTANDING CITIZEN WITH NO CRIMINAL RECORD.
THIS IS A DAMN SHAME.
YOUR NOBBY WAYS DISGUST ME, MISTER BOTTOM!! I COMMAND YOU TO DO MY HEINOUS BIDDING ON THIS EARTH OR I SHALL WREAK PAIN AND TORTURE UPON YOUR EVERLASTING SOUL!! START TEARING SHIT UP OR I'LL COME ROUND AND SMASH ALL YOUR LIGHTBULBS YOU BIG GURL.
CLICK
HEE HEE. WHEEE, YAYYYY!!
ACTUALLY THAT WAS KINDA NASTY, BEAR. YOU COULD REALLY SCARE SOMEONE WITH THAT.
ROBOT BEE!!
AH SHUSH, YOU'RE THE ONE WHO TOLD ME TO TERRIFY SOMEONE.
THAT WAS JUST MANLY BRAVADO TALK. I DIDN'T MEAN FOR YOU TO ACTUALLY MENTALLY TORMENT SOMEONE.
SHHH!! IT'S A PERSPECTIVE TRICK!
I DON'T THINK IT WAS ANY MEANER THAN PHONING THAT OLD LADY AND TELLING HER YOU HAD HER DOGGY.
HOW WAS I TO KNOW HER DOGGY WAS MISSING?
WILL YOU BITCHES KEEP IT DOWN? WE ALL CHILLIN' N' YOU ALL ILLIN'.
FO' SHIZZY.

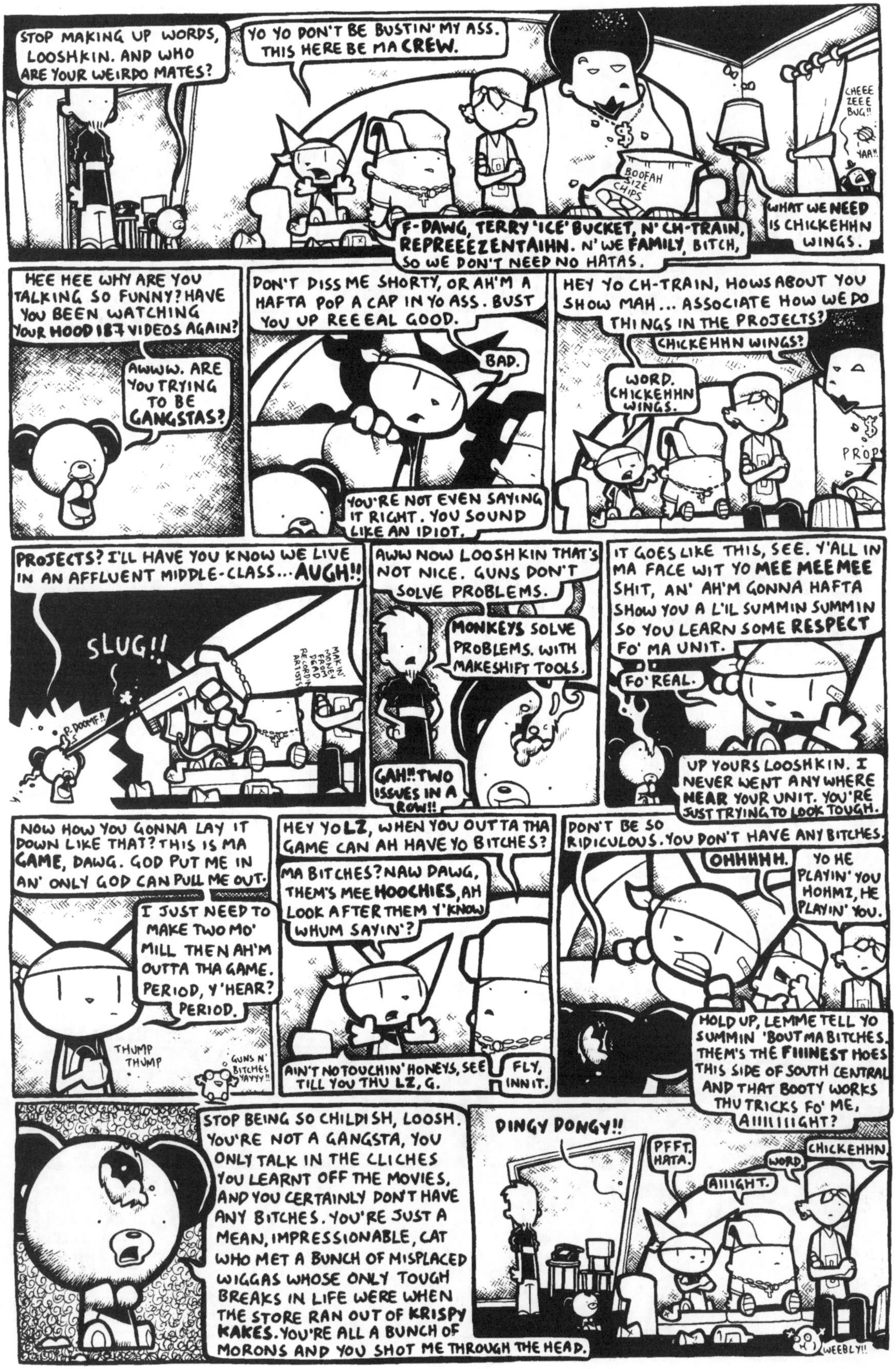

STOP MAKING UP WORDS, LOOSHKIN. AND WHO ARE YOUR WEIRDO MATES?
YO YO DON'T BE BUSTIN' MY ASS. THIS HERE BE MA CREW.
BOOFAH SIZE CHIPS
CHEEE ZEEE BUG!!
YAA!!
F-DAWG, TERRY 'ICE' BUCKET, N' CH-TRAIN, REPREEEZENTAIHN. N' WE FAMILY, BITCH, SO WE DON'T NEED NO HATAS.
WHAT WE NEED IS CHICKEHHN WINGS.
HEE HEE WHY ARE YOU TALKING SO FUNNY? HAVE YOU BEEN WATCHING YOUR HOOD 187 VIDEOS AGAIN?
AWWW. ARE YOU TRYING TO BE GANGSTAS?
DON'T DISS ME SHORTY, OR AH'M A HAFTA POP A CAP IN YO ASS. BUST YOU UP REEEAL GOOD.
BAD.
YOU'RE NOT EVEN SAYING IT RIGHT. YOU SOUND LIKE AN IDIOT.
HEY YO CH-TRAIN, HOWS ABOUT YOU SHOW MAH... ASSOCIATE HOW WE DO THINGS IN THE PROJECTS?
CHICKEHHN WINGS?
WORD. CHICKEHHN WINGS.
PROPS
PROJECTS? I'LL HAVE YOU KNOW WE LIVE IN AN AFFLUENT MIDDLE-CLASS... AUGH!!
SLUG!!
P. DOOMF!!
MAKIN' MONEY FROM DEAD RECORDIN' ARTISTS
AWW NOW LOOSHKIN THAT'S NOT NICE. GUNS DON'T SOLVE PROBLEMS.
MONKEYS SOLVE PROBLEMS. WITH MAKESHIFT TOOLS.
GAH!! TWO ISSUES IN A ROW!!
IT GOES LIKE THIS, SEE. Y'ALL IN MA FACE WIT YO MEE MEE MEE SHIT, AN' AH'M GONNA HAFTA SHOW YOU A L'IL SUMMIN SUMMIN SO YOU LEARN SOME RESPECT FO' MA UNIT.
FO' REAL.
UP YOURS LOOSHKIN. I NEVER WENT ANYWHERE NEAR YOUR UNIT. YOU'RE JUST TRYING TO LOOK TOUGH.
NOW HOW YOU GONNA LAY IT DOWN LIKE THAT? THIS IS MA GAME, DAWG. GOD PUT ME IN AN' ONLY GOD CAN PULL ME OUT.
I JUST NEED TO MAKE TWO MO' MILL THEN AH'M OUTTA THA GAME. PERIOD, Y'HEAR? PERIOD.
THUMP THUMP
GUNS N' BITCHES YAYYY!!
HEY YO LZ, WHEN YOU OUTTA THA GAME CAN AH HAVE YO BITCHES?
MA BITCHES? NAW DAWG, THEM'S MEE HOOCHIES, AH LOOK AFTER THEM Y'KNOW WHUM SAYIN'?
AIN'T NO TOUCHIN' HONEYS, SEE TILL YOU THU LZ, G.
FLY, INNIT.
DON'T BE SO RIDICULOUS. YOU DON'T HAVE ANY BITCHES.
OHHHHH.
YO HE PLAYIN' YOU HOHMZ, HE PLAYIN' YOU.
HOLD UP, LEMME TELL YO SUMMIN 'BOUT MA BITCHES. THEM'S THE FIIINEST HOES THIS SIDE OF SOUTH CENTRAL AND THAT BOOTY WORKS THU TRICKS FO' ME, AIIIIIIIGHT?
STOP BEING SO CHILDISH, LOOSH. YOU'RE NOT A GANGSTA, YOU ONLY TALK IN THE CLICHES YOU LEARNT OFF THE MOVIES, AND YOU CERTAINLY DON'T HAVE ANY BITCHES. YOU'RE JUST A MEAN, IMPRESSIONABLE, CAT WHO MET A BUNCH OF MISPLACED WIGGAS WHOSE ONLY TOUGH BREAKS IN LIFE WERE WHEN THE STORE RAN OUT OF KRISPY KAKES. YOU'RE ALL A BUNCH OF MORONS AND YOU SHOT ME THROUGH THE HEAD.
DINGY DONGY!!
PFFT. HATA.
AIIIGHT.
WORD.
CHICKEHHN.
WEEBLY!!

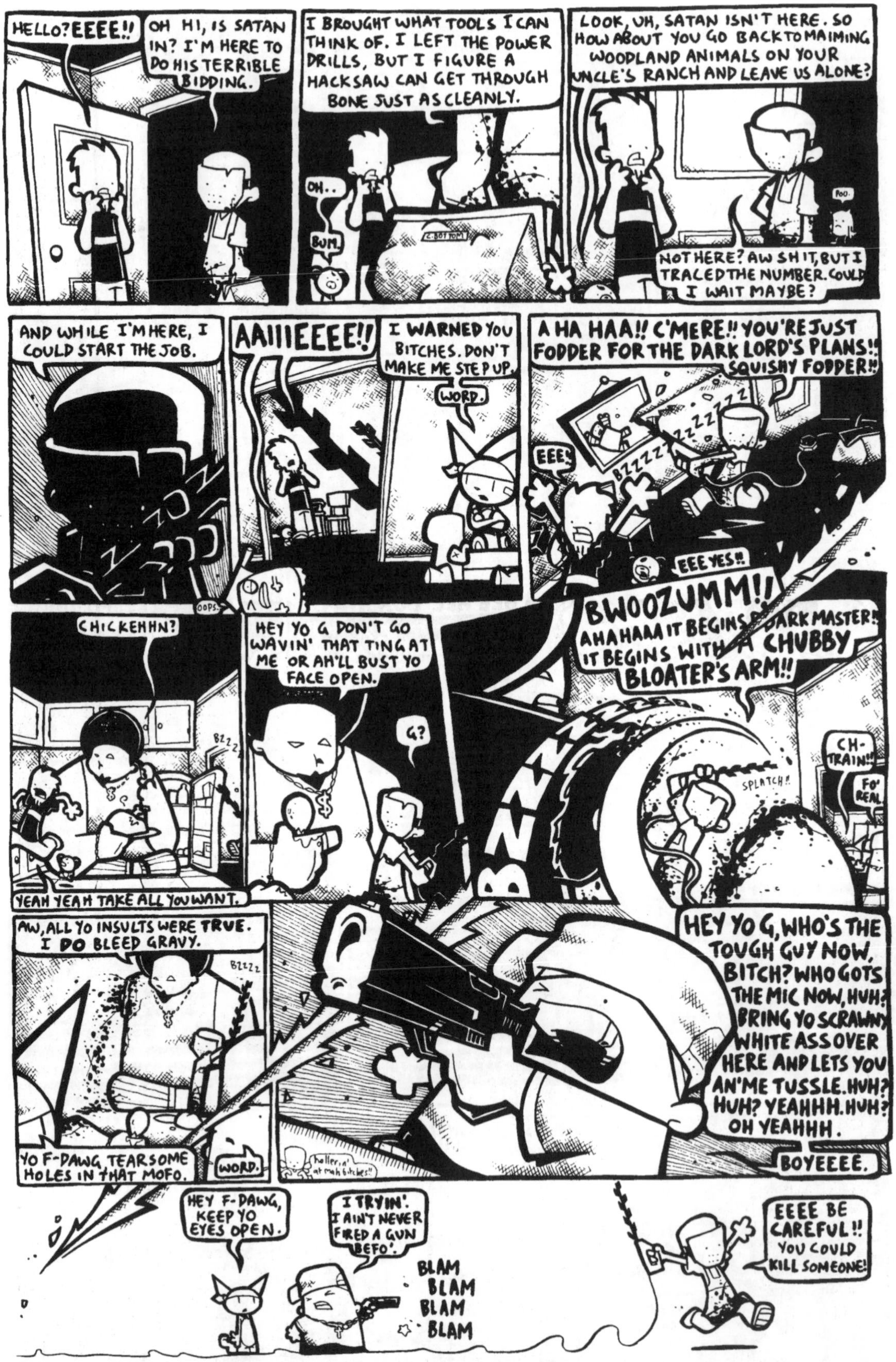
HELLO? EEEE!!
OH HI, IS SATAN IN? I'M HERE TO DO HIS TERRIBLE BIDDING.
I BROUGHT WHAT TOOLS I CAN THINK OF. I LEFT THE POWER DRILLS, BUT I FIGURE A HACKSAW CAN GET THROUGH BONE JUST AS CLEANLY.
OH..
BUM.
C-BOTTOM
LOOK, UH, SATAN ISN'T HERE. SO HOW ABOUT YOU GO BACK TO MAIMING WOODLAND ANIMALS ON YOUR UNCLE'S RANCH AND LEAVE US ALONE?
POO.
NOT HERE? AW SHIT, BUT I TRACED THE NUMBER. COULD I WAIT MAYBE?
AND WHILE I'M HERE, I COULD START THE JOB.
AAIIIEEEE!!
I WARNED YOU BITCHES. DON'T MAKE ME STEP UP.
WORD.
OOPS.
A HA HAA!! C'MERE!! YOU'RE JUST FODDER FOR THE DARK LORD'S PLANS!! SQUISHY FODDER!!
EEE!
EEE YES!!
CHICKEHHN?
YEAH YEAH TAKE ALL YOU WANT.
HEY YO G DON'T GO WAVIN' THAT TING AT ME OR AH'LL BUST YO FACE OPEN.
G?
BWOOZUMM!!
AHAHAAA IT BEGINS DARK MASTER!! IT BEGINS WITH A CHUBBY BLOATER'S ARM!!
SPLATCH!!
CH-TRAIN!!
FO' REAL.
AW, ALL YO INSULTS WERE TRUE. I DO BLEED GRAVY.
YO F-DAWG, TEAR SOME HOLES IN THAT MOFO.
WORD.
hollerin' at mah bitches!!
HEY YO G, WHO'S THE TOUGH GUY NOW, BITCH? WHO GOTS THE MIC NOW, HUH? BRING YO SCRAWNY WHITE ASS OVER HERE AND LETS YOU AN'ME TUSSLE. HUH? HUH? YEAHHH. HUH? OH YEAHHH.
BOYEEEE.
HEY F-DAWG, KEEP YO EYES OPEN.
I TRYIN'. I AIN'T NEVER FIRED A GUN BEFO'.
BLAM BLAM BLAM BLAM
EEEE BE CAREFUL!! YOU COULD KILL SOMEONE!

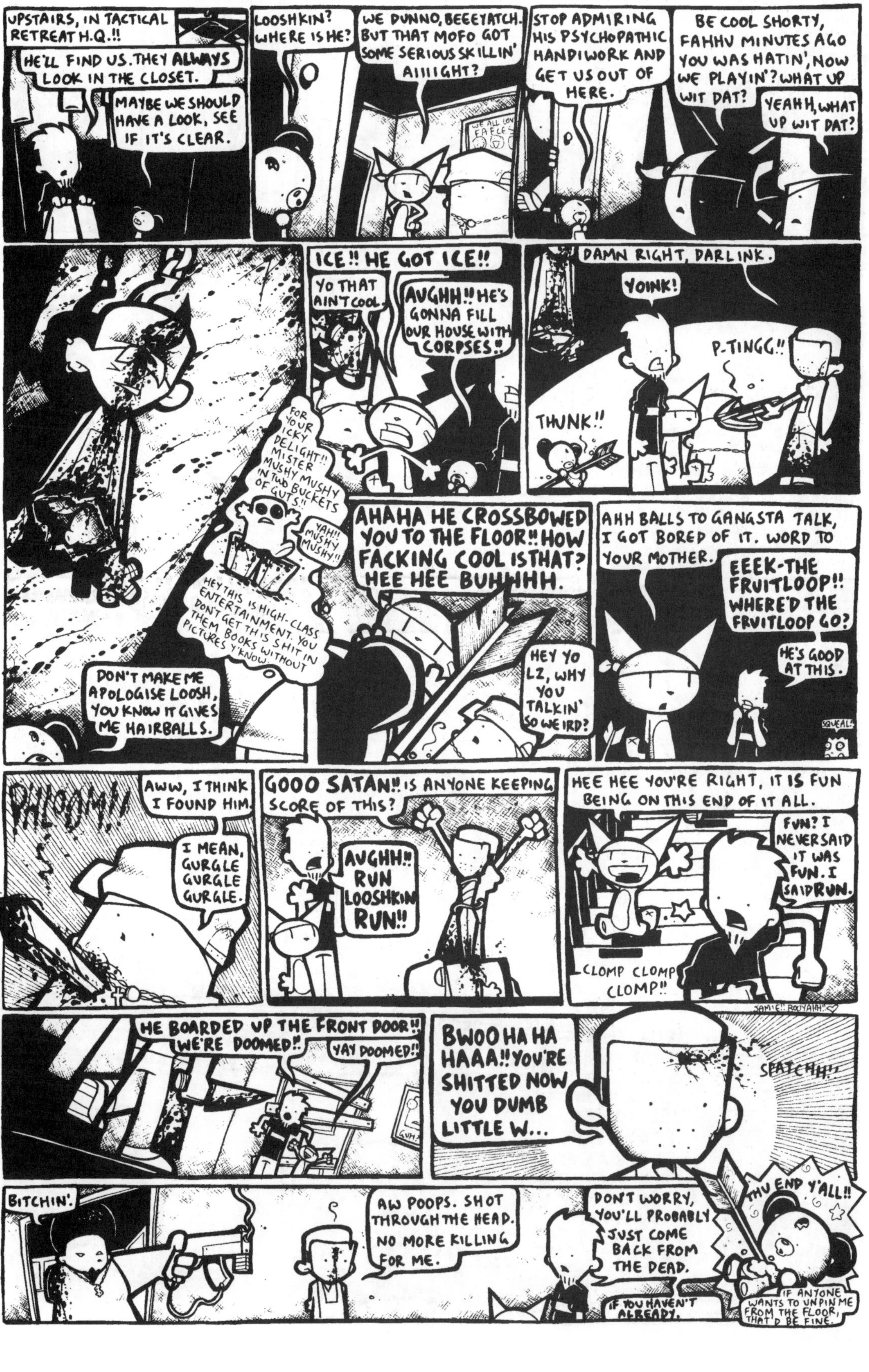
UPSTAIRS, IN TACTICAL RETREAT H.Q.!!
HE'LL FIND US. THEY ALWAYS LOOK IN THE CLOSET.
MAYBE WE SHOULD HAVE A LOOK, SEE IF IT'S CLEAR.
LOOSHKIN? WHERE IS HE?
WE DUNNO, BEEEYATCH. BUT THAT MOFO GOT SOME SERIOUS SKILLIN' AIIIIGHT?
STOP ADMIRING HIS PSYCHOPATHIC HANDIWORK AND GET US OUT OF HERE.
BE COOL SHORTY, FAHHV MINUTES AGO YOU WAS HATIN', NOW WE PLAYIN'? WHAT UP WIT DAT?
YEAHH, WHAT UP WIT DAT?
ICE!! HE GOT ICE!!
YO THAT AIN'T COOL.
AUGHH!! HE'S GONNA FILL OUR HOUSE WITH CORPSES!!
DAMN RIGHT, DARLINK.
YOINK!
P-TINGG!!
THUNK!!
FOR YOUR ICKY DELIGHT!! MISTER MUSHY MUSHY IN TWO BUCKETS OF GUTS!!
YAH!! MUSHY MUSHY!!
HEY THIS IS HIGH-CLASS ENTERTAINMENT. YOU DON'T GET THIS SHIT IN THEM BOOKS WITHOUT PICTURES Y'KNOW.
DON'T MAKE ME APOLOGISE LOOSH, YOU KNOW IT GIVES ME HAIRBALLS.
AHAHA HE CROSSBOWED YOU TO THE FLOOR!! HOW FACKING COOL IS THAT? HEE HEE BUHHHH.
HEY YO LZ, WHY YOU TALKIN' SO WEIRD?
AHH BALLS TO GANGSTA TALK, I GOT BORED OF IT. WORD TO YOUR MOTHER.
EEEK-THE FRUITLOOP!! WHERE'D THE FRUITLOOP GO?
HE'S GOOD AT THIS.
SQUEAL!
PHLOOM!!
AWW, I THINK I FOUND HIM.
I MEAN, GURGLE GURGLE GURGLE.
GOOO SATAN!! IS ANYONE KEEPING SCORE OF THIS?
AUGHH!! RUN LOOSHKIN RUN!!
HEE HEE YOU'RE RIGHT, IT IS FUN BEING ON THIS END OF IT ALL.
FUN? I NEVER SAID IT WAS FUN. I SAID RUN.
CLOMP CLOMP CLOMP!!
HE BOARDED UP THE FRONT DOOR!! WE'RE DOOMED!!
YAY DOOMED!!
BWOO HA HA HAAA!! YOU'RE SHITTED NOW YOU DUMB LITTLE W...
SPATCHH!!
BITCHIN'.
AW POOPS. SHOT THROUGH THE HEAD. NO MORE KILLING FOR ME.
DON'T WORRY, YOU'LL PROBABLY JUST COME BACK FROM THE DEAD.
IF YOU HAVEN'T ALREADY.
THU END Y'ALL!!
IF ANYONE WANTS TO UNPIN ME FROM THE FLOOR, THAT'D BE FINE.

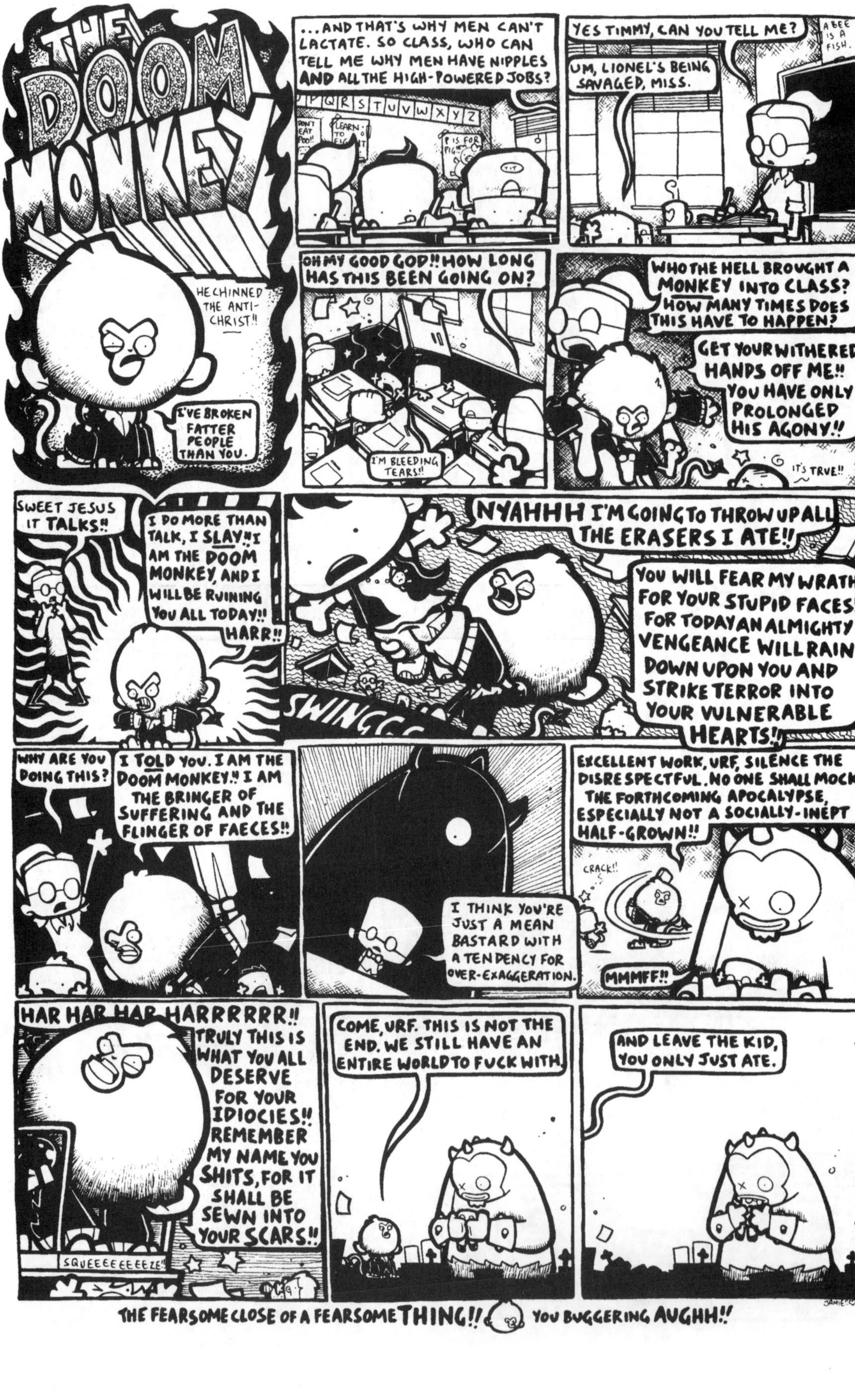
THE DOOM MONKEY
HE CHINNED THE ANTI-CHRIST!!
I'VE BROKEN FATTER PEOPLE THAN YOU.
...AND THAT'S WHY MEN CAN'T LACTATE. SO CLASS, WHO CAN TELL ME WHY MEN HAVE NIPPLES AND ALL THE HIGH-POWERED JOBS?
YES TIMMY, CAN YOU TELL ME?
A BEE IS A FISH.
UM, LIONEL'S BEING SAVAGED, MISS.
OH MY GOOD GOD!! HOW LONG HAS THIS BEEN GOING ON?
I'M BLEEDING TEARS!!
WHO THE HELL BROUGHT A MONKEY INTO CLASS? HOW MANY TIMES DOES THIS HAVE TO HAPPEN?
GET YOUR WITHERED HANDS OFF ME!! YOU HAVE ONLY PROLONGED HIS AGONY!!
IT'S TRUE!!
SWEET JESUS IT TALKS!!
I DO MORE THAN TALK, I SLAY!! I AM THE DOOM MONKEY, AND I WILL BE RUINING YOU ALL TODAY!! HARR!!
NYAHHH I'M GOING TO THROW UP ALL THE ERASERS I ATE!!
YOU WILL FEAR MY WRATH FOR YOUR STUPID FACES!! FOR TODAY AN ALMIGHTY VENGEANCE WILL RAIN DOWN UPON YOU AND STRIKE TERROR INTO YOUR VULNERABLE HEARTS!!
WHY ARE YOU DOING THIS?
I TOLD YOU. I AM THE DOOM MONKEY!! I AM THE BRINGER OF SUFFERING AND THE FLINGER OF FAECES!!
I THINK YOU'RE JUST A MEAN BASTARD WITH A TENDENCY FOR OVER-EXAGGERATION.
EXCELLENT WORK, URF, SILENCE THE DISRESPECTFUL. NO ONE SHALL MOCK THE FORTHCOMING APOCALYPSE, ESPECIALLY NOT A SOCIALLY-INEPT HALF-GROWN!!
CRACK!!
MMMFF!!
HAR HAR HAR HARRRRRR!!
TRULY THIS IS WHAT YOU ALL DESERVE FOR YOUR IDIOCIES!! REMEMBER MY NAME YOU SHITS, FOR IT SHALL BE SEWN INTO YOUR SCARS!!
SQUEEEEEEEEZE!!
COME, URF. THIS IS NOT THE END. WE STILL HAVE AN ENTIRE WORLD TO FUCK WITH.
AND LEAVE THE KID, YOU ONLY JUST ATE.

THE FEARSOME CLOSE OF A FEARSOME THING!! YOU BUGGERING AUGHH!!

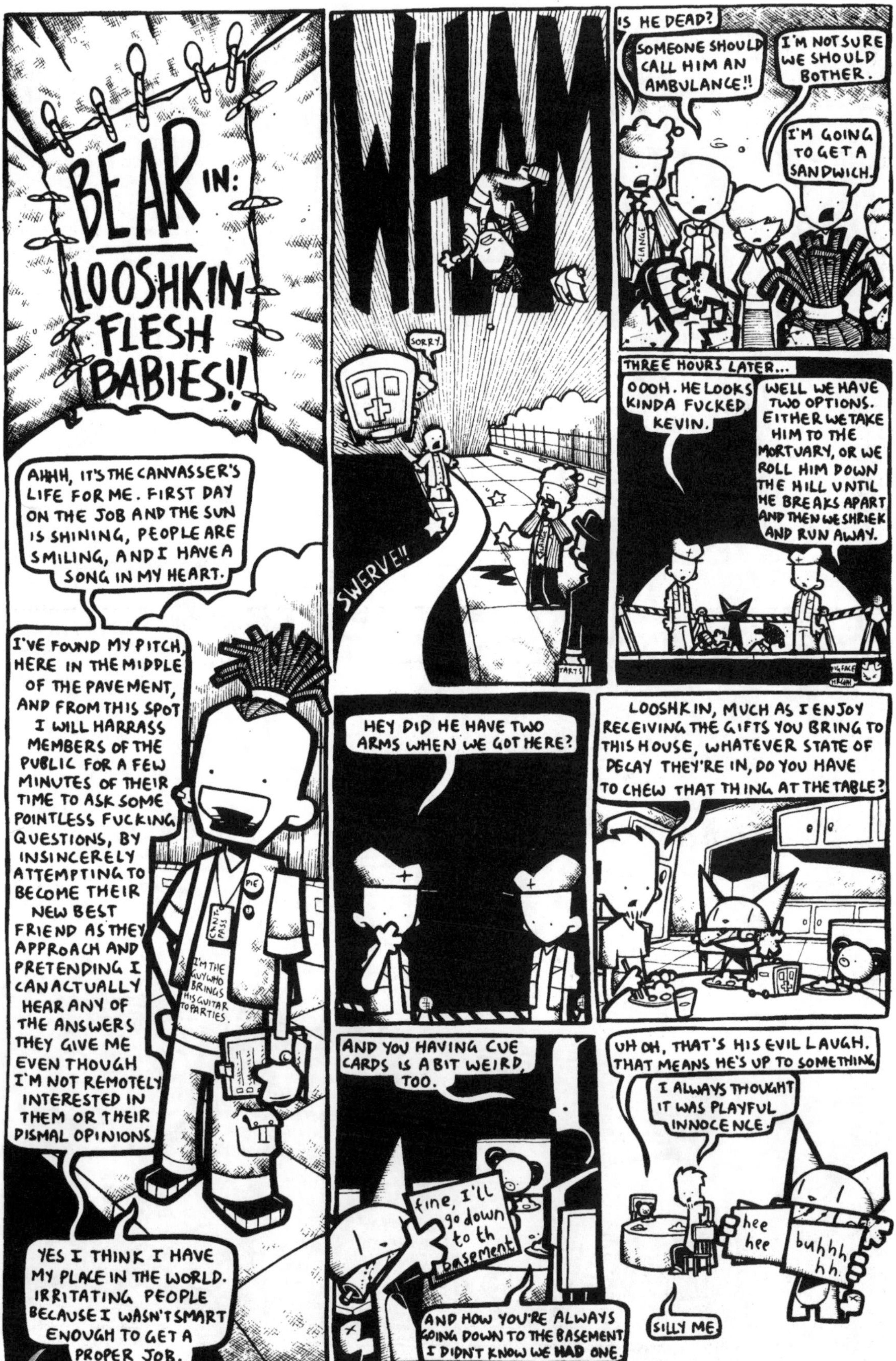
BEAR IN:
LOOSHKIN FLESH BABIES!!
AHHH, IT'S THE CANVASSER'S LIFE FOR ME. FIRST DAY ON THE JOB AND THE SUN IS SHINING, PEOPLE ARE SMILING, AND I HAVE A SONG IN MY HEART.
I'VE FOUND MY PITCH, HERE IN THE MIDDLE OF THE PAVEMENT, AND FROM THIS SPOT I WILL HARRASS MEMBERS OF THE PUBLIC FOR A FEW MINUTES OF THEIR TIME TO ASK SOME POINTLESS FUCKING QUESTIONS, BY INSINCERELY ATTEMPTING TO BECOME THEIR NEW BEST FRIEND AS THEY APPROACH AND PRETENDING I CAN ACTUALLY HEAR ANY OF THE ANSWERS THEY GIVE ME EVEN THOUGH I'M NOT REMOTELY INTERESTED IN THEM OR THEIR DISMAL OPINIONS.
PIE
CANT-PASS
I'M THE GUY WHO BRINGS HIS GUITAR TO PARTIES.
YES I THINK I HAVE MY PLACE IN THE WORLD. IRRITATING PEOPLE BECAUSE I WASN'T SMART ENOUGH TO GET A PROPER JOB.
WHAM
SORRY.
SWERVE!!
TARTS
IS HE DEAD?
SOMEONE SHOULD CALL HIM AN AMBULANCE!!
I'M NOT SURE WE SHOULD BOTHER.
I'M GOING TO GET A SANDWICH.
FLANGE
THREE HOURS LATER...
OOOH. HE LOOKS KINDA FUCKED KEVIN.
WELL WE HAVE TWO OPTIONS. EITHER WE TAKE HIM TO THE MORTUARY, OR WE ROLL HIM DOWN THE HILL UNTIL HE BREAKS APART AND THEN WE SHRIEK AND RUN AWAY.
HEY DID HE HAVE TWO ARMS WHEN WE GOT HERE?
LOOSHKIN, MUCH AS I ENJOY RECEIVING THE GIFTS YOU BRING TO THIS HOUSE, WHATEVER STATE OF DECAY THEY'RE IN, DO YOU HAVE TO CHEW THAT THING AT THE TABLE?
AND YOU HAVING CUE CARDS IS A BIT WEIRD, TOO.
fine, I'll go down to th basement
AND HOW YOU'RE ALWAYS GOING DOWN TO THE BASEMENT I DIDN'T KNOW WE HAD ONE.
UH OH, THAT'S HIS EVIL LAUGH. THAT MEANS HE'S UP TO SOMETHING.
I ALWAYS THOUGHT IT WAS PLAYFUL INNOCENCE.
hee hee
buhhh hh.
SILLY ME.

HE'S UNDER MY WINDOW NOW!! THE FUCKER!! HE WON'T FUCKING SHUT UP!!

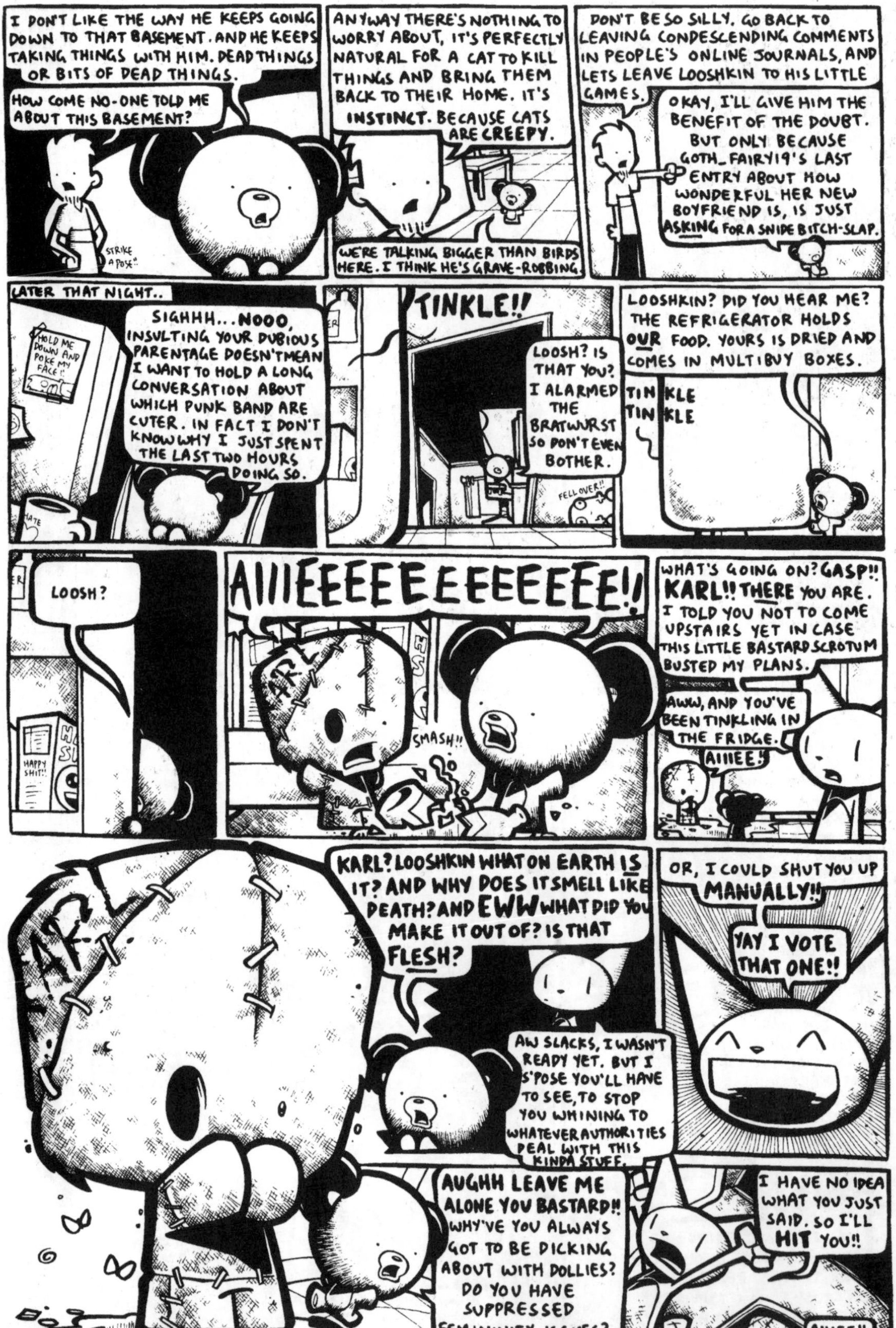
I DON'T LIKE THE WAY HE KEEPS GOING DOWN TO THAT BASEMENT. AND HE KEEPS TAKING THINGS WITH HIM. DEAD THINGS OR BITS OF DEAD THINGS.
HOW COME NO-ONE TOLD ME ABOUT THIS BASEMENT?
STRIKE A POSE!!
ANYWAY THERE'S NOTHING TO WORRY ABOUT, IT'S PERFECTLY NATURAL FOR A CAT TO KILL THINGS AND BRING THEM BACK TO THEIR HOME. IT'S INSTINCT. BECAUSE CATS ARE CREEPY.
WE'RE TALKING BIGGER THAN BIRDS HERE. I THINK HE'S GRAVE-ROBBING.
DON'T BE SO SILLY. GO BACK TO LEAVING CONDESCENDING COMMENTS IN PEOPLE'S ONLINE JOURNALS, AND LETS LEAVE LOOSHKIN TO HIS LITTLE GAMES.
OKAY, I'LL GIVE HIM THE BENEFIT OF THE DOUBT. BUT ONLY BECAUSE GOTH_FAIRY19'S LAST ENTRY ABOUT HOW WONDERFUL HER NEW BOYFRIEND IS, IS JUST ASKING FOR A SNIDE BITCH-SLAP.
LATER THAT NIGHT..
HOLD ME DOWN AND POKE MY FACE!!
SIGHHH...NOOO, INSULTING YOUR DUBIOUS PARENTAGE DOESN'T MEAN I WANT TO HOLD A LONG CONVERSATION ABOUT WHICH PUNK BAND ARE CUTER. IN FACT I DON'T KNOW WHY I JUST SPENT THE LAST TWO HOURS DOING SO.
HATE
TINKLE!!
LOOSH? IS THAT YOU? I ALARMED THE BRATWURST SO DON'T EVEN BOTHER.
FELL OVER!!
LOOSHKIN? DID YOU HEAR ME? THE REFRIGERATOR HOLDS OUR FOOD. YOURS IS DRIED AND COMES IN MULTIBUY BOXES.
TINKLE
TINKLE
LOOSH?
HAPPY SHIT!!
AIIIEEEEEEEEEEEEEE!!
SMASH!!
WHAT'S GOING ON? GASP!! KARL!! THERE YOU ARE. I TOLD YOU NOT TO COME UPSTAIRS YET IN CASE THIS LITTLE BASTARD SCROTUM BUSTED MY PLANS.
AWW, AND YOU'VE BEEN TINKLING IN THE FRIDGE.
AIIIEE!
KARL? LOOSHKIN WHAT ON EARTH IS IT? AND WHY DOES IT SMELL LIKE DEATH? AND EWW WHAT DID YOU MAKE IT OUT OF? IS THAT FLESH?
AW SLACKS, I WASN'T READY YET. BUT I S'POSE YOU'LL HAVE TO SEE, TO STOP YOU WHINING TO WHATEVER AUTHORITIES DEAL WITH THIS KINDA STUFF.
OR, I COULD SHUT YOU UP MANUALLY!!
YAY I VOTE THAT ONE!!
AUGHH LEAVE ME ALONE YOU BASTARD!! WHY'VE YOU ALWAYS GOT TO BE DICKING ABOUT WITH DOLLIES? DO YOU HAVE SUPPRESSED FEMININITY ISSUES?
I HAVE NO IDEA WHAT YOU JUST SAID. SO I'LL HIT YOU!!
AIIIEE!!

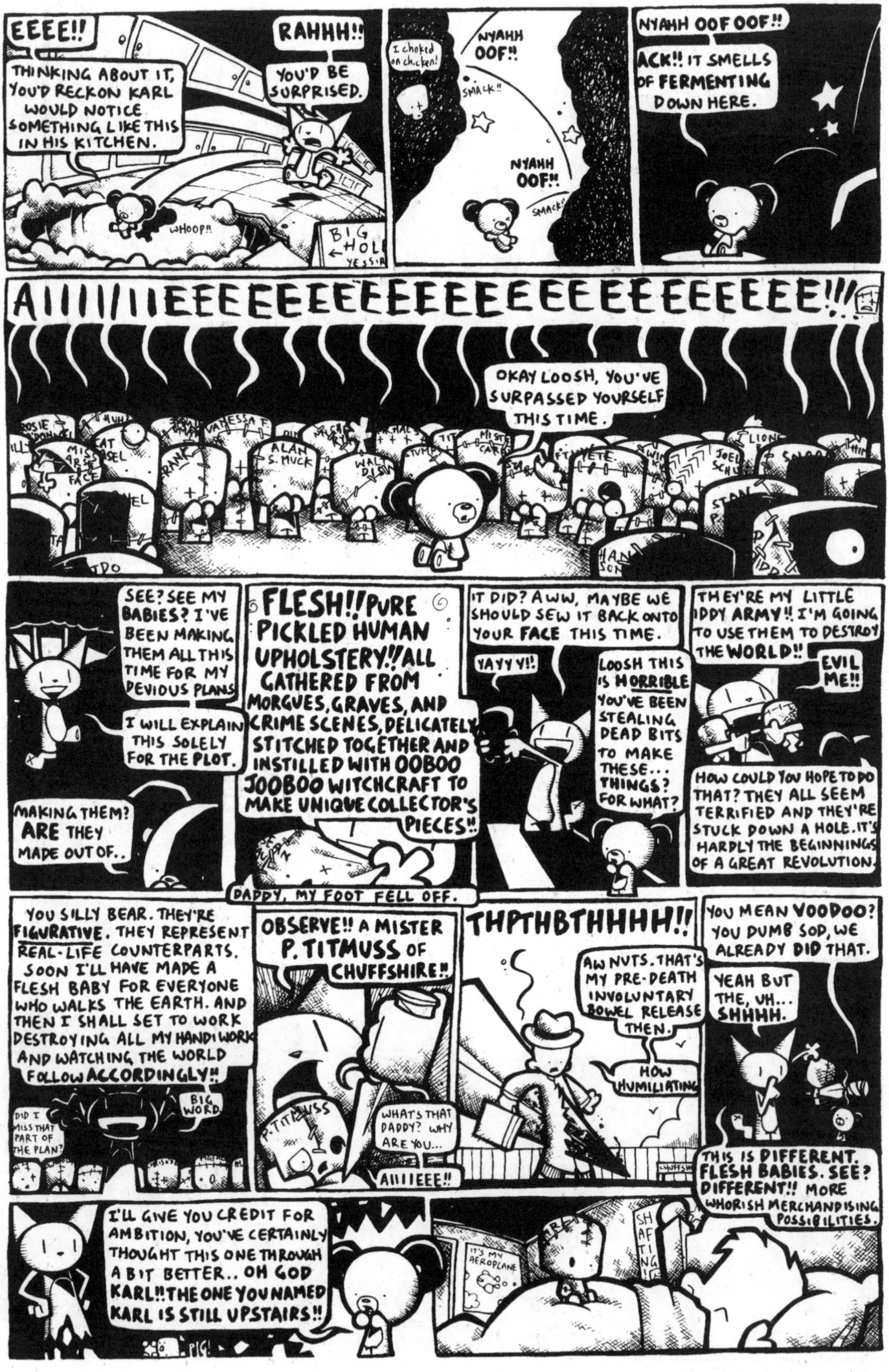
EEEE!!
THINKING ABOUT IT, YOU'D RECKON KARL WOULD NOTICE SOMETHING LIKE THIS IN HIS KITCHEN.
RAHHH!!
YOU'D BE SURPRISED.
WHOOP!!
I choked on chicken!
NYAHH OOF!!
SMACK!!
NYAHH OOF!!
SMACK!!
NYAHH OOF OOF!!
ACK!! IT SMELLS OF FERMENTING DOWN HERE.
AIIIIIIIEEEEEEEEEEEEEEEEEEEEEE!!!
OKAY LOOSH, YOU'VE SURPASSED YOURSELF THIS TIME.
SEE? SEE MY BABIES? I'VE BEEN MAKING THEM ALL THIS TIME FOR MY DEVIOUS PLANS
I WILL EXPLAIN THIS SOLELY FOR THE PLOT.
MAKING THEM? ARE THEY MADE OUT OF..
FLESH!! PURE PICKLED HUMAN UPHOLSTERY!! ALL GATHERED FROM MORGUES, GRAVES, AND CRIME SCENES, DELICATELY STITCHED TOGETHER AND INSTILLED WITH OOBOO JOOBOO WITCHCRAFT TO MAKE UNIQUE COLLECTOR'S PIECES!!
DADDY, MY FOOT FELL OFF.
IT DID? AWW, MAYBE WE SHOULD SEW IT BACK ONTO YOUR FACE THIS TIME.
YAYYY!!
LOOSH THIS IS HORRIBLE. YOU'VE BEEN STEALING DEAD BITS TO MAKE THESE... THINGS? FOR WHAT?
THEY'RE MY LITTLE IDDY ARMY!! I'M GOING TO USE THEM TO DESTROY THE WORLD!!
EVIL ME!!
HOW COULD YOU HOPE TO DO THAT? THEY ALL SEEM TERRIFIED AND THEY'RE STUCK DOWN A HOLE. IT'S HARDLY THE BEGINNINGS OF A GREAT REVOLUTION.
YOU SILLY BEAR. THEY'RE FIGURATIVE. THEY REPRESENT REAL-LIFE COUNTERPARTS. SOON I'LL HAVE MADE A FLESH BABY FOR EVERYONE WHO WALKS THE EARTH. AND THEN I SHALL SET TO WORK DESTROYING ALL MY HANDIWORK AND WATCHING THE WORLD FOLLOW ACCORDINGLY!!
BIG WORD.
DID I MISS THAT PART OF THE PLAN?
OBSERVE!! A MISTER P. TITMUSS OF CHUFFSHIRE!!
P. TITMUSS
WHAT'S THAT DADDY? WHY ARE YOU...
AIIIIEEE!!
THPTHBTHHHH!!
AW NUTS. THAT'S MY PRE-DEATH INVOLUNTARY BOWEL RELEASE THEN.
HOW HUMILIATING.
YOU MEAN VOODOO? YOU DUMB SOD, WE ALREADY DID THAT.
YEAH BUT THE, UH... SHHHH.
THIS IS DIFFERENT. FLESH BABIES. SEE? DIFFERENT!! MORE WHORISH MERCHANDISING POSSIBILITIES.
I'LL GIVE YOU CREDIT FOR AMBITION, YOU'VE CERTAINLY THOUGHT THIS ONE THROUGH A BIT BETTER.. OH GOD KARL!! THE ONE YOU NAMED KARL IS STILL UPSTAIRS!!
IT'S MY AEROPLANE
SHAFTING!

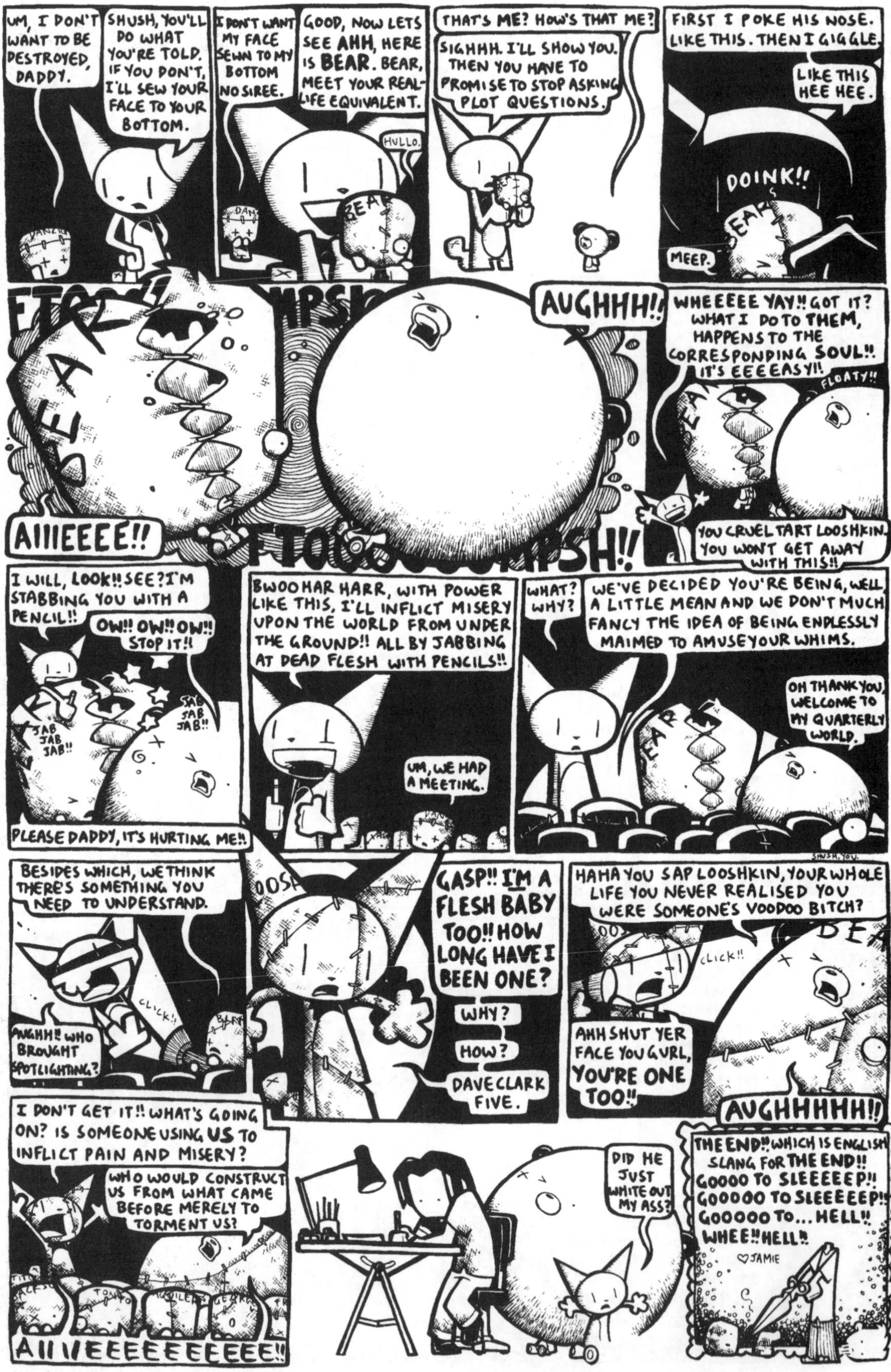
UM, I DON'T WANT TO BE DESTROYED, DADDY.
SHUSH, YOU'LL DO WHAT YOU'RE TOLD. IF YOU DON'T, I'LL SEW YOUR FACE TO YOUR BOTTOM.
I DON'T WANT MY FACE SEWN TO MY BOTTOM NO SIREE.
GOOD, NOW LETS SEE AHH, HERE IS BEAR. BEAR, MEET YOUR REAL-LIFE EQUIVALENT.
HULLO.
BEAR
THAT'S ME? HOW'S THAT ME?
SIGHHH. I'LL SHOW YOU. THEN YOU HAVE TO PROMISE TO STOP ASKING PLOT QUESTIONS.
FIRST I POKE HIS NOSE. LIKE THIS. THEN I GIGGLE.
LIKE THIS HEE HEE.
DOINK!!
MEEP.
AIIIEEEE!!
AUGHHH!!
WHEEEEE YAY!! GOT IT? WHAT I DO TO THEM, HAPPENS TO THE CORRESPONDING SOUL!! IT'S EEEEASY!!
FLOATY!!
YOU CRUEL TART LOOSHKIN. YOU WON'T GET AWAY WITH THIS!!
I WILL, LOOK!! SEE? I'M STABBING YOU WITH A PENCIL!!
OW!! OW!! OW!! STOP IT!!
JAB JAB JAB!!
JAB JAB JAB!!
PLEASE DADDY, IT'S HURTING ME!!
BWOOHAR HARR, WITH POWER LIKE THIS, I'LL INFLICT MISERY UPON THE WORLD FROM UNDER THE GROUND!! ALL BY JABBING AT DEAD FLESH WITH PENCILS!!
UM, WE HAD A MEETING.
WHAT? WHY?
WE'VE DECIDED YOU'RE BEING, WELL, A LITTLE MEAN AND WE DON'T MUCH FANCY THE IDEA OF BEING ENDLESSLY MAIMED TO AMUSE YOUR WHIMS.
OH THANK YOU, WELCOME TO MY QUARTERLY WORLD.
SHUSH, YOU.
BESIDES WHICH, WE THINK THERE'S SOMETHING YOU NEED TO UNDERSTAND.
CLICK!!
AUGHH!! WHO BROUGHT SPOTLIGHTING?
GASP!! I'M A FLESH BABY TOO!! HOW LONG HAVE I BEEN ONE?
WHY?
HOW?
DAVE CLARK FIVE.
HAHA YOU SAP LOOSHKIN, YOUR WHOLE LIFE YOU NEVER REALISED YOU WERE SOMEONE'S VOODOO BITCH?
CLICK!!
AHH SHUT YER FACE YOU GURL, YOU'RE ONE TOO!!
AUGHHHHH!!
I DON'T GET IT!! WHAT'S GOING ON? IS SOMEONE USING US TO INFLICT PAIN AND MISERY?
WHO WOULD CONSTRUCT US FROM WHAT CAME BEFORE MERELY TO TORMENT US?
AIIIEEEEEEEEEEE!!
DID HE JUST WHITE OUT MY ASS?
THE END!! WHICH IS ENGLISH SLANG FOR THE END!! GOOOO TO SLEEEEEP!! GOOOOO TO SLEEEEEP!! GOOOOO TO... HELL!! WHEE!! HELL!!
♡JAMIE

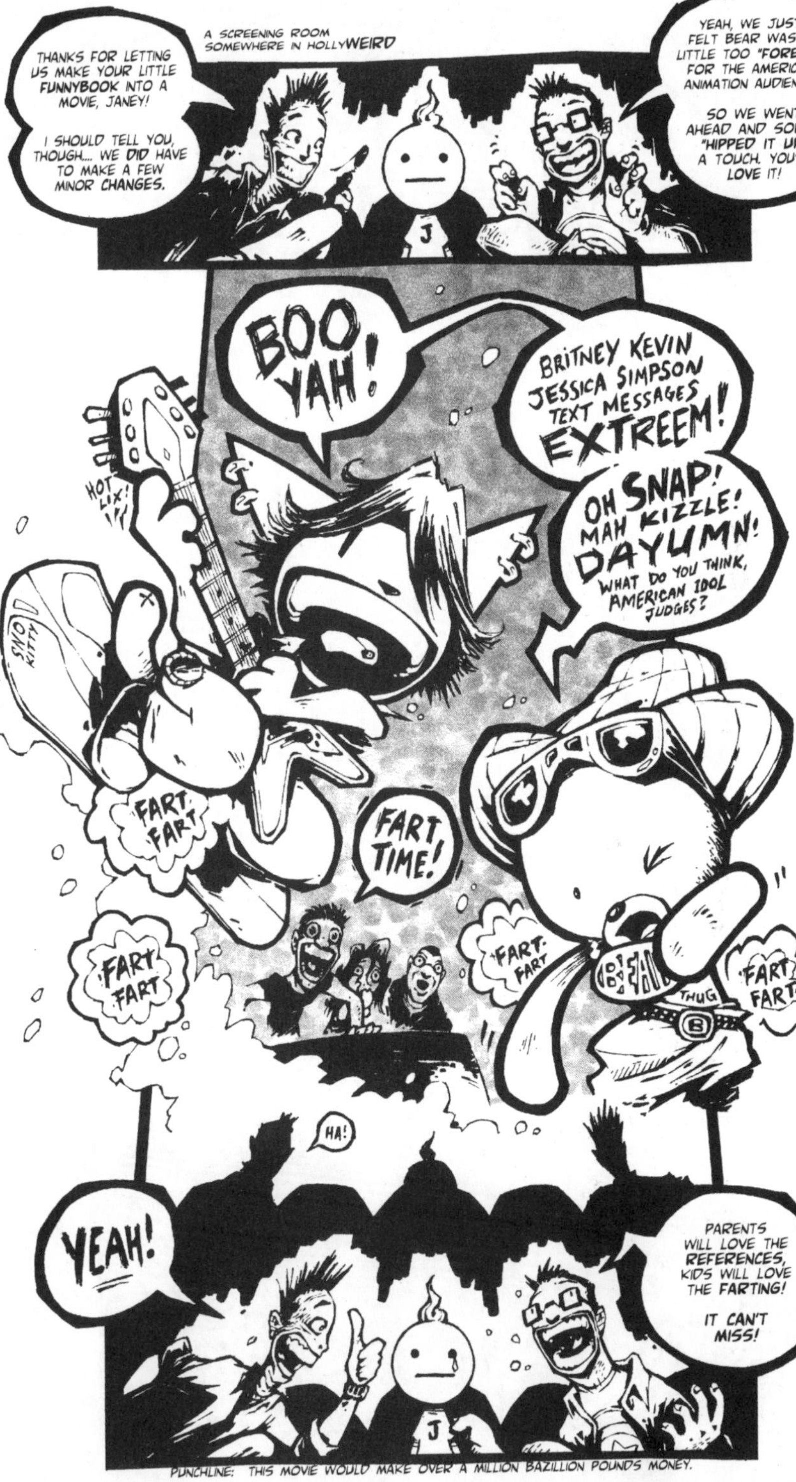

PUNCHLINE: THIS MOVIE WOULD MAKE OVER A MILLION BAZILLION POUNDS MONEY.

by aaron a
www.heartshapedskull.com

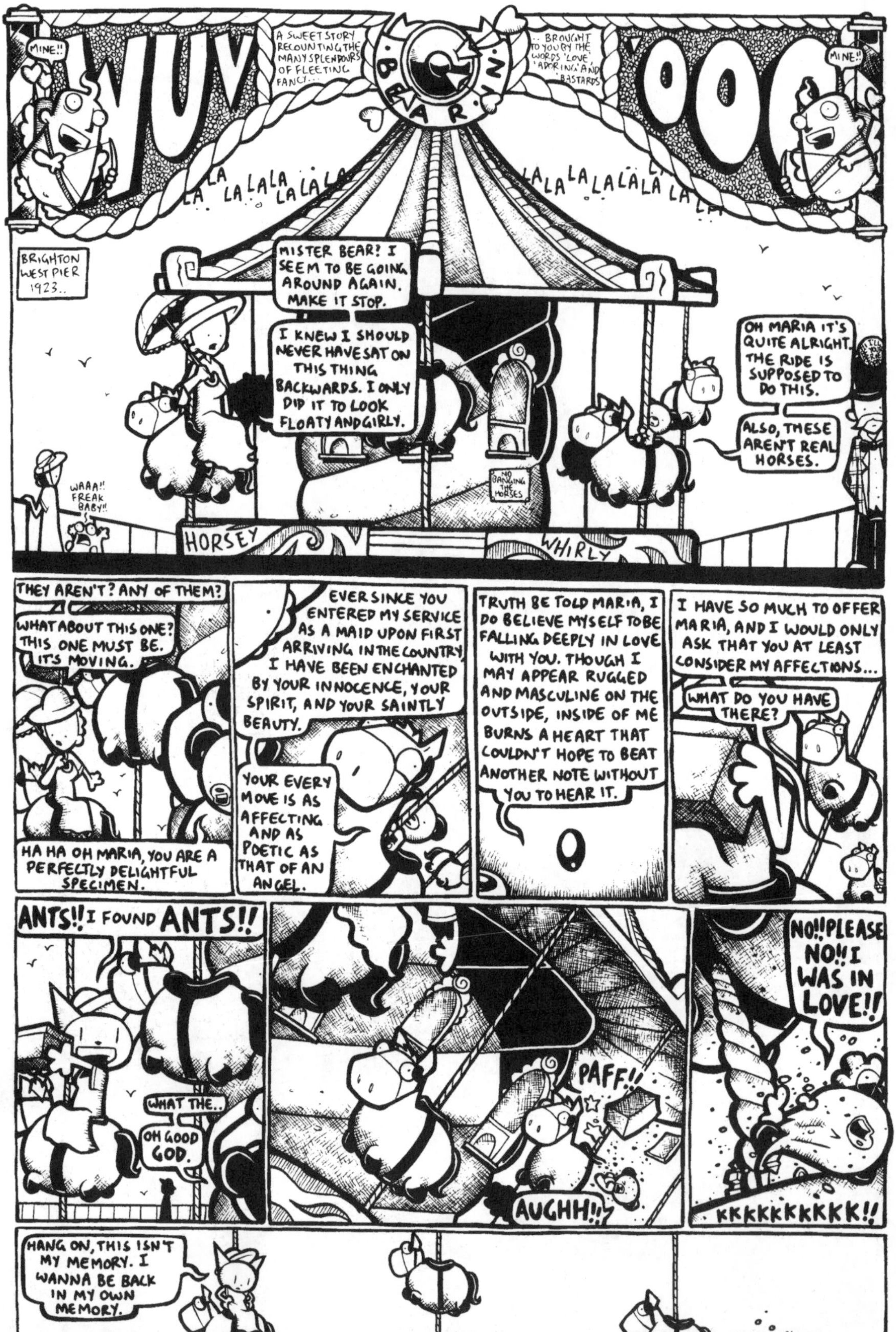
MINE!!
WUV
A SWEET STORY RECOUNTING THE MANY SPLENDOURS OF FLEETING FANCY...
BEARN
.. BROUGHT TO YOU BY THE WORDS 'LOVE', 'ADORING' AND 'BASTARDS'
OOO
MINE!!
LA LA LA LA LA LA LA LA
LA LA LA LA LA LA LA LA
BRIGHTON WEST PIER 1923..
MISTER BEAR? I SEEM TO BE GOING AROUND AGAIN. MAKE IT STOP.
I KNEW I SHOULD NEVER HAVE SAT ON THIS THING BACKWARDS. I ONLY DID IT TO LOOK FLOATY AND GIRLY.
OH MARIA IT'S QUITE ALRIGHT. THE RIDE IS SUPPOSED TO DO THIS.
ALSO, THESE AREN'T REAL HORSES.
WAAA!! FREAK BABY!!
NO BANGING THE HORSES
HORSEY
WHIRLY
THEY AREN'T? ANY OF THEM?
WHAT ABOUT THIS ONE? THIS ONE MUST BE. IT'S MOVING.
HA HA OH MARIA, YOU ARE A PERFECTLY DELIGHTFUL SPECIMEN.
EVER SINCE YOU ENTERED MY SERVICE AS A MAID UPON FIRST ARRIVING IN THE COUNTRY, I HAVE BEEN ENCHANTED BY YOUR INNOCENCE, YOUR SPIRIT, AND YOUR SAINTLY BEAUTY.
YOUR EVERY MOVE IS AS AFFECTING AND AS POETIC AS THAT OF AN ANGEL.
TRUTH BE TOLD MARIA, I DO BELIEVE MYSELF TO BE FALLING DEEPLY IN LOVE WITH YOU. THOUGH I MAY APPEAR RUGGED AND MASCULINE ON THE OUTSIDE, INSIDE OF ME BURNS A HEART THAT COULDN'T HOPE TO BEAT ANOTHER NOTE WITHOUT YOU TO HEAR IT.
I HAVE SO MUCH TO OFFER MARIA, AND I WOULD ONLY ASK THAT YOU AT LEAST CONSIDER MY AFFECTIONS...
WHAT DO YOU HAVE THERE?
ANTS!! I FOUND ANTS!!
WHAT THE..
OH GOOD GOD.
PAFF!!
AUGHH!!
NO!! PLEASE NO!! I WAS IN LOVE!!
KKKKKKKKK!!
HANG ON, THIS ISN'T MY MEMORY. I WANNA BE BACK IN MY OWN MEMORY.
KKKKKKK..

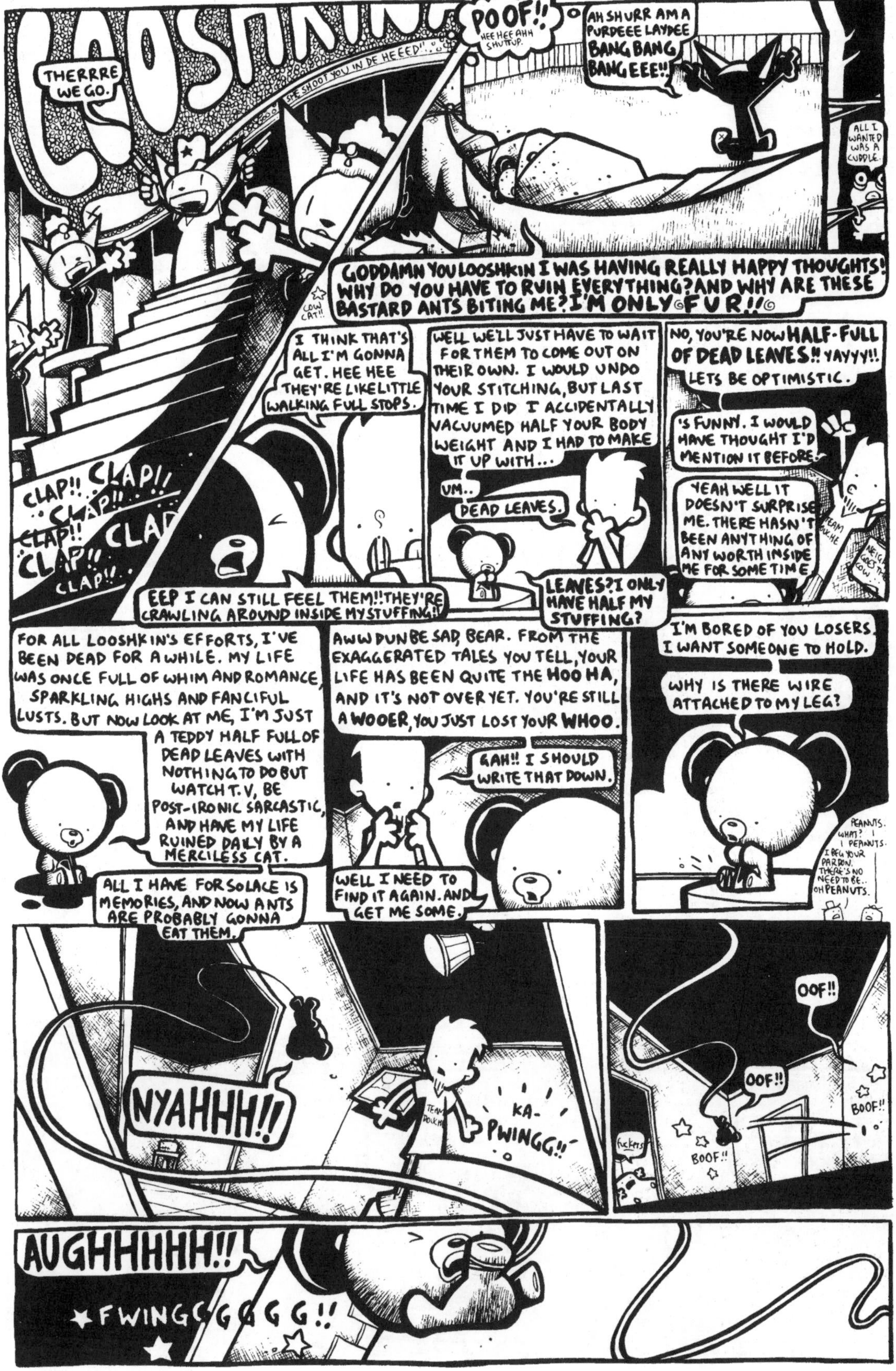

LOOSHKIN!
THERRRE WE GO.
SHE SHOOT YOU IN DE HEEED!!
POOF!!
HEE HEE AHH SHUTUP.
AH SHURR AM A PURDEEE LAYDEE BANG BANG BANG EEE!!
ALL I WANTED WAS A CUDDLE.
GODDAMN YOU LOOSHKIN I WAS HAVING REALLY HAPPY THOUGHTS! WHY DO YOU HAVE TO RUIN EVERYTHING? AND WHY ARE THESE BASTARD ANTS BITING ME? I'M ONLY FUR!!
COW CAT!!
CLAP!! CLAP!! CLAP!! CLAP!! CLAP!! CLAP CLAP!!
I THINK THAT'S ALL I'M GONNA GET. HEE HEE THEY'RE LIKE LITTLE WALKING FULL STOPS.
EEP I CAN STILL FEEL THEM!! THEY'RE CRAWLING AROUND INSIDE MY STUFFING!
WELL WE'LL JUST HAVE TO WAIT FOR THEM TO COME OUT ON THEIR OWN. I WOULD UNDO YOUR STITCHING, BUT LAST TIME I DID I ACCIDENTALLY VACUUMED HALF YOUR BODY WEIGHT AND I HAD TO MAKE IT UP WITH...
UM..
DEAD LEAVES.
LEAVES? I ONLY HAVE HALF MY STUFFING?
NO, YOU'RE NOW HALF-FULL OF DEAD LEAVES!! YAYYY!! LETS BE OPTIMISTIC.
'S FUNNY. I WOULD HAVE THOUGHT I'D MENTION IT BEFORE.
YEAH WELL IT DOESN'T SURPRISE ME. THERE HASN'T BEEN ANYTHING OF ANY WORTH INSIDE ME FOR SOME TIME.
TEAM DOUCHE
NEIGH GOES THE COW
FOR ALL LOOSHKIN'S EFFORTS, I'VE BEEN DEAD FOR A WHILE. MY LIFE WAS ONCE FULL OF WHIM AND ROMANCE, SPARKLING HIGHS AND FANCIFUL LUSTS. BUT NOW LOOK AT ME, I'M JUST A TEDDY HALF FULL OF DEAD LEAVES WITH NOTHING TO DO BUT WATCH T.V, BE POST-IRONIC SARCASTIC, AND HAVE MY LIFE RUINED DAILY BY A MERCILESS CAT.
ALL I HAVE FOR SOLACE IS MEMORIES, AND NOW ANTS ARE PROBABLY GONNA EAT THEM.
AWW DUN BE SAD, BEAR. FROM THE EXAGGERATED TALES YOU TELL, YOUR LIFE HAS BEEN QUITE THE HOO HA, AND IT'S NOT OVER YET. YOU'RE STILL A WOOER, YOU JUST LOST YOUR WHOO.
GAH!! I SHOULD WRITE THAT DOWN.
WELL I NEED TO FIND IT AGAIN. AND GET ME SOME.
I'M BORED OF YOU LOSERS. I WANT SOMEONE TO HOLD.
WHY IS THERE WIRE ATTACHED TO MY LEG?
PEANUTS.
WHAT? I PEANUTS.
I BEG YOUR PARDON. THERE'S NO NEED TO BE..
OH PEANUTS.
NYAHHH!!
KA-PWINGG!!
OOF!!
OOF!!
BOOF!!
BOOF!!
fuckers
AUGHHHHH!!
FWINGGGGGG!!

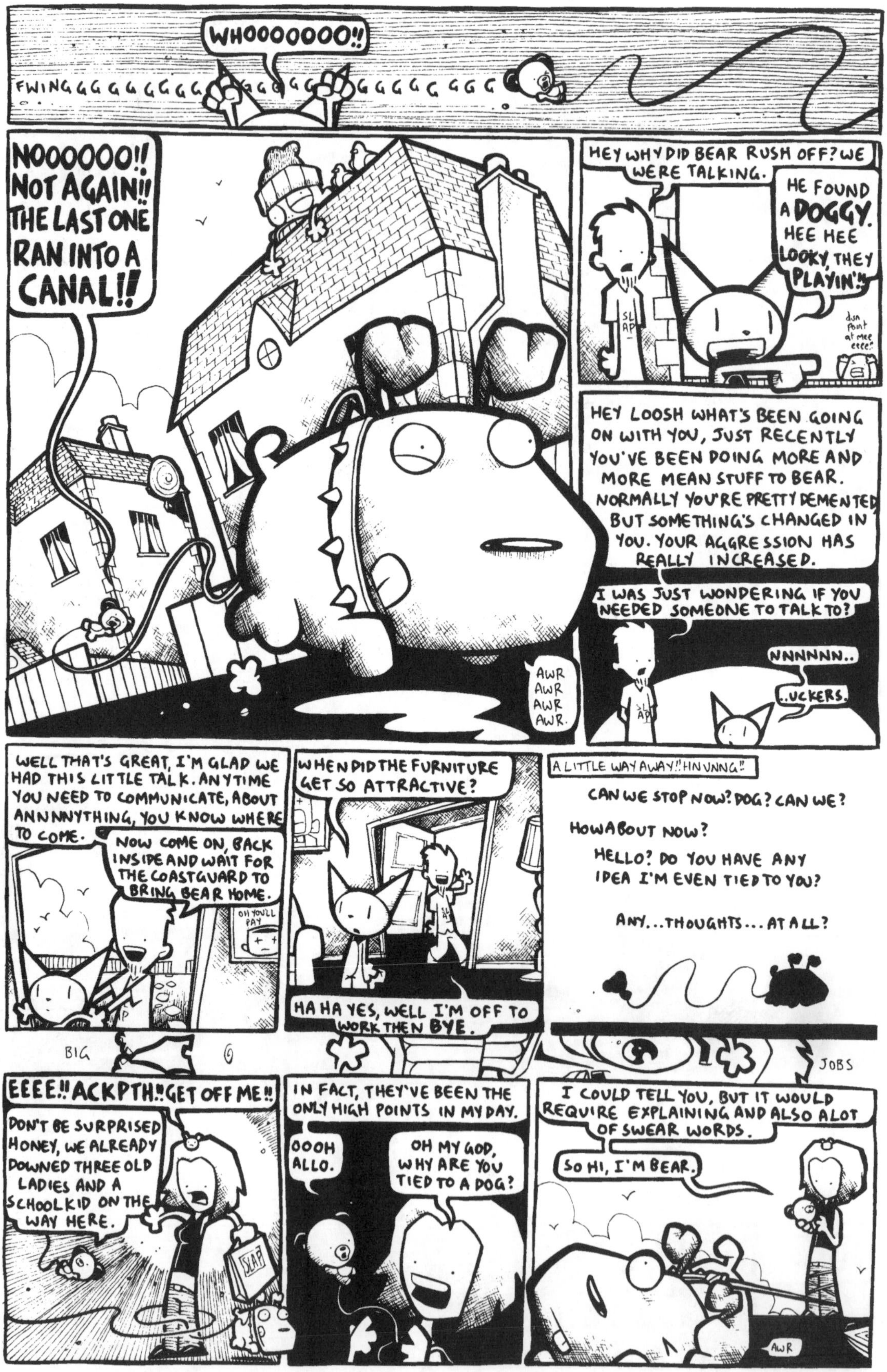
WHOOOOOOO!!
FWINGGGGGGGGGGGGGGGGGGGGGGGG
NOOOOOO!! NOT AGAIN!! THE LAST ONE RAN INTO A CANAL!!
AWR AWR AWR AWR.
HEY WHY DID BEAR RUSH OFF? WE WERE TALKING.
HE FOUND A DOGGY. HEE HEE LOOKY, THEY PLAYIN'!!
dsn point at mee eeee!
HEY LOOSH WHAT'S BEEN GOING ON WITH YOU, JUST RECENTLY YOU'VE BEEN DOING MORE AND MORE MEAN STUFF TO BEAR. NORMALLY YOU'RE PRETTY DEMENTED, BUT SOMETHING'S CHANGED IN YOU. YOUR AGGRESSION HAS REALLY INCREASED.
I WAS JUST WONDERING IF YOU NEEDED SOMEONE TO TALK TO?
NNNNNN..
..UCKERS.
WELL THAT'S GREAT, I'M GLAD WE HAD THIS LITTLE TALK. ANYTIME YOU NEED TO COMMUNICATE, ABOUT ANNNNYTHING, YOU KNOW WHERE TO COME.
NOW COME ON, BACK INSIDE AND WAIT FOR THE COASTGUARD TO BRING BEAR HOME.
OH YOU'LL PAY
WHEN DID THE FURNITURE GET SO ATTRACTIVE?
HA HA YES, WELL I'M OFF TO WORK THEN BYE.
A LITTLE WAY AWAY!! HNVNNG!!
CAN WE STOP NOW? DOG? CAN WE?
HOW ABOUT NOW?
HELLO? DO YOU HAVE ANY IDEA I'M EVEN TIED TO YOU?
ANY... THOUGHTS... AT ALL?
BIG
JOBS
EEEE!! ACKPTH!! GET OFF ME!!
DON'T BE SURPRISED HONEY, WE ALREADY DOWNED THREE OLD LADIES AND A SCHOOLKID ON THE WAY HERE.
SLAP
IN FACT, THEY'VE BEEN THE ONLY HIGH POINTS IN MY DAY.
OOOH ALLO.
OH MY GOD, WHY ARE YOU TIED TO A DOG?
I COULD TELL YOU, BUT IT WOULD REQUIRE EXPLAINING AND ALSO ALOT OF SWEAR WORDS.
SO HI, I'M BEAR.
AWR

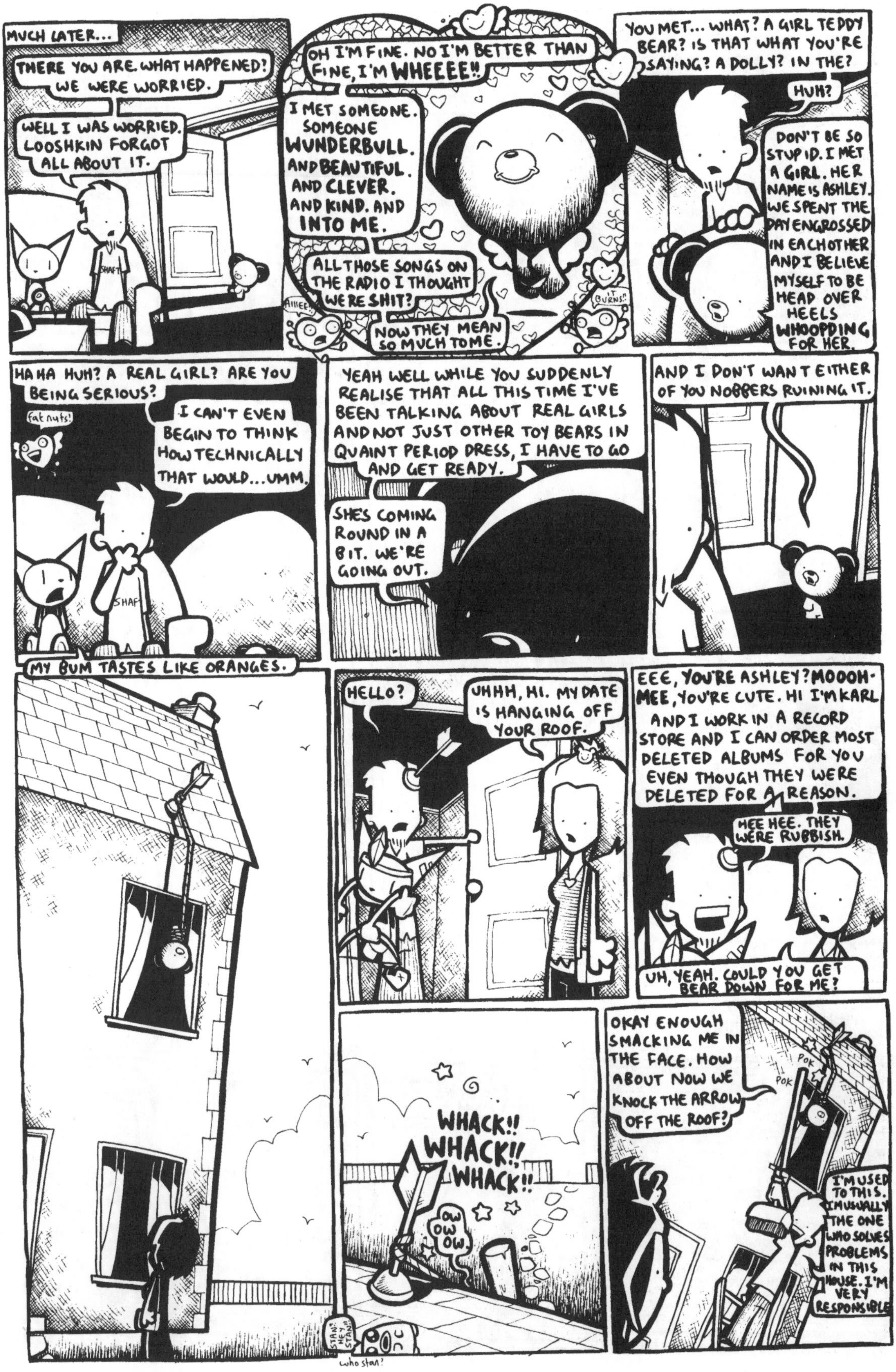
MUCH LATER...
THERE YOU ARE. WHAT HAPPENED? WE WERE WORRIED.
WELL I WAS WORRIED. LOOSHKIN FORGOT ALL ABOUT IT.
SHAFT
OH I'M FINE. NO I'M BETTER THAN FINE, I'M WHEEEE!!
I MET SOMEONE. SOMEONE WUNDERBULL. AND BEAUTIFUL. AND CLEVER. AND KIND. AND INTO ME.
ALL THOSE SONGS ON THE RADIO I THOUGHT WERE SHIT?
NOW THEY MEAN SO MUCH TO ME.
IT BURNS!!
YOU MET... WHAT? A GIRL TEDDY BEAR? IS THAT WHAT YOU'RE SAYING? A DOLLY? IN THE?
HUH?
DON'T BE SO STUPID. I MET A GIRL. HER NAME IS ASHLEY. WE SPENT THE DAY ENGROSSED IN EACH OTHER AND I BELIEVE MYSELF TO BE HEAD OVER HEELS WHOOPDING FOR HER.
HA HA HUH? A REAL GIRL? ARE YOU BEING SERIOUS?
fat nuts!
I CAN'T EVEN BEGIN TO THINK HOW TECHNICALLY THAT WOULD... UMM.
SHAFT
MY BUM TASTES LIKE ORANGES.
YEAH WELL WHILE YOU SUDDENLY REALISE THAT ALL THIS TIME I'VE BEEN TALKING ABOUT REAL GIRLS AND NOT JUST OTHER TOY BEARS IN QUAINT PERIOD DRESS, I HAVE TO GO AND GET READY.
SHE'S COMING ROUND IN A BIT. WE'RE GOING OUT.
AND I DON'T WANT EITHER OF YOU NOBBERS RUINING IT.
HELLO?
UHHH, HI. MY DATE IS HANGING OFF YOUR ROOF.
EEE, YOU'RE ASHLEY? MOOOH-MEE, YOU'RE CUTE. HI I'M KARL AND I WORK IN A RECORD STORE AND I CAN ORDER MOST DELETED ALBUMS FOR YOU EVEN THOUGH THEY WERE DELETED FOR A REASON.
HEE HEE. THEY WERE RUBBISH.
UH, YEAH. COULD YOU GET BEAR DOWN FOR ME?
WHACK!! WHACK!! WHACK!!
OW OW OW.
who stan?
OKAY ENOUGH SMACKING ME IN THE FACE. HOW ABOUT NOW WE KNOCK THE ARROW OFF THE ROOF?
POK
POK
I'M USED TO THIS. I'M USUALLY THE ONE WHO SOLVES PROBLEMS IN THIS HOUSE. I'M VERY RESPONSIBLE.

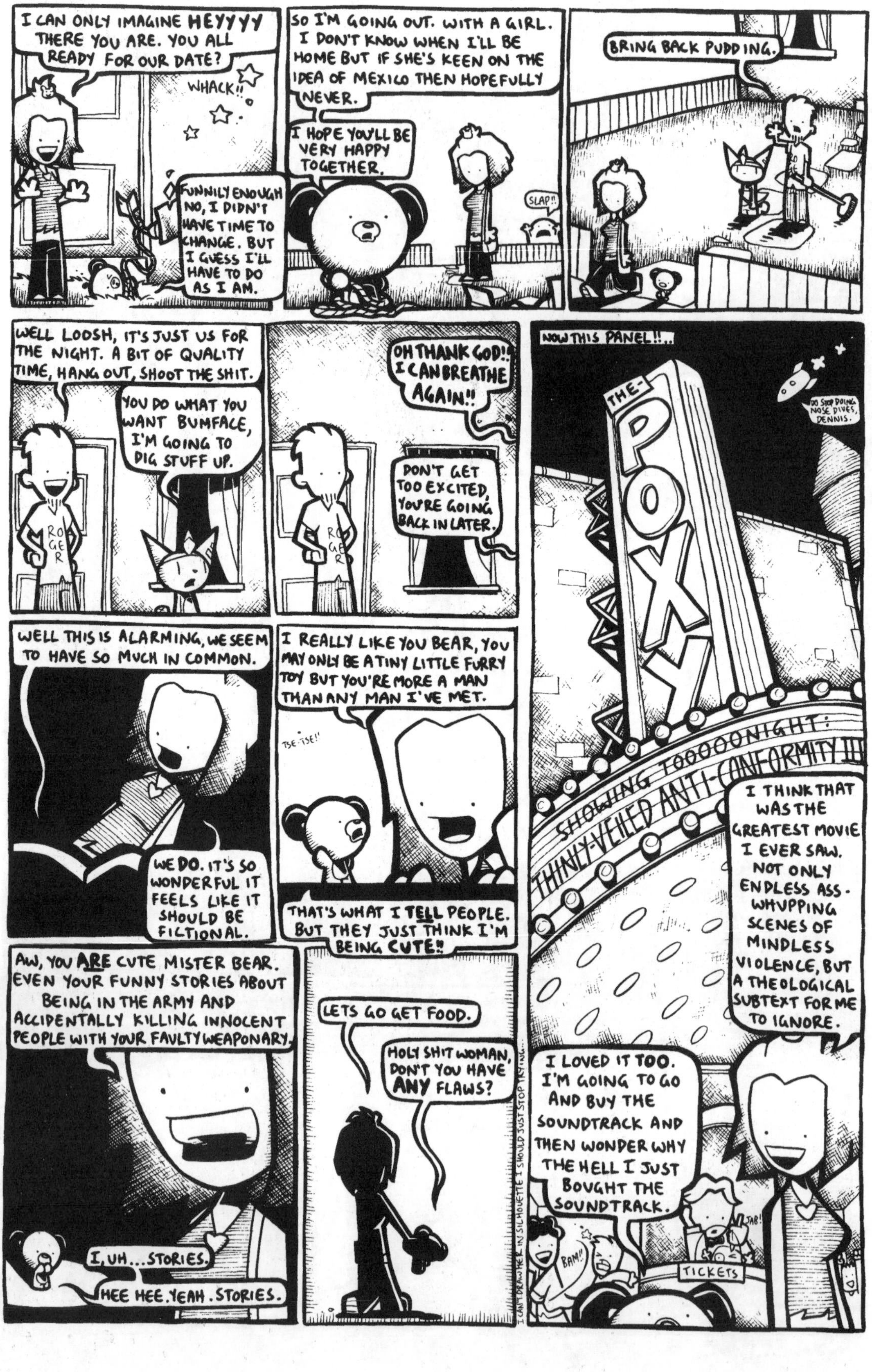

I CAN ONLY IMAGINE HEYYYY THERE YOU ARE. YOU ALL READY FOR OUR DATE?
WHACK!!
FUNNILY ENOUGH NO, I DIDN'T HAVE TIME TO CHANGE. BUT I GUESS I'LL HAVE TO DO AS I AM.
SO I'M GOING OUT. WITH A GIRL. I DON'T KNOW WHEN I'LL BE HOME BUT IF SHE'S KEEN ON THE IDEA OF MEXICO THEN HOPEFULLY NEVER.
I HOPE YOU'LL BE VERY HAPPY TOGETHER.
SLAP!!
BRING BACK PUDDING.
WELL LOOSH, IT'S JUST US FOR THE NIGHT. A BIT OF QUALITY TIME, HANG OUT, SHOOT THE SHIT.
YOU DO WHAT YOU WANT BUMFACE, I'M GOING TO DIG STUFF UP.
ROGER
OH THANK GOD!! I CAN BREATHE AGAIN!!
DON'T GET TOO EXCITED, YOU'RE GOING BACK IN LATER.
WELL THIS IS ALARMING, WE SEEM TO HAVE SO MUCH IN COMMON.
WE DO. IT'S SO WONDERFUL IT FEELS LIKE IT SHOULD BE FICTIONAL.
I REALLY LIKE YOU BEAR, YOU MAY ONLY BE A TINY LITTLE FURRY TOY BUT YOU'RE MORE A MAN THAN ANY MAN I'VE MET.
TSE-TSE!!
THAT'S WHAT I TELL PEOPLE. BUT THEY JUST THINK I'M BEING CUTE!!
NOW THIS PANEL!!..
DO STOP DOING NOSE DIVES, DENNIS.
THE- POXY
SHOWING TOOOOONIGHT: THINLY-VEILED ANTI-CONFORMITY III
I THINK THAT WAS THE GREATEST MOVIE I EVER SAW. NOT ONLY ENDLESS ASS-WHUPPING SCENES OF MINDLESS VIOLENCE, BUT A THEOLOGICAL SUBTEXT FOR ME TO IGNORE.
I LOVED IT TOO. I'M GOING TO GO AND BUY THE SOUNDTRACK AND THEN WONDER WHY THE HELL I JUST BOUGHT THE SOUNDTRACK.
BAM!!
JAB!
TICKETS
AW, YOU ARE CUTE MISTER BEAR. EVEN YOUR FUNNY STORIES ABOUT BEING IN THE ARMY AND ACCIDENTALLY KILLING INNOCENT PEOPLE WITH YOUR FAULTY WEAPONARY.
I, UH... STORIES.
HEE HEE. YEAH. STORIES.
LETS GO GET FOOD.
HOLY SHIT WOMAN, DON'T YOU HAVE ANY FLAWS?
I CAN'T DRAW HER IN SILHOUETTE I SHOULD JUST STOP TRYING...

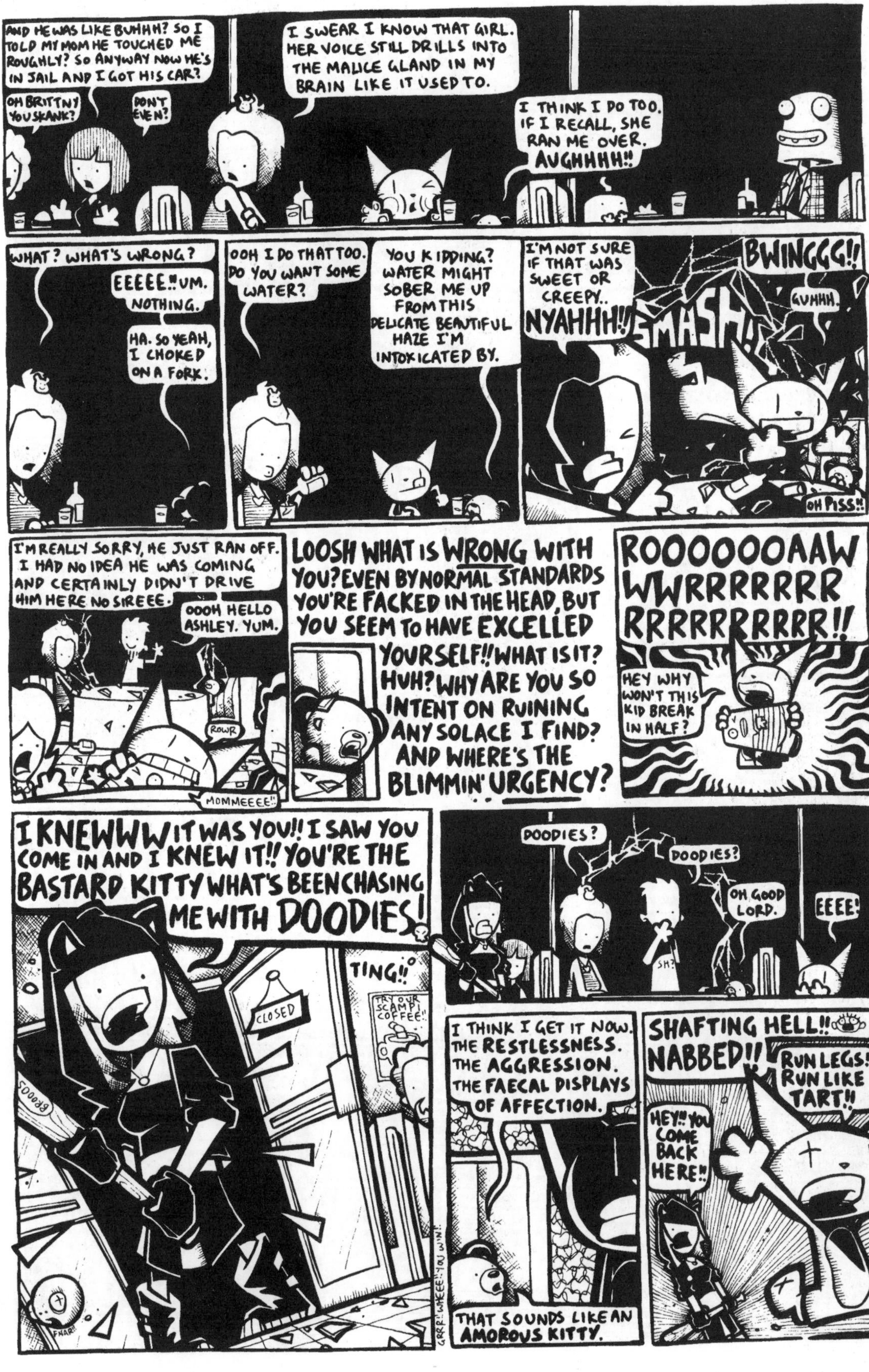
AND HE WAS LIKE BUHHH? SO I TOLD MY MOM HE TOUCHED ME ROUGHLY? SO ANYWAY NOW HE'S IN JAIL AND I GOT HIS CAR?
OH BRITTNY YOU SKANK?
DON'T EVEN?
I SWEAR I KNOW THAT GIRL. HER VOICE STILL DRILLS INTO THE MALICE GLAND IN MY BRAIN LIKE IT USED TO.
I THINK I DO TOO. IF I RECALL, SHE RAN ME OVER. AUGHHHH!!
WHAT? WHAT'S WRONG?
EEEEE!! UM. NOTHING.
HA. SO YEAH, I CHOKED ON A FORK.
OOH I DO THAT TOO. DO YOU WANT SOME WATER?
YOU KIDDING? WATER MIGHT SOBER ME UP FROM THIS DELICATE BEAUTIFUL HAZE I'M INTOXICATED BY.
I'M NOT SURE IF THAT WAS SWEET OR CREEPY.. NYAHHH!!
BWINGGG!!
SMASH!!
GUHHH.
OH PISS!!
I'M REALLY SORRY, HE JUST RAN OFF. I HAD NO IDEA HE WAS COMING AND CERTAINLY DIDN'T DRIVE HIM HERE NO SIREEE.
OOOH HELLO ASHLEY. YUM.
ROWR
MOMMEEEE!!
LOOSH WHAT IS WRONG WITH YOU? EVEN BY NORMAL STANDARDS YOU'RE FACKED IN THE HEAD, BUT YOU SEEM TO HAVE EXCELLED YOURSELF!! WHAT IS IT? HUH? WHY ARE YOU SO INTENT ON RUINING ANY SOLACE I FIND? AND WHERE'S THE BLIMMIN' URGENCY?
ROOOOOOAAW WWRRRRRRR RRRRRRRRRR!!
HEY WHY WON'T THIS KID BREAK IN HALF?
I KNEWWW IT WAS YOU!! I SAW YOU COME IN AND I KNEW IT!! YOU'RE THE BASTARD KITTY WHAT'S BEEN CHASING ME WITH DOODIES!
TING!!
CLOSED
TRY OUR SCAMPI COFFEE!!
FNAR!
DOODIES?
DOODIES?
OH GOOD LORD.
EEEE!
I THINK I GET IT NOW. THE RESTLESSNESS. THE AGGRESSION. THE FAECAL DISPLAYS OF AFFECTION.
THAT SOUNDS LIKE AN AMOROUS KITTY.
SHAFTING HELL!! NABBED!!
RUN LEGS!! RUN LIKE TART!!
HEY!! YOU COME BACK HERE!!

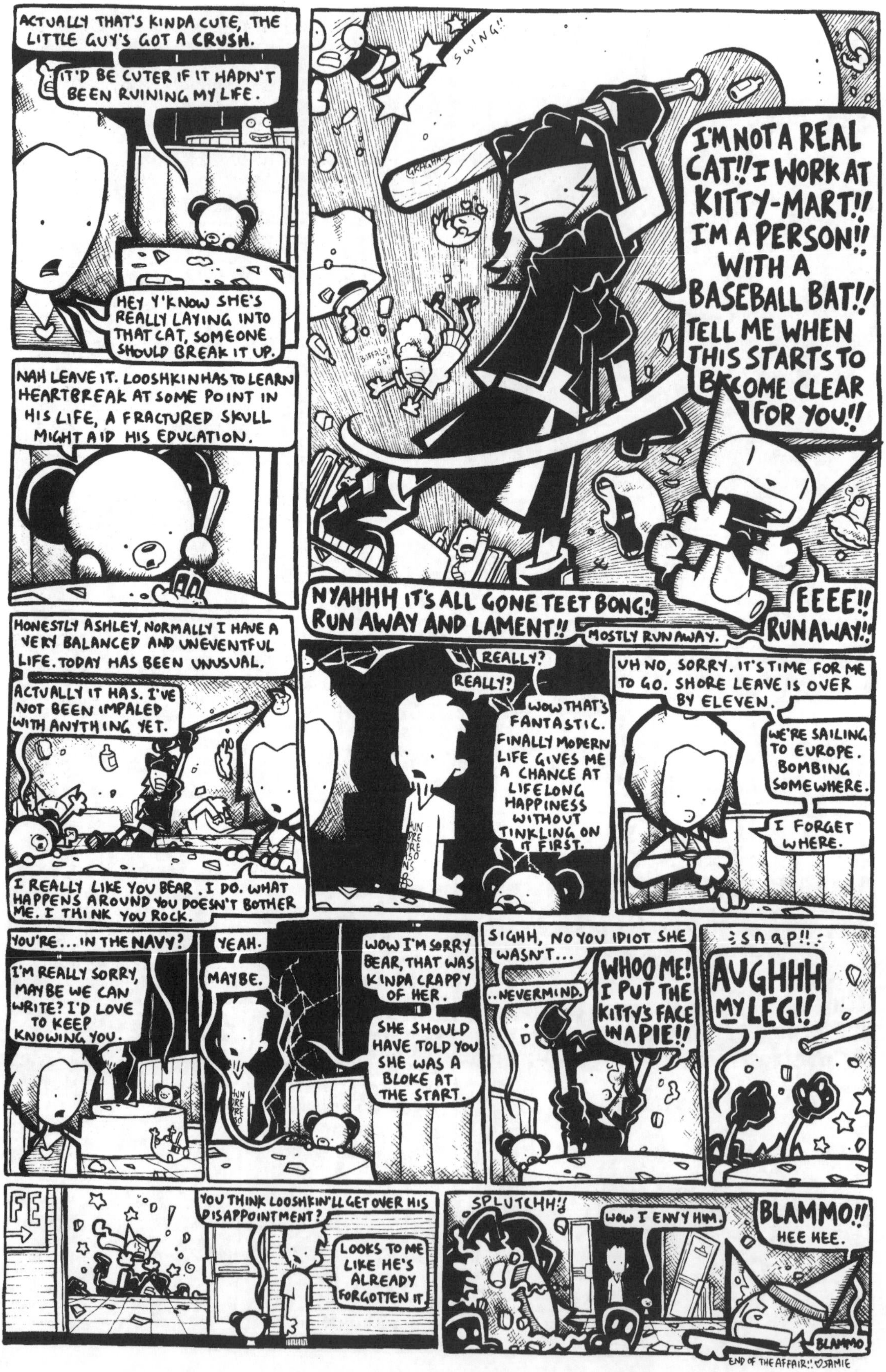
ACTUALLY THAT'S KINDA CUTE, THE LITTLE GUY'S GOT A CRUSH.
IT'D BE CUTER IF IT HADN'T BEEN RUINING MY LIFE.
HEY Y'KNOW SHE'S REALLY LAYING INTO THAT CAT, SOMEONE SHOULD BREAK IT UP.
SWING!!
I'M NOT A REAL CAT!! I WORK AT KITTY-MART!! I'M A PERSON!! WITH A BASEBALL BAT!! TELL ME WHEN THIS STARTS TO BECOME CLEAR FOR YOU!!
NAH LEAVE IT. LOOSHKIN HAS TO LEARN HEARTBREAK AT SOME POINT IN HIS LIFE, A FRACTURED SKULL MIGHT AID HIS EDUCATION.
NYAHHH IT'S ALL GONE TEET BONG! RUN AWAY AND LAMENT!!
MOSTLY RUN AWAY.
EEEE!! RUN AWAY!!
HONESTLY ASHLEY, NORMALLY I HAVE A VERY BALANCED AND UNEVENTFUL LIFE. TODAY HAS BEEN UNUSUAL.
ACTUALLY IT HAS. I'VE NOT BEEN IMPALED WITH ANYTHING YET.
I REALLY LIKE YOU BEAR. I DO. WHAT HAPPENS AROUND YOU DOESN'T BOTHER ME. I THINK YOU ROCK.
REALLY?
REALLY?
WOW THAT'S FANTASTIC. FINALLY MODERN LIFE GIVES ME A CHANCE AT LIFELONG HAPPINESS WITHOUT TINKLING ON IT FIRST.
UH NO, SORRY. IT'S TIME FOR ME TO GO. SHORE LEAVE IS OVER BY ELEVEN.
WE'RE SAILING TO EUROPE. BOMBING SOMEWHERE.
I FORGET WHERE.
YOU'RE... IN THE NAVY?
I'M REALLY SORRY, MAYBE WE CAN WRITE? I'D LOVE TO KEEP KNOWING YOU.
YEAH.
MAYBE.
WOW I'M SORRY BEAR, THAT WAS KINDA CRAPPY OF HER.
SHE SHOULD HAVE TOLD YOU SHE WAS A BLOKE AT THE START.
SIGHH, NO YOU IDIOT SHE WASN'T...
..NEVERMIND.
WHOO ME! I PUT THE KITTY'S FACE IN A PIE!!
snap!!
AUGHHH MY LEG!!
YOU THINK LOOSHKIN'LL GET OVER HIS DISAPPOINTMENT?
LOOKS TO ME LIKE HE'S ALREADY FORGOTTEN IT.
SPLUTCHH!!
WOW I ENVY HIM.
BLAMMO!! HEE HEE.
BLAMMO.
END OF THE AFFAIR!! ♡JAMIE

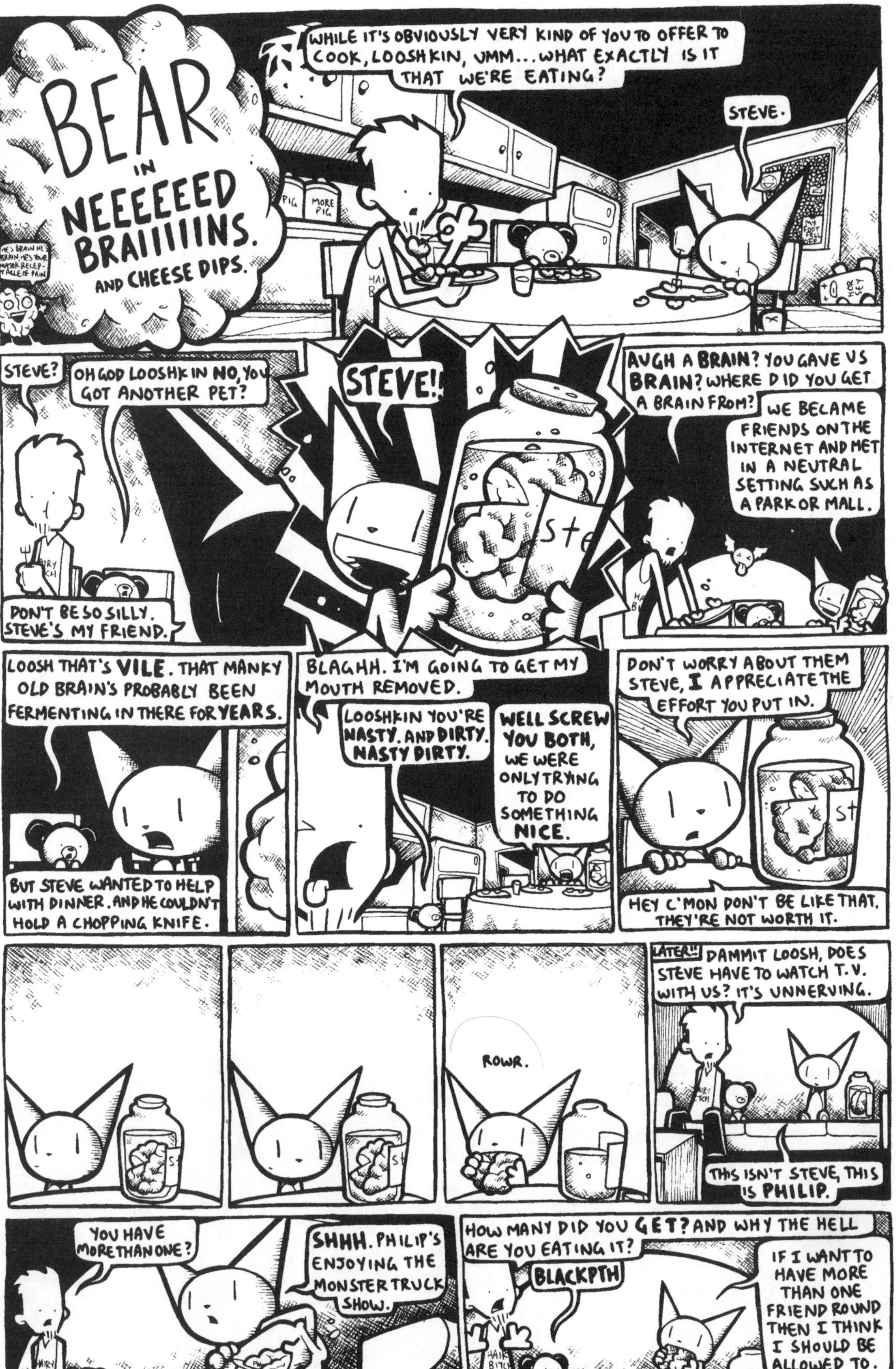
BEAR
IN
NEEEEEED BRAIIIIIINS.
AND CHEESE DIPS.
HE'S BRAIN HE'S BRAIN, HE'S YOUR MAJOR RECEP-TACLE OF PAIN
WHILE IT'S OBVIOUSLY VERY KIND OF YOU TO OFFER TO COOK, LOOSHKIN, UMM... WHAT EXACTLY IS IT THAT WE'RE EATING?
STEVE.
PIG
MORE PIG
STEVE?
OH GOD LOOSHKIN NO, YOU GOT ANOTHER PET?
DON'T BE SO SILLY. STEVE'S MY FRIEND.
STEVE!!
AUGH A BRAIN? YOU GAVE US BRAIN? WHERE DID YOU GET A BRAIN FROM?
WE BECAME FRIENDS ON THE INTERNET AND MET IN A NEUTRAL SETTING SUCH AS A PARK OR MALL.
LOOSH THAT'S VILE. THAT MANKY OLD BRAIN'S PROBABLY BEEN FERMENTING IN THERE FOR YEARS.
BUT STEVE WANTED TO HELP WITH DINNER. AND HE COULDN'T HOLD A CHOPPING KNIFE.
BLAGHH. I'M GOING TO GET MY MOUTH REMOVED.
LOOSHKIN YOU'RE NASTY. AND DIRTY. NASTY DIRTY.
WELL SCREW YOU BOTH, WE WERE ONLY TRYING TO DO SOMETHING NICE.
DON'T WORRY ABOUT THEM STEVE, I APPRECIATE THE EFFORT YOU PUT IN.
HEY C'MON DON'T BE LIKE THAT. THEY'RE NOT WORTH IT.
ROWR.
LATER!!
DAMMIT LOOSH, DOES STEVE HAVE TO WATCH T.V. WITH US? IT'S UNNERVING.
THIS ISN'T STEVE, THIS IS PHILIP.
YOU HAVE MORE THAN ONE?
SHHH. PHILIP'S ENJOYING THE MONSTER TRUCK SHOW.
YUR!!
HOW MANY DID YOU GET? AND WHY THE HELL ARE YOU EATING IT?
BLACKPTH
IF I WANT TO HAVE MORE THAN ONE FRIEND ROUND THEN I THINK I SHOULD BE ALLOWED TO.

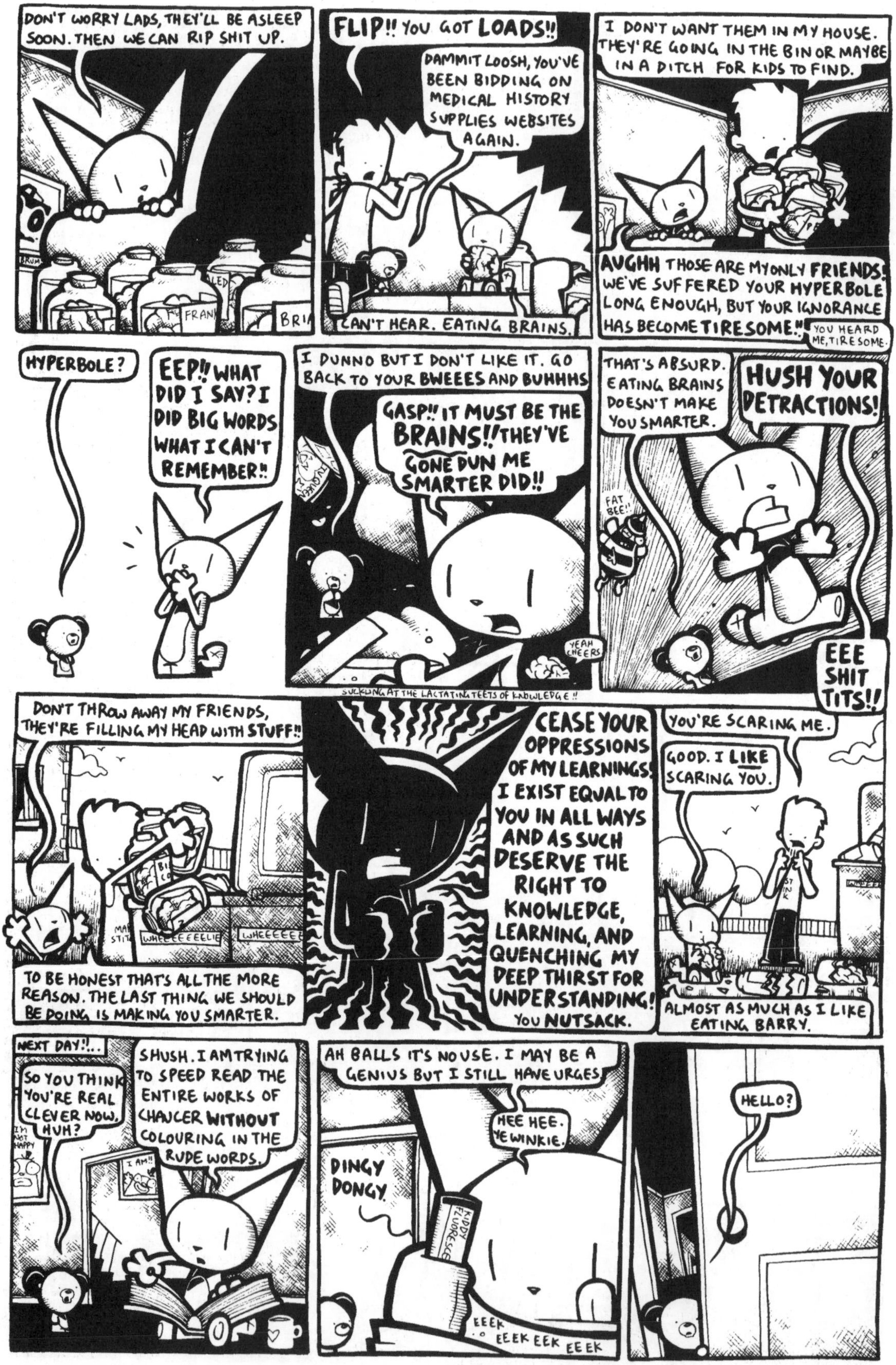
DON'T WORRY LADS, THEY'LL BE ASLEEP SOON. THEN WE CAN RIP SHIT UP.
FLIP!! YOU GOT LOADS!!
DAMMIT LOOSH, YOU'VE BEEN BIDDING ON MEDICAL HISTORY SUPPLIES WEBSITES AGAIN.
CAN'T HEAR. EATING BRAINS.
I DON'T WANT THEM IN MY HOUSE. THEY'RE GOING IN THE BIN OR MAYBE IN A DITCH FOR KIDS TO FIND.
AUGHH THOSE ARE MY ONLY FRIENDS! WE'VE SUFFERED YOUR HYPERBOLE LONG ENOUGH, BUT YOUR IGNORANCE HAS BECOME TIRESOME!!
YOU HEARD ME, TIRESOME.
HYPERBOLE?
EEP!! WHAT DID I SAY? I DID BIG WORDS WHAT I CAN'T REMEMBER!!
I DUNNO BUT I DON'T LIKE IT. GO BACK TO YOUR BWEEES AND BUHHHS
GASP!! IT MUST BE THE BRAINS!! THEY'VE GONE DUN ME SMARTER DID!!
YEAH CHEERS
THAT'S ABSURD. EATING BRAINS DOESN'T MAKE YOU SMARTER.
HUSH YOUR DETRACTIONS!
FAT BEE!!
EEE SHIT TITS!!
SUCKLING AT THE LACTATING TEETS OF KNOWLEDGE !!
DON'T THROW AWAY MY FRIENDS, THEY'RE FILLING MY HEAD WITH STUFF!!
TO BE HONEST THAT'S ALL THE MORE REASON. THE LAST THING WE SHOULD BE DOING IS MAKING YOU SMARTER.
CEASE YOUR OPPRESSIONS OF MY LEARNINGS! I EXIST EQUAL TO YOU IN ALL WAYS AND AS SUCH DESERVE THE RIGHT TO KNOWLEDGE, LEARNING, AND QUENCHING MY DEEP THIRST FOR UNDERSTANDING! YOU NUTSACK.
YOU'RE SCARING ME.
GOOD. I LIKE SCARING YOU.
ALMOST AS MUCH AS I LIKE EATING BARRY.
NEXT DAY!...
SO YOU THINK YOU'RE REAL CLEVER NOW, HUH?
I'M NOT HAPPY
I AM!!
SHUSH. I AM TRYING TO SPEED READ THE ENTIRE WORKS OF CHAUCER WITHOUT COLOURING IN THE RUDE WORDS.
AH BALLS IT'S NO USE. I MAY BE A GENIUS BUT I STILL HAVE URGES.
HEE HEE. YE WINKIE.
DINGY DONGY.
EEEK EEEK EEK EEEK
HELLO?

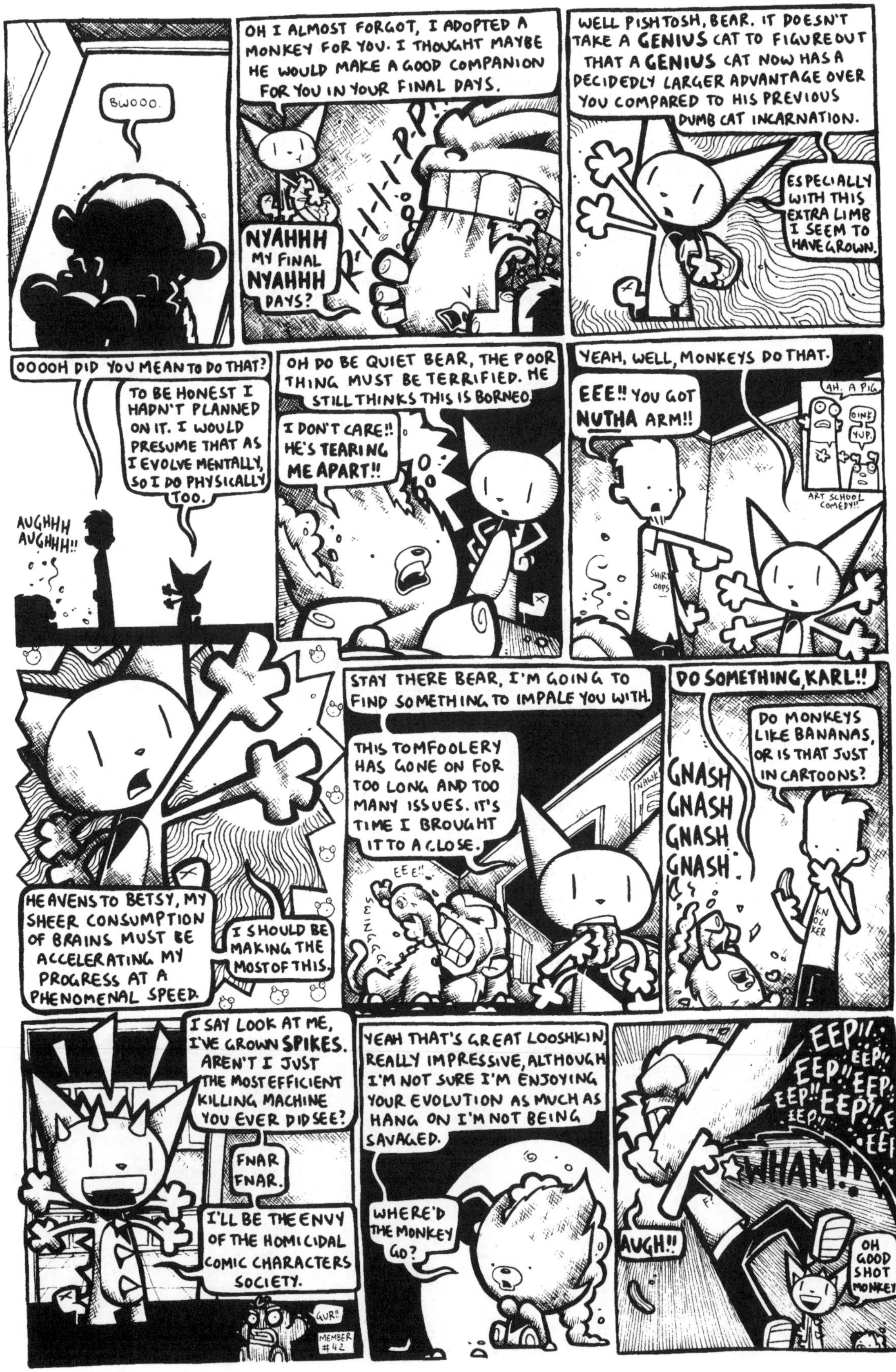
BWOOO.
OH I ALMOST FORGOT, I ADOPTED A MONKEY FOR YOU. I THOUGHT MAYBE HE WOULD MAKE A GOOD COMPANION FOR YOU IN YOUR FINAL DAYS.
NYAHHH MY FINAL NYAHHH DAYS?
WELL PISHTOSH, BEAR. IT DOESN'T TAKE A GENIUS CAT TO FIGURE OUT THAT A GENIUS CAT NOW HAS A DECIDEDLY LARGER ADVANTAGE OVER YOU COMPARED TO HIS PREVIOUS DUMB CAT INCARNATION.
ESPECIALLY WITH THIS EXTRA LIMB I SEEM TO HAVE GROWN.
OOOOH DID YOU MEAN TO DO THAT?
TO BE HONEST I HADN'T PLANNED ON IT. I WOULD PRESUME THAT AS I EVOLVE MENTALLY, SO I DO PHYSICALLY TOO.
AUGHHH AUGHHH!!
OH DO BE QUIET BEAR, THE POOR THING MUST BE TERRIFIED. HE STILL THINKS THIS IS BORNEO.
I DON'T CARE!! HE'S TEARING ME APART!!
YEAH, WELL, MONKEYS DO THAT.
EEE!! YOU GOT NUTHA ARM!!
AH. A PIG.
OINK
YUP.
ART SCHOOL COMEDY!!
SHIRT OOPS
HEAVENS TO BETSY, MY SHEER CONSUMPTION OF BRAINS MUST BE ACCELERATING MY PROGRESS AT A PHENOMENAL SPEED.
I SHOULD BE MAKING THE MOST OF THIS.
STAY THERE BEAR, I'M GOING TO FIND SOMETHING TO IMPALE YOU WITH.
THIS TOMFOOLERY HAS GONE ON FOR TOO LONG AND TOO MANY ISSUES. IT'S TIME I BROUGHT IT TO A CLOSE.
EEE!!
SWINGG
DO SOMETHING, KARL!!
DO MONKEYS LIKE BANANAS, OR IS THAT JUST IN CARTOONS?
GNASH GNASH GNASH GNASH
KNOCKER
I SAY LOOK AT ME, I'VE GROWN SPIKES. AREN'T I JUST THE MOST EFFICIENT KILLING MACHINE YOU EVER DID SEE?
FNAR FNAR.
I'LL BE THE ENVY OF THE HOMICIDAL COMIC CHARACTERS SOCIETY.
GUR!!
MEMBER #42
YEAH THAT'S GREAT LOOSHKIN, REALLY IMPRESSIVE, ALTHOUGH I'M NOT SURE I'M ENJOYING YOUR EVOLUTION AS MUCH AS HANG ON I'M NOT BEING SAVAGED.
WHERE'D THE MONKEY GO?
EEP!! EEP!! EEP!! EEP!! EEP!! EEP!! EEP!!
WHAM!!
AUGH!!
OH GOOD SHOT MONKEY.

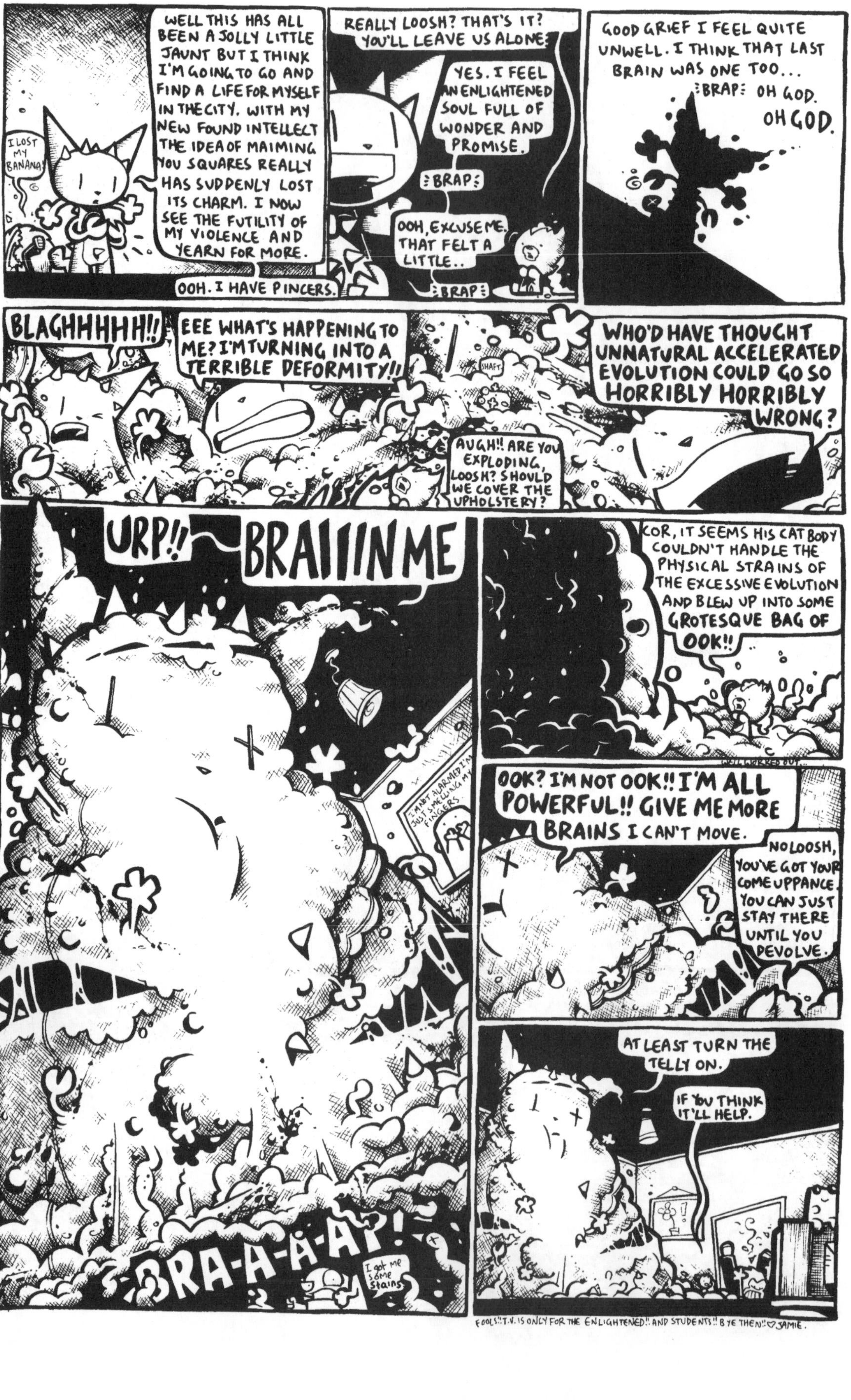
WELL THIS HAS ALL BEEN A JOLLY LITTLE JAUNT BUT I THINK I'M GOING TO GO AND FIND A LIFE FOR MYSELF IN THE CITY. WITH MY NEW FOUND INTELLECT THE IDEA OF MAIMING YOU SQUARES REALLY HAS SUDDENLY LOST ITS CHARM. I NOW SEE THE FUTILITY OF MY VIOLENCE AND YEARN FOR MORE.
I LOST MY BANANA!
OOH. I HAVE PINCERS.
REALLY LOOSH? THAT'S IT? YOU'LL LEAVE US ALONE?
YES. I FEEL AN ENLIGHTENED SOUL FULL OF WONDER AND PROMISE.
BRAP
OOH, EXCUSE ME. THAT FELT A LITTLE..
BRAP
GOOD GRIEF I FEEL QUITE UNWELL. I THINK THAT LAST BRAIN WAS ONE TOO...
BRAP
OH GOD.
OH GOD.
BLAGHHHHH!!
EEE WHAT'S HAPPENING TO ME? I'M TURNING INTO A TERRIBLE DEFORMITY!!
SHAFT
AUGH!! ARE YOU EXPLODING, LOOSH? SHOULD WE COVER THE UPHOLSTERY?
WHO'D HAVE THOUGHT UNNATURAL ACCELERATED EVOLUTION COULD GO SO HORRIBLY HORRIBLY WRONG?
URP!!
BRAIIINME
I'M NOT ALARMED I'M JUST SMELLING MY FINGERS
BRA-A-A-AP!
I got me some stains
COR, IT SEEMS HIS CAT BODY COULDN'T HANDLE THE PHYSICAL STRAINS OF THE EXCESSIVE EVOLUTION AND BLEW UP INTO SOME GROTESQUE BAG OF OOK!!
WELL WORKED OUT...
OOK? I'M NOT OOK!! I'M ALL POWERFUL!! GIVE ME MORE BRAINS I CAN'T MOVE.
NO LOOSH, YOU'VE GOT YOUR COMEUPPANCE. YOU CAN JUST STAY THERE UNTIL YOU DEVOLVE.
AT LEAST TURN THE TELLY ON.
IF YOU THINK IT'LL HELP.
FOOLS!! T.V. IS ONLY FOR THE ENLIGHTENED!! AND STUDENTS!! BYE THEN!! ♡ JAMIE.

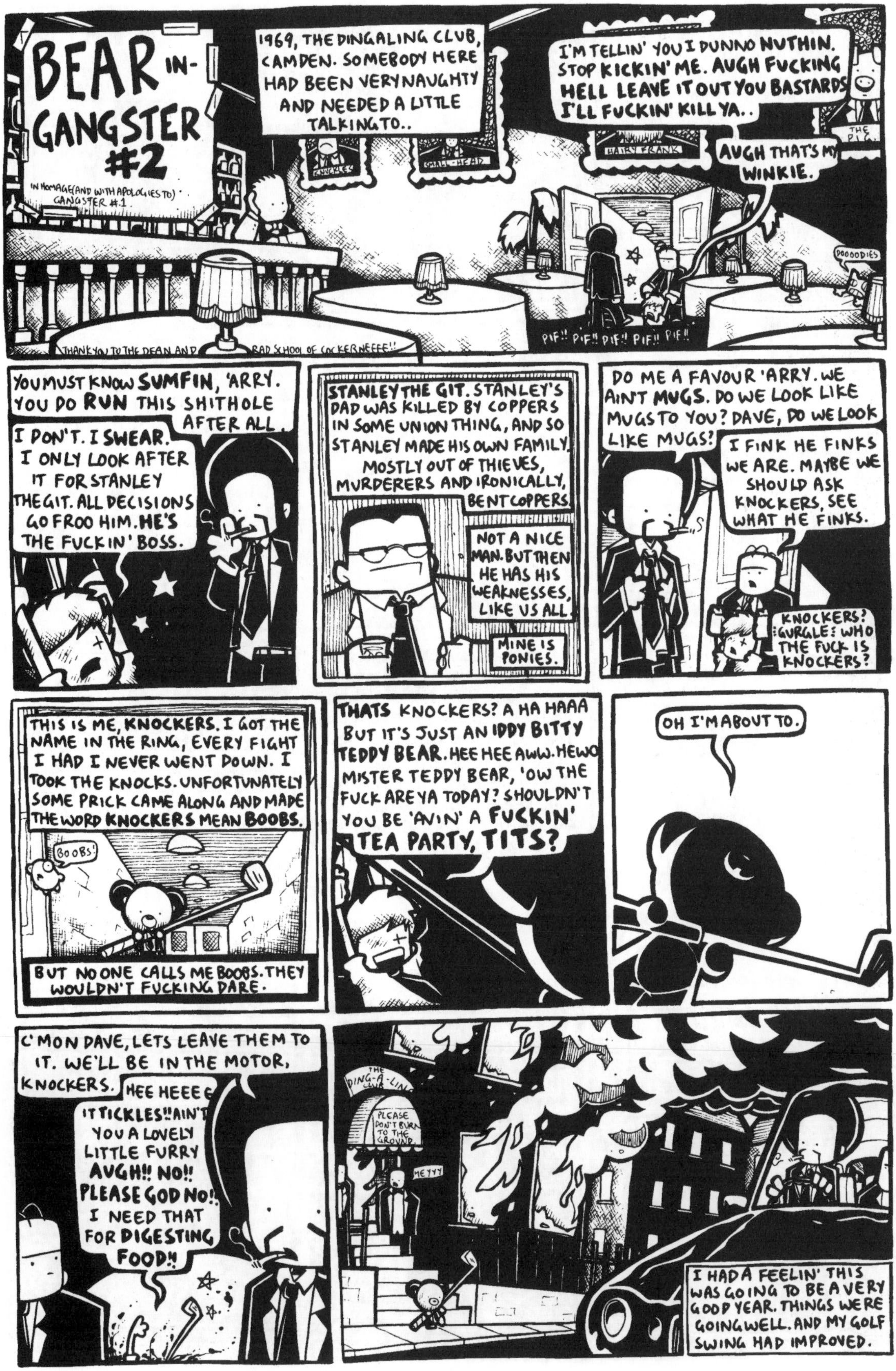

BEAR IN-GANGSTER #2
IN HOMAGE (AND WITH APOLOGIES TO) GANGSTER #1.
1969, THE DINGALING CLUB, CAMDEN. SOMEBODY HERE HAD BEEN VERY NAUGHTY AND NEEDED A LITTLE TALKING TO..
KNUCKLES
SMALL-HEAD
HAIRY FRANK
I'M TELLIN' YOU I DUNNO NUTHIN. STOP KICKIN' ME. AUGH FUCKING HELL LEAVE IT OUT YOU BASTARDS I'LL FUCKIN' KILL YA..
THE PIG.
AUGH THAT'S MY WINKIE.
DOOOODIES
PIF!! PIF!! PIF!! PIF!! PIF!!
THANK YOU TO THE DEAN AND BAD SCHOOL OF COCKERNEEEE!!
YOU MUST KNOW SUMFIN, 'ARRY. YOU DO RUN THIS SHITHOLE AFTER ALL.
I DON'T. I SWEAR. I ONLY LOOK AFTER IT FOR STANLEY THE GIT. ALL DECISIONS GO FROO HIM. HE'S THE FUCKIN' BOSS.
STANLEY THE GIT. STANLEY'S DAD WAS KILLED BY COPPERS IN SOME UNION THING, AND SO STANLEY MADE HIS OWN FAMILY, MOSTLY OUT OF THIEVES, MURDERERS AND IRONICALLY, BENT COPPERS.
NOT A NICE MAN. BUT THEN HE HAS HIS WEAKNESSES, LIKE US ALL.
MINE IS PONIES.
DO ME A FAVOUR 'ARRY. WE AIN'T MUGS. DO WE LOOK LIKE MUGS TO YOU? DAVE, DO WE LOOK LIKE MUGS?
I FINK HE FINKS WE ARE. MAYBE WE SHOULD ASK KNOCKERS, SEE WHAT HE FINKS.
KNOCKERS? GURGLE! WHO THE FUCK IS KNOCKERS?
THIS IS ME, KNOCKERS. I GOT THE NAME IN THE RING, EVERY FIGHT I HAD I NEVER WENT DOWN. I TOOK THE KNOCKS. UNFORTUNATELY SOME PRICK CAME ALONG AND MADE THE WORD KNOCKERS MEAN BOOBS.
BOOBS!
BUT NO ONE CALLS ME BOOBS. THEY WOULDN'T FUCKING DARE.
THATS KNOCKERS? A HA HAAA BUT IT'S JUST AN IDDY BITTY TEDDY BEAR. HEE HEE AWW. HEWO MISTER TEDDY BEAR, 'OW THE FUCK ARE YA TODAY? SHOULDN'T YOU BE 'AVIN' A FUCKIN' TEA PARTY, TITS?
OH I'M ABOUT TO.
C'MON DAVE, LETS LEAVE THEM TO IT. WE'LL BE IN THE MOTOR, KNOCKERS.
HEE HEEEE IT TICKLES!! AIN'T YOU A LOVELY LITTLE FURRY AUGH!! NO!! PLEASE GOD NO!! I NEED THAT FOR DIGESTING FOOD!!
THE DING-A-LING CLUB
PLEASE DON'T BURN TO THE GROUND
HEYYY
I HAD A FEELIN' THIS WAS GOING TO BE A VERY GOOD YEAR. THINGS WERE GOING WELL. AND MY GOLF SWING HAD IMPROVED.

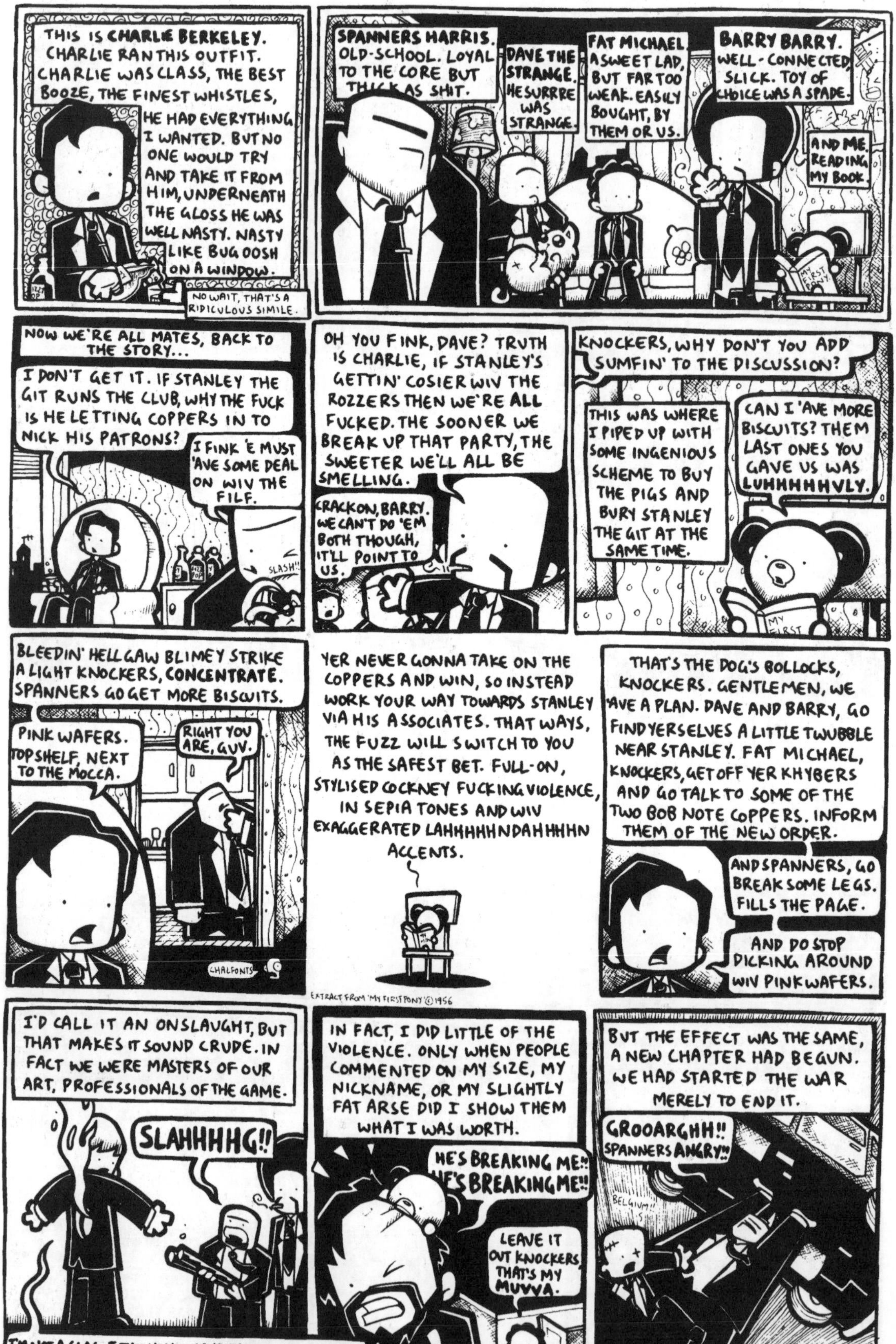
THIS IS CHARLIE BERKELEY. CHARLIE RAN THIS OUTFIT. CHARLIE WAS CLASS, THE BEST BOOZE, THE FINEST WHISTLES,
HE HAD EVERYTHING I WANTED. BUT NO ONE WOULD TRY AND TAKE IT FROM HIM, UNDERNEATH THE GLOSS HE WAS WELL NASTY. NASTY LIKE BUG OOSH ON A WINDOW.
NO WAIT, THAT'S A RIDICULOUS SIMILE.
SPANNERS HARRIS. OLD-SCHOOL. LOYAL TO THE CORE BUT THICK AS SHIT.
DAVE THE STRANGE. HE SURRRE WAS STRANGE.
FAT MICHAEL. A SWEET LAD, BUT FAR TOO WEAK. EASILY BOUGHT, BY THEM OR US.
BARRY BARRY. WELL-CONNECTED, SLICK. TOY OF CHOICE WAS A SPADE.
AND ME. READING MY BOOK.
MY FIRST PONY
NOW WE'RE ALL MATES, BACK TO THE STORY...
I DON'T GET IT. IF STANLEY THE GIT RUNS THE CLUB, WHY THE FUCK IS HE LETTING COPPERS IN TO NICK HIS PATRONS?
I FINK 'E MUST 'AVE SOME DEAL ON WIV THE FILF.
SLASH!!
OH YOU FINK, DAVE? TRUTH IS CHARLIE, IF STANLEY'S GETTIN' COSIER WIV THE ROZZERS THEN WE'RE ALL FUCKED. THE SOONER WE BREAK UP THAT PARTY, THE SWEETER WE'LL ALL BE SMELLING.
CRACK ON, BARRY. WE CAN'T DO 'EM BOTH THOUGH, IT'LL POINT TO US.
KNOCKERS, WHY DON'T YOU ADD SUMFIN' TO THE DISCUSSION?
THIS WAS WHERE I PIPED UP WITH SOME INGENIOUS SCHEME TO BUY THE PIGS AND BURY STANLEY THE GIT AT THE SAME TIME.
CAN I 'AVE MORE BISCUITS? THEM LAST ONES YOU GAVE US WAS LUHHHHHVLY.
BLEEDIN' HELLGAW BLIMEY STRIKE A LIGHT KNOCKERS, CONCENTRATE. SPANNERS GO GET MORE BISCUITS.
PINK WAFERS. TOP SHELF, NEXT TO THE MOCCA.
RIGHT YOU ARE, GUV.
CHALFONTS
YER NEVER GONNA TAKE ON THE COPPERS AND WIN, SO INSTEAD WORK YOUR WAY TOWARDS STANLEY VIA HIS ASSOCIATES. THAT WAYS, THE FUZZ WILL SWITCH TO YOU AS THE SAFEST BET. FULL-ON, STYLISED COCKNEY FUCKING VIOLENCE, IN SEPIA TONES AND WIV EXAGGERATED LAHHHHHNDAHHHHN ACCENTS.
EXTRACT FROM 'MY FIRST PONY' © 1956
THAT'S THE DOG'S BOLLOCKS, KNOCKERS. GENTLEMEN, WE 'AVE A PLAN. DAVE AND BARRY, GO FIND YERSELVES A LITTLE TWUBBLE NEAR STANLEY. FAT MICHAEL, KNOCKERS, GET OFF YER KHYBERS AND GO TALK TO SOME OF THE TWO BOB NOTE COPPERS. INFORM THEM OF THE NEW ORDER.
AND SPANNERS, GO BREAK SOME LEGS. FILLS THE PAGE.
AND DO STOP DICKING AROUND WIV PINK WAFERS.
I'D CALL IT AN ONSLAUGHT, BUT THAT MAKES IT SOUND CRUDE. IN FACT WE WERE MASTERS OF OUR ART, PROFESSIONALS OF THE GAME.
SLAHHHHG!!
I'M NOT A SLAG. I THINK YOU HAVE THE WRONG PERSON.
IN FACT, I DID LITTLE OF THE VIOLENCE. ONLY WHEN PEOPLE COMMENTED ON MY SIZE, MY NICKNAME, OR MY SLIGHTLY FAT ARSE DID I SHOW THEM WHAT I WAS WORTH.
HE'S BREAKING ME!! HE'S BREAKING ME!!
LEAVE IT OUT KNOCKERS, THAT'S MY MUVVA.
BUT THE EFFECT WAS THE SAME, A NEW CHAPTER HAD BEGUN. WE HAD STARTED THE WAR MERELY TO END IT.
GROOARGHH!! SPANNERS ANGRY!!
BELGIUM!!

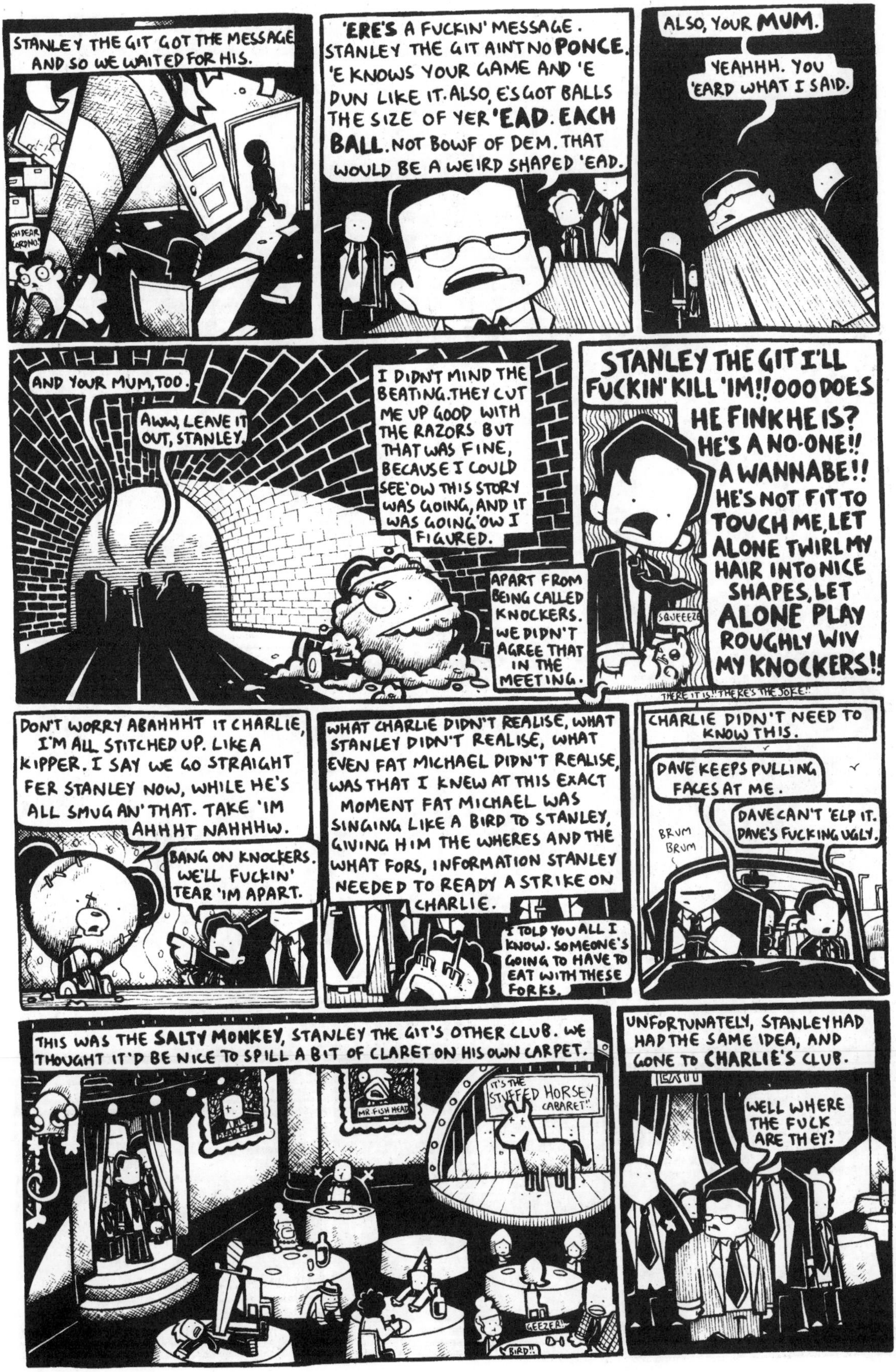
STANLEY THE GIT GOT THE MESSAGE AND SO WE WAITED FOR HIS.
OH DEAR LORDNO!
'ERE'S A FUCKIN' MESSAGE. STANLEY THE GIT AIN'T NO PONCE. 'E KNOWS YOUR GAME AND 'E DUN LIKE IT. ALSO, E'S GOT BALLS THE SIZE OF YER 'EAD. EACH BALL. NOT BOWF OF DEM. THAT WOULD BE A WEIRD SHAPED 'EAD.
ALSO, YOUR MUM.
YEAHHH. YOU 'EARD WHAT I SAID.
AND YOUR MUM, TOO.
AWW, LEAVE IT OUT, STANLEY.
I DIDN'T MIND THE BEATING. THEY CUT ME UP GOOD WITH THE RAZORS BUT THAT WAS FINE, BECAUSE I COULD SEE 'OW THIS STORY WAS GOING, AND IT WAS GOING 'OW I FIGURED.
APART FROM BEING CALLED KNOCKERS. WE DIDN'T AGREE THAT IN THE MEETING.
STANLEY THE GIT I'LL FUCKIN' KILL 'IM!! OOO DOES HE FINK HE IS? HE'S A NO-ONE!! A WANNABE!! HE'S NOT FIT TO TOUCH ME, LET ALONE TWIRL MY HAIR INTO NICE SHAPES, LET ALONE PLAY ROUGHLY WIV MY KNOCKERS!!
SQUEEEZE
THERE IT IS!! THERE'S THE JOKE!!
DON'T WORRY ABAHHHT IT CHARLIE, I'M ALL STITCHED UP. LIKE A KIPPER. I SAY WE GO STRAIGHT FER STANLEY NOW, WHILE HE'S ALL SMUG AN' THAT. TAKE 'IM AHHHT NAHHHW.
BANG ON KNOCKERS. WE'LL FUCKIN' TEAR 'IM APART.
WHAT CHARLIE DIDN'T REALISE, WHAT STANLEY DIDN'T REALISE, WHAT EVEN FAT MICHAEL DIDN'T REALISE, WAS THAT I KNEW AT THIS EXACT MOMENT FAT MICHAEL WAS SINGING LIKE A BIRD TO STANLEY, GIVING HIM THE WHERES AND THE WHAT FORS, INFORMATION STANLEY NEEDED TO READY A STRIKE ON CHARLIE.
I TOLD YOU ALL I KNOW. SOMEONE'S GOING TO HAVE TO EAT WITH THESE FORKS.
CHARLIE DIDN'T NEED TO KNOW THIS.
DAVE KEEPS PULLING FACES AT ME.
BRUM BRUM
DAVE CAN'T 'ELP IT. DAVE'S FUCKING UGLY.
THIS WAS THE SALTY MONKEY, STANLEY THE GIT'S OTHER CLUB. WE THOUGHT IT'D BE NICE TO SPILL A BIT OF CLARET ON HIS OWN CARPET.
MR FISH HEAD
IT'S THE STUFFED HORSEY CABARET!!
GEEZER!
BIRD!!
UNFORTUNATELY, STANLEY HAD HAD THE SAME IDEA, AND GONE TO CHARLIE'S CLUB.
WELL WHERE THE FUCK ARE THEY?

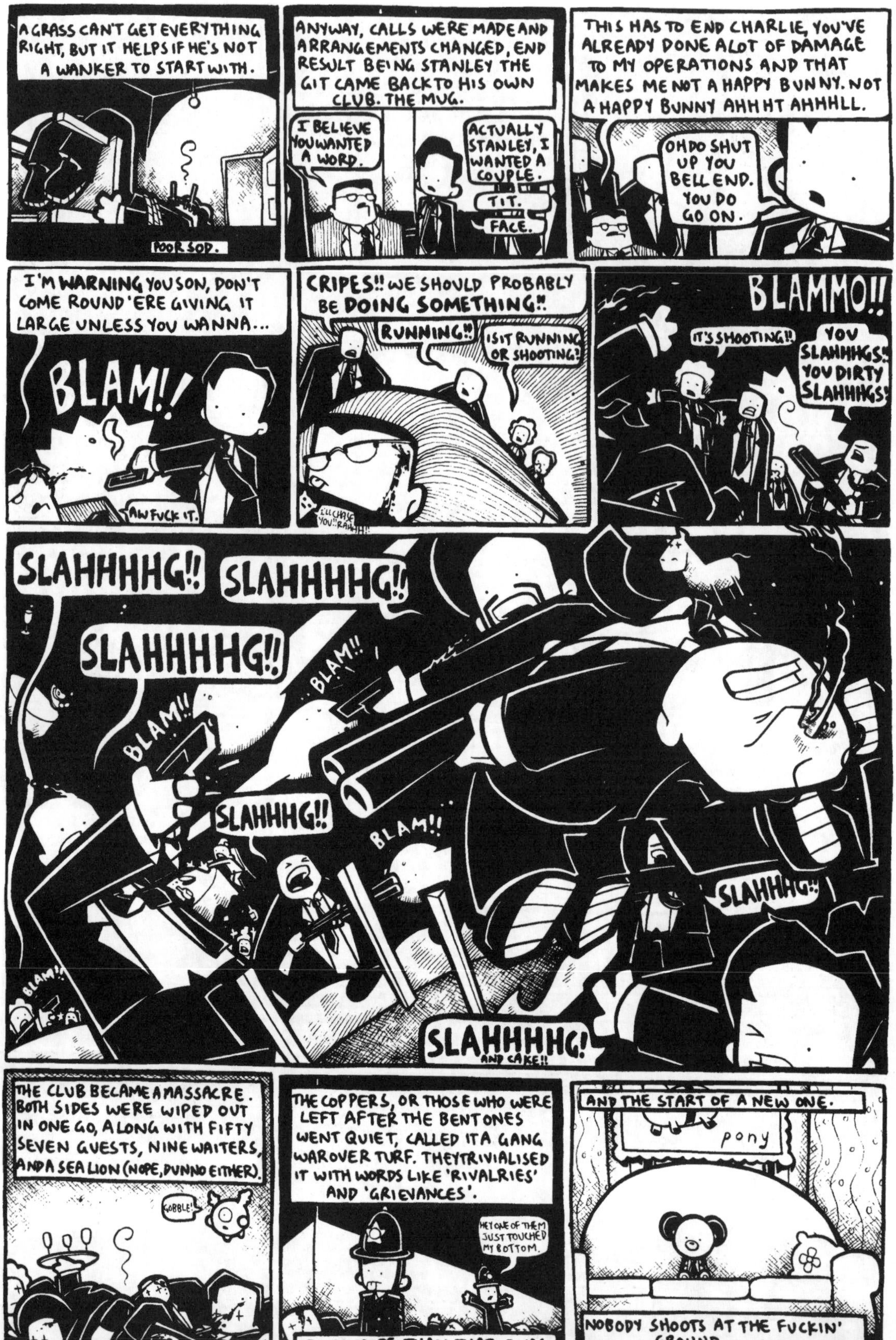
A GRASS CAN'T GET EVERYTHING RIGHT, BUT IT HELPS IF HE'S NOT A WANKER TO START WITH.
POOR SOD.
ANYWAY, CALLS WERE MADE AND ARRANGEMENTS CHANGED, END RESULT BEING STANLEY THE GIT CAME BACK TO HIS OWN CLUB. THE MUG.
I BELIEVE YOU WANTED A WORD.
ACTUALLY STANLEY, I WANTED A COUPLE.
TIT.
FACE.
THIS HAS TO END CHARLIE, YOU'VE ALREADY DONE ALOT OF DAMAGE TO MY OPERATIONS AND THAT MAKES ME NOT A HAPPY BUNNY. NOT A HAPPY BUNNY AHHHT AHHHLL.
OH DO SHUT UP YOU BELL END. YOU DO GO ON.
I'M WARNING YOU SON, DON'T COME ROUND 'ERE GIVING IT LARGE UNLESS YOU WANNA...
BLAM!!
AW FUCK IT.
CRIPES!! WE SHOULD PROBABLY BE DOING SOMETHING!!
RUNNING!!
IS IT RUNNING OR SHOOTING?
I'LL CHASE YOU!! RAHHHH!!
BLAMMO!!
IT'S SHOOTING!!
YOU SLAHHHGS!! YOU DIRTY SLAHHHGS!
SLAHHHHG!!
SLAHHHHG!!
SLAHHHHG!!
BLAM!!
BLAM!!
SLAHHHG!!
BLAM!!
SLAHHHG!!
BLAM!!
SLAHHHHG!
AND CAKE!!
THE CLUB BECAME A MASSACRE. BOTH SIDES WERE WIPED OUT IN ONE GO, ALONG WITH FIFTY SEVEN GUESTS, NINE WAITERS, AND A SEA LION (NOPE, DUNNO EITHER).
GOBBLE!
THE COPPERS, OR THOSE WHO WERE LEFT AFTER THE BENT ONES WENT QUIET, CALLED IT A GANG WAR OVER TURF. THEY TRIVIALISED IT WITH WORDS LIKE 'RIVALRIES' AND 'GRIEVANCES'.
HEY ONE OF THEM JUST TOUCHED MY BOTTOM.
IT WAS MORE THAN THAT, IT WAS THE END OF AN ERA.
AND THE START OF A NEW ONE.
pony
NOBODY SHOOTS AT THE FUCKIN' GROUND.
THE END!! AND I DIDN'T EVEN SAY CU
♡JAMIE!!

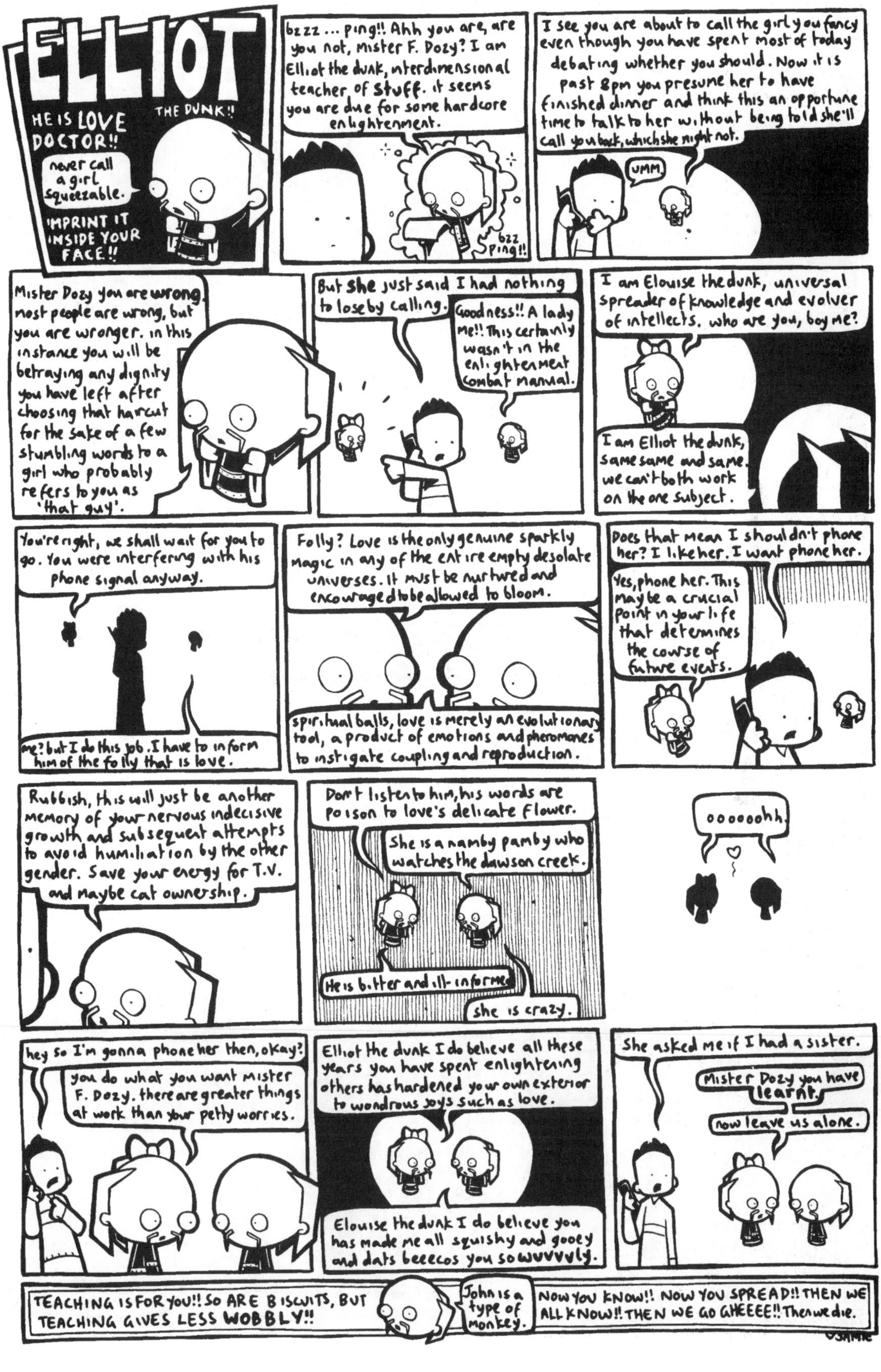
ELLIOT
THE DUNK!!
HE IS LOVE DOCTOR!!
never call a girl squeezable.
'IMPRINT IT INSIDE YOUR FACE!!
bzzz... ping!! Ahh you are, are you not, mister F. Dozy? I am Elliot the dunk, interdimensional teacher of stuff. it seems you are due for some hardcore enlightenment.
bzz ping!!
I see you are about to call the girl you fancy even though you have spent most of today debating whether you should. Now it is past 8pm you presume her to have finished dinner and think this an opportune time to talk to her without being told she'll call you back, which she might not.
UMM.
Mister Dozy you are wrong. most people are wrong, but you are wronger. in this instance you will be betraying any dignity you have left after choosing that haircut for the sake of a few stumbling words to a girl who probably refers to you as 'that guy'.
But she just said I had nothing to lose by calling.
Goodness!! A lady me!! This certainly wasn't in the enlightenment combat manual.
I am Elouise the dunk, universal spreader of knowledge and evolver of intellects. who are you, boy me?
I am Elliot the dunk, same same and same. we can't both work on the one subject.
You're right, we shall wait for you to go. You were interfering with his phone signal anyway.
me? but I do this job. I have to inform him of the folly that is love.
Folly? Love is the only genuine sparkly magic in any of the entire empty desolate universes. It must be nurtured and encouraged to be allowed to bloom.
spiritual balls, love is merely an evolutionary tool, a product of emotions and pheromones to instigate coupling and reproduction.
Does that mean I shouldn't phone her? I like her. I want phone her.
Yes, phone her. This may be a crucial point in your life that determines the course of future events.
Rubbish, this will just be another memory of your nervous indecisive growth and subsequent attempts to avoid humiliation by the other gender. Save your energy for T.V. and maybe cat ownership.
Don't listen to him, his words are poison to love's delicate flower.
She is a namby pamby who watches the dawson creek.
He is bitter and ill-informed
she is crazy.
ooooooohh.
hey so I'm gonna phone her then, okay?
you do what you want mister F. Dozy. there are greater things at work than your petty worries.
Elliot the dunk I do believe all these years you have spent enlightening others has hardened your own exterior to wondrous joys such as love.
Elouise the dunk I do believe you has made me all squishy and gooey and dats beeecos you so wuvvvvly.
She asked me if I had a sister.
Mister Dozy you have learnt.
now leave us alone.
TEACHING IS FOR YOU!! SO ARE BISCUITS, BUT TEACHING GIVES LESS WOBBLY!!
John is a type of monkey.
NOW YOU KNOW!! NOW YOU SPREAD!! THEN WE ALL KNOW!! THEN WE GO GHEEEE!! Then we die.

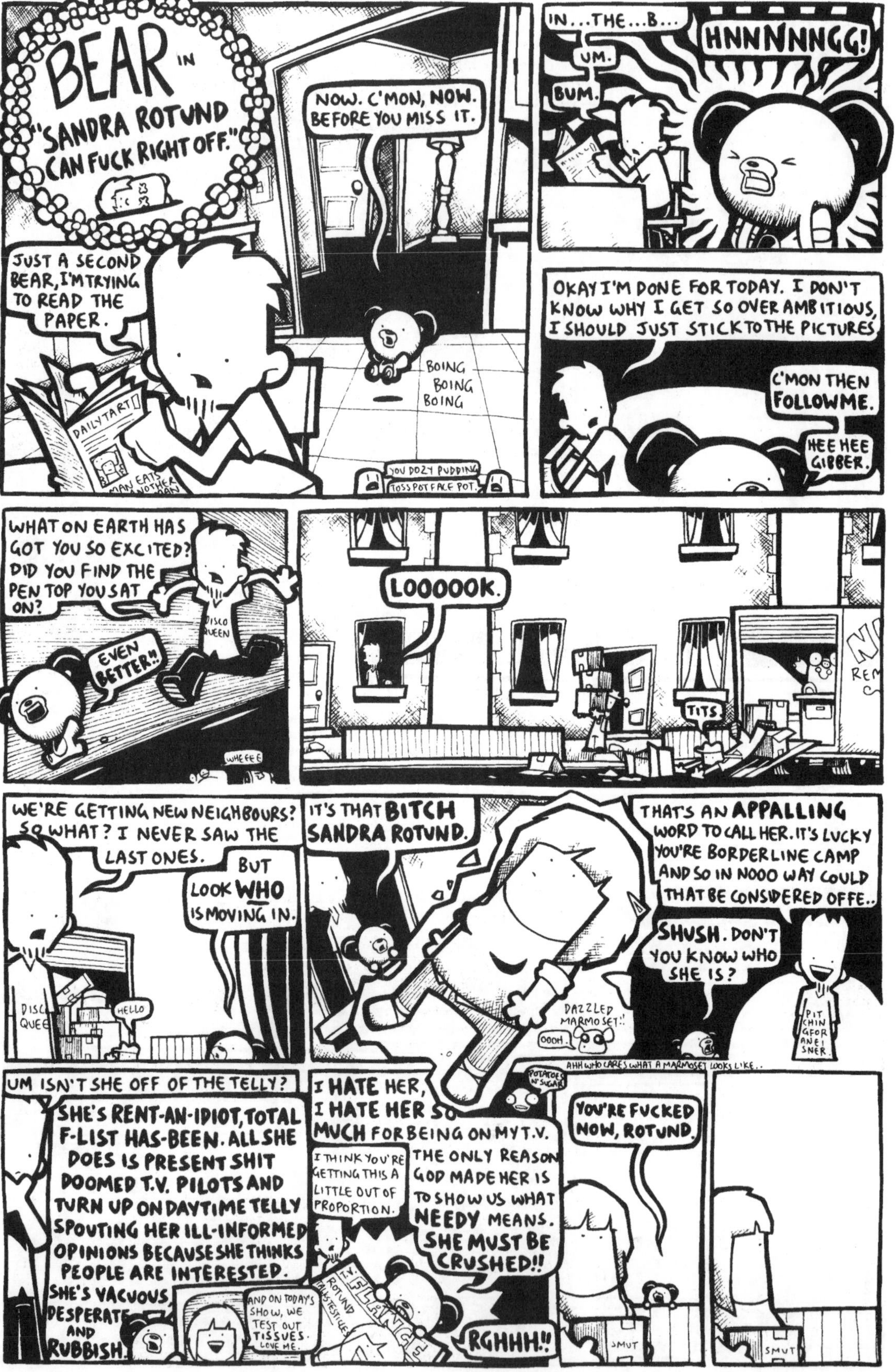
BEAR IN
"SANDRA ROTUND CAN FUCK RIGHT OFF."
NOW. C'MON, NOW. BEFORE YOU MISS IT.
JUST A SECOND BEAR, I'M TRYING TO READ THE PAPER.
DAILY TART
BOING BOING BOING
YOU DOZY PUDDING
TOSS POT FACE POT.
IN...THE...B...
UM.
BUM.
HNNNNNGG!
OKAY I'M DONE FOR TODAY. I DON'T KNOW WHY I GET SO OVER AMBITIOUS, I SHOULD JUST STICK TO THE PICTURES.
C'MON THEN FOLLOW ME.
HEE HEE GIBBER.
WHAT ON EARTH HAS GOT YOU SO EXCITED? DID YOU FIND THE PEN TOP YOU SAT ON?
DISCO QUEEN
EVEN BETTER!!
WHEEEE
LOOOOOK.
TITS.
WE'RE GETTING NEW NEIGHBOURS? SO WHAT? I NEVER SAW THE LAST ONES.
BUT LOOK WHO IS MOVING IN.
HELLO
IT'S THAT BITCH SANDRA ROTUND.
THAT'S AN APPALLING WORD TO CALL HER. IT'S LUCKY YOU'RE BORDERLINE CAMP AND SO IN NOOO WAY COULD THAT BE CONSIDERED OFFE..
SHUSH. DON'T YOU KNOW WHO SHE IS?
DAZZLED MARMOSET!!
OOOH.
AHH WHO CARES WHAT A MARMOSET LOOKS LIKE..
UM ISN'T SHE OFF OF THE TELLY?
SHE'S RENT-AN-IDIOT, TOTAL F-LIST HAS-BEEN. ALL SHE DOES IS PRESENT SHIT DOOMED T.V. PILOTS AND TURN UP ON DAYTIME TELLY SPOUTING HER ILL-INFORMED OPINIONS BECAUSE SHE THINKS PEOPLE ARE INTERESTED.
SHE'S VACUOUS, DESPERATE AND RUBBISH.
AND ON TODAY'S SHOW, WE TEST OUT TISSUES. LOVE ME.
I HATE HER, I HATE HER SO MUCH FOR BEING ON MY T.V.
I THINK YOU'RE GETTING THIS A LITTLE OUT OF PROPORTION.
THE ONLY REASON GOD MADE HER IS TO SHOW US WHAT NEEDY MEANS. SHE MUST BE CRUSHED!!
POTATOES N' SUGAR
RGHHH!!
YOU'RE FUCKED NOW, ROTUND.
SMUT
SMUT

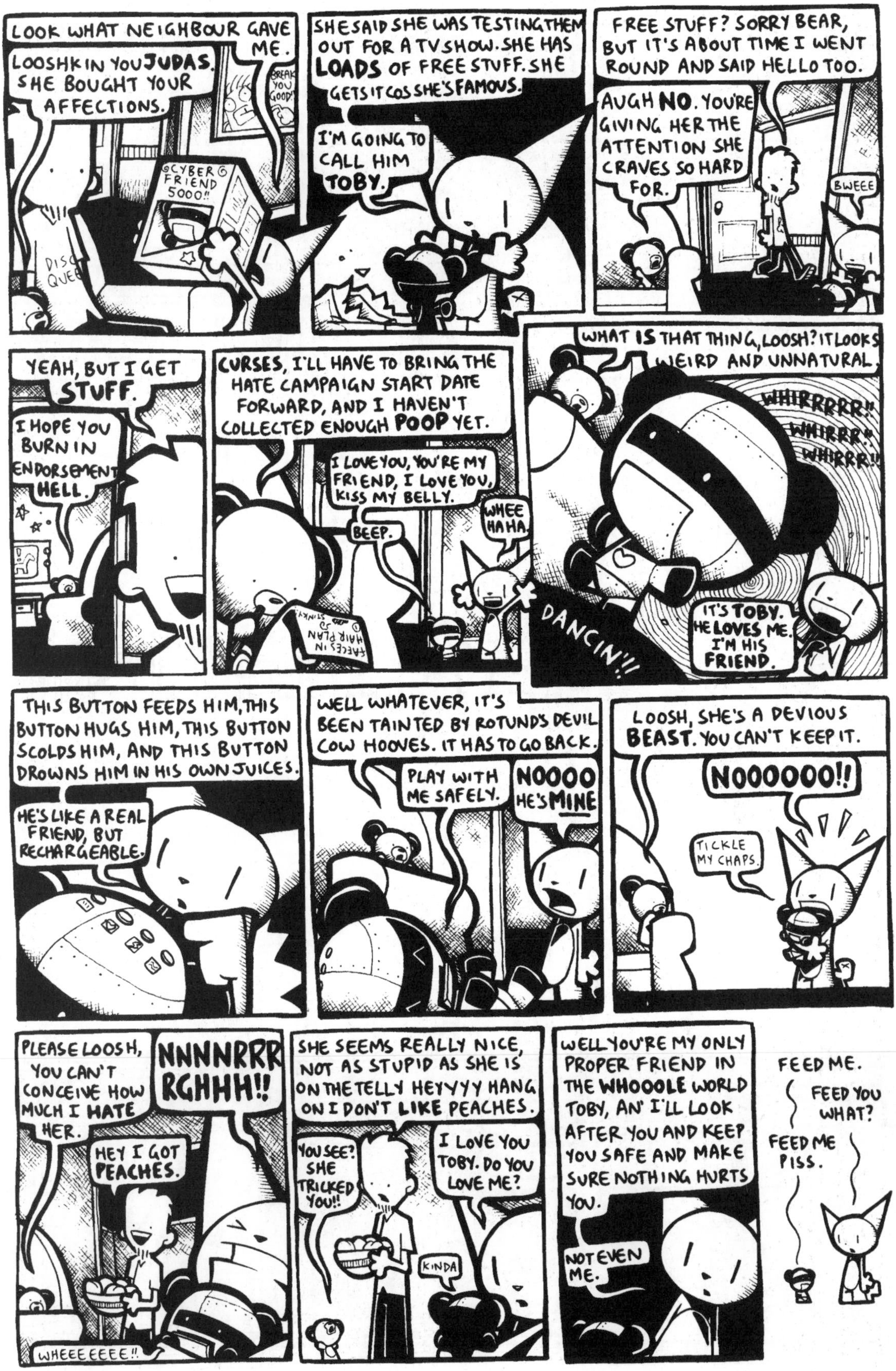
LOOK WHAT NEIGHBOUR GAVE ME.
LOOSHKIN YOU JUDAS. SHE BOUGHT YOUR AFFECTIONS.
BREAK YOU GOOD!
CYBER FRIEND 5000!!
DISCO QUEE
SHE SAID SHE WAS TESTING THEM OUT FOR A TV SHOW. SHE HAS LOADS OF FREE STUFF. SHE GETS IT COS SHE'S FAMOUS.
I'M GOING TO CALL HIM TOBY.
FREE STUFF? SORRY BEAR, BUT IT'S ABOUT TIME I WENT ROUND AND SAID HELLO TOO.
AUGH NO. YOU'RE GIVING HER THE ATTENTION SHE CRAVES SO HARD FOR.
BWEEE
YEAH, BUT I GET STUFF.
I HOPE YOU BURN IN ENDORSEMENT HELL.
CURSES, I'LL HAVE TO BRING THE HATE CAMPAIGN START DATE FORWARD, AND I HAVEN'T COLLECTED ENOUGH POOP YET.
I LOVE YOU, YOU'RE MY FRIEND, I LOVE YOU, KISS MY BELLY.
BEEP.
WHEE HAHA.
1 FAECES IN HAIR PLAN 2 STINKY
WHAT IS THAT THING, LOOSH? IT LOOKS WEIRD AND UNNATURAL.
WHIRRRRR!! WHIRRR!! WHIRRR!!
DANCIN'!!
IT'S TOBY. HE LOVES ME. I'M HIS FRIEND.
THIS BUTTON FEEDS HIM, THIS BUTTON HUGS HIM, THIS BUTTON SCOLDS HIM, AND THIS BUTTON DROWNS HIM IN HIS OWN JUICES.
HE'S LIKE A REAL FRIEND, BUT RECHARGEABLE.
WELL WHATEVER, IT'S BEEN TAINTED BY ROTUND'S DEVIL COW HOOVES. IT HAS TO GO BACK.
PLAY WITH ME SAFELY.
NOOOO HE'S MINE
LOOSH, SHE'S A DEVIOUS BEAST. YOU CAN'T KEEP IT.
NOOOOOO!!
TICKLE MY CHAPS.
PLEASE LOOSH, YOU CAN'T CONCEIVE HOW MUCH I HATE HER.
NNNNRRR RGHHH!!
HEY I GOT PEACHES.
WHEEEEEEE!!
SHE SEEMS REALLY NICE, NOT AS STUPID AS SHE IS ON THE TELLY HEYYYY HANG ON I DON'T LIKE PEACHES.
YOU SEE? SHE TRICKED YOU!!
I LOVE YOU TOBY. DO YOU LOVE ME?
KINDA
WELL YOU'RE MY ONLY PROPER FRIEND IN THE WHOOOLE WORLD TOBY, AN' I'LL LOOK AFTER YOU AND KEEP YOU SAFE AND MAKE SURE NOTHING HURTS YOU.
NOT EVEN ME.
FEED ME.
FEED YOU WHAT?
FEED ME PISS.

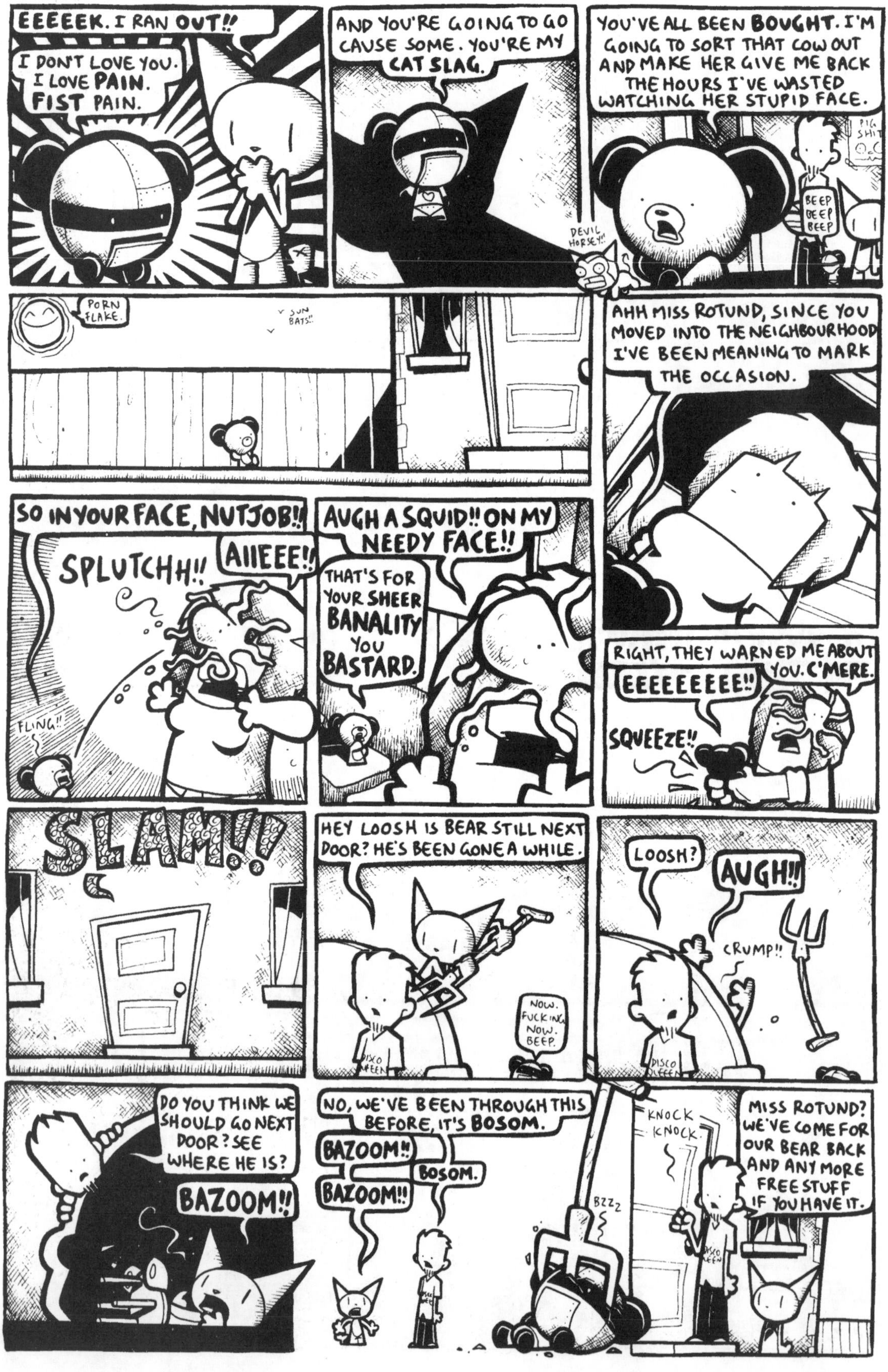
EEEEEK. I RAN OUT!!
I DON'T LOVE YOU. I LOVE PAIN. FIST PAIN.
AND YOU'RE GOING TO GO CAUSE SOME. YOU'RE MY CAT SLAG.
YOU'VE ALL BEEN BOUGHT. I'M GOING TO SORT THAT COW OUT AND MAKE HER GIVE ME BACK THE HOURS I'VE WASTED WATCHING HER STUPID FACE.
PIG SHIT
BEEP BEEP BEEP
DEVIL HORSEY!!
PORN FLAKE.
SUN BATS!!
AHH MISS ROTUND, SINCE YOU MOVED INTO THE NEIGHBOURHOOD I'VE BEEN MEANING TO MARK THE OCCASION.
SO IN YOUR FACE, NUTJOB!!
SPLUTCHH!!
AIIEEE!!
FLING!!
AUGH A SQUID!! ON MY NEEDY FACE!!
THAT'S FOR YOUR SHEER BANALITY YOU BASTARD.
RIGHT, THEY WARNED ME ABOUT YOU. C'MERE.
EEEEEEEEE!!
SQUEEZE!!
SLAM!!
HEY LOOSH IS BEAR STILL NEXT DOOR? HE'S BEEN GONE A WHILE.
NOW. FUCKING NOW. BEEP.
DISCO QUEEN
LOOSH?
AUGH!!
CRUMP!!
DISCO QUEEN
DO YOU THINK WE SHOULD GO NEXT DOOR? SEE WHERE HE IS?
BAZOOM!!
NO, WE'VE BEEN THROUGH THIS BEFORE, IT'S BOSOM.
BAZOOM!!
BAZOOM!!
BOSOM.
KNOCK KNOCK.
BZZZ
MISS ROTUND? WE'VE COME FOR OUR BEAR BACK AND ANY MORE FREE STUFF IF YOU HAVE IT.
DISCO QUEEN

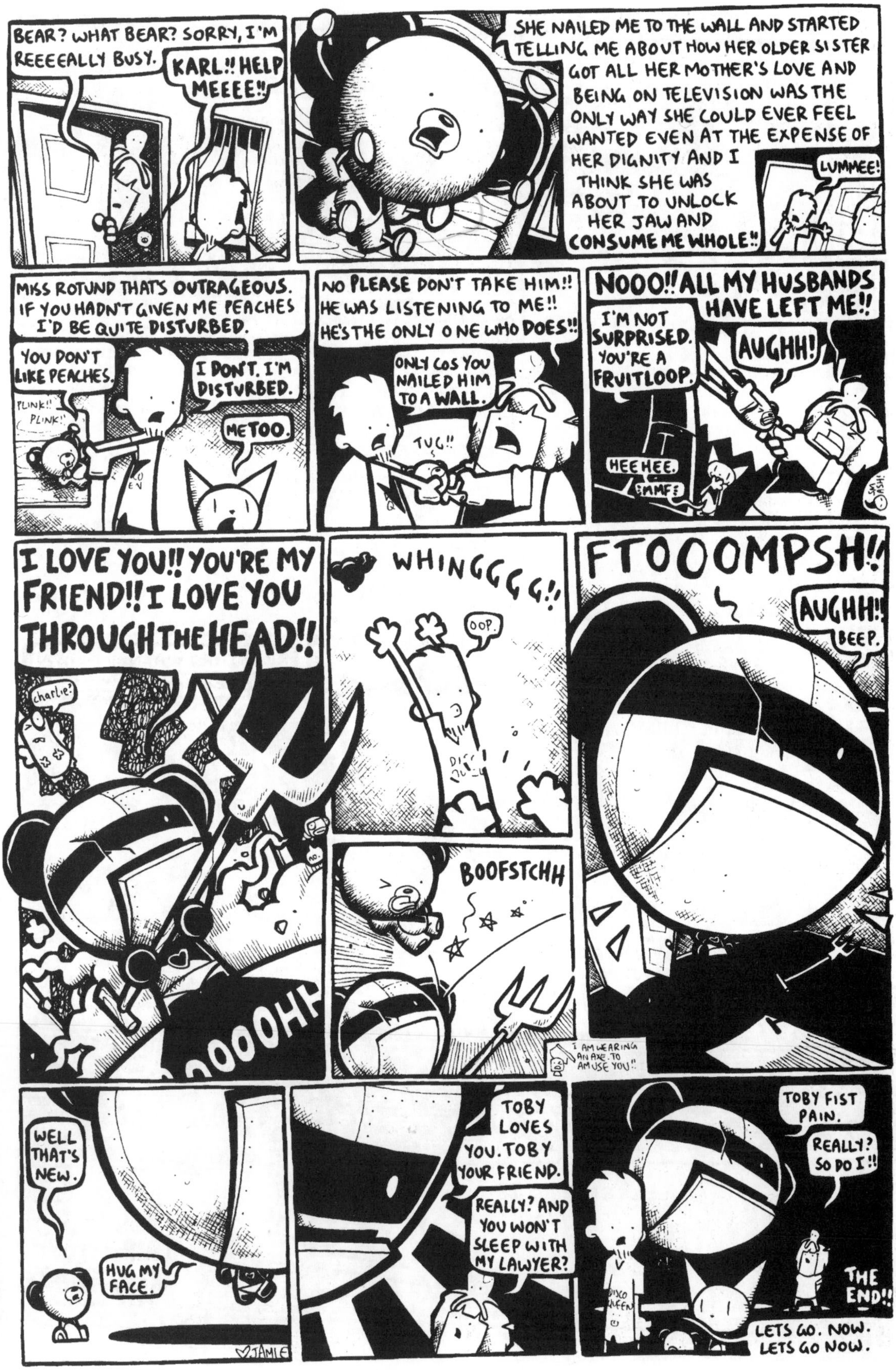
BEAR? WHAT BEAR? SORRY, I'M REEEEALLY BUSY.
KARL!! HELP MEEEE!!
SHE NAILED ME TO THE WALL AND STARTED TELLING ME ABOUT HOW HER OLDER SISTER GOT ALL HER MOTHER'S LOVE AND BEING ON TELEVISION WAS THE ONLY WAY SHE COULD EVER FEEL WANTED EVEN AT THE EXPENSE OF HER DIGNITY AND I THINK SHE WAS ABOUT TO UNLOCK HER JAW AND CONSUME ME WHOLE!!
LUMMEE!
MISS ROTUND THAT'S OUTRAGEOUS. IF YOU HADN'T GIVEN ME PEACHES I'D BE QUITE DISTURBED.
YOU DON'T LIKE PEACHES.
I DON'T. I'M DISTURBED.
PLINK!! PLINK!!
ME TOO.
NO PLEASE DON'T TAKE HIM!! HE WAS LISTENING TO ME!! HE'S THE ONLY ONE WHO DOES!!
ONLY COS YOU NAILED HIM TO A WALL.
TUG!!
NOOO!! ALL MY HUSBANDS HAVE LEFT ME!!
I'M NOT SURPRISED. YOU'RE A FRUITLOOP.
AUGHH!
HEE HEE.
MMF
SMASH!
I LOVE YOU!! YOU'RE MY FRIEND!! I LOVE YOU THROUGH THE HEAD!!
charlie?
NO.
OOOOHH
WHINGGGGG!!
OOP.
BOOFSTCHH
I AM WEARING AN AXE TO AMUSE YOU!!
FTOOOMPSH!!
AUGHH!!
BEEP.
WELL THAT'S NEW.
HUG MY FACE.
JAMIE
TOBY LOVES YOU. TOBY YOUR FRIEND.
REALLY? AND YOU WON'T SLEEP WITH MY LAWYER?
TOBY FIST PAIN.
REALLY? SO DO I!!
THE END!!
LETS GO. NOW. LETS GO NOW.

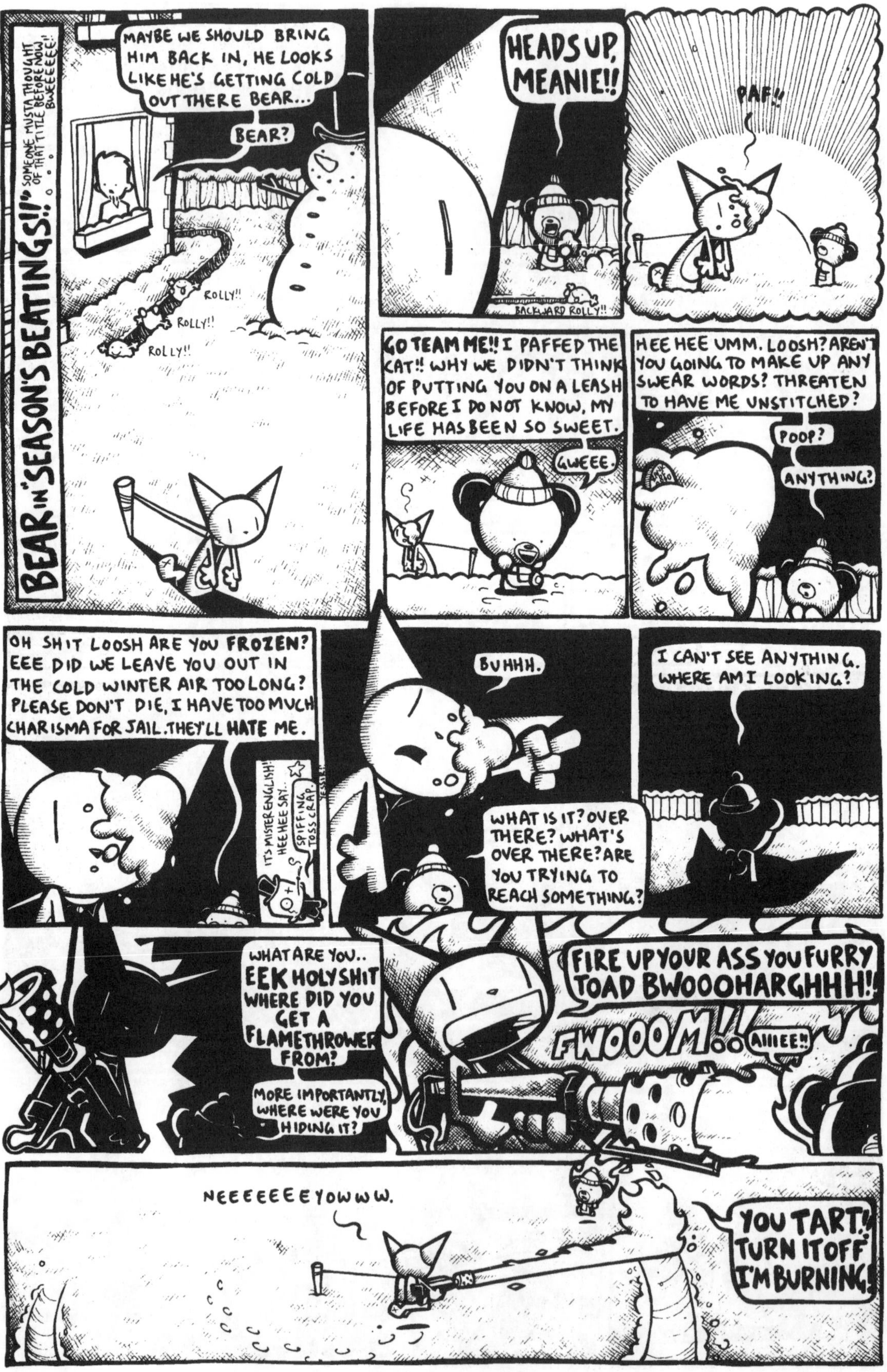
BEAR IN "SEASON'S BEATINGS!!"
SOMEONE MUSTA THOUGHT OF THAT TITLE BEFORE NOW BWEEEEEE!!
MAYBE WE SHOULD BRING HIM BACK IN, HE LOOKS LIKE HE'S GETTING COLD OUT THERE BEAR...
BEAR?
ROLLY!!
ROLLY!!
ROLLY!!
HEADS UP, MEANIE!!
BACKWARD ROLLY!!
PAF!!
GO TEAM ME!! I PAFFED THE CAT!! WHY WE DIDN'T THINK OF PUTTING YOU ON A LEASH BEFORE I DO NOT KNOW, MY LIFE HAS BEEN SO SWEET.
GWEEE.
HEE HEE UMM. LOOSH? AREN'T YOU GOING TO MAKE UP ANY SWEAR WORDS? THREATEN TO HAVE ME UNSTITCHED?
POOP?
ANYTHING?
OH SHIT LOOSH ARE YOU FROZEN? EEE DID WE LEAVE YOU OUT IN THE COLD WINTER AIR TOO LONG? PLEASE DON'T DIE, I HAVE TOO MUCH CHARISMA FOR JAIL. THEY'LL HATE ME.
IT'S MISTER ENGLISH! HEE HEE SAY..
SPIFFING TOSS CRAP.
BUHHH.
WHAT IS IT? OVER THERE? WHAT'S OVER THERE? ARE YOU TRYING TO REACH SOMETHING?
I CAN'T SEE ANYTHING. WHERE AM I LOOKING?
WHAT ARE YOU.. EEK HOLY SHIT WHERE DID YOU GET A FLAMETHROWER FROM?
MORE IMPORTANTLY, WHERE WERE YOU HIDING IT?
FIRE UP YOUR ASS YOU FURRY TOAD BWOOOHARGHHH!!
FWOOOM!!
AIIIEE!!
NEEEEEEEYOWWW.
YOU TART!! TURN IT OFF I'M BURNING!

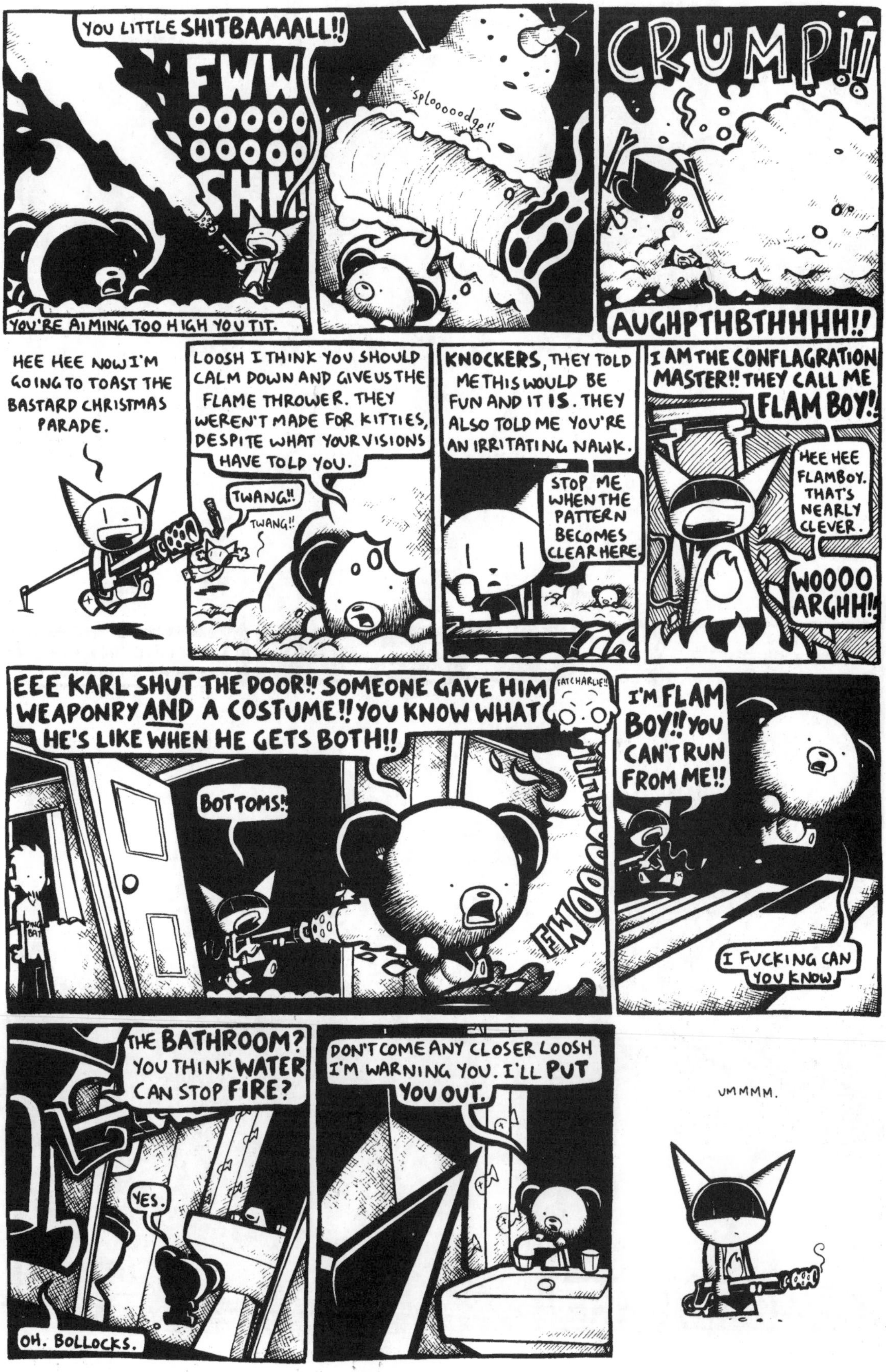

YOU LITTLE SHITBAAAALL!!
FWW OOOOO OOOOO SHH!!
YOU'RE AIMING TOO HIGH YOU TIT.
sploooooodge!!
CRUMP!!
AUGHPTHBTHHHH!!
HEE HEE NOW I'M GOING TO TOAST THE BASTARD CHRISTMAS PARADE.
LOOSH I THINK YOU SHOULD CALM DOWN AND GIVE US THE FLAME THROWER. THEY WEREN'T MADE FOR KITTIES, DESPITE WHAT YOUR VISIONS HAVE TOLD YOU.
TWANG!!
TWANG!!
KNOCKERS, THEY TOLD ME THIS WOULD BE FUN AND IT IS. THEY ALSO TOLD ME YOU'RE AN IRRITATING NAWK.
STOP ME WHEN THE PATTERN BECOMES CLEAR HERE.
I AM THE CONFLAGRATION MASTER!! THEY CALL ME FLAM BOY!!
HEE HEE FLAMBOY. THAT'S NEARLY CLEVER.
WOOOO ARGHH!!
EEE KARL SHUT THE DOOR!! SOMEONE GAVE HIM WEAPONRY AND A COSTUME!! YOU KNOW WHAT HE'S LIKE WHEN HE GETS BOTH!!
FATCHARLIE!!
BOTTOMS!!
FWOOOOOOM!!
I'M FLAM BOY!! YOU CAN'T RUN FROM ME!!
I FUCKING CAN YOU KNOW.
THE BATHROOM? YOU THINK WATER CAN STOP FIRE?
YES.
OH. BOLLOCKS.
DON'T COME ANY CLOSER LOOSH I'M WARNING YOU. I'LL PUT YOU OUT.
UMMMM.

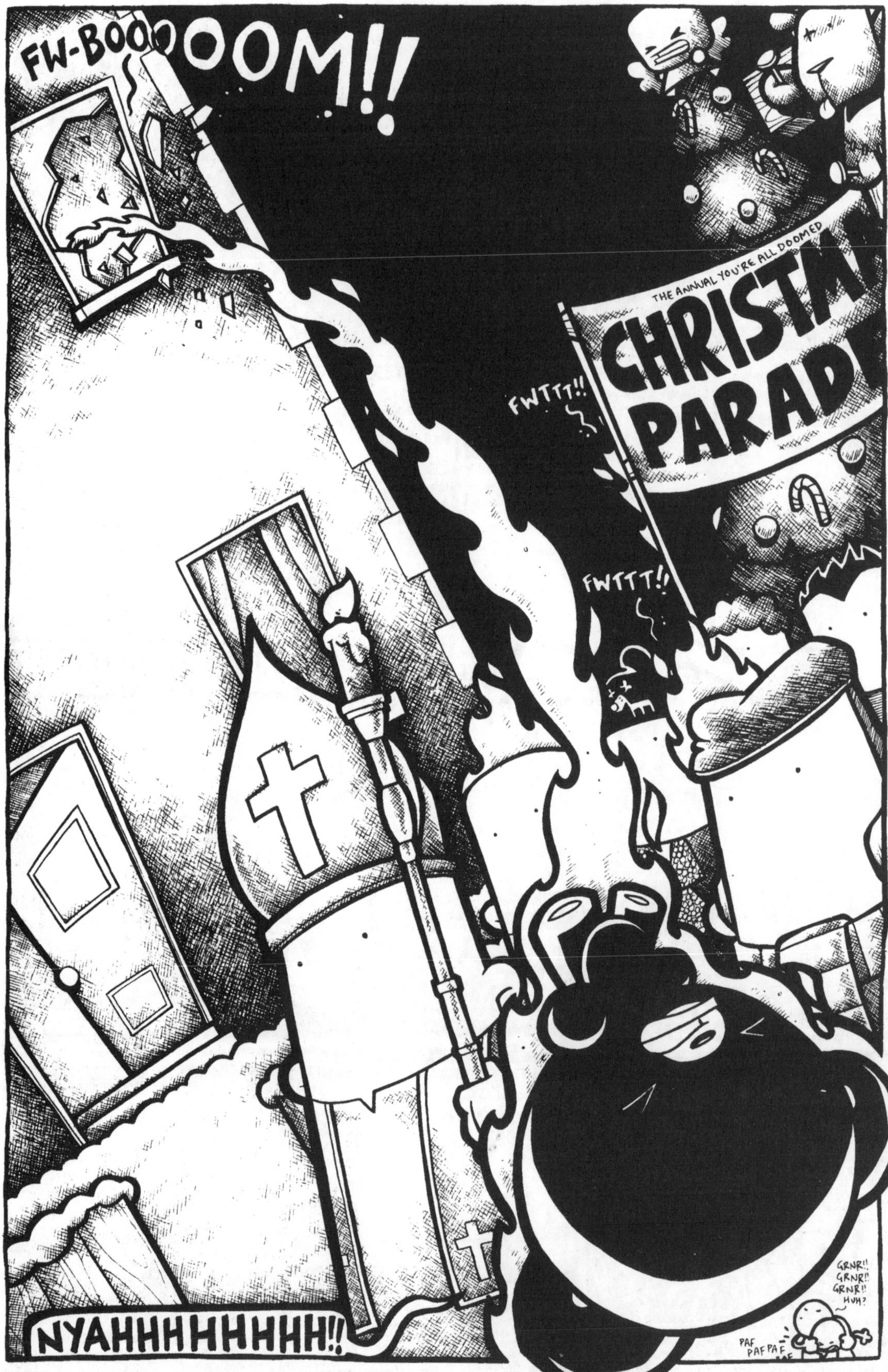
FW-BOOOOOM!!
THE ANNUAL YOU'RE ALL DOOMED
CHRISTM
PARAD
FWTTT!!
FWTTT!!
NYAHHHHHHHHH!!
GRNR!! GRNR!! GRNR!!
HUH?
PAF PAF PAF

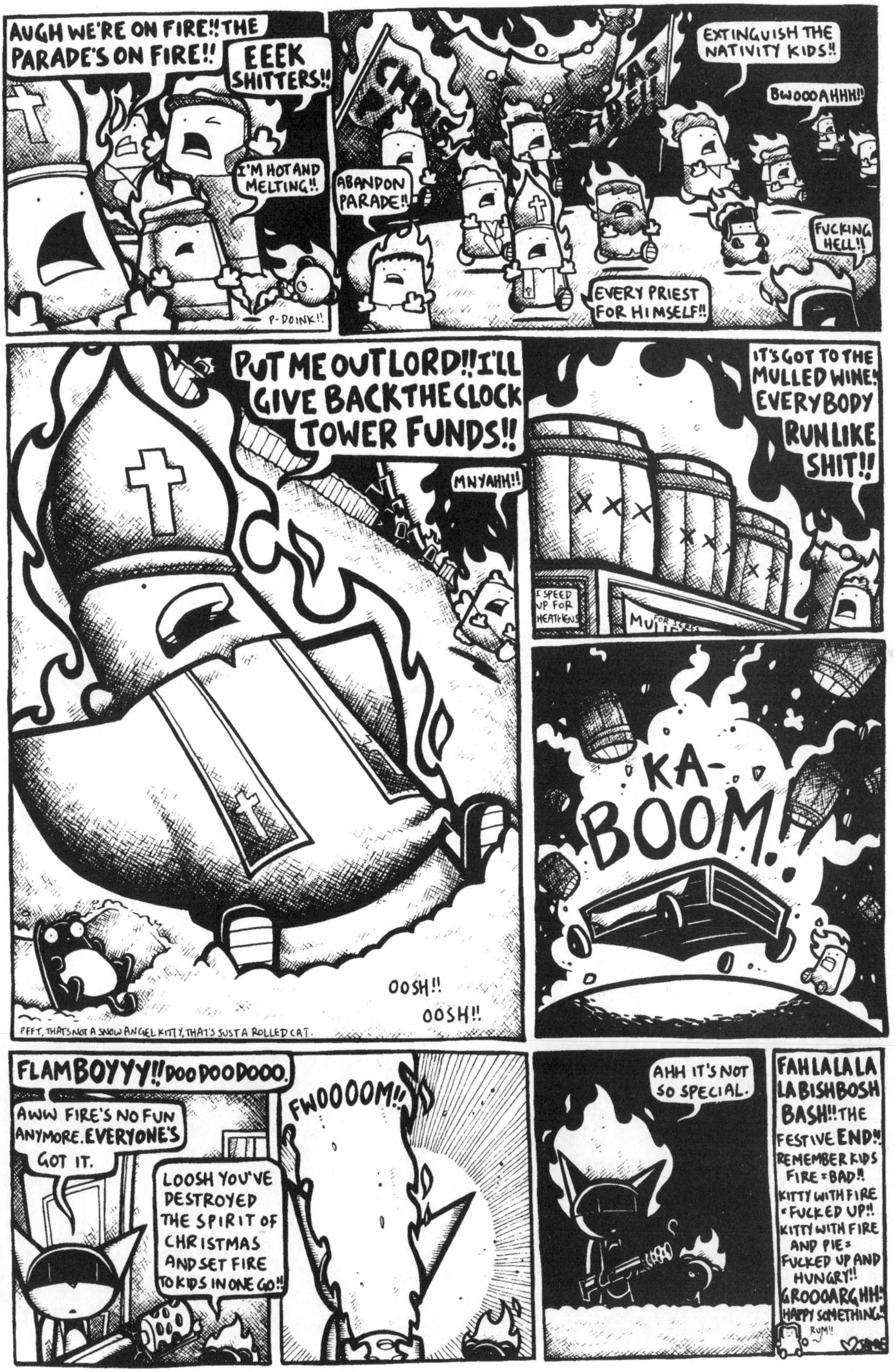
AUGH WE'RE ON FIRE!! THE PARADE'S ON FIRE!!
EEEK SHITTERS!!
I'M HOT AND MELTING!!
P-DOINK!!
EXTINGUISH THE NATIVITY KIDS!!
BWOOOAHHH!!
ABANDON PARADE!!
FUCKING HELL!!
EVERY PRIEST FOR HIMSELF!!
PUT ME OUT LORD!! I'LL GIVE BACK THE CLOCK TOWER FUNDS!!
MNYAHH!!
OOSH!!
OOSH!!
PFFT, THAT'S NOT A SNOW ANGEL KITTY, THAT'S JUST A ROLLED CAT.
IT'S GOT TO THE MULLED WINE!! EVERYBODY RUN LIKE SHIT!!
I SPEED UP FOR HEATHENS
KA-BOOM!!
FLAMBOYYY!! DOO DOO DOOO.
AWW FIRE'S NO FUN ANYMORE. EVERYONE'S GOT IT.
LOOSH YOU'VE DESTROYED THE SPIRIT OF CHRISTMAS AND SET FIRE TO KIDS IN ONE GO!!
FWOOOOM!!
AHH IT'S NOT SO SPECIAL.
FAH LA LA LA LA BISH BOSH BASH!! THE FESTIVE END!! REMEMBER KIDS FIRE = BAD!! KITTY WITH FIRE = FUCKED UP!! KITTY WITH FIRE AND PIE = FUCKED UP AND HUNGRY!! GROOOARGHH!! HAPPY SOMETHING!!
RUM!!

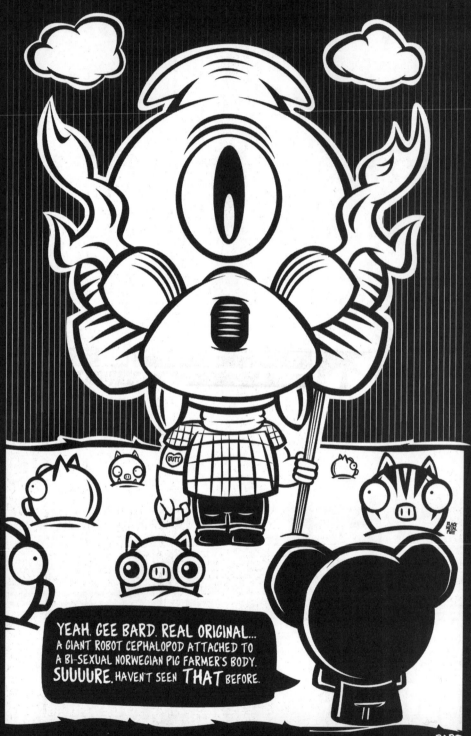

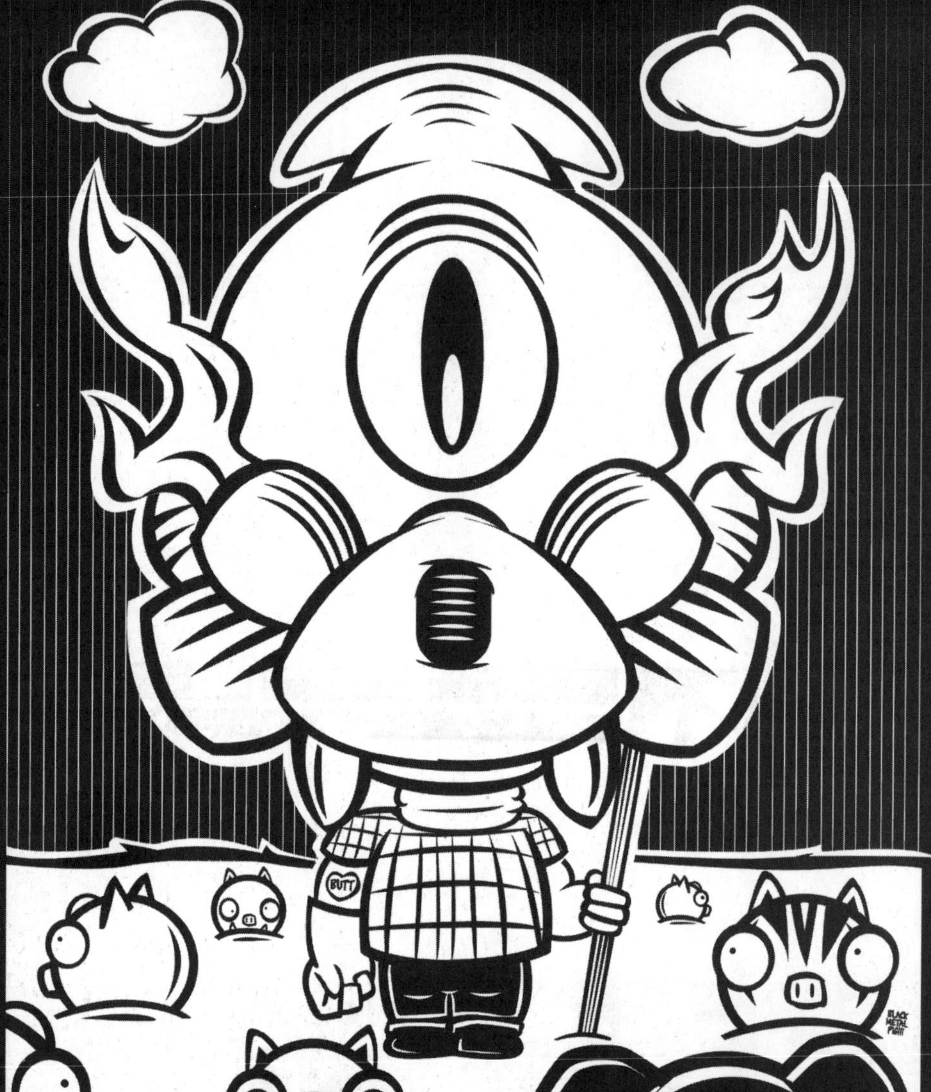
BUTT
YEAH. GEE BARD. REAL ORIGINAL... A GIANT ROBOT CEPHALOPOD ATTACHED TO A BI-SEXUAL NORWEGIAN PIG FARMER'S BODY. SUUUURE. HAVEN'T SEEN THAT BEFORE.
BARD

by bard
www.hellobard.com

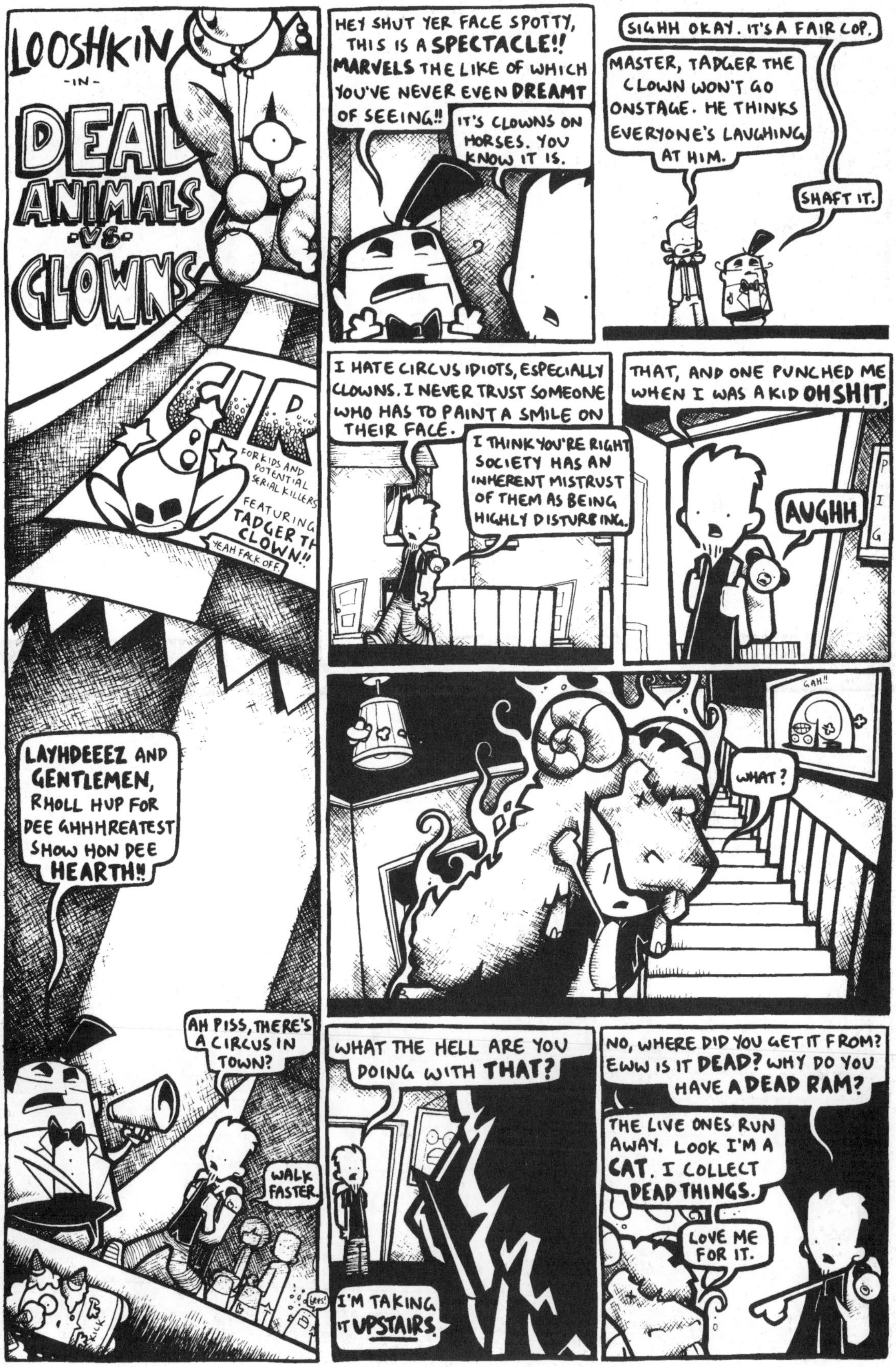
LOOSHKIN
-IN-
DEAD ANIMALS -VS- CLOWNS
CIR
FOR KIDS AND POTENTIAL SERIAL KILLERS
FEATURING TADGER TH CLOWN!!
YEAH FACK OFF.
LAYHDEEEZ AND GENTLEMEN, RHOLL HUP FOR DEE GHHHREATEST SHOW HON DEE HEARTH!!
AH PISS, THERE'S A CIRCUS IN TOWN?
WALK FASTER.
HEY SHUT YER FACE SPOTTY, THIS IS A SPECTACLE!! MARVELS THE LIKE OF WHICH YOU'VE NEVER EVEN DREAMT OF SEEING!!
IT'S CLOWNS ON HORSES. YOU KNOW IT IS.
SIGHH OKAY. IT'S A FAIR COP.
MASTER, TADGER THE CLOWN WON'T GO ONSTAGE. HE THINKS EVERYONE'S LAUGHING AT HIM.
SHAFT IT.
I HATE CIRCUS IDIOTS, ESPECIALLY CLOWNS. I NEVER TRUST SOMEONE WHO HAS TO PAINT A SMILE ON THEIR FACE.
I THINK YOU'RE RIGHT SOCIETY HAS AN INHERENT MISTRUST OF THEM AS BEING HIGHLY DISTURBING.
THAT, AND ONE PUNCHED ME WHEN I WAS A KID OH SHIT.
AUGHH.
GAH!!
WHAT?
WHAT THE HELL ARE YOU DOING WITH THAT?
I'M TAKING IT UPSTAIRS.
NO, WHERE DID YOU GET IT FROM? EWW IS IT DEAD? WHY DO YOU HAVE A DEAD RAM?
THE LIVE ONES RUN AWAY. LOOK I'M A CAT. I COLLECT DEAD THINGS.
LOVE ME FOR IT.

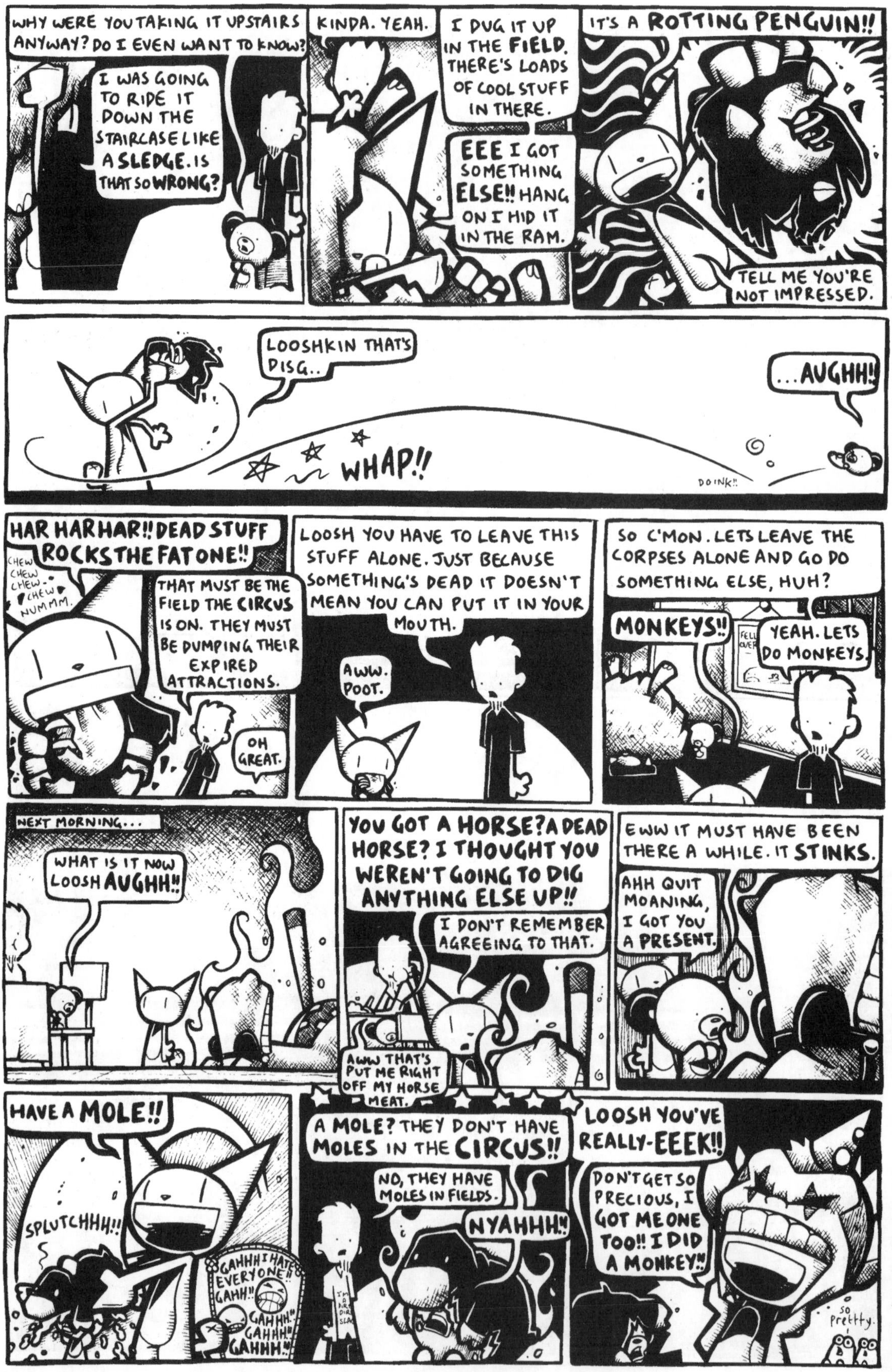
WHY WERE YOU TAKING IT UPSTAIRS ANYWAY? DO I EVEN WANT TO KNOW?
I WAS GOING TO RIDE IT DOWN THE STAIRCASE LIKE A SLEDGE. IS THAT SO WRONG?
KINDA. YEAH.
I DUG IT UP IN THE FIELD. THERE'S LOADS OF COOL STUFF IN THERE.
EEE I GOT SOMETHING ELSE!! HANG ON I HID IT IN THE RAM.
IT'S A ROTTING PENGUIN!!
TELL ME YOU'RE NOT IMPRESSED.
LOOSHKIN THAT'S DISG..
WHAP!!
...AUGHH!!
DOINK!!
HAR HAR HAR!! DEAD STUFF ROCKS THE FAT ONE!!
CHEW CHEW CHEW CHEW NUMMM.
THAT MUST BE THE FIELD THE CIRCUS IS ON. THEY MUST BE DUMPING THEIR EXPIRED ATTRACTIONS.
OH GREAT.
LOOSH YOU HAVE TO LEAVE THIS STUFF ALONE. JUST BECAUSE SOMETHING'S DEAD IT DOESN'T MEAN YOU CAN PUT IT IN YOUR MOUTH.
AWW. POOT.
SO C'MON. LETS LEAVE THE CORPSES ALONE AND GO DO SOMETHING ELSE, HUH?
MONKEYS!!
YEAH. LETS DO MONKEYS.
NEXT MORNING...
WHAT IS IT NOW LOOSH AUGHH!!
YOU GOT A HORSE? A DEAD HORSE? I THOUGHT YOU WEREN'T GOING TO DIG ANYTHING ELSE UP!!
I DON'T REMEMBER AGREEING TO THAT.
AWW THAT'S PUT ME RIGHT OFF MY HORSE MEAT.
EWW IT MUST HAVE BEEN THERE A WHILE. IT STINKS.
AHH QUIT MOANING, I GOT YOU A PRESENT.
HAVE A MOLE!!
SPLUTCHHH!!
GAHHH I HATE EVERYONE!! GAHH!! GAHHH!! GAHHH!! GAHHH!!
A MOLE? THEY DON'T HAVE MOLES IN THE CIRCUS!!
NO, THEY HAVE MOLES IN FIELDS.
NYAHHH!!
LOOSH YOU'VE REALLY-EEEK!!
DON'T GET SO PRECIOUS, I GOT ME ONE TOO!! I DID A MONKEY!!
so prettty.

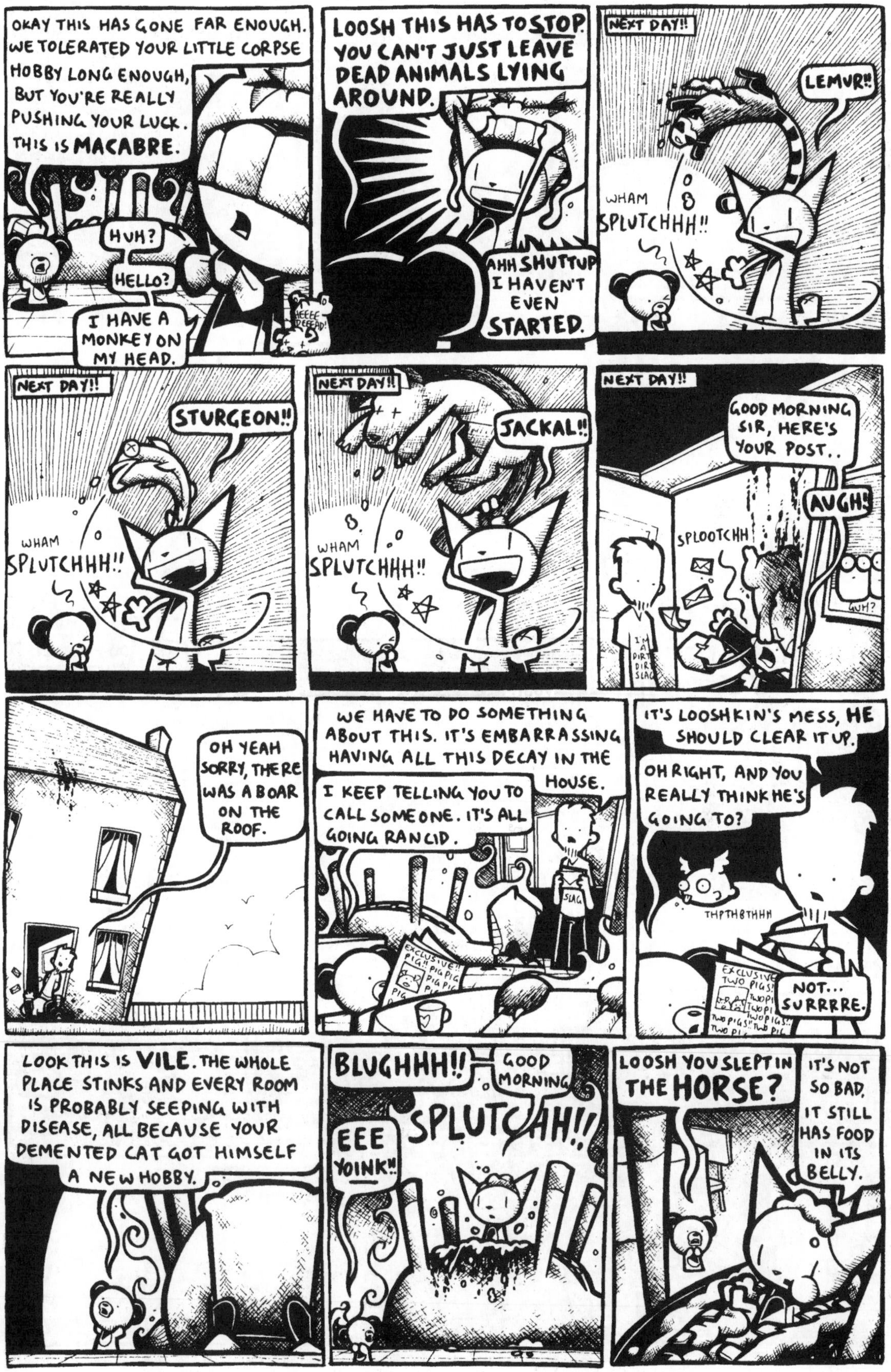
OKAY THIS HAS GONE FAR ENOUGH. WE TOLERATED YOUR LITTLE CORPSE HOBBY LONG ENOUGH, BUT YOU'RE REALLY PUSHING YOUR LUCK. THIS IS MACABRE.
HUH?
HELLO?
I HAVE A MONKEY ON MY HEAD.
HEEEE DEEEAD!
LOOSH THIS HAS TO STOP. YOU CAN'T JUST LEAVE DEAD ANIMALS LYING AROUND.
AHH SHUTTUP I HAVEN'T EVEN STARTED.
NEXT DAY!!
LEMUR!!
WHAM
SPLUTCHHH!!
NEXT DAY!!
STURGEON!!
WHAM
SPLUTCHHH!!
NEXT DAY!!
JACKAL!!
WHAM
SPLUTCHHH!!
NEXT DAY!!
GOOD MORNING SIR, HERE'S YOUR POST..
SPLOOTCHH
AUGH!
GUH?
OH YEAH SORRY, THERE WAS A BOAR ON THE ROOF.
WE HAVE TO DO SOMETHING ABOUT THIS. IT'S EMBARRASSING HAVING ALL THIS DECAY IN THE HOUSE.
I KEEP TELLING YOU TO CALL SOMEONE. IT'S ALL GOING RANCID.
SLAG
EXCLUSIVE!! PIG!! PIG PIG PIG PIG
IT'S LOOSHKIN'S MESS, HE SHOULD CLEAR IT UP.
OH RIGHT, AND YOU REALLY THINK HE'S GOING TO?
THPTHBTHHH
EXCLUSIVE TWO PIGS!!
NOT... SURRRRE.
LOOK THIS IS VILE. THE WHOLE PLACE STINKS AND EVERY ROOM IS PROBABLY SEEPING WITH DISEASE, ALL BECAUSE YOUR DEMENTED CAT GOT HIMSELF A NEW HOBBY.
BLUGHHH!!
GOOD MORNING
SPLUTCHH!!
EEE
YOINK!!
LOOSH YOU SLEPT IN THE HORSE?
IT'S NOT SO BAD, IT STILL HAS FOOD IN ITS BELLY.

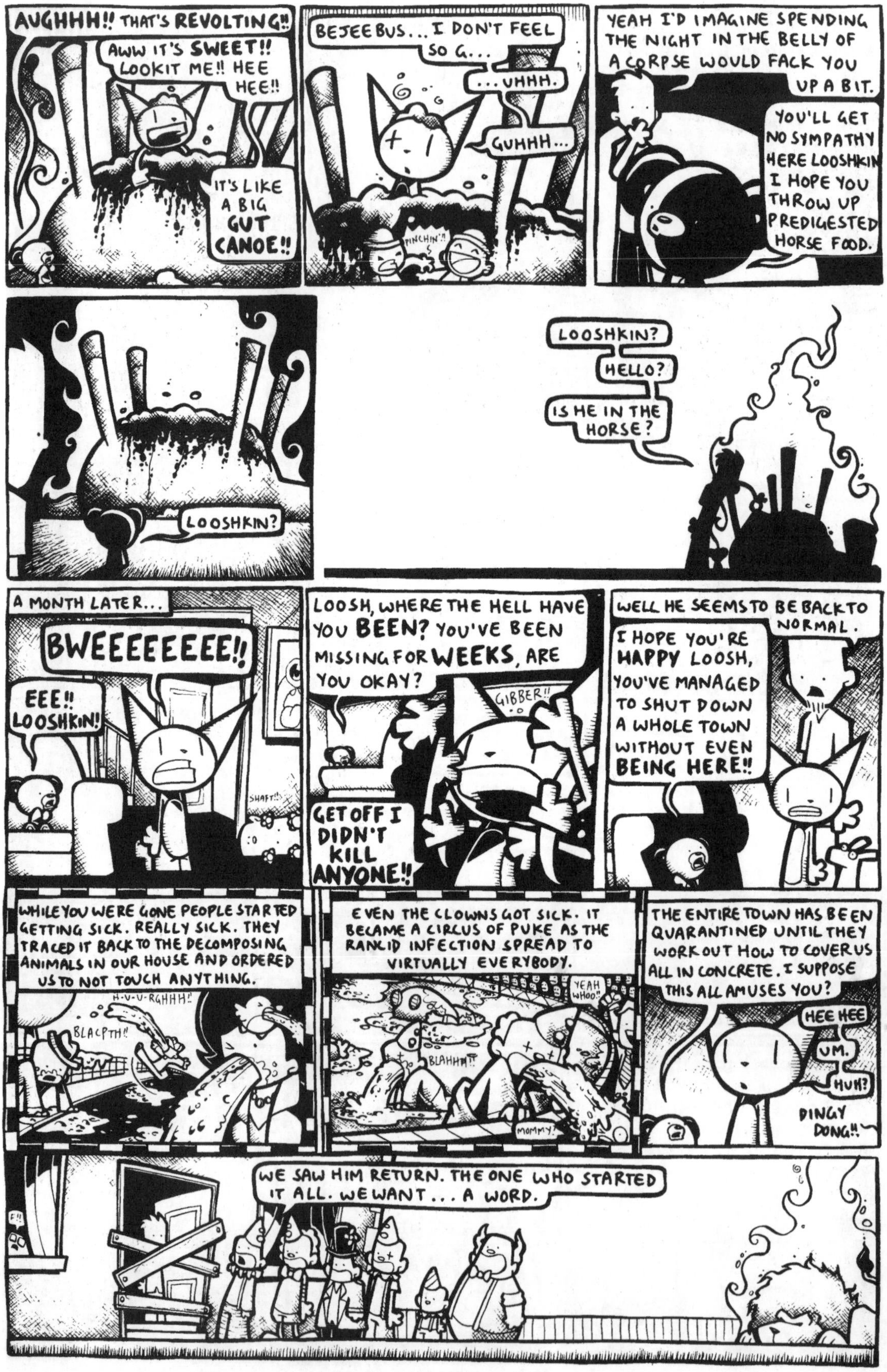
AUGHHH!! THAT'S REVOLTING!!
AWW IT'S SWEET!! LOOKIT ME!! HEE HEE!!
IT'S LIKE A BIG GUT CANOE!!
BEJEEBUS... I DON'T FEEL SO G...
...UHHH.
GUHHH...
PINCHIN'!!
YEAH I'D IMAGINE SPENDING THE NIGHT IN THE BELLY OF A CORPSE WOULD FACK YOU UP A BIT.
YOU'LL GET NO SYMPATHY HERE LOOSHKIN I HOPE YOU THROW UP PREDIGESTED HORSE FOOD.
LOOSHKIN?
LOOSHKIN?
HELLO?
IS HE IN THE HORSE?
A MONTH LATER...
BWEEEEEEEEE!!
EEE!! LOOSHKIN!
SHAFT!!
LOOSH, WHERE THE HELL HAVE YOU BEEN? YOU'VE BEEN MISSING FOR WEEKS, ARE YOU OKAY?
GIBBER!!
GET OFF I DIDN'T KILL ANYONE!!
WELL HE SEEMS TO BE BACK TO NORMAL.
I HOPE YOU'RE HAPPY LOOSH, YOU'VE MANAGED TO SHUT DOWN A WHOLE TOWN WITHOUT EVEN BEING HERE!!
WHILE YOU WERE GONE PEOPLE STARTED GETTING SICK. REALLY SICK. THEY TRACED IT BACK TO THE DECOMPOSING ANIMALS IN OUR HOUSE AND ORDERED US TO NOT TOUCH ANYTHING.
H-U-U-RGHHH!!
BLACPTH!!
EVEN THE CLOWNS GOT SICK. IT BECAME A CIRCUS OF PUKE AS THE RANCID INFECTION SPREAD TO VIRTUALLY EVERYBODY.
YEAH WHOO!!
BLAHHH!!
MOMMY!
THE ENTIRE TOWN HAS BEEN QUARANTINED UNTIL THEY WORK OUT HOW TO COVER US ALL IN CONCRETE. I SUPPOSE THIS ALL AMUSES YOU?
HEE HEE
UM.
HUH?
DINGY DONG!!
WE SAW HIM RETURN. THE ONE WHO STARTED IT ALL. WE WANT... A WORD.

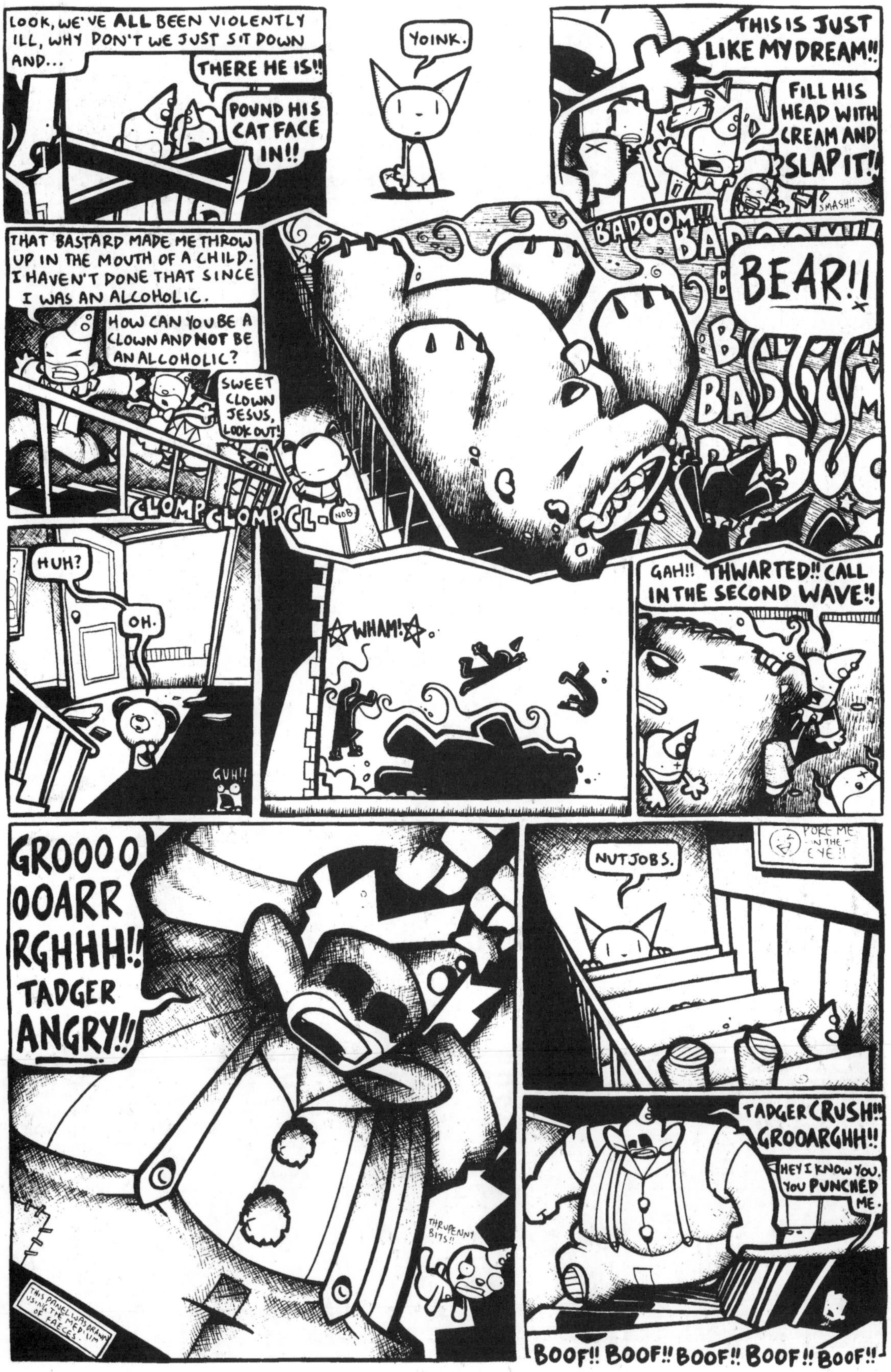
LOOK, WE'VE ALL BEEN VIOLENTLY ILL, WHY DON'T WE JUST SIT DOWN AND...
THERE HE IS!!
POUND HIS CAT FACE IN!!
YOINK.
THIS IS JUST LIKE MY DREAM!!
FILL HIS HEAD WITH CREAM AND SLAP IT!!
SMASH!!
THAT BASTARD MADE ME THROW UP IN THE MOUTH OF A CHILD. I HAVEN'T DONE THAT SINCE I WAS AN ALCOHOLIC.
HOW CAN YOU BE A CLOWN AND NOT BE AN ALCOHOLIC?
SWEET CLOWN JESUS, LOOK OUT!
CLOMP CLOMP CL-
NOB.
BADOOM!!
BEAR!!
HUH?
OH.
GUH!!
WHAM!
GAH!! THWARTED!! CALL IN THE SECOND WAVE!!
GROOOO OOARR RGHHH!! TADGER ANGRY!!
THRUPENNY BITS!!
THIS PANEL WAS DRAWN USING THE MEDIUM OF FAECES.
NUTJOBS.
POKE ME IN THE EYE!!
TADGER CRUSH!! GROOARGHH!!
HEY I KNOW YOU. YOU PUNCHED ME.
BOOF!! BOOF!! BOOF!! BOOF!! BOOF!!

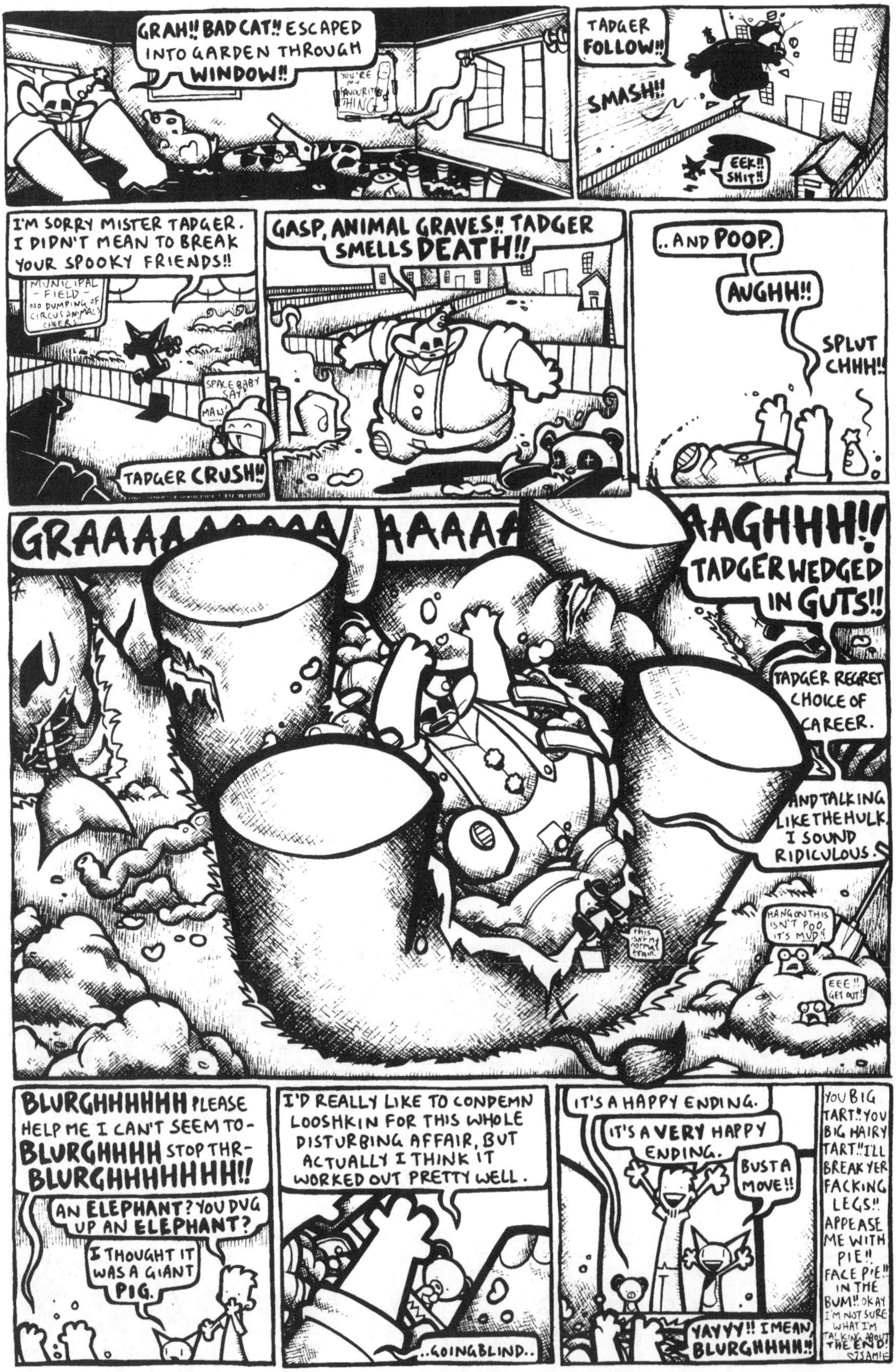
GRAH!! BAD CAT!! ESCAPED INTO GARDEN THROUGH WINDOW!!
YOU'RE MY FAVOURITE THING
TADGER FOLLOW!!
SMASH!!
EEK!! SHIT!!
I'M SORRY MISTER TADGER. I DIDN'T MEAN TO BREAK YOUR SPOOKY FRIENDS!!
MUNICIPAL - FIELD - NO DUMPING OF CIRCUS ANIMALS CHEERS
SPACE BABY SAY!
MAW!
TADGER CRUSH!!
GASP, ANIMAL GRAVES!! TADGER SMELLS DEATH!!
..AND POOP.
AUGHH!!
SPLUT CHHH!!
GRAAAAAAAAAAAAAAAAGHHH!!
TADGER WEDGED IN GUTS!!
TADGER REGRET CHOICE OF CAREER.
AND TALKING LIKE THE HULK. I SOUND RIDICULOUS.
this isn't my normal train.
HANG ON THIS ISN'T POO, IT'S MUD!!
EEE!! GET OUT!!
BLURGHHHHHH PLEASE HELP ME I CAN'T SEEM TO- BLURGHHHH STOP THR- BLURGHHHHHHH!!
AN ELEPHANT? YOU DUG UP AN ELEPHANT?
I THOUGHT IT WAS A GIANT PIG.
I'D REALLY LIKE TO CONDEMN LOOSHKIN FOR THIS WHOLE DISTURBING AFFAIR, BUT ACTUALLY I THINK IT WORKED OUT PRETTY WELL.
..GOING BLIND..
IT'S A HAPPY ENDING.
IT'S A VERY HAPPY ENDING.
BUSTA MOVE!!
YAYYY!! I MEAN, BLURGHHHH!!
YOU BIG TART!! YOU BIG HAIRY TART!! I'LL BREAK YER FACKING LEGS!! APPEASE ME WITH PIE!! FACE PIE!! IN THE BUM!! OKAY I'M NOT SURE WHAT I'M TALKING ABOUT
THE END!
JAMIE

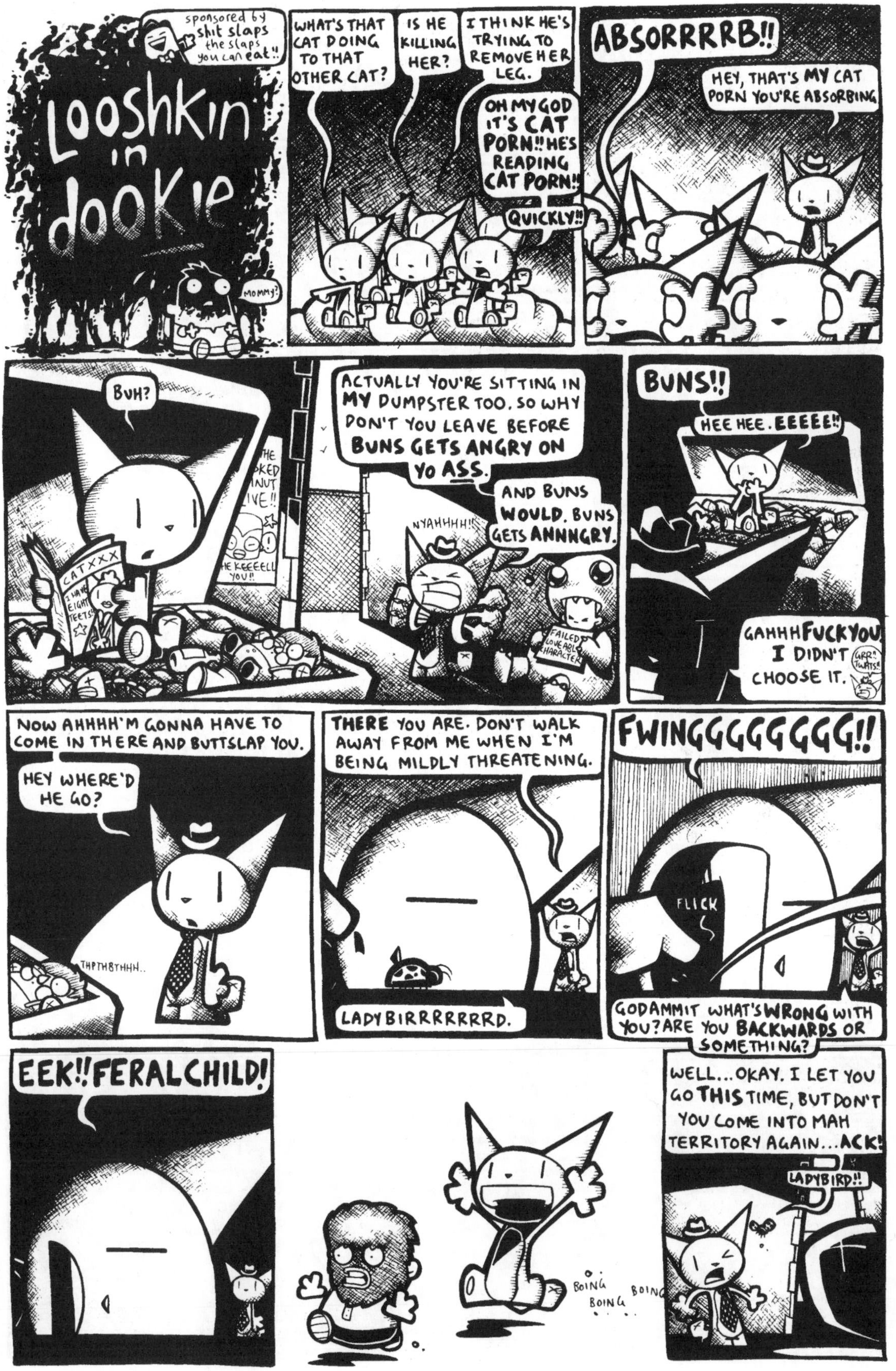
sponsored by shit slaps the slaps you can eat!!
Looshkin in dooKie
MOMMY?
WHAT'S THAT CAT DOING TO THAT OTHER CAT?
IS HE KILLING HER?
I THINK HE'S TRYING TO REMOVE HER LEG.
OH MY GOD IT'S CAT PORN!! HE'S READING CAT PORN!!
QUICKLY!!
ABSORRRRRB!!
HEY, THAT'S MY CAT PORN YOU'RE ABSORBING
BUH?
CAT XXX
ACTUALLY YOU'RE SITTING IN MY DUMPSTER TOO. SO WHY DON'T YOU LEAVE BEFORE BUNS GETS ANGRY ON YO ASS.
AND BUNS WOULD. BUNS GETS ANNNGRY.
NYAHHHH!!
BUNS!!
HEE HEE. EEEEE!!
GAHHH FUCK YOU. I DIDN'T CHOOSE IT.
NOW AHHHH'M GONNA HAVE TO COME IN THERE AND BUTTSLAP YOU.
HEY WHERE'D HE GO?
THPTHBTHHH..
THERE YOU ARE. DON'T WALK AWAY FROM ME WHEN I'M BEING MILDLY THREATENING.
LADYBIRRRRRRRD.
FWINGGGGGGGGG!!
FLICK
GODAMMIT WHAT'S WRONG WITH YOU? ARE YOU BACKWARDS OR SOMETHING?
EEK!! FERALCHILD!
BOING
BOING
BOING
WELL... OKAY. I LET YOU GO THIS TIME, BUT DON'T YOU COME INTO MAH TERRITORY AGAIN... ACK!
LADYBIRD!!

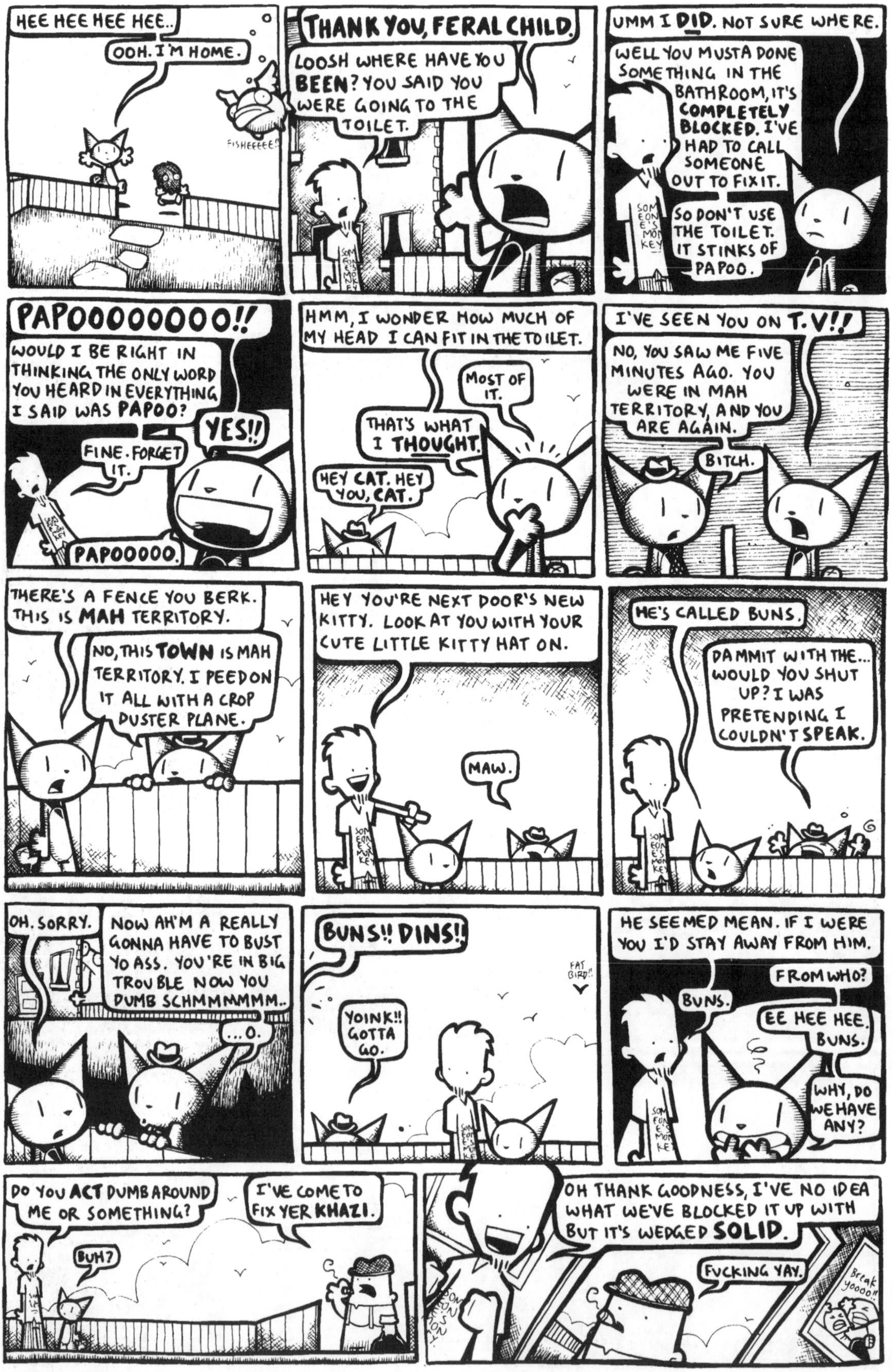
HEE HEE HEE HEE..
OOH. I'M HOME.
FISHEEEEE!!
THANK YOU, FERAL CHILD.
LOOSH WHERE HAVE YOU BEEN? YOU SAID YOU WERE GOING TO THE TOILET.
UMM I DID. NOT SURE WHERE.
WELL YOU MUSTA DONE SOMETHING IN THE BATHROOM, IT'S COMPLETELY BLOCKED. I'VE HAD TO CALL SOMEONE OUT TO FIX IT.
SO DON'T USE THE TOILET. IT STINKS OF PAPOO.
PAPOOOOOOOO!!
WOULD I BE RIGHT IN THINKING THE ONLY WORD YOU HEARD IN EVERYTHING I SAID WAS PAPOO?
YES!!
FINE. FORGET IT.
PAPOOOOO.
HMM, I WONDER HOW MUCH OF MY HEAD I CAN FIT IN THE TOILET.
MOST OF IT.
THAT'S WHAT I THOUGHT.
HEY CAT. HEY YOU, CAT.
I'VE SEEN YOU ON T.V!!
NO, YOU SAW ME FIVE MINUTES AGO. YOU WERE IN MAH TERRITORY, AND YOU ARE AGAIN.
BITCH.
THERE'S A FENCE YOU BERK. THIS IS MAH TERRITORY.
NO, THIS TOWN IS MAH TERRITORY. I PEED ON IT ALL WITH A CROP DUSTER PLANE.
HEY YOU'RE NEXT DOOR'S NEW KITTY. LOOK AT YOU WITH YOUR CUTE LITTLE KITTY HAT ON.
MAW.
HE'S CALLED BUNS.
DAMMIT WITH THE... WOULD YOU SHUT UP? I WAS PRETENDING I COULDN'T SPEAK.
OH. SORRY.
NOW AH'M A REALLY GONNA HAVE TO BUST YO ASS. YOU'RE IN BIG TROUBLE NOW YOU DUMB SCHMMMMMM..
...O.
BUNS!! DINS!!
YOINK!! GOTTA GO.
FAT BIRD!!
HE SEEMED MEAN. IF I WERE YOU I'D STAY AWAY FROM HIM.
FROM WHO?
BUNS.
EE HEE HEE. BUNS.
WHY, DO WE HAVE ANY?
DO YOU ACT DUMB AROUND ME OR SOMETHING?
BUH?
I'VE COME TO FIX YER KHAZI.
OH THANK GOODNESS, I'VE NO IDEA WHAT WE'VE BLOCKED IT UP WITH BUT IT'S WEDGED SOLID.
FUCKING YAY.
Break yoooo!!

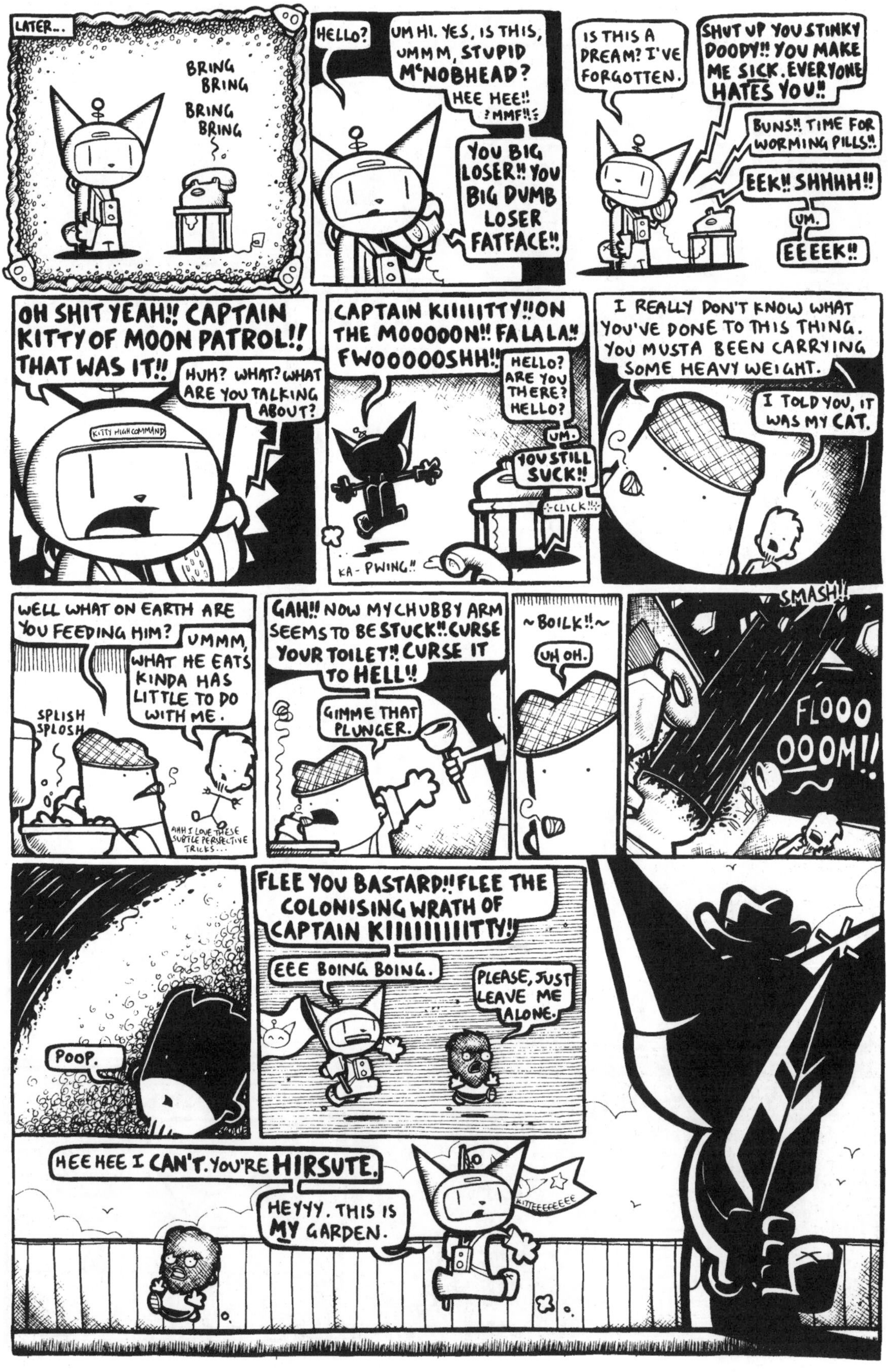
LATER...
BRING BRING
BRING BRING
HELLO?
UM HI. YES, IS THIS, UMMM, STUPID McNOBHEAD?
HEE HEE!! ?MMF!!?
YOU BIG LOSER!! YOU BIG DUMB LOSER FATFACE!!
IS THIS A DREAM? I'VE FORGOTTEN.
SHUT UP YOU STINKY DOODY!! YOU MAKE ME SICK. EVERYONE HATES YOU!!
BUNS!! TIME FOR WORMING PILLS!!
EEK!! SHHHH!!
UM.
EEEEK!!
OH SHIT YEAH!! CAPTAIN KITTY OF MOON PATROL!! THAT WAS IT!!
HUH? WHAT? WHAT ARE YOU TALKING ABOUT?
KITTY HIGH COMMAND
CAPTAIN KIIIIITTY!! ON THE MOOOOON!! FA LA LA!! FWOOOOOSHH!!
HELLO? ARE YOU THERE? HELLO?
UM.
YOU STILL SUCK!!
CLICK
KA-PWING!!
I REALLY DON'T KNOW WHAT YOU'VE DONE TO THIS THING. YOU MUSTA BEEN CARRYING SOME HEAVY WEIGHT.
I TOLD YOU, IT WAS MY CAT.
WELL WHAT ON EARTH ARE YOU FEEDING HIM?
UMMM, WHAT HE EATS KINDA HAS LITTLE TO DO WITH ME.
SPLISH SPLOSH
AHH I LOVE THESE SUBTLE PERSPECTIVE TRICKS...
GAH!! NOW MY CHUBBY ARM SEEMS TO BE STUCK!! CURSE YOUR TOILET!! CURSE IT TO HELL!!
GIMME THAT PLUNGER.
~BOILK!!~
UH OH.
SMASH!!
FLOOO OOOM!!
POOP.
FLEE YOU BASTARD!! FLEE THE COLONISING WRATH OF CAPTAIN KIIIIIIIIITTY!!
EEE BOING BOING.
PLEASE, JUST LEAVE ME ALONE.
HEE HEE I CAN'T. YOU'RE HIRSUTE.
HEYYY. THIS IS MY GARDEN.
KITTEEEEEEEE

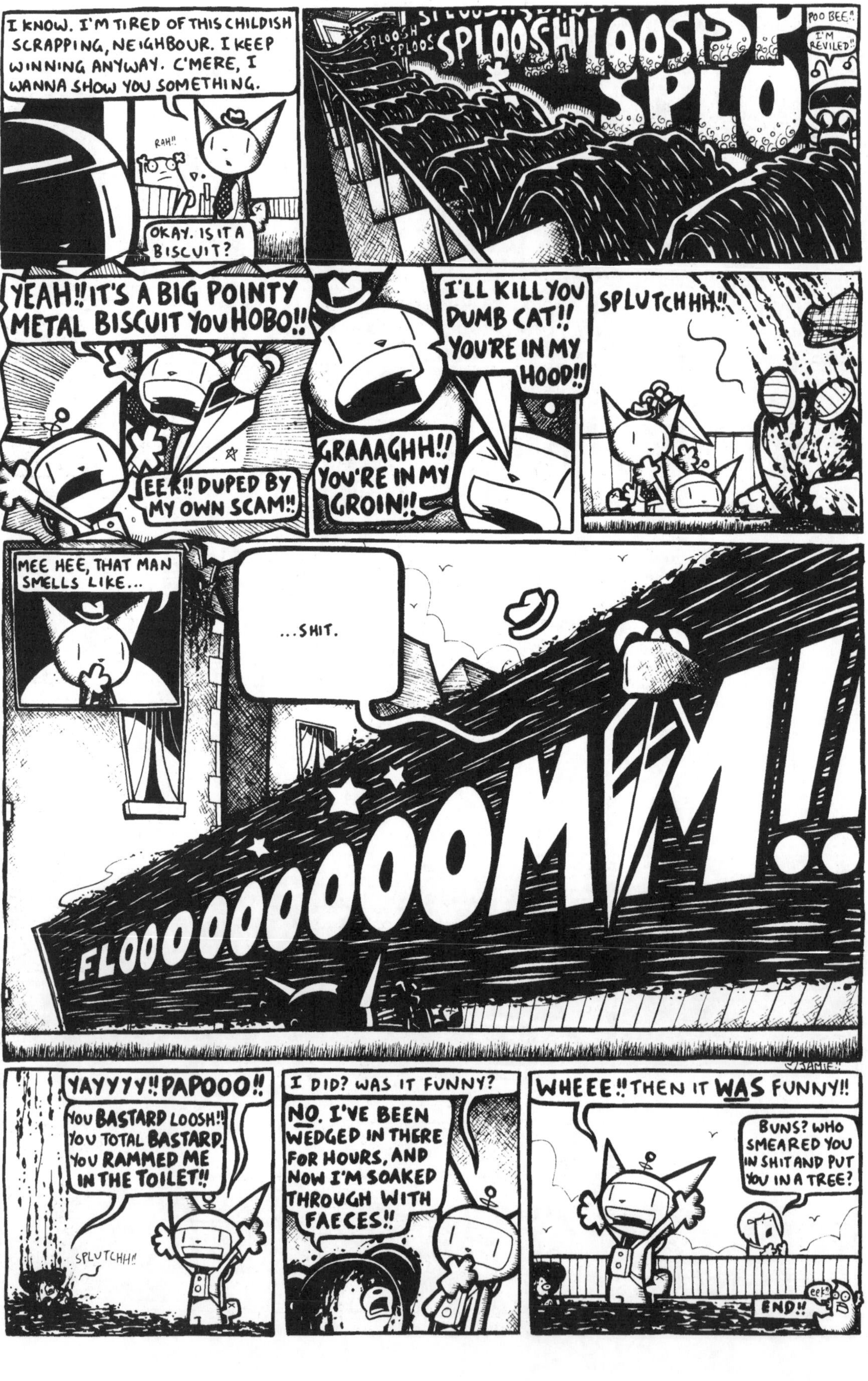
I KNOW. I'M TIRED OF THIS CHILDISH SCRAPPING, NEIGHBOUR. I KEEP WINNING ANYWAY. C'MERE, I WANNA SHOW YOU SOMETHING.
RAH!!
OKAY. IS IT A BISCUIT?
SPLOOSH SPLOOS SPLOOSH LOOSPSP SPLO
POO BEE.
I'M REVILED!!
YEAH!! IT'S A BIG POINTY METAL BISCUIT YOU HOBO!!
EEK!! DUPED BY MY OWN SCAM!!
I'LL KILL YOU DUMB CAT!! YOU'RE IN MY HOOD!!
GRAAAGHH!! YOU'RE IN MY GROIN!!
SPLUTCHHH!!
MEE HEE, THAT MAN SMELLS LIKE...
...SHIT.
FLOOOOOOOOOOMM!!
JAMIE
YAYYYY!! PAPOOO!!
YOU BASTARD LOOSH!! YOU TOTAL BASTARD. YOU RAMMED ME IN THE TOILET!!
SPLUTCHH!!
I DID? WAS IT FUNNY?
NO. I'VE BEEN WEDGED IN THERE FOR HOURS, AND NOW I'M SOAKED THROUGH WITH FAECES!!
WHEEE!! THEN IT WAS FUNNY!!
BUNS? WHO SMEARED YOU IN SHIT AND PUT YOU IN A TREE?
eek!!
END!!

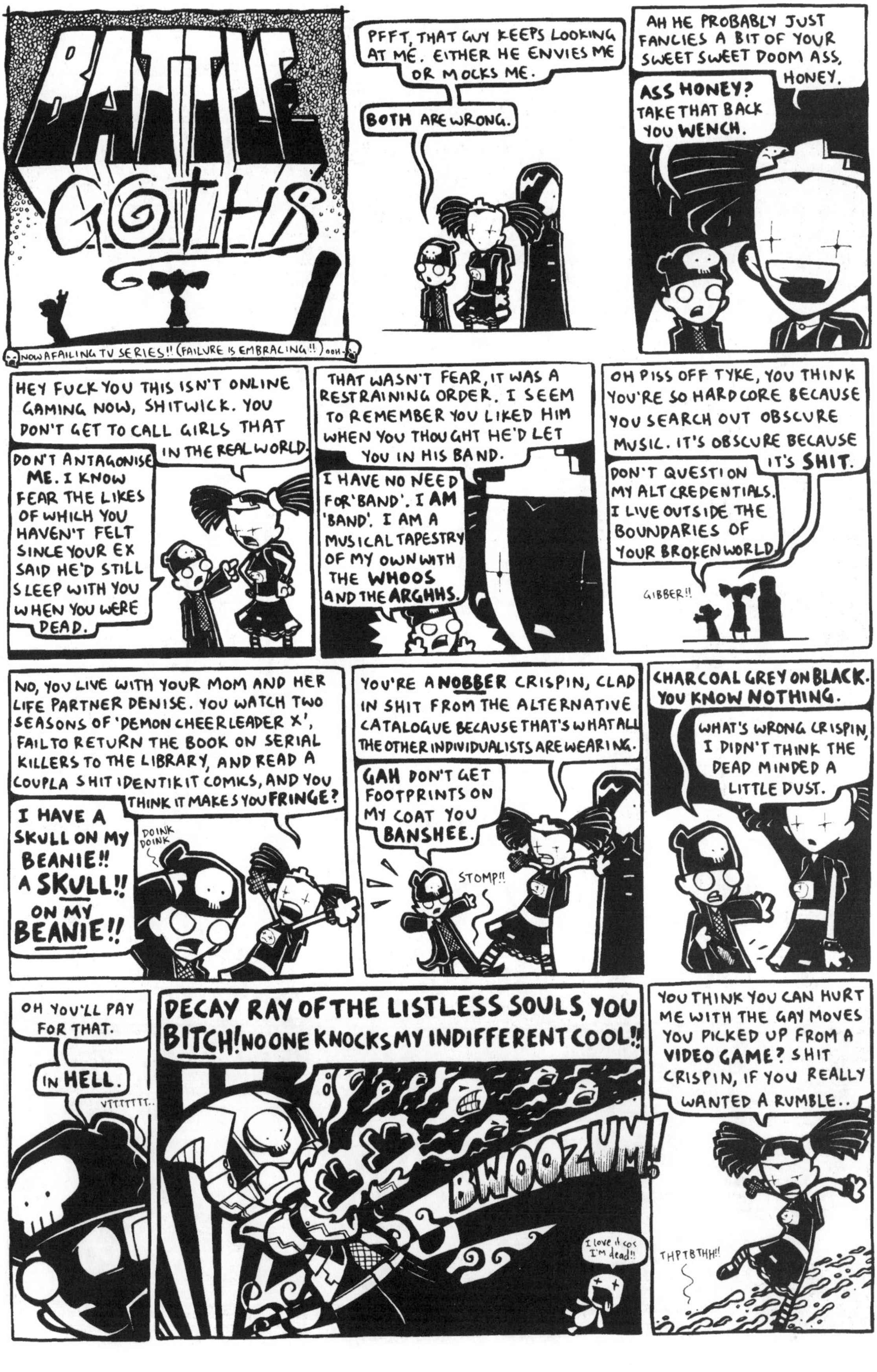
BATTLE GOTHS
NOW A FAILING TV SERIES!! (FAILURE IS EMBRACING!!) OOH-
PFFT, THAT GUY KEEPS LOOKING AT ME. EITHER HE ENVIES ME OR MOCKS ME.
BOTH ARE WRONG.
AH HE PROBABLY JUST FANCIES A BIT OF YOUR SWEET SWEET DOOM ASS, HONEY.
ASS HONEY? TAKE THAT BACK YOU WENCH.
HEY FUCK YOU THIS ISN'T ONLINE GAMING NOW, SHITWICK. YOU DON'T GET TO CALL GIRLS THAT IN THE REAL WORLD.
DON'T ANTAGONISE ME. I KNOW FEAR THE LIKES OF WHICH YOU HAVEN'T FELT SINCE YOUR EX SAID HE'D STILL SLEEP WITH YOU WHEN YOU WERE DEAD.
THAT WASN'T FEAR, IT WAS A RESTRAINING ORDER. I SEEM TO REMEMBER YOU LIKED HIM WHEN YOU THOUGHT HE'D LET YOU IN HIS BAND.
I HAVE NO NEED FOR 'BAND'. I AM 'BAND'. I AM A MUSICAL TAPESTRY OF MY OWN WITH THE WHOOS AND THE ARGHHS.
OH PISS OFF TYKE, YOU THINK YOU'RE SO HARDCORE BECAUSE YOU SEARCH OUT OBSCURE MUSIC. IT'S OBSCURE BECAUSE IT'S SHIT.
DON'T QUESTION MY ALT CREDENTIALS. I LIVE OUTSIDE THE BOUNDARIES OF YOUR BROKEN WORLD.
GIBBER!!
NO, YOU LIVE WITH YOUR MOM AND HER LIFE PARTNER DENISE. YOU WATCH TWO SEASONS OF 'DEMON CHEERLEADER X', FAIL TO RETURN THE BOOK ON SERIAL KILLERS TO THE LIBRARY, AND READ A COUPLA SHIT IDENTIKIT COMICS, AND YOU THINK IT MAKES YOU FRINGE?
I HAVE A SKULL ON MY BEANIE!! A SKULL!! ON MY BEANIE!!
DOINK DOINK
YOU'RE A NOBBER CRISPIN, CLAD IN SHIT FROM THE ALTERNATIVE CATALOGUE BECAUSE THAT'S WHAT ALL THE OTHER INDIVIDUALISTS ARE WEARING.
GAH DON'T GET FOOTPRINTS ON MY COAT YOU BANSHEE.
STOMP!!
CHARCOAL GREY ON BLACK. YOU KNOW NOTHING.
WHAT'S WRONG CRISPIN, I DIDN'T THINK THE DEAD MINDED A LITTLE DUST.
OH YOU'LL PAY FOR THAT.
IN HELL.
VTTTTTTT..
DECAY RAY OF THE LISTLESS SOULS, YOU BITCH! NO ONE KNOCKS MY INDIFFERENT COOL!!
BWOOZUM!
I love it cos I'm dead!!
YOU THINK YOU CAN HURT ME WITH THE GAY MOVES YOU PICKED UP FROM A VIDEO GAME? SHIT CRISPIN, IF YOU REALLY WANTED A RUMBLE..
THPTBTHH!!

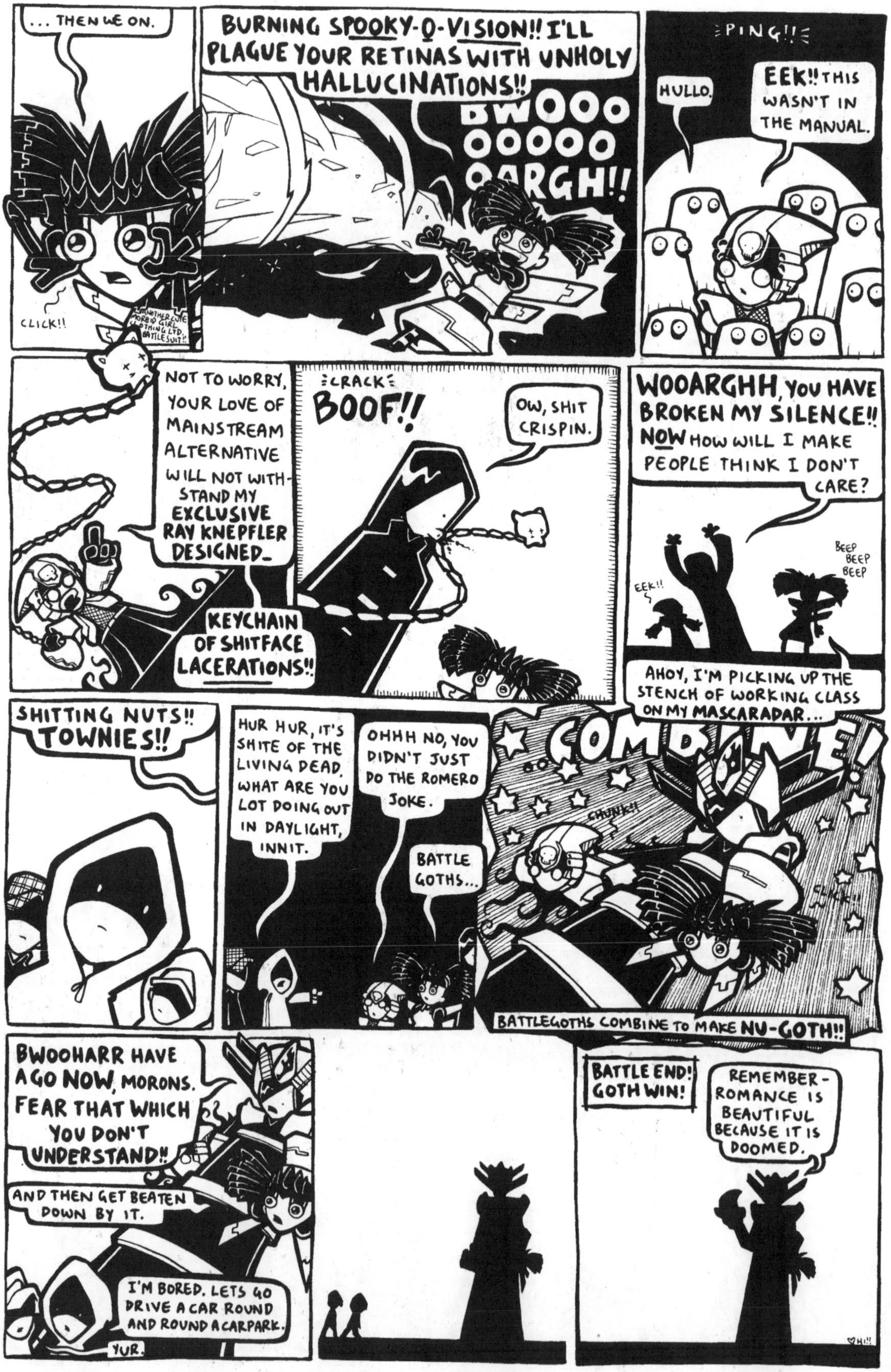
... THEN WE ON.
CLICK!!
ANOTHER CUTE MORBID GIRL CLOTHING LTD. BATTLESUIT!!
BURNING SPOOKY-Q-VISION!! I'LL PLAGUE YOUR RETINAS WITH UNHOLY HALLUCINATIONS!!
BWOOOOOOOOOARGH!!
PING!!
HULLO.
EEK!! THIS WASN'T IN THE MANUAL.
NOT TO WORRY, YOUR LOVE OF MAINSTREAM ALTERNATIVE WILL NOT WITHSTAND MY EXCLUSIVE RAY KNEPFLER DESIGNED_
KEYCHAIN OF SHITFACE LACERATIONS!!
CRACK
BOOF!!
OW, SHIT CRISPIN.
WOOARGHH, YOU HAVE BROKEN MY SILENCE!! NOW HOW WILL I MAKE PEOPLE THINK I DON'T CARE?
EEK!!
BEEP BEEP BEEP
AHOY, I'M PICKING UP THE STENCH OF WORKING CLASS ON MY MASCARADAR...
SHITTING NUTS!! TOWNIES!!
HUR HUR, IT'S SHITE OF THE LIVING DEAD. WHAT ARE YOU LOT DOING OUT IN DAYLIGHT, INNIT.
OHHH NO, YOU DIDN'T JUST DO THE ROMERO JOKE.
BATTLE GOTHS...
COMBINE!
CHUNK!!
CLICK!!
BATTLEGOTHS COMBINE TO MAKE NU-GOTH!!
BWOOHARR HAVE A GO NOW, MORONS. FEAR THAT WHICH YOU DON'T UNDERSTAND!!
AND THEN GET BEATEN DOWN BY IT.
I'M BORED. LETS GO DRIVE A CAR ROUND AND ROUND A CARPARK.
YUR.
BATTLE END! GOTH WIN!
REMEMBER - ROMANCE IS BEAUTIFUL BECAUSE IT IS DOOMED.
♡HI!!

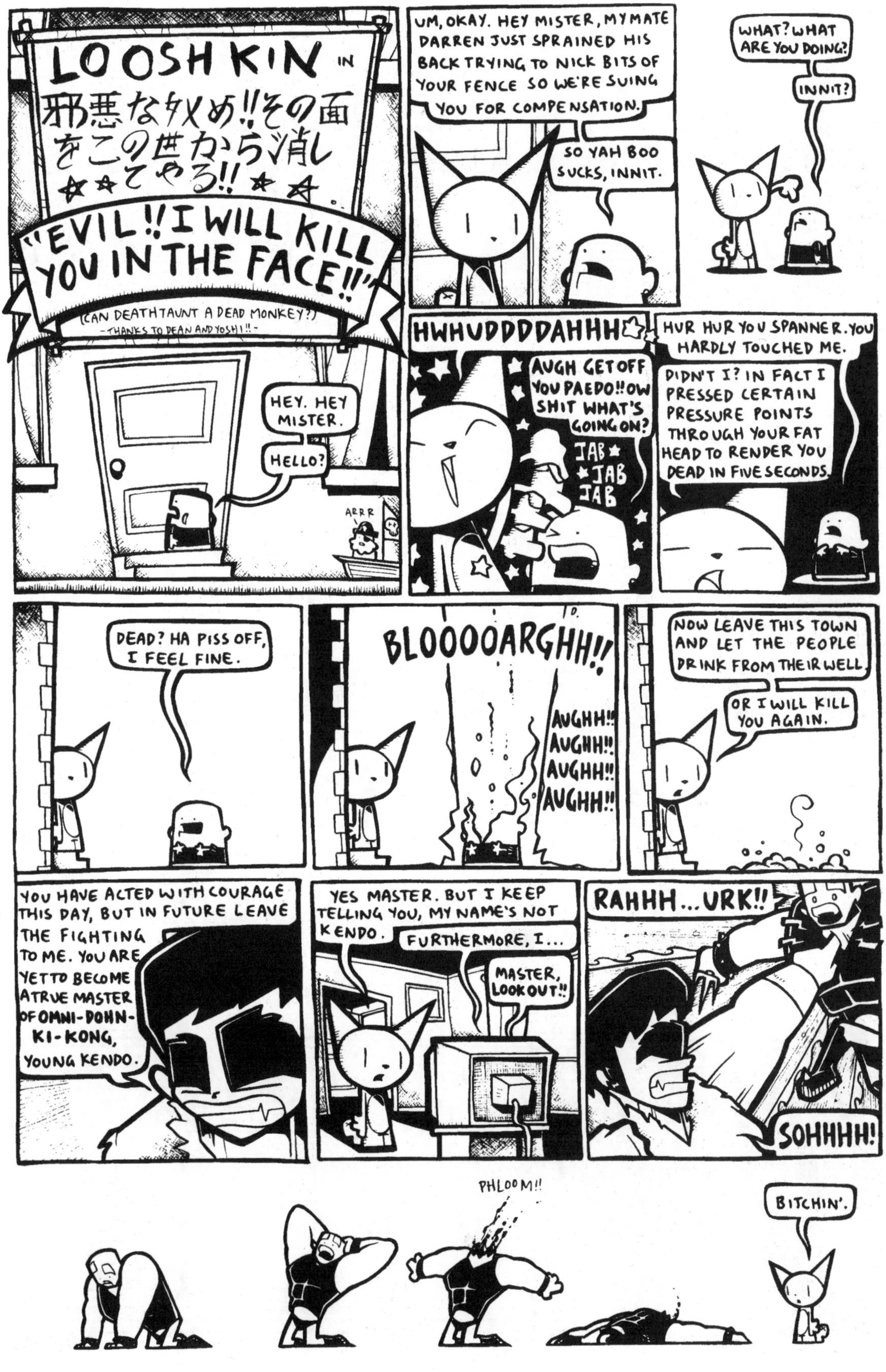

LOOSH KIN IN
邪悪な奴め!!その面をこの世から消してやる!!
"EVIL!! I WILL KILL YOU IN THE FACE!!"
(CAN DEATH TAUNT A DEAD MONKEY?)
- THANKS TO DEAN AND YOSHI!! -
HEY. HEY MISTER.
HELLO?
ARRR
UM, OKAY. HEY MISTER, MY MATE DARREN JUST SPRAINED HIS BACK TRYING TO NICK BITS OF YOUR FENCE SO WE'RE SUING YOU FOR COMPENSATION.
SO YAH BOO SUCKS, INNIT.
WHAT? WHAT ARE YOU DOING?
INNIT?
HWHUDDDDAHHH
AUGH GET OFF YOU PAEDO!! OW SHIT WHAT'S GOING ON?
JAB JAB JAB
HUR HUR YOU SPANNER. YOU HARDLY TOUCHED ME.
DIDN'T I? IN FACT I PRESSED CERTAIN PRESSURE POINTS THROUGH YOUR FAT HEAD TO RENDER YOU DEAD IN FIVE SECONDS.
DEAD? HA PISS OFF, I FEEL FINE.
BLOOOOARGHH!!
AUGHH!! AUGHH!! AUGHH!! AUGHH!!
NOW LEAVE THIS TOWN AND LET THE PEOPLE DRINK FROM THEIR WELL.
OR I WILL KILL YOU AGAIN.
YOU HAVE ACTED WITH COURAGE THIS DAY, BUT IN FUTURE LEAVE THE FIGHTING TO ME. YOU ARE YET TO BECOME A TRUE MASTER OF OMNI-DOHN-KI-KONG, YOUNG KENDO.
YES MASTER. BUT I KEEP TELLING YOU, MY NAME'S NOT KENDO.
FURTHERMORE, I...
MASTER, LOOK OUT!!
RAHHH...URK!!
SOHHHH!
PHLOOM!!
BITCHIN'.

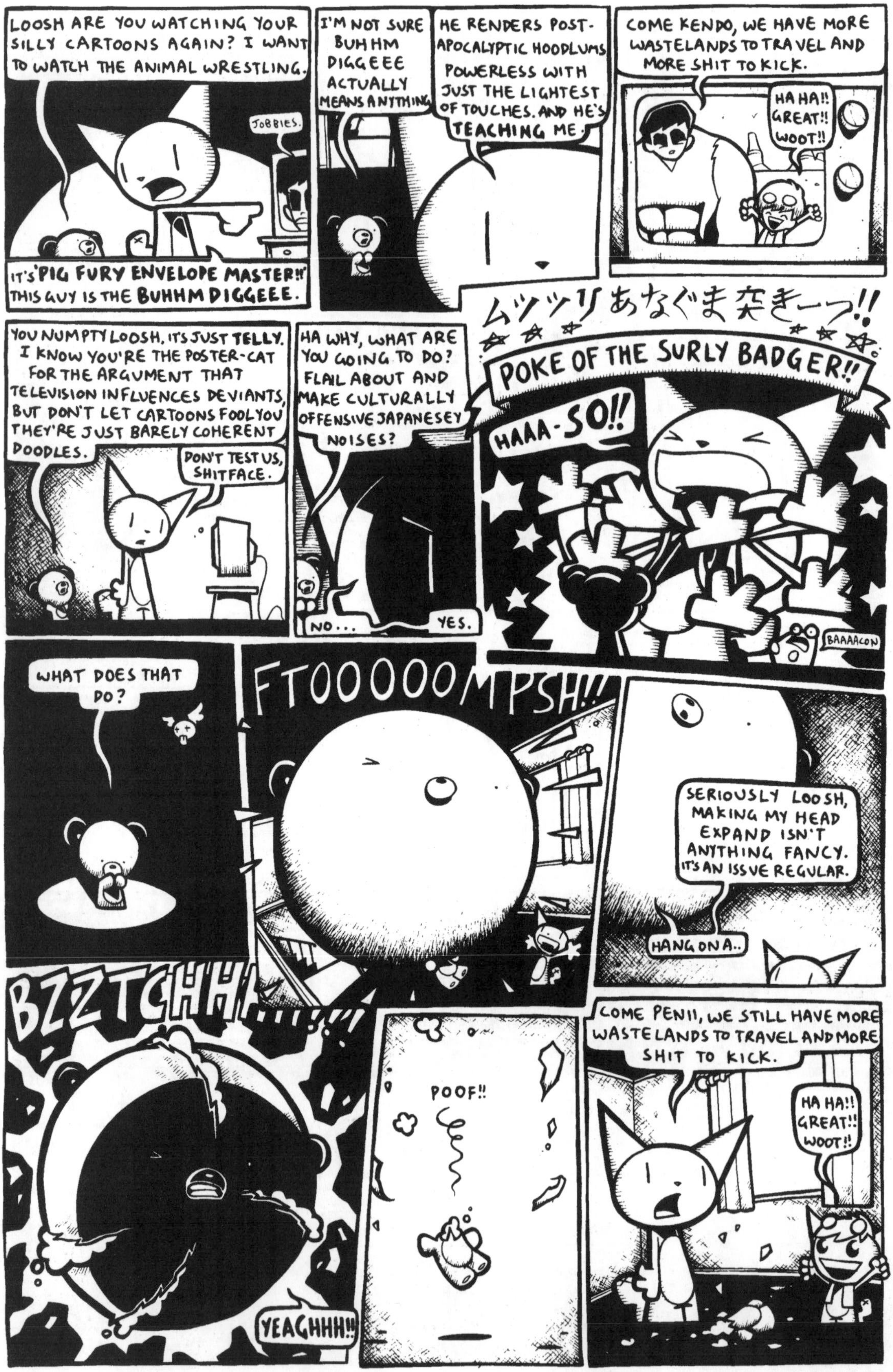
LOOSH ARE YOU WATCHING YOUR SILLY CARTOONS AGAIN? I WANT TO WATCH THE ANIMAL WRESTLING.
JOBBIES.
IT'S 'PIG FURY ENVELOPE MASTER!!' THIS GUY IS THE BUHHM DIGGEEE.
I'M NOT SURE BUHHM DIGGEEE ACTUALLY MEANS ANYTHING.
HE RENDERS POST-APOCALYPTIC HOODLUMS POWERLESS WITH JUST THE LIGHTEST OF TOUCHES. AND HE'S TEACHING ME.
COME KENDO, WE HAVE MORE WASTELANDS TO TRAVEL AND MORE SHIT TO KICK.
HA HA!! GREAT!! WOOT!!
YOU NUMPTY LOOSH, IT'S JUST TELLY. I KNOW YOU'RE THE POSTER-CAT FOR THE ARGUMENT THAT TELEVISION INFLUENCES DEVIANTS, BUT DON'T LET CARTOONS FOOL YOU THEY'RE JUST BARELY COHERENT DOODLES.
DON'T TEST US, SHITFACE.
HA WHY, WHAT ARE YOU GOING TO DO? FLAIL ABOUT AND MAKE CULTURALLY OFFENSIVE JAPANESEY NOISES?
NO...
YES.
ムッツリあなぐま突きーっ!!
POKE OF THE SURLY BADGER!!
HAAA-SO!!
BAAAACON
WHAT DOES THAT DO?
FTOOOOOMPSH!!
SERIOUSLY LOOSH, MAKING MY HEAD EXPAND ISN'T ANYTHING FANCY. IT'S AN ISSUE REGULAR.
HANG ON A..
BZZTCHH!!
YEAGHHH!!
POOF!!
COME PENII, WE STILL HAVE MORE WASTELANDS TO TRAVEL AND MORE SHIT TO KICK.
HA HA!! GREAT!! WOOT!!

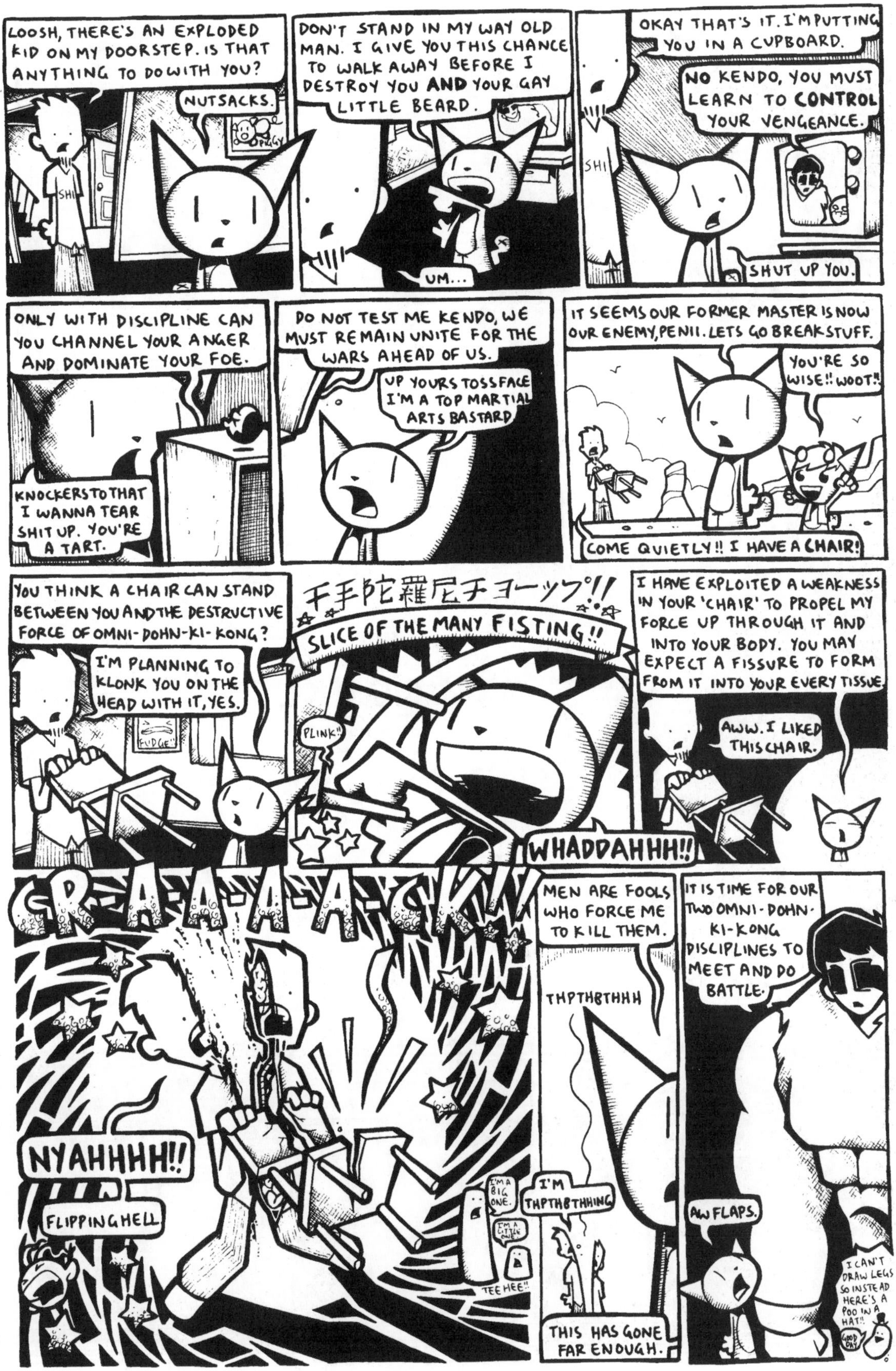
LOOSH, THERE'S AN EXPLODED KID ON MY DOORSTEP. IS THAT ANYTHING TO DO WITH YOU?
NUTSACKS.
PIGGY
DON'T STAND IN MY WAY OLD MAN. I GIVE YOU THIS CHANCE TO WALK AWAY BEFORE I DESTROY YOU AND YOUR GAY LITTLE BEARD.
UM...
OKAY THAT'S IT. I'M PUTTING YOU IN A CUPBOARD.
NO KENDO, YOU MUST LEARN TO CONTROL YOUR VENGEANCE.
SHUT UP YOU.
ONLY WITH DISCIPLINE CAN YOU CHANNEL YOUR ANGER AND DOMINATE YOUR FOE.
KNOCKERS TO THAT I WANNA TEAR SHIT UP. YOU'RE A TART.
DO NOT TEST ME KENDO, WE MUST REMAIN UNITE FOR THE WARS AHEAD OF US.
UP YOURS TOSSFACE I'M A TOP MARTIAL ARTS BASTARD.
IT SEEMS OUR FORMER MASTER IS NOW OUR ENEMY, PENII. LETS GO BREAK STUFF.
YOU'RE SO WISE!! WOOT!!
COME QUIETLY!! I HAVE A CHAIR!
YOU THINK A CHAIR CAN STAND BETWEEN YOU AND THE DESTRUCTIVE FORCE OF OMNI-DOHN-KI-KONG?
I'M PLANNING TO KLONK YOU ON THE HEAD WITH IT, YES.
FUDGE
千手陀羅尼チョーップ!!
SLICE OF THE MANY FISTING!!
PLINK!!
WHADDAHHH!!
I HAVE EXPLOITED A WEAKNESS IN YOUR 'CHAIR' TO PROPEL MY FORCE UP THROUGH IT AND INTO YOUR BODY. YOU MAY EXPECT A FISSURE TO FORM FROM IT INTO YOUR EVERY TISSUE.
AWW. I LIKED THIS CHAIR.
G-R-A-A-A-C-K!!
NYAHHHH!!
FLIPPING HELL.
I'M A BIG ONE.
I'M A LITTLE ONE.
TEE HEE!!
MEN ARE FOOLS WHO FORCE ME TO KILL THEM.
THPTHBTHHH
I'M THPTHBTHHING
THIS HAS GONE FAR ENOUGH.
IT IS TIME FOR OUR TWO OMNI-DOHN-KI-KONG DISCIPLINES TO MEET AND DO BATTLE.
AW FLAPS.
I CAN'T DRAW LEGS SO INSTEAD HERE'S A POO IN A HAT!!
GOOD DAY.

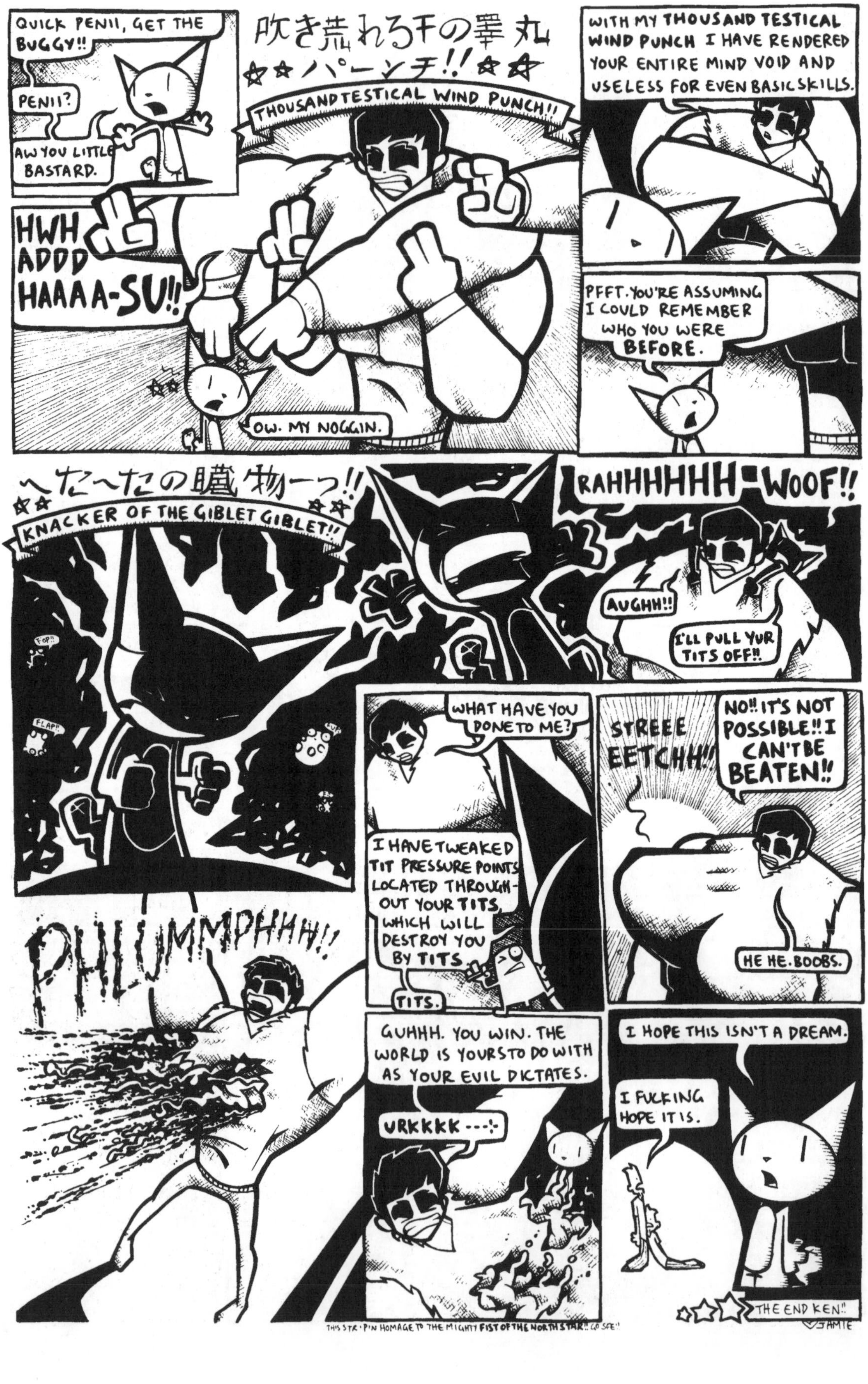

QUICK PENII, GET THE BUGGY!!
PENII?
AW YOU LITTLE BASTARD.
吹き荒れる千の睾丸
☆☆パーンチ!!☆☆
THOUSAND TESTICAL WIND PUNCH!!
HWH ADDD HAAAA-SU!!
OW. MY NOGGIN.
WITH MY THOUSAND TESTICAL WIND PUNCH I HAVE RENDERED YOUR ENTIRE MIND VOID AND USELESS FOR EVEN BASIC SKILLS.
PFFT. YOU'RE ASSUMING I COULD REMEMBER WHO YOU WERE BEFORE.
へたへたの臓物ーっ!!
KNACKER OF THE GIBLET GIBLET!!
RAHHHHHH-WOOF!!
AUGHH!!
I'LL PULL YUR TITS OFF!!
WHAT HAVE YOU DONE TO ME?
I HAVE TWEAKED TIT PRESSURE POINTS LOCATED THROUGHOUT YOUR TITS, WHICH WILL DESTROY YOU BY TITS.
TITS.
STREEE EETCHH!!
NO!! IT'S NOT POSSIBLE!! I CAN'T BE BEATEN!!
HE HE. BOOBS.
PHLUMMPHHH!!
GUHHH. YOU WIN. THE WORLD IS YOURS TO DO WITH AS YOUR EVIL DICTATES.
URKKKK ---
I HOPE THIS ISN'T A DREAM.
I FUCKING HOPE IT IS.
THE END KEN!!
THIS STRIP IN HOMAGE TO THE MIGHTY FIST OF THE NORTH STAR!! GO SEE!!
♡JAMIE

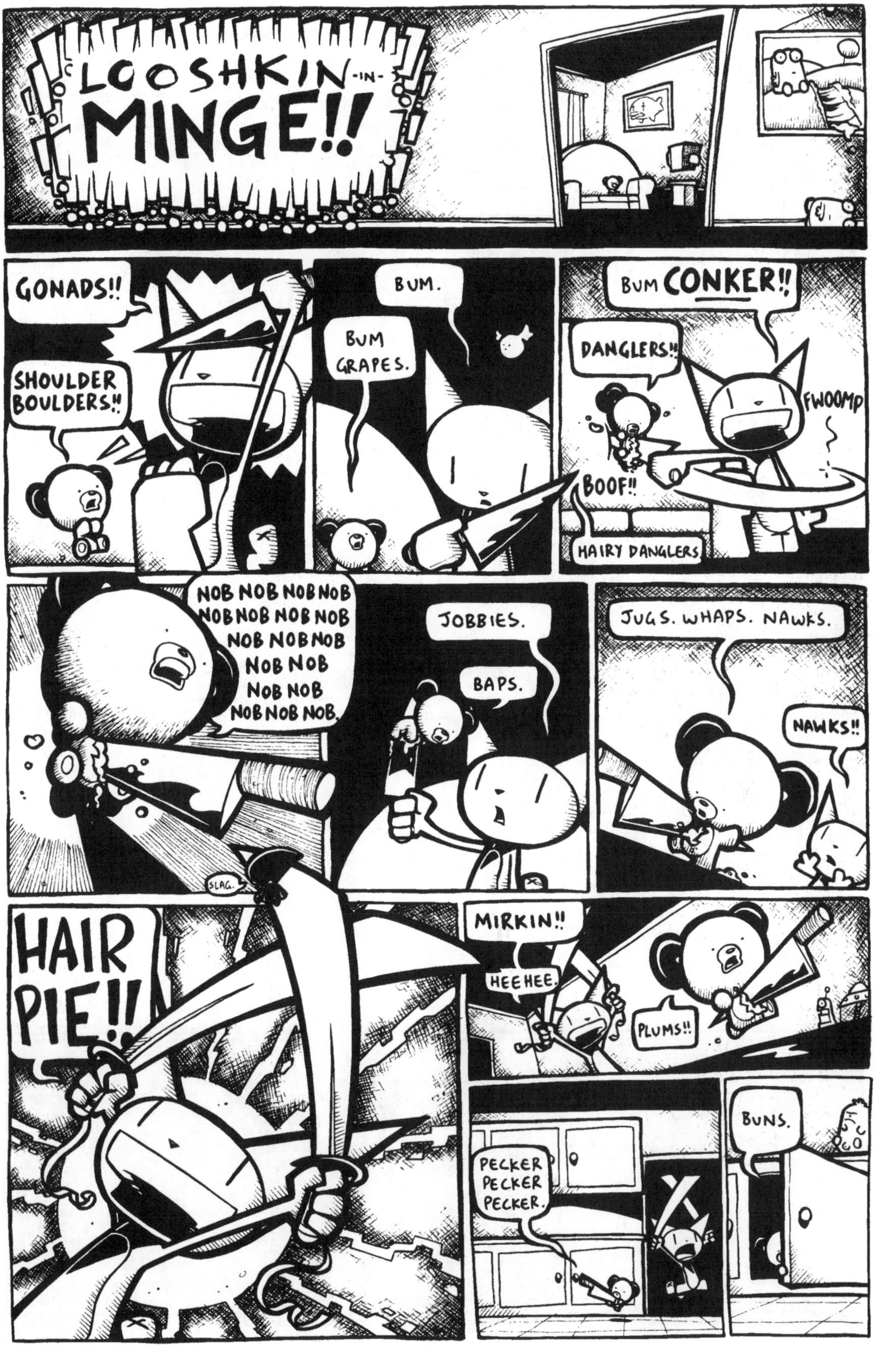
LOOSHKIN -IN- MINGE!!
GONADS!!
SHOULDER BOULDERS!!
BUM.
BUM GRAPES.
BUM CONKER!!
DANGLERS!!
FWOOMP
BOOF!!
HAIRY DANGLERS
NOB NOB NOB NOB NOB NOB NOB NOB NOB NOB NOB NOB NOB NOB NOB NOB NOB NOB NOB.
JOBBIES.
BAPS.
JUGS. WHAPS. NAWKS.
NAWKS!!
SLAG.
HAIR PIE!!
MIRKIN!!
HEEHEE.
PLUMS!!
BUNS.
PECKER PECKER PECKER PECKER.

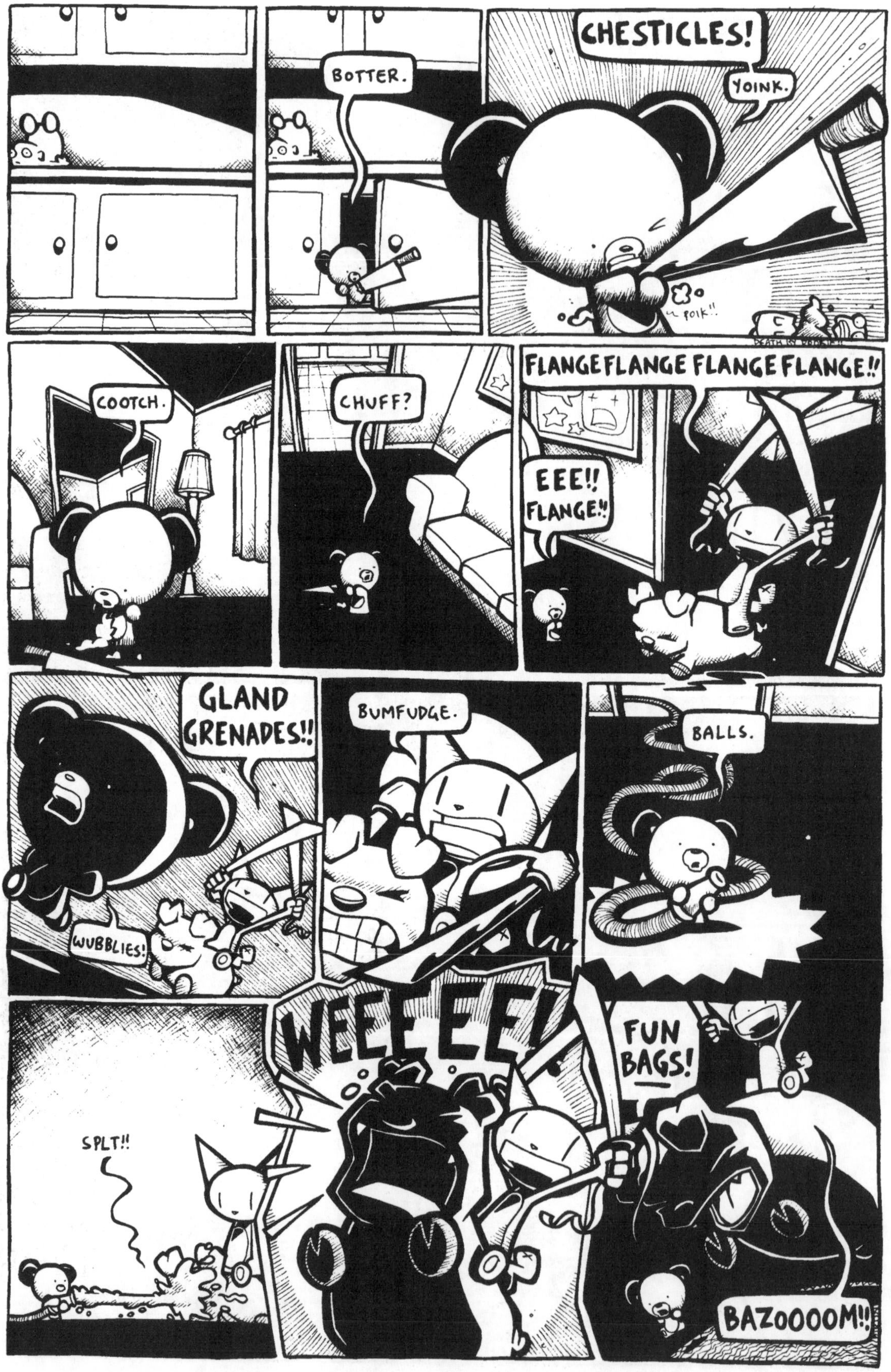

BOTTER.
CHESTICLES!
YOINK.
POIK!!
COOTCH.
CHUFF?
FLANGEFLANGE FLANGE FLANGE!!
EEE!! FLANGE!!
GLAND GRENADES!!
WUBBLIES!
BUMFUDGE.
BALLS.
SPLT!!
WEEEEE!
FUN BAGS!
BAZOOOOM!!

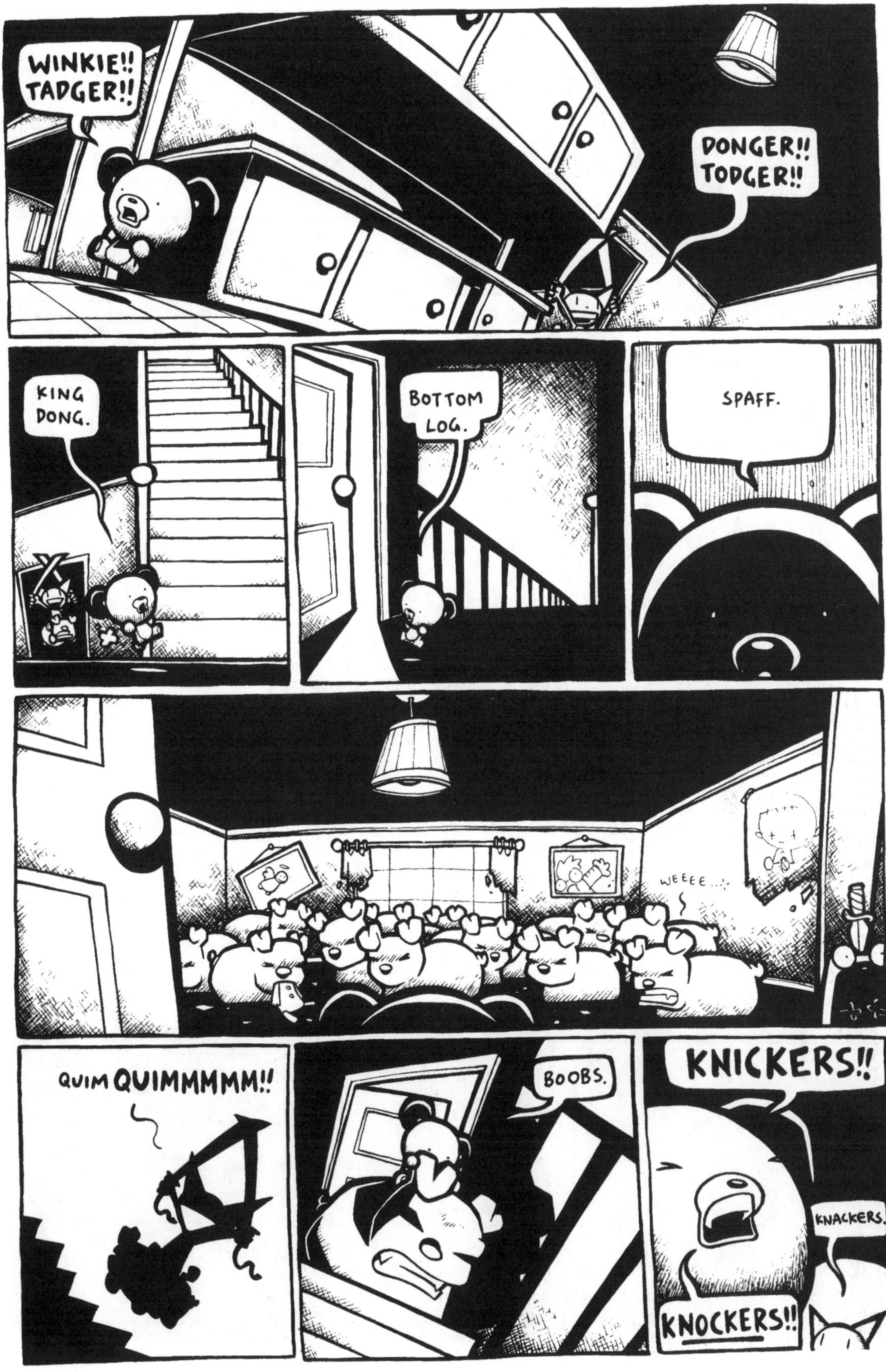
WINKIE!! TADGER!!
DONGER!! TODGER!!
KING DONG.
BOTTOM LOG.
SPAFF.
WEEEE...
QUIM QUIMMMMM!!
BOOBS.
KNICKERS!!
KNACKERS.
KNOCKERS!!

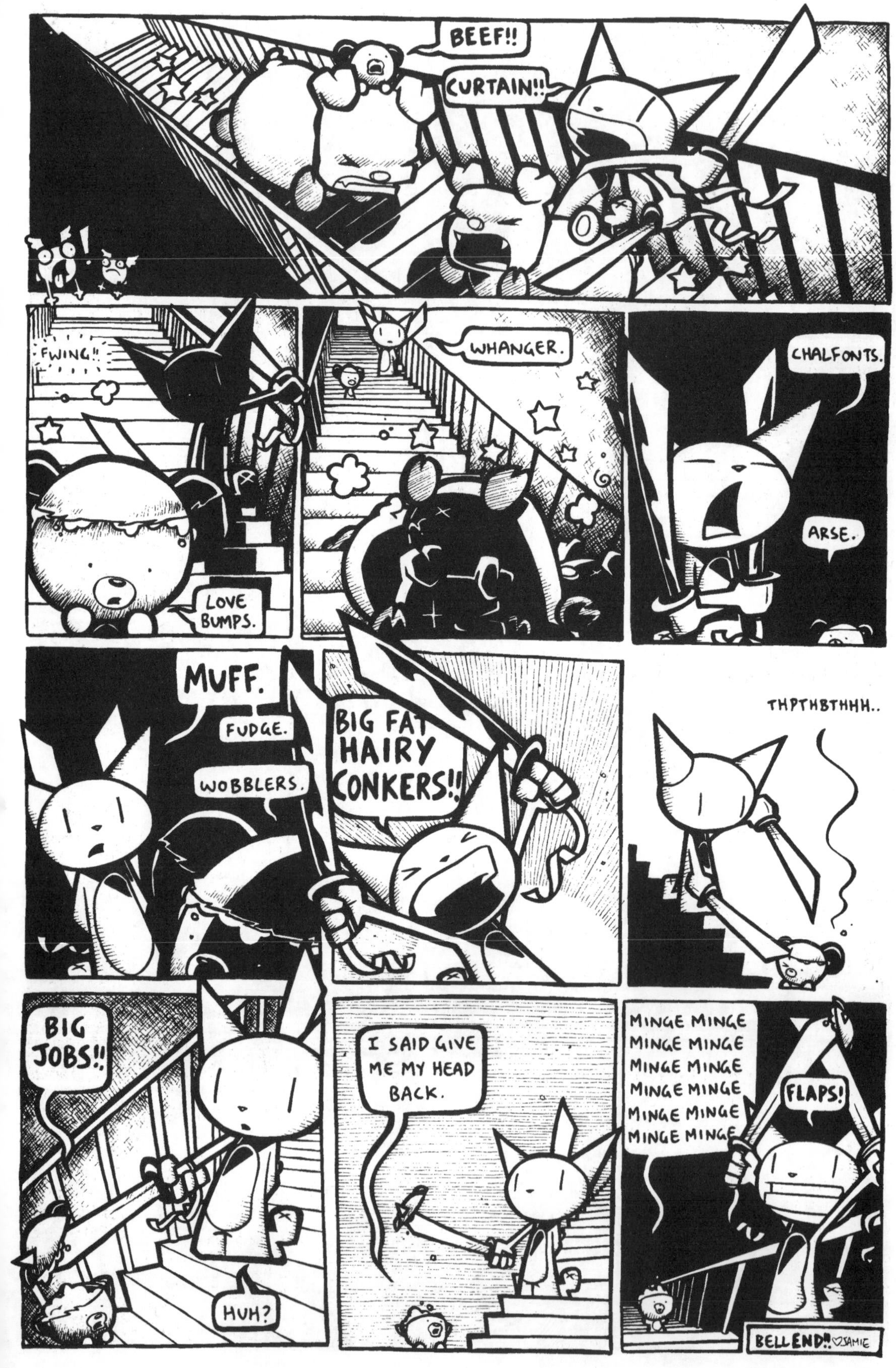

BEEF!!
CURTAIN!!
FWING!!
LOVE BUMPS.
WHANGER.
CHALFONTS.
ARSE.
MUFF.
FUDGE.
WOBBLERS.
BIG FAT HAIRY CONKERS!!
THPTHBTHHH..
BIG JOBS!!
HUH?
I SAID GIVE ME MY HEAD BACK.
MINGE MINGE MINGE MINGE MINGE MINGE MINGE MINGE MINGE MINGE MINGE MINGE
FLAPS!
BELLEND!!
JAMIE

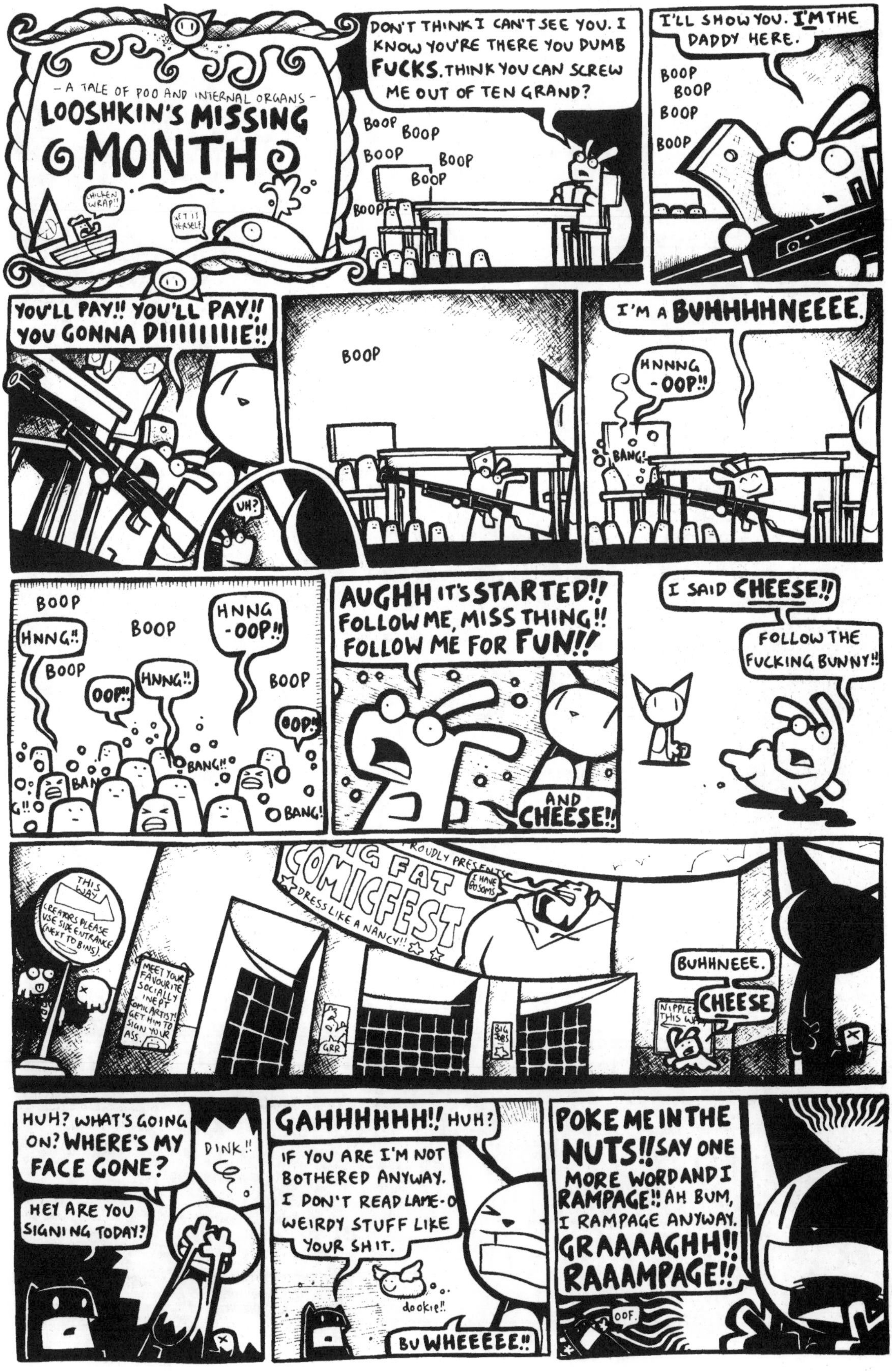
- A TALE OF POO AND INTERNAL ORGANS -
LOOSHKIN'S MISSING MONTH
CHICKEN WRAP!!
GET IT YERSELF
DON'T THINK I CAN'T SEE YOU. I KNOW YOU'RE THERE YOU DUMB FUCKS. THINK YOU CAN SCREW ME OUT OF TEN GRAND?
BOOP BOOP BOOP BOOP BOOP BOOP
I'LL SHOW YOU. I'M THE DADDY HERE.
BOOP BOOP BOOP BOOP
YOU'LL PAY!! YOU'LL PAY!! YOU GONNA DIIIIIIIIE!!
UH?
BOOP
I'M A BUHHHHNEEEE.
HNNG -OOP!!
BANG!
BOOP
HNNG!!
BOOP
BOOP
OOP!!
HNNG!!
HNNG -OOP!!
BOOP
OOP!!
BANG!!
BANG!
AUGHH IT'S STARTED!! FOLLOW ME, MISS THING!! FOLLOW ME FOR FUN!!
AND CHEESE!!
I SAID CHEESE!!
FOLLOW THE FUCKING BUNNY!!
PROUDLY PRESENTS
BIG FAT COMICFEST
DRESS LIKE A NANCY!!
I HAVE BOSOMS
THIS WAY
CREATORS PLEASE USE SIDE ENTRANCE (NEXT TO BINS).
MEET YOUR FAVOURITE SOCIALLY INEPT COMIC ARTIST!! GET HIM TO SIGN YOUR ASS.
GRR
BIG JOBS
NIPPLES THIS WAY
BUHHNEEE.
CHEESE
HUH? WHAT'S GOING ON? WHERE'S MY FACE GONE?
DINK!!
HEY ARE YOU SIGNING TODAY?
GAHHHHHH!! HUH?
IF YOU ARE I'M NOT BOTHERED ANYWAY. I DON'T READ LAME-O WEIRDY STUFF LIKE YOUR SHIT.
dookie!!
BUWHEEEEE!!
POKE ME IN THE NUTS!! SAY ONE MORE WORD AND I RAMPAGE!! AH BUM, I RAMPAGE ANYWAY. GRAAAAGHH!! RAAAMPAGE!!
OOF.

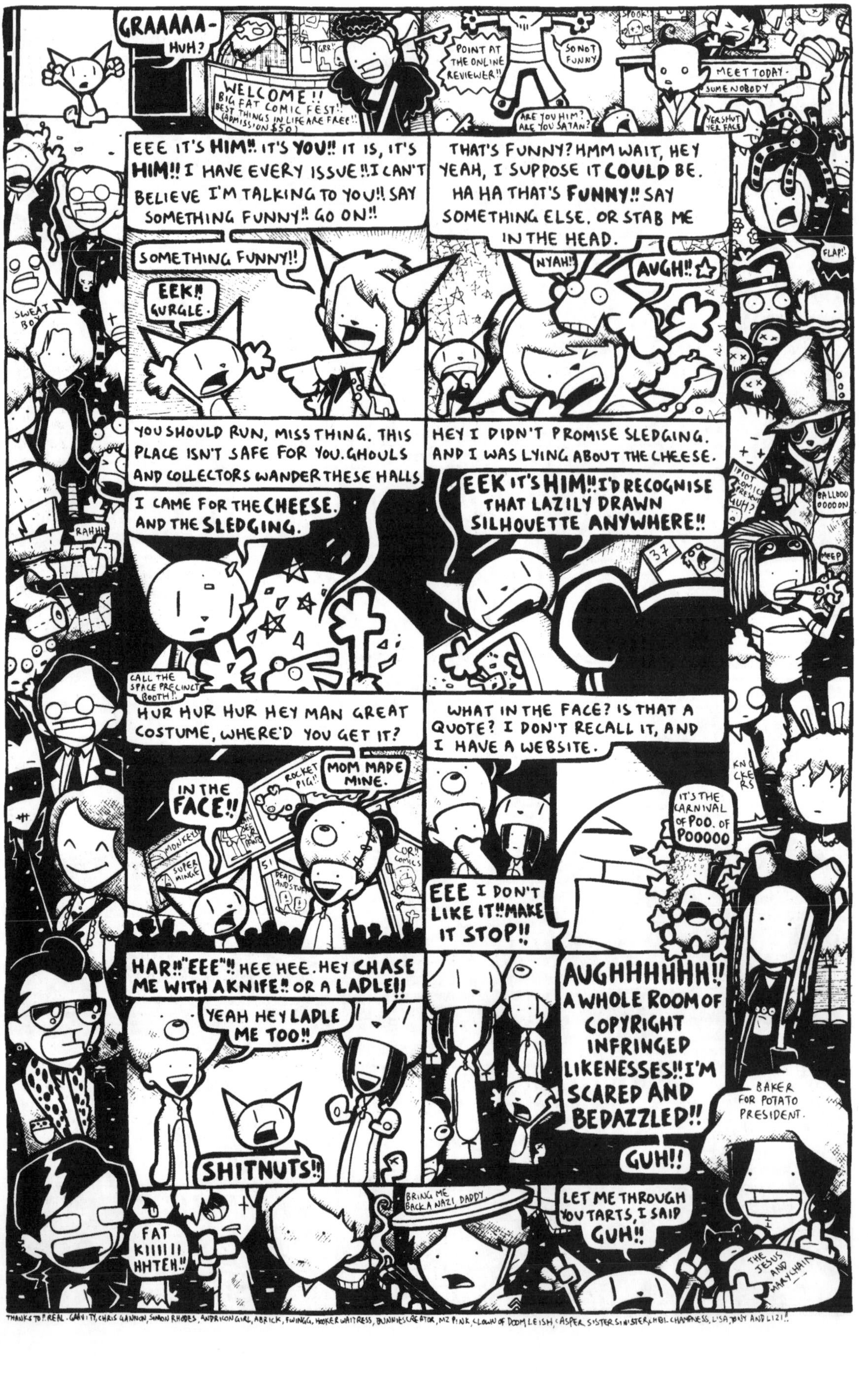

GRAAAAA-
HUH?
WELCOME!! BIG FAT COMIC FEST!! BEST THINGS IN LIFE ARE FREE!! (ADMISSION $50)
GRR
POINT AT THE ONLINE REVIEWER!!
SO NOT FUNNY
ARE YOU HIM? ARE YOU SATAN?
MEET TODAY - SOME NOBODY
YER SHUT YER FACE
EEE IT'S HIM!! IT'S YOU!! IT IS, IT'S HIM!! I HAVE EVERY ISSUE!! I CAN'T BELIEVE I'M TALKING TO YOU!! SAY SOMETHING FUNNY!! GO ON!!
SOMETHING FUNNY!!
EEK!! GURGLE.
THAT'S FUNNY? HMM WAIT, HEY YEAH, I SUPPOSE IT COULD BE. HA HA THAT'S FUNNY!! SAY SOMETHING ELSE. OR STAB ME IN THE HEAD.
NYAH!!
AUGH!!
SWEAT BOY
FLAP!!
YOU SHOULD RUN, MISS THING. THIS PLACE ISN'T SAFE FOR YOU. GHOULS AND COLLECTORS WANDER THESE HALLS.
I CAME FOR THE CHEESE. AND THE SLEDGING.
HEY I DIDN'T PROMISE SLEDGING. AND I WAS LYING ABOUT THE CHEESE.
EEK IT'S HIM!! I'D RECOGNISE THAT LAZILY DRAWN SILHOUETTE ANYWHERE!!
37
RAHHH
BALLOOOOOOON
MEEP
CALL THE SPACE PRECINCT BOOTH!!
HUR HUR HUR HEY MAN GREAT COSTUME, WHERE'D YOU GET IT?
IN THE FACE!!
ROCKET PIG!!
MOM MADE MINE.
MONKEYS
SUPER MINGE
51
DEAD AND STUFF
COR!! COMICS
WHAT IN THE FACE? IS THAT A QUOTE? I DON'T RECALL IT, AND I HAVE A WEBSITE.
IT'S THE CARNIVAL OF POO. OF POOOOO
EEE I DON'T LIKE IT!! MAKE IT STOP!!
KNOCKERS
HAR!! "EEE"!! HEE HEE. HEY CHASE ME WITH A KNIFE!! OR A LADLE!!
YEAH HEY LADLE ME TOO!!
SHITNUTS!!
AUGHHHHHH!! A WHOLE ROOM OF COPYRIGHT INFRINGED LIKENESSES!! I'M SCARED AND BEDAZZLED!!
BAKER FOR POTATO PRESIDENT.
GUH!!
LET ME THROUGH YOU TARTS, I SAID GUH!!
FAT KIIIIII HHTEH!!
BRING ME BACK A NAZI, DADDY.
THE JESUS AND MARY CHAIN

THANKS TO!! REAL. GANVITY, CHRIS GANNON, SIMON RHODES, ANDRICON GIRL, ABRICK, FWINGG, HOOKER WAITRESS, BUNNIESCREATOR, MZ PINK, CLOWN OF DOOM LEISH, CASPER SISTER SINISTER, CHIBI-CHAMPNESS, LISA, TONY AND LIZI!!

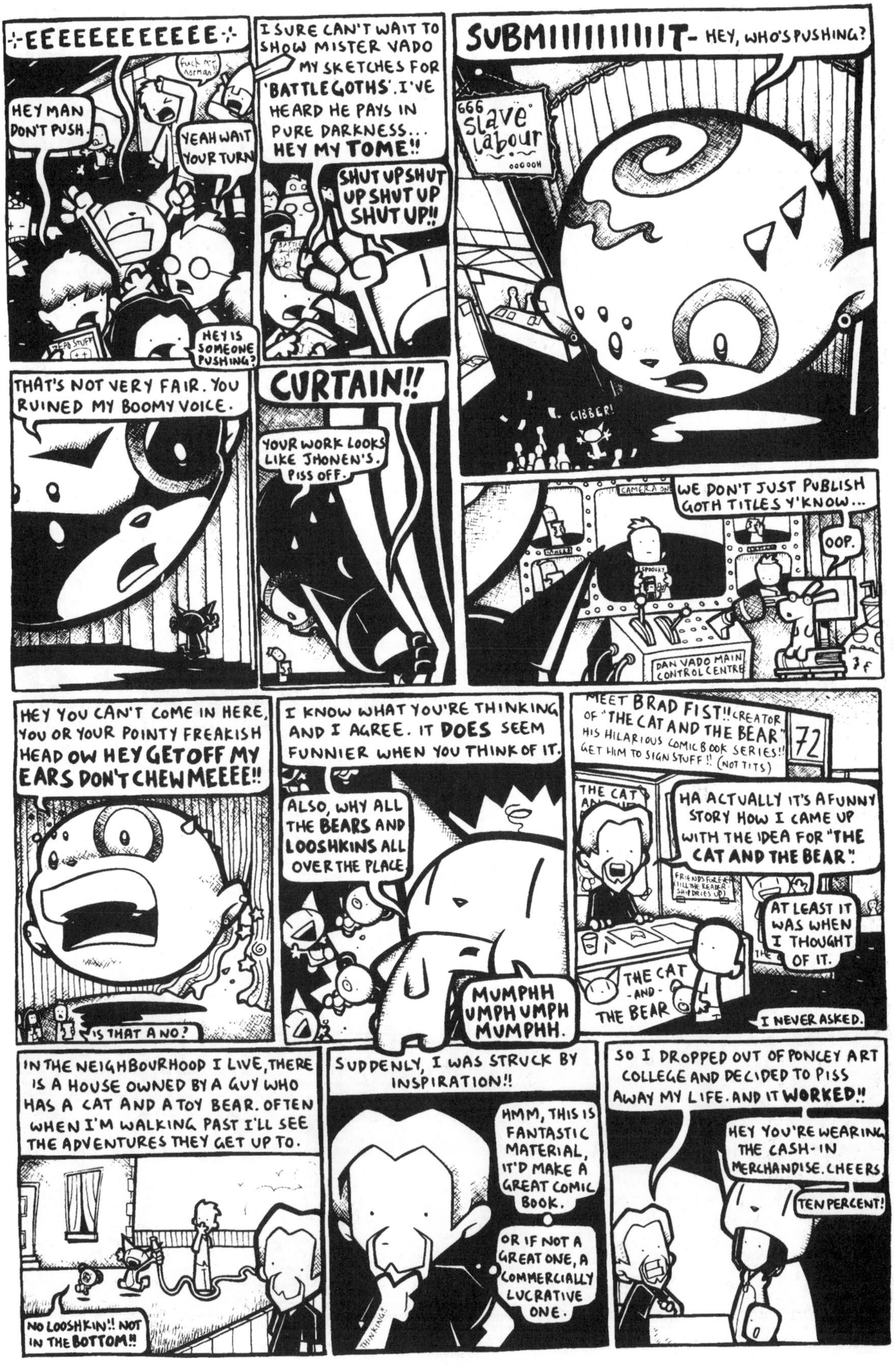

EEEEEEEEEEEE
Fuck it Norman!!
HEY MAN DON'T PUSH.
YEAH WAIT YOUR TURN
HEY IS SOMEONE PUSHING?
I SURE CAN'T WAIT TO SHOW MISTER VADO MY SKETCHES FOR 'BATTLEGOTHS'. I'VE HEARD HE PAYS IN PURE DARKNESS... HEY MY TOME!!
SHUT UP SHUT UP SHUT UP SHUT UP!!
SUBMIIIIIIIIIIT- HEY, WHO'S PUSHING?
666 slave labour oooooh
GIBBER!
THAT'S NOT VERY FAIR. YOU RUINED MY BOOMY VOICE.
CURTAIN!!
YOUR WORK LOOKS LIKE JHONEN'S. PISS OFF.
WE DON'T JUST PUBLISH GOTH TITLES Y'KNOW...
OOP.
DAN VADO MAIN CONTROL CENTRE
HEY YOU CAN'T COME IN HERE, YOU OR YOUR POINTY FREAKISH HEAD OW HEY GET OFF MY EARS DON'T CHEW MEEEE!!
IS THAT A NO?
I KNOW WHAT YOU'RE THINKING AND I AGREE. IT DOES SEEM FUNNIER WHEN YOU THINK OF IT.
ALSO, WHY ALL THE BEARS AND LOOSHKINS ALL OVER THE PLACE.
MUMPHH UMPH UMPH MUMPHH.
MEET BRAD FIST!! CREATOR OF "THE CAT AND THE BEAR" HIS HILARIOUS COMIC BOOK SERIES!! GET HIM TO SIGN STUFF!! (NOT TITS)
72
HA ACTUALLY IT'S A FUNNY STORY HOW I CAME UP WITH THE IDEA FOR "THE CAT AND THE BEAR".
AT LEAST IT WAS WHEN I THOUGHT OF IT.
THE CAT -AND- THE BEAR
I NEVER ASKED.
IN THE NEIGHBOURHOOD I LIVE, THERE IS A HOUSE OWNED BY A GUY WHO HAS A CAT AND A TOY BEAR. OFTEN WHEN I'M WALKING PAST I'LL SEE THE ADVENTURES THEY GET UP TO.
NO LOOSHKIN!! NOT IN THE BOTTOM!!
SUDDENLY, I WAS STRUCK BY INSPIRATION!!
HMM, THIS IS FANTASTIC MATERIAL, IT'D MAKE A GREAT COMIC BOOK.
OR IF NOT A GREAT ONE, A COMMERCIALLY LUCRATIVE ONE.
SO I DROPPED OUT OF PONCEY ART COLLEGE AND DECIDED TO PISS AWAY MY LIFE. AND IT WORKED!!
HEY YOU'RE WEARING THE CASH-IN MERCHANDISE. CHEERS.
TEN PERCENT!

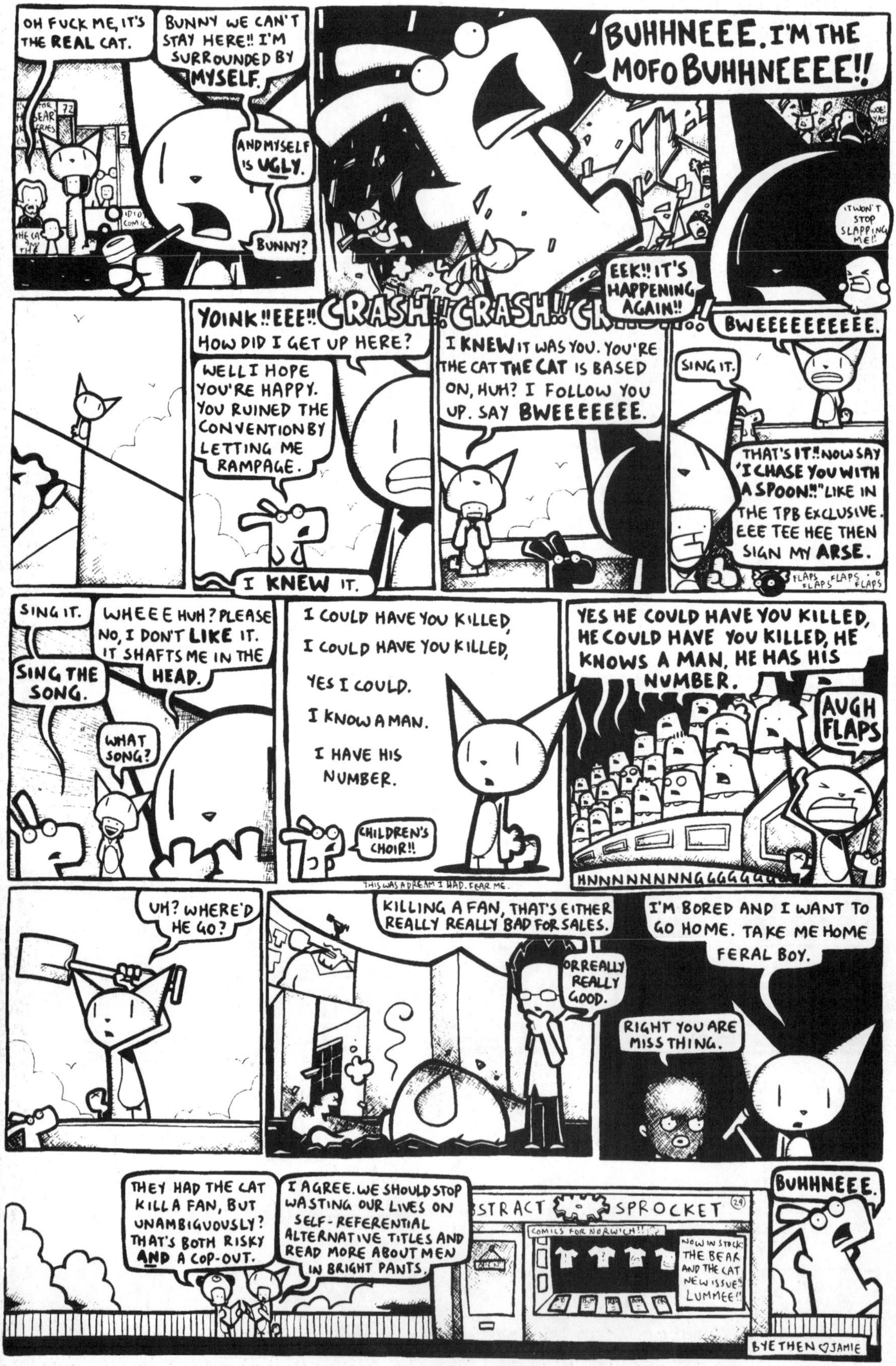

OH FUCK ME, IT'S THE REAL CAT.
BUNNY WE CAN'T STAY HERE!! I'M SURROUNDED BY MYSELF.
AND MYSELF IS UGLY.
BUNNY?
BUHHNEEE. I'M THE MOFO BUHHNEEEE!!
IT WON'T STOP SLAPPING ME!!
EEK!! IT'S HAPPENING AGAIN!!
CRASH!! CRASH!!
YOINK!! EEE!! HOW DID I GET UP HERE?
WELL I HOPE YOU'RE HAPPY. YOU RUINED THE CONVENTION BY LETTING ME RAMPAGE.
I KNEW IT.
I KNEW IT WAS YOU. YOU'RE THE CAT THE CAT IS BASED ON, HUH? I FOLLOW YOU UP. SAY BWEEEEEEE.
BWEEEEEEEEEE.
SING IT.
THAT'S IT!! NOW SAY "I CHASE YOU WITH A SPOON!!" LIKE IN THE TPB EXCLUSIVE. EEE TEE HEE THEN SIGN MY ARSE.
FLAPS FLAPS FLAPS FLAPS
SING IT.
WHEEE HUH? PLEASE NO, I DON'T LIKE IT. IT SHAFTS ME IN THE HEAD.
SING THE SONG.
WHAT SONG?
I COULD HAVE YOU KILLED, I COULD HAVE YOU KILLED, YES I COULD. I KNOW A MAN. I HAVE HIS NUMBER.
CHILDREN'S CHOIR!!
THIS WAS A DREAM I HAD. FEAR ME.
YES HE COULD HAVE YOU KILLED, HE COULD HAVE YOU KILLED, HE KNOWS A MAN, HE HAS HIS NUMBER.
AUGH FLAPS
HNNNNNNNNGGGGGG
UH? WHERE'D HE GO?
KILLING A FAN, THAT'S EITHER REALLY REALLY BAD FOR SALES.
OR REALLY REALLY GOOD.
I'M BORED AND I WANT TO GO HOME. TAKE ME HOME FERAL BOY.
RIGHT YOU ARE MISS THING.
THEY HAD THE CAT KILL A FAN, BUT UNAMBIGUOUSLY? THAT'S BOTH RISKY AND A COP-OUT.
I AGREE. WE SHOULD STOP WASTING OUR LIVES ON SELF-REFERENTIAL ALTERNATIVE TITLES AND READ MORE ABOUT MEN IN BRIGHT PANTS.
BSTRACT SPROCKET
COMICS FOR NORWICH!!
NOW IN STOCK: THE BEAR AND THE CAT NEW ISSUE!! LUMMEE!!
BUHHNEEE.
BYE THEN ♡ JAMIE

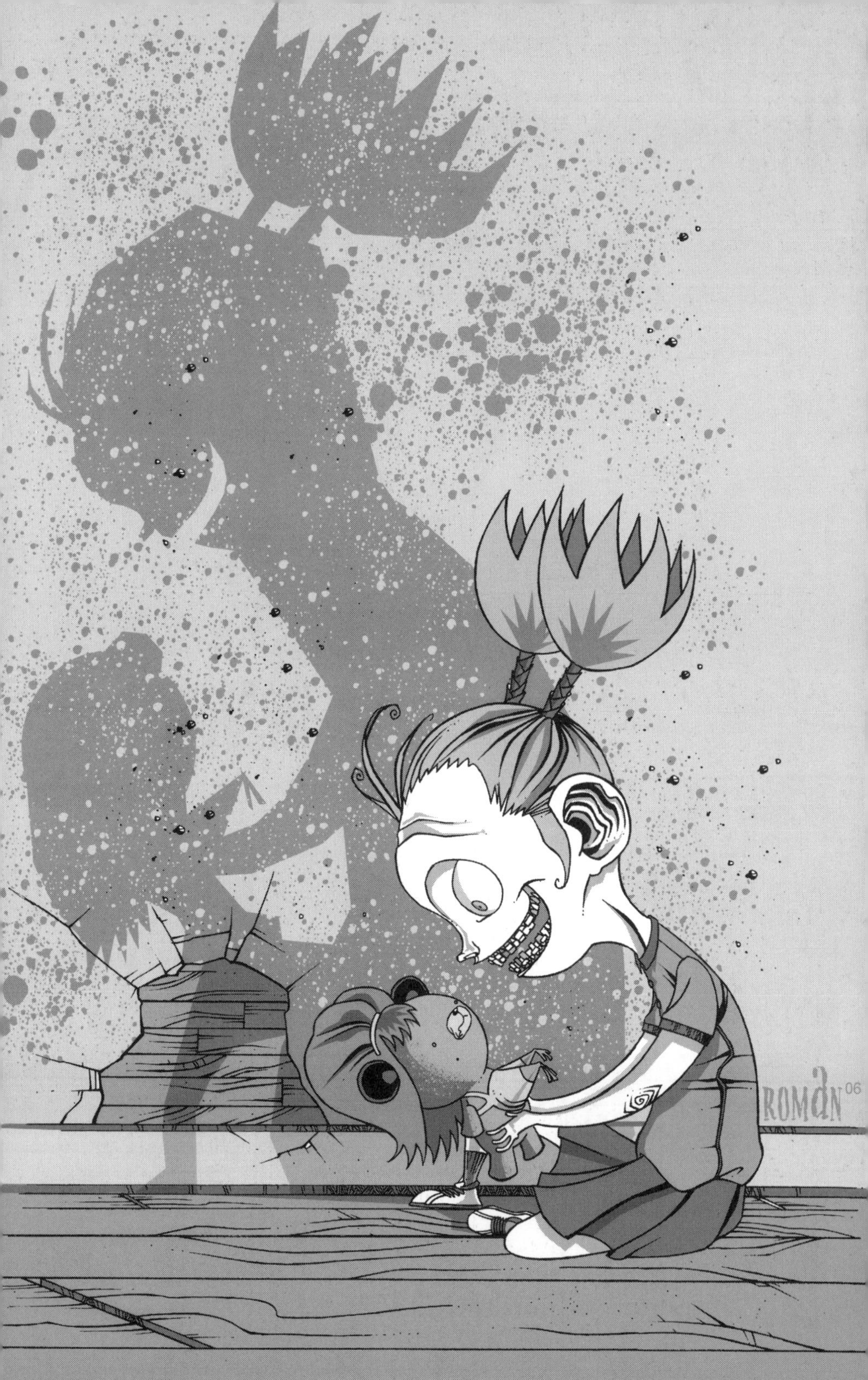
ROMAN 06

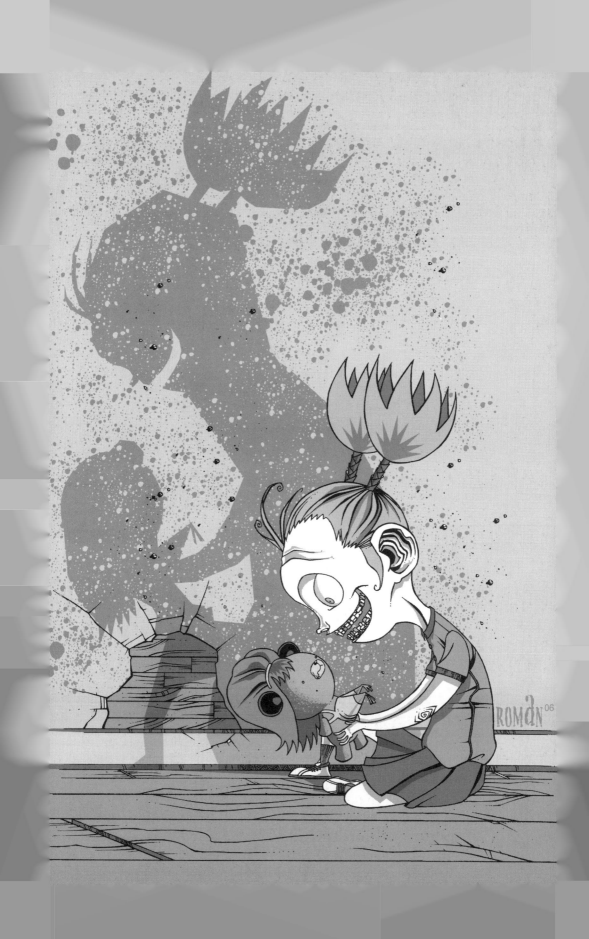

BEAR
(BASTARDS)

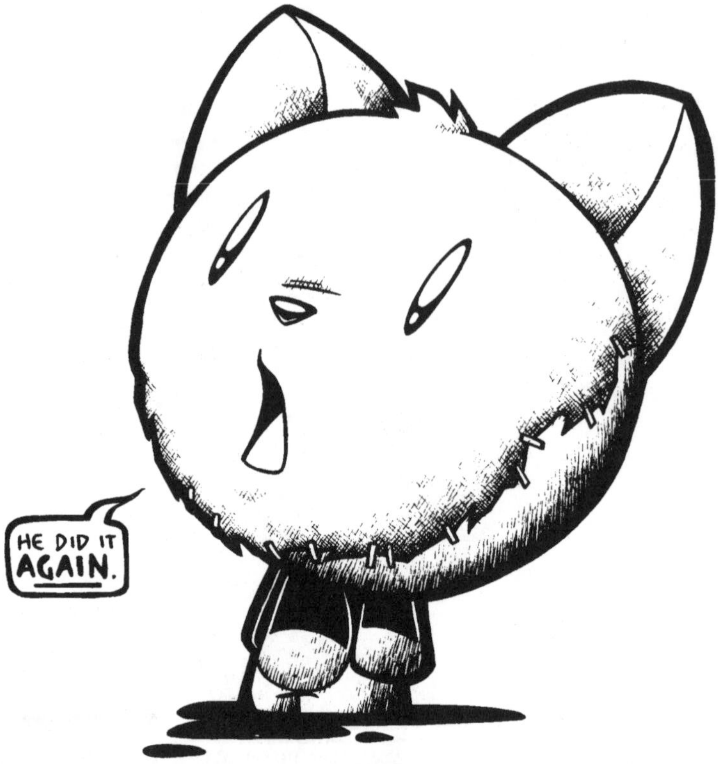

HE DID IT AGAIN.

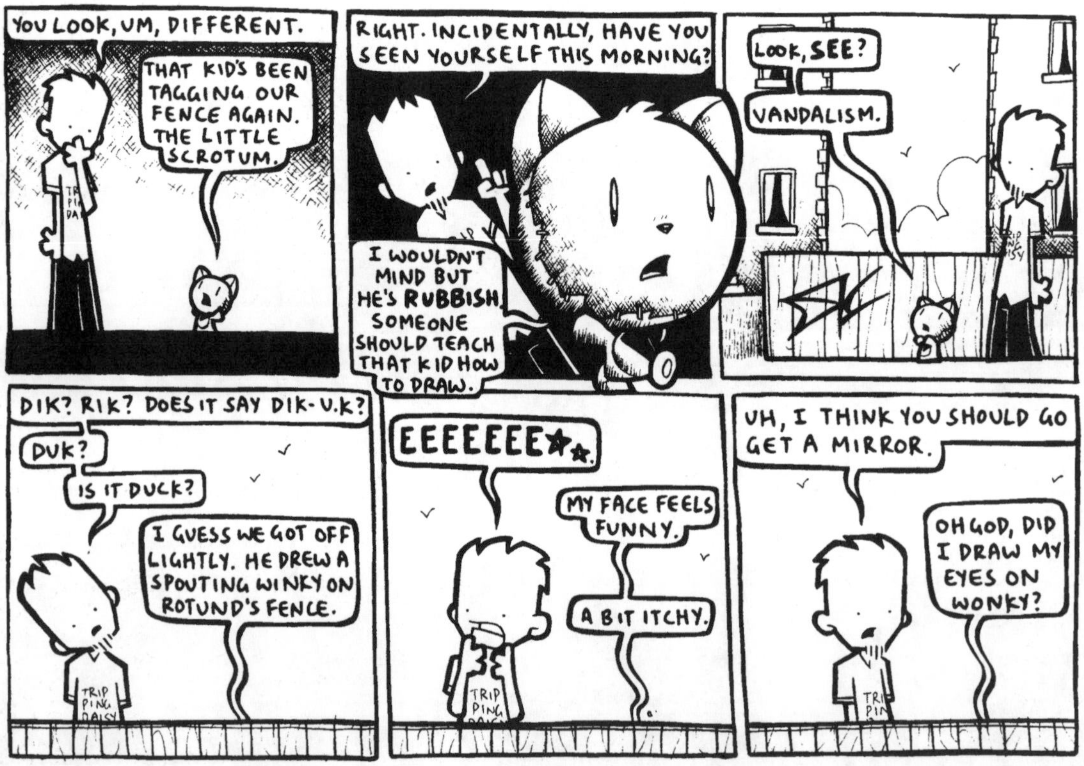

YOU LOOK, UM, DIFFERENT.
THAT KID'S BEEN TAGGING OUR FENCE AGAIN. THE LITTLE SCROTUM.
TRIP PIN DAI
RIGHT. INCIDENTALLY, HAVE YOU SEEN YOURSELF THIS MORNING?
I WOULDN'T MIND BUT HE'S RUBBISH. SOMEONE SHOULD TEACH THAT KID HOW TO DRAW.
LOOK, SEE?
VANDALISM.
DIK? RIK? DOES IT SAY DIK-U.K?
DUK?
IS IT DUCK?
I GUESS WE GOT OFF LIGHTLY. HE DREW A SPOUTING WINKY ON ROTUND'S FENCE.
TRIP PING DAISY
EEEEEEE★★.
MY FACE FEELS FUNNY.
A BIT ITCHY.
TRIP PING
UH, I THINK YOU SHOULD GO GET A MIRROR.
OH GOD, DID I DRAW MY EYES ON WONKY?
TRI PIN

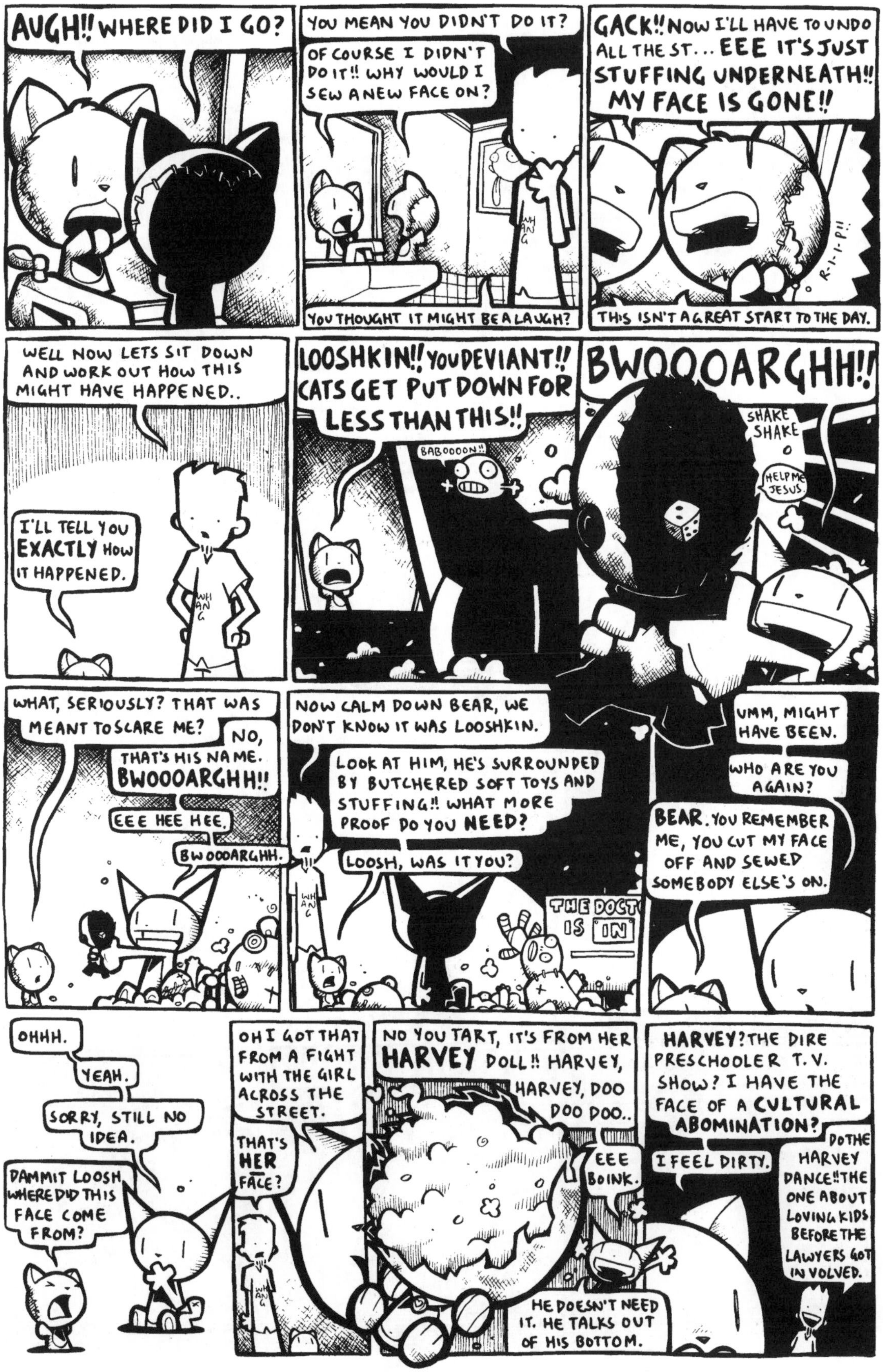
AUGH!! WHERE DID I GO?
YOU MEAN YOU DIDN'T DO IT?
OF COURSE I DIDN'T DO IT!! WHY WOULD I SEW A NEW FACE ON?
YOU THOUGHT IT MIGHT BE A LAUGH?
GACK!! NOW I'LL HAVE TO UNDO ALL THE ST... EEE IT'S JUST STUFFING UNDERNEATH!! MY FACE IS GONE!!
R-I-I-P!!
THIS ISN'T A GREAT START TO THE DAY.
WELL NOW LETS SIT DOWN AND WORK OUT HOW THIS MIGHT HAVE HAPPENED..
I'LL TELL YOU EXACTLY HOW IT HAPPENED.
LOOSHKIN!! YOU DEVIANT!! CATS GET PUT DOWN FOR LESS THAN THIS!!
BABOOOON!!
BWOOOARGHH!!
SHAKE SHAKE
HELP ME JESUS.
WHAT, SERIOUSLY? THAT WAS MEANT TO SCARE ME?
NO, THAT'S HIS NAME. BWOOOARGHH!!
EEE HEE HEE.
BWOOOARGHH.
NOW CALM DOWN BEAR, WE DON'T KNOW IT WAS LOOSHKIN.
LOOK AT HIM, HE'S SURROUNDED BY BUTCHERED SOFT TOYS AND STUFFING!! WHAT MORE PROOF DO YOU NEED?
LOOSH, WAS IT YOU?
THE DOCT IS IN
UMM, MIGHT HAVE BEEN.
WHO ARE YOU AGAIN?
BEAR. YOU REMEMBER ME, YOU CUT MY FACE OFF AND SEWED SOMEBODY ELSE'S ON.
OHHH.
YEAH.
SORRY, STILL NO IDEA.
DAMMIT LOOSH WHERE DID THIS FACE COME FROM?
OH I GOT THAT FROM A FIGHT WITH THE GIRL ACROSS THE STREET.
THAT'S HER FACE?
NO YOU TART, IT'S FROM HER HARVEY DOLL!! HARVEY, HARVEY, DOO DOO DOO..
EEE BOINK.
HE DOESN'T NEED IT. HE TALKS OUT OF HIS BOTTOM.
HARVEY? THE DIRE PRESCHOOLER T.V. SHOW? I HAVE THE FACE OF A CULTURAL ABOMINATION?
I FEEL DIRTY.
DO THE HARVEY DANCE!! THE ONE ABOUT LOVING KIDS BEFORE THE LAWYERS GOT INVOLVED.

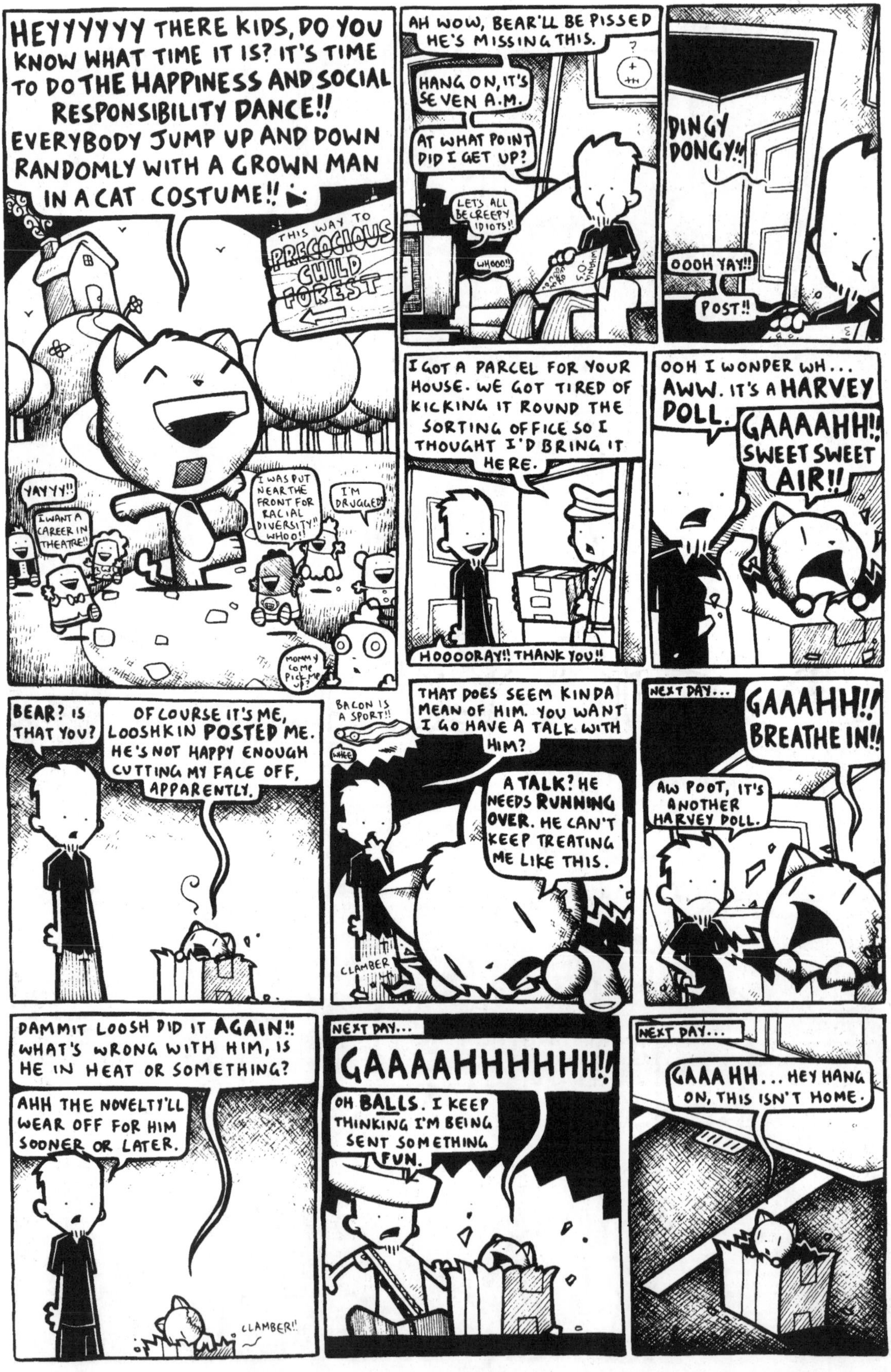
HEYYYYYY THERE KIDS, DO YOU KNOW WHAT TIME IT IS? IT'S TIME TO DO THE HAPPINESS AND SOCIAL RESPONSIBILITY DANCE!! EVERYBODY JUMP UP AND DOWN RANDOMLY WITH A GROWN MAN IN A CAT COSTUME!!
THIS WAY TO PRECOCIOUS CHILD FOREST
YAYYY!!
I WANT A CAREER IN THEATRE!!
I WAS PUT NEAR THE FRONT FOR RACIAL DIVERSITY!! WHOO!!
I'M DRUGGED!
MOMMY COME PICK ME UP?
AH WOW, BEAR'LL BE PISSED HE'S MISSING THIS.
HANG ON, IT'S SEVEN A.M.
AT WHAT POINT DID I GET UP?
LET'S ALL BE CREEPY IDIOTS!!
WHOOO!!
DINGY DONGY!!
OOOH YAY!!
POST!!
I GOT A PARCEL FOR YOUR HOUSE. WE GOT TIRED OF KICKING IT ROUND THE SORTING OFFICE SO I THOUGHT I'D BRING IT HERE.
HOOOORAY!! THANK YOU!!
OOH I WONDER WH... AWW. IT'S A HARVEY DOLL.
GAAAAHH!! SWEET SWEET AIR!!
BEAR? IS THAT YOU?
OF COURSE IT'S ME, LOOSHKIN POSTED ME. HE'S NOT HAPPY ENOUGH CUTTING MY FACE OFF, APPARENTLY.
BACON IS A SPORT!!
WHEE
THAT DOES SEEM KINDA MEAN OF HIM. YOU WANT I GO HAVE A TALK WITH HIM?
A TALK? HE NEEDS RUNNING OVER. HE CAN'T KEEP TREATING ME LIKE THIS.
CLAMBER
NEXT DAY...
GAAAHH!! BREATHE IN!!
AW POOT, IT'S ANOTHER HARVEY DOLL.
DAMMIT LOOSH DID IT AGAIN!! WHAT'S WRONG WITH HIM, IS HE IN HEAT OR SOMETHING?
AHH THE NOVELTY'LL WEAR OFF FOR HIM SOONER OR LATER.
CLAMBER!!
NEXT DAY...
GAAAAHHHHHH!!
OH BALLS. I KEEP THINKING I'M BEING SENT SOMETHING FUN.
NEXT DAY...
GAAAHH... HEY HANG ON, THIS ISN'T HOME.

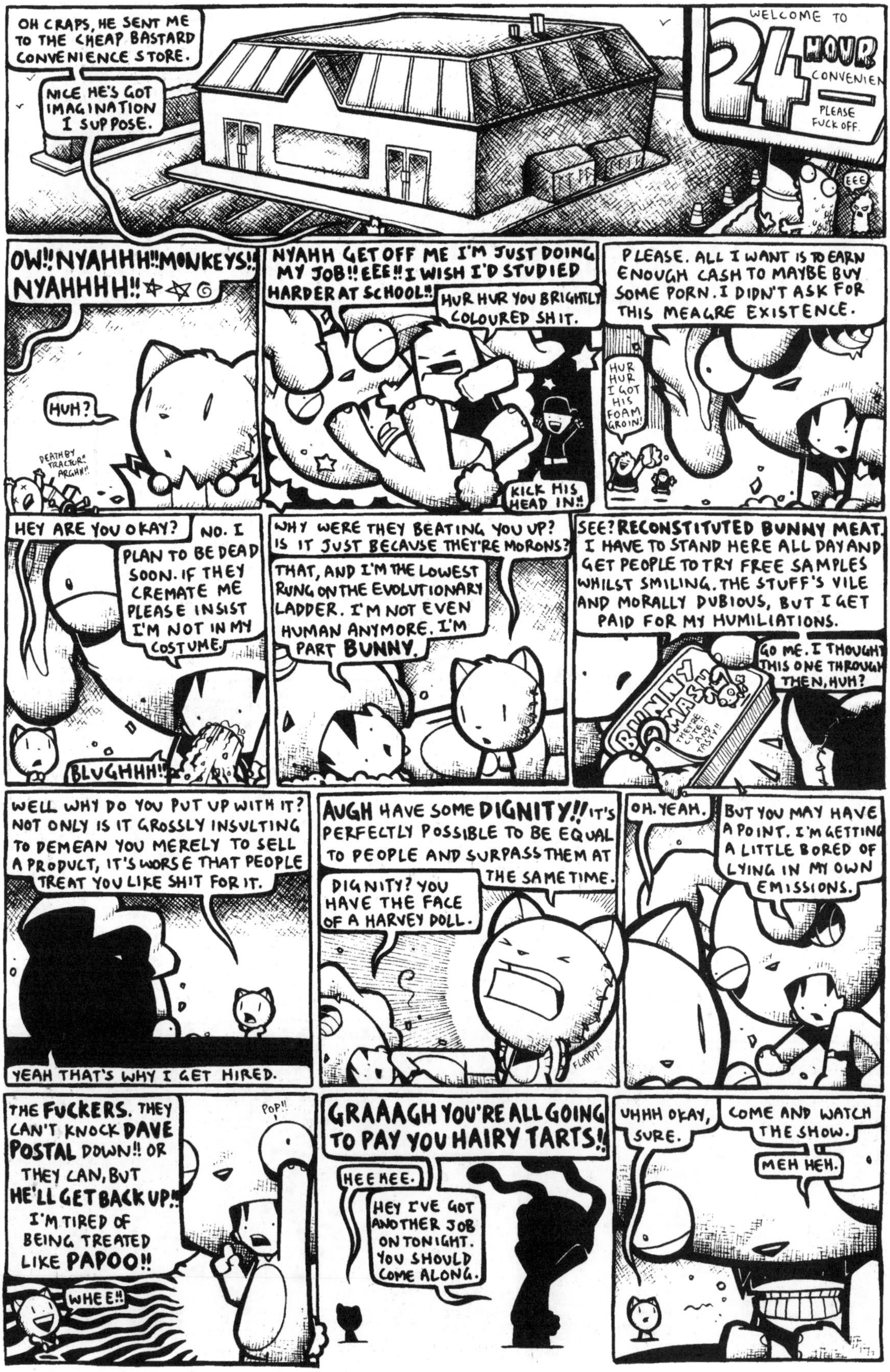
OH CRAPS, HE SENT ME TO THE CHEAP BASTARD CONVENIENCE STORE.
NICE HE'S GOT IMAGINATION I SUPPOSE.
WELCOME TO 24 HOUR CONVENIEN
PLEASE FUCK OFF.
EEE
OW!! NYAHHH!! MONKEYS!! NYAHHHH!!
HUH?
DEATH BY TRACTOR! ARGHH!!
NYAHH GET OFF ME I'M JUST DOING MY JOB!! EEE!! I WISH I'D STUDIED HARDER AT SCHOOL!!
HUR HUR YOU BRIGHTLY COLOURED SHIT.
KICK HIS HEAD IN!!
PLEASE. ALL I WANT IS TO EARN ENOUGH CASH TO MAYBE BUY SOME PORN. I DIDN'T ASK FOR THIS MEAGRE EXISTENCE.
HUR HUR I GOT HIS FOAM GROIN!
HEY ARE YOU OKAY?
NO. I PLAN TO BE DEAD SOON. IF THEY CREMATE ME PLEASE INSIST I'M NOT IN MY COSTUME.
BLUGHHH!!
WHY WERE THEY BEATING YOU UP? IS IT JUST BECAUSE THEY'RE MORONS?
THAT, AND I'M THE LOWEST RUNG ON THE EVOLUTIONARY LADDER. I'M NOT EVEN HUMAN ANYMORE. I'M PART BUNNY.
SEE? RECONSTITUTED BUNNY MEAT. I HAVE TO STAND HERE ALL DAY AND GET PEOPLE TO TRY FREE SAMPLES WHILST SMILING. THE STUFF'S VILE AND MORALLY DUBIOUS, BUT I GET PAID FOR MY HUMILIATIONS.
GO ME. I THOUGHT THIS ONE THROUGH THEN, HUH?
BUNNY MASH
THEY'RE CUTE! AND TASTY!!
WELL WHY DO YOU PUT UP WITH IT? NOT ONLY IS IT GROSSLY INSULTING TO DEMEAN YOU MERELY TO SELL A PRODUCT, IT'S WORSE THAT PEOPLE TREAT YOU LIKE SHIT FOR IT.
YEAH THAT'S WHY I GET HIRED.
AUGH HAVE SOME DIGNITY!! IT'S PERFECTLY POSSIBLE TO BE EQUAL TO PEOPLE AND SURPASS THEM AT THE SAME TIME.
DIGNITY? YOU HAVE THE FACE OF A HARVEY DOLL.
FLAPPY!!
OH. YEAH.
BUT YOU MAY HAVE A POINT. I'M GETTING A LITTLE BORED OF LYING IN MY OWN EMISSIONS.
THE FUCKERS. THEY CAN'T KNOCK DAVE POSTAL DOWN!! OR THEY CAN, BUT HE'LL GET BACK UP!! I'M TIRED OF BEING TREATED LIKE PAPOO!!
POP!!
WHEE!!
GRAAAGH YOU'RE ALL GOING TO PAY YOU HAIRY TARTS!!
HEE HEE.
HEY I'VE GOT ANOTHER JOB ON TONIGHT. YOU SHOULD COME ALONG.
UHHH OKAY, SURE.
COME AND WATCH THE SHOW.
MEH HEH.

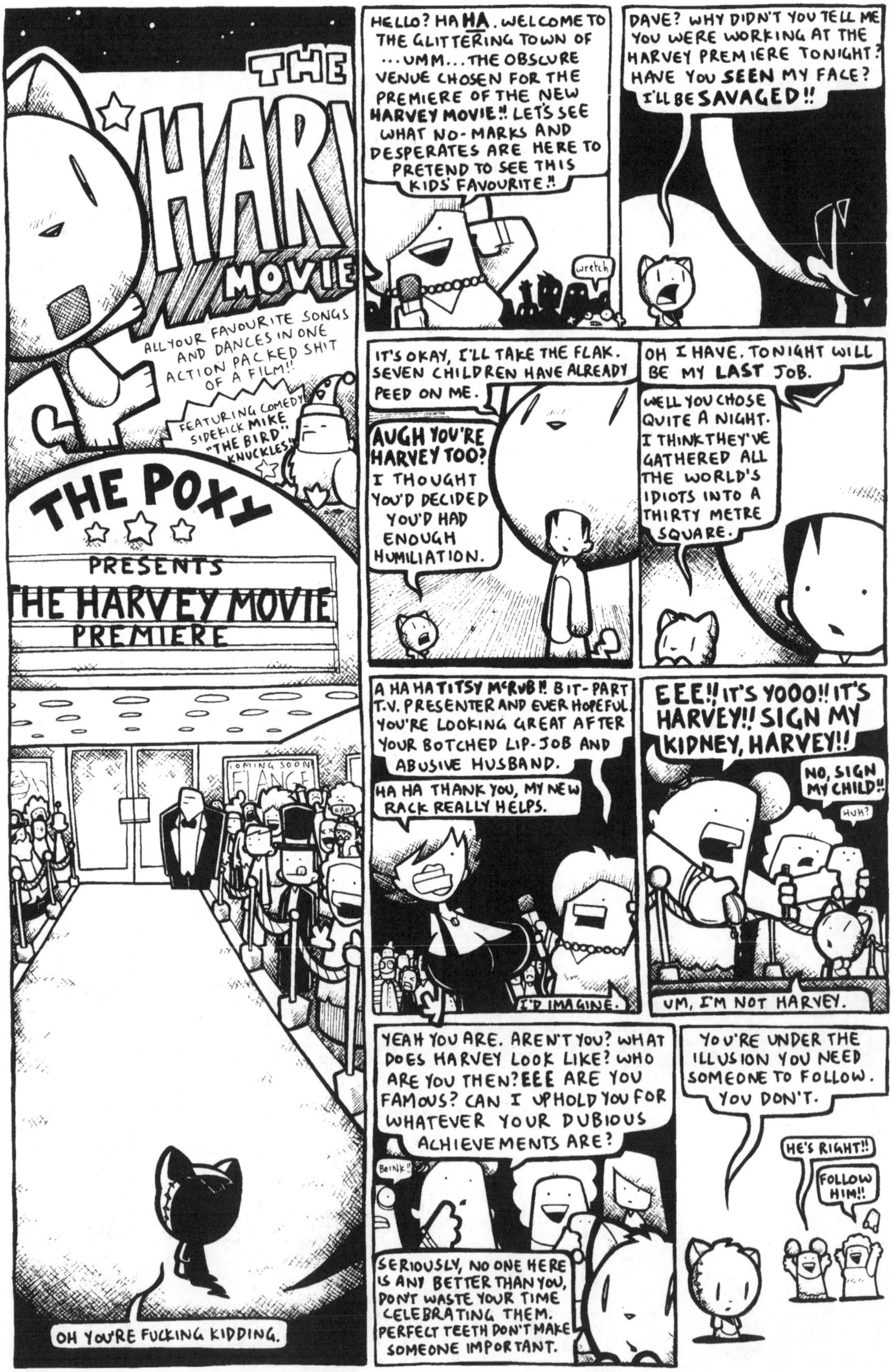
THE
MOVIE
ALL YOUR FAVOURITE SONGS AND DANCES IN ONE ACTION PACKED SHIT OF A FILM!!
FEATURING COMEDY SIDEKICK MIKE "THE BIRD" KNUCKLES!!
THE POXY
PRESENTS
THE HARVEY MOVIE
PREMIERE
COMING SOON
FLANGE
RAH
OH YOU'RE FUCKING KIDDING.
HELLO? HA HA. WELCOME TO THE GLITTERING TOWN OF ...UMM... THE OBSCURE VENUE CHOSEN FOR THE PREMIERE OF THE NEW HARVEY MOVIE!! LET'S SEE WHAT NO-MARKS AND DESPERATES ARE HERE TO PRETEND TO SEE THIS KIDS' FAVOURITE!!
wretch
DAVE? WHY DIDN'T YOU TELL ME YOU WERE WORKING AT THE HARVEY PREMIERE TONIGHT? HAVE YOU SEEN MY FACE? I'LL BE SAVAGED!!
IT'S OKAY, I'LL TAKE THE FLAK. SEVEN CHILDREN HAVE ALREADY PEED ON ME.
AUGH YOU'RE HARVEY TOO? I THOUGHT YOU'D DECIDED YOU'D HAD ENOUGH HUMILIATION.
OH I HAVE. TONIGHT WILL BE MY LAST JOB.
WELL YOU CHOSE QUITE A NIGHT. I THINK THEY'VE GATHERED ALL THE WORLD'S IDIOTS INTO A THIRTY METRE SQUARE.
A HA HA TITSY McRUB!! BIT-PART T.V. PRESENTER AND EVER HOPEFUL. YOU'RE LOOKING GREAT AFTER YOUR BOTCHED LIP-JOB AND ABUSIVE HUSBAND.
HA HA THANK YOU, MY NEW RACK REALLY HELPS.
I'D IMAGINE.
EEE!! IT'S YOOO!! IT'S HARVEY!! SIGN MY KIDNEY, HARVEY!!
NO, SIGN MY CHILD!!
HUH?
UM, I'M NOT HARVEY.
YEAH YOU ARE. AREN'T YOU? WHAT DOES HARVEY LOOK LIKE? WHO ARE YOU THEN? EEE ARE YOU FAMOUS? CAN I UPHOLD YOU FOR WHATEVER YOUR DUBIOUS ACHIEVEMENTS ARE?
BOINK!
SERIOUSLY, NO ONE HERE IS ANY BETTER THAN YOU, DON'T WASTE YOUR TIME CELEBRATING THEM. PERFECT TEETH DON'T MAKE SOMEONE IMPORTANT.
YOU'RE UNDER THE ILLUSION YOU NEED SOMEONE TO FOLLOW. YOU DON'T.
HE'S RIGHT!!
FOLLOW HIM!!

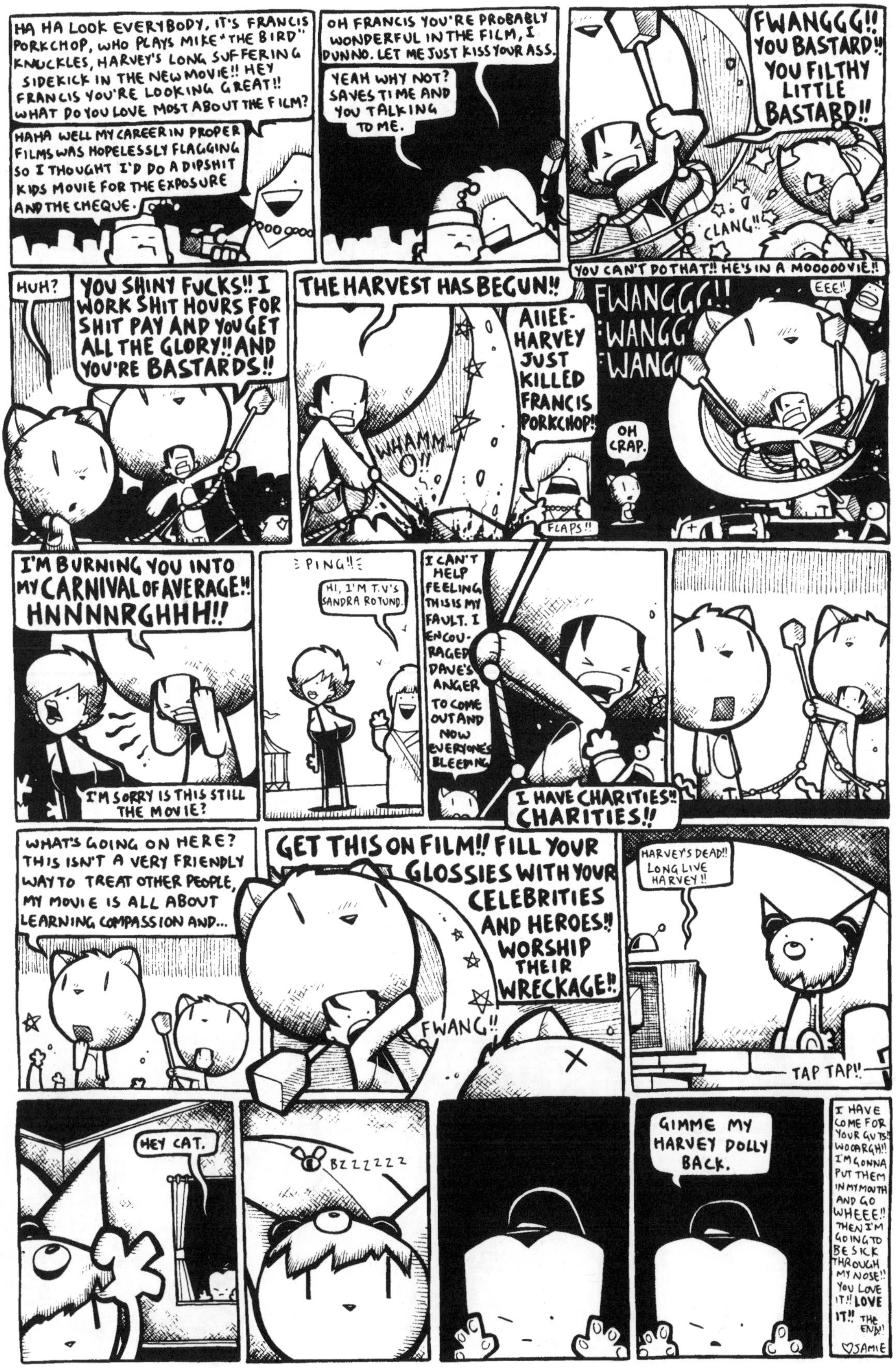

HA HA LOOK EVERYBODY, IT'S FRANCIS PORKCHOP, WHO PLAYS MIKE "THE BIRD" KNUCKLES, HARVEY'S LONG SUFFERING SIDEKICK IN THE NEW MOVIE!! HEY FRANCIS YOU'RE LOOKING GREAT!! WHAT DO YOU LOVE MOST ABOUT THE FILM?
HAHA WELL MY CAREER IN PROPER FILMS WAS HOPELESSLY FLAGGING SO I THOUGHT I'D DO A DIPSHIT KIDS MOVIE FOR THE EXPOSURE AND THE CHEQUE.
OH FRANCIS YOU'RE PROBABLY WONDERFUL IN THE FILM, I DUNNO. LET ME JUST KISS YOUR ASS.
YEAH WHY NOT? SAVES TIME AND YOU TALKING TO ME.
FWANGGG!! YOU BASTARD!! YOU FILTHY LITTLE BASTARD!!
CLANG!!
YOU CAN'T DO THAT!! HE'S IN A MOOOOOVIE!!
HUH?
YOU SHINY FUCKS!! I WORK SHIT HOURS FOR SHIT PAY AND YOU GET ALL THE GLORY!! AND YOU'RE BASTARDS!!
THE HARVEST HAS BEGUN!!
WHAMM!!
AIIEE- HARVEY JUST KILLED FRANCIS PORKCHOP!!
FLAPS!!
FWANGGG!! WANGG WANG
EEE!!
OH CRAP.
I'M BURNING YOU INTO MY CARNIVAL OF AVERAGE!! HNNNNRGHHH!!
I'M SORRY IS THIS STILL THE MOVIE?
PING!!
HI, I'M T.V.'S SANDRA ROTUND.
I CAN'T HELP FEELING THIS IS MY FAULT. I ENCOURAGED DAVE'S ANGER TO COME OUT AND NOW EVERYONE'S BLEEDING
I HAVE CHARITIES!! CHARITIES!!
WHAT'S GOING ON HERE? THIS ISN'T A VERY FRIENDLY WAY TO TREAT OTHER PEOPLE, MY MOVIE IS ALL ABOUT LEARNING COMPASSION AND...
GET THIS ON FILM!! FILL YOUR GLOSSIES WITH YOUR CELEBRITIES AND HEROES!! WORSHIP THEIR WRECKAGE!!
FWANG!!
HARVEY'S DEAD!! LONG LIVE HARVEY!!
TAP TAP!!
HEY CAT.
BZZZZZZ
GIMME MY HARVEY DOLLY BACK.
I HAVE COME FOR YOUR GUTS!! WOOARGH!! I'M GONNA PUT THEM IN MY MOUTH AND GO WHEEE!! THEN I'M GOING TO BE SICK THROUGH MY NOSE!! YOU LOVE IT!! LOVE IT!!
THE END!
♡JAMIE

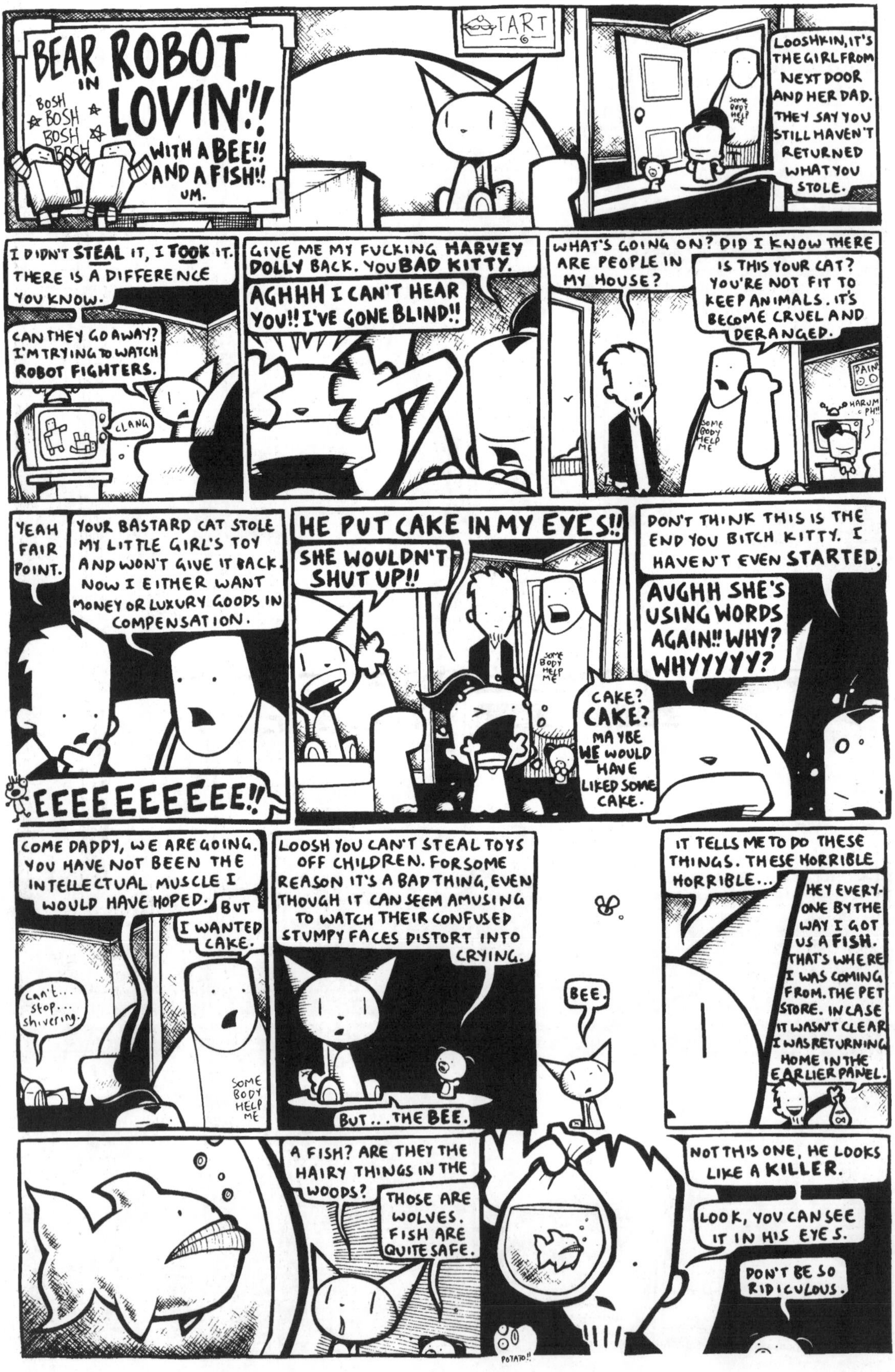
BEAR ROBOT IN LOVIN'!!
BOSH BOSH BOSH BOSH
WITH A BEE!! AND A FISH!! UM.
TART
LOOSHKIN, IT'S THE GIRL FROM NEXT DOOR AND HER DAD. THEY SAY YOU STILL HAVEN'T RETURNED WHAT YOU STOLE.
SOME BODY HELP ME
I DIDN'T STEAL IT, I TOOK IT. THERE IS A DIFFERENCE YOU KNOW.
CAN THEY GO AWAY? I'M TRYING TO WATCH ROBOT FIGHTERS.
CLANG
GIVE ME MY FUCKING HARVEY DOLLY BACK. YOU BAD KITTY.
AGHHH I CAN'T HEAR YOU!! I'VE GONE BLIND!!
WHAT'S GOING ON? DID I KNOW THERE ARE PEOPLE IN MY HOUSE?
IS THIS YOUR CAT? YOU'RE NOT FIT TO KEEP ANIMALS. IT'S BECOME CRUEL AND DERANGED.
SOME BODY HELP ME
PAIN
HARUMPH!!
YEAH FAIR POINT.
YOUR BASTARD CAT STOLE MY LITTLE GIRL'S TOY AND WON'T GIVE IT BACK. NOW I EITHER WANT MONEY OR LUXURY GOODS IN COMPENSATION.
EEEEEEEEEE!!
HE PUT CAKE IN MY EYES!!
SHE WOULDN'T SHUT UP!!
SOME BODY HELP ME
CAKE? CAKE? MAYBE WE WOULD HAVE LIKED SOME CAKE.
DON'T THINK THIS IS THE END YOU BITCH KITTY. I HAVEN'T EVEN STARTED.
AUGHH SHE'S USING WORDS AGAIN!! WHY? WHYYYYY?
COME DADDY, WE ARE GOING. YOU HAVE NOT BEEN THE INTELLECTUAL MUSCLE I WOULD HAVE HOPED.
BUT I WANTED CAKE.
can't... stop... shivering.
SOME BODY HELP ME
LOOSH YOU CAN'T STEAL TOYS OFF CHILDREN. FOR SOME REASON IT'S A BAD THING, EVEN THOUGH IT CAN SEEM AMUSING TO WATCH THEIR CONFUSED STUMPY FACES DISTORT INTO CRYING.
BUT... THE BEE.
BEE.
IT TELLS ME TO DO THESE THINGS. THESE HORRIBLE HORRIBLE...
HEY EVERYONE BY THE WAY I GOT US A FISH. THAT'S WHERE I WAS COMING FROM. THE PET STORE. IN CASE IT WASN'T CLEAR I WAS RETURNING HOME IN THE EARLIER PANEL.
A FISH? ARE THEY THE HAIRY THINGS IN THE WOODS?
THOSE ARE WOLVES. FISH ARE QUITE SAFE.
POTATO!!
NOT THIS ONE, HE LOOKS LIKE A KILLER.
LOOK, YOU CAN SEE IT IN HIS EYES.
DON'T BE SO RIDICULOUS.

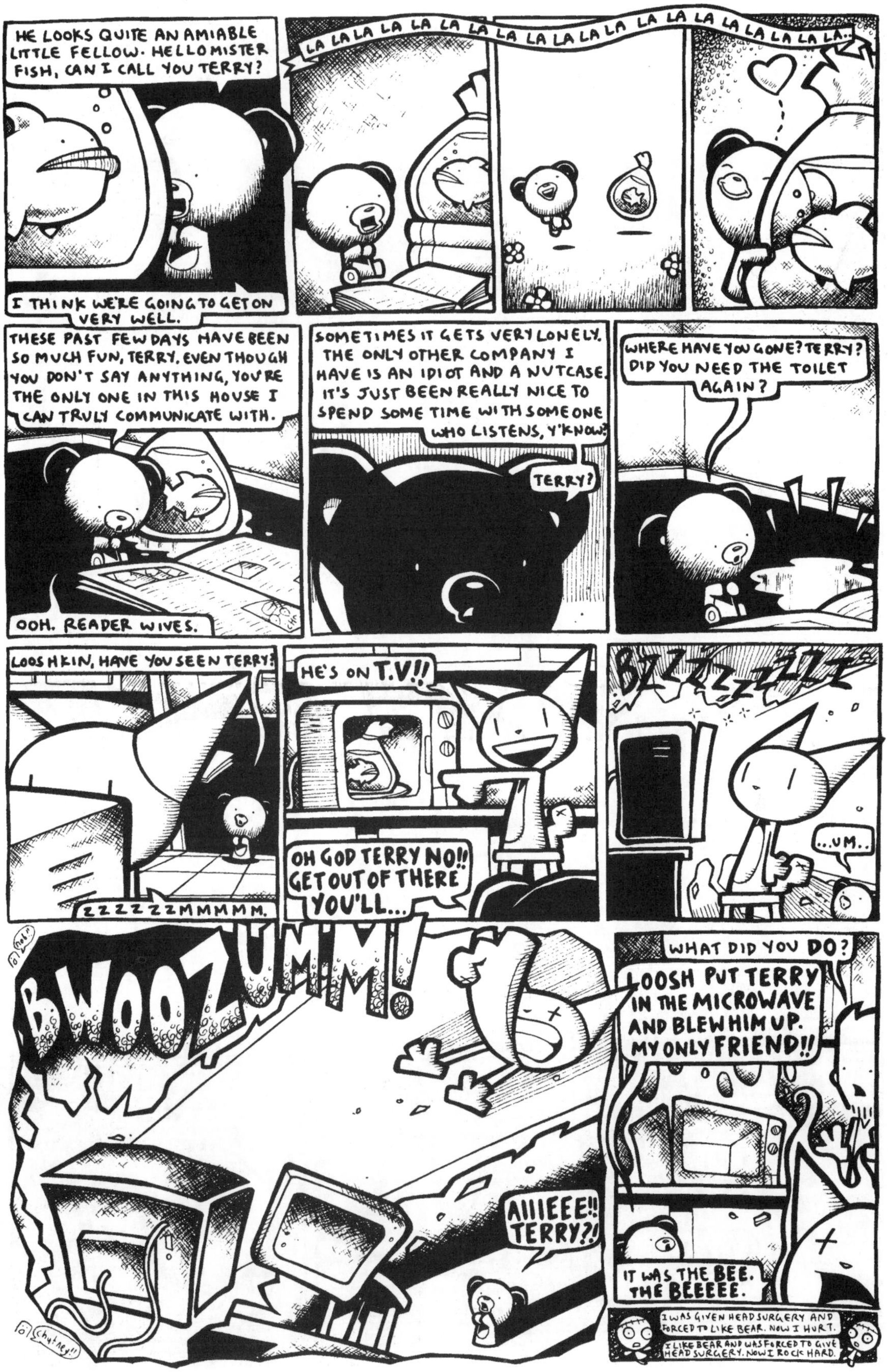

HE LOOKS QUITE AN AMIABLE LITTLE FELLOW. HELLO MISTER FISH, CAN I CALL YOU TERRY?
I THINK WE'RE GOING TO GET ON VERY WELL.
LA LA LA LA LA LA LA LA LA LA LA LA LA LA LA LA LA LA LA LA..
THESE PAST FEW DAYS HAVE BEEN SO MUCH FUN, TERRY. EVEN THOUGH YOU DON'T SAY ANYTHING, YOU'RE THE ONLY ONE IN THIS HOUSE I CAN TRULY COMMUNICATE WITH.
OOH. READER WIVES.
SOMETIMES IT GETS VERY LONELY. THE ONLY OTHER COMPANY I HAVE IS AN IDIOT AND A NUTCASE. IT'S JUST BEEN REALLY NICE TO SPEND SOME TIME WITH SOMEONE WHO LISTENS, Y'KNOW?
TERRY?
WHERE HAVE YOU GONE? TERRY? DID YOU NEED THE TOILET AGAIN?
LOOSHKIN, HAVE YOU SEEN TERRY?
ZZZZZZMMMMM.
HE'S ON T.V!!
OH GOD TERRY NO!! GET OUT OF THERE YOU'LL...
BZZZZZZZZZ
...UM..
BWOOZUMM!
AIIIEEE!! TERRY?!
WHAT DID YOU DO?
LOOSH PUT TERRY IN THE MICROWAVE AND BLEW HIM UP. MY ONLY FRIEND!!
IT WAS THE BEE. THE BEEEEE.
I WAS GIVEN HEAD SURGERY AND FORCED TO LIKE BEAR. NOW I HURT.
I LIKE BEAR AND WAS FORCED TO GIVE HEAD SURGERY. NOW I ROCK HARD.
chutney!!

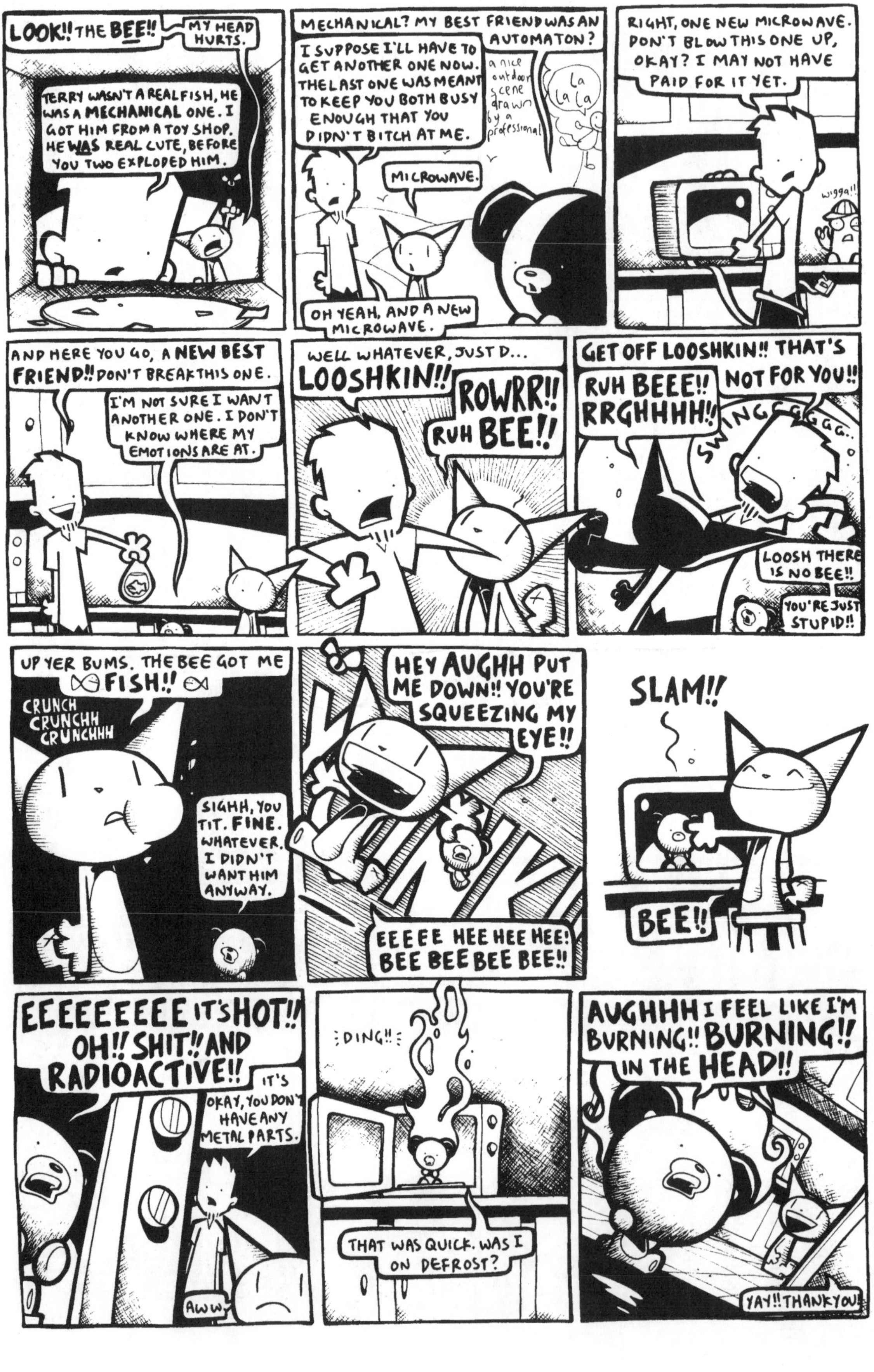
LOOK!! THE BEE!!
MY HEAD HURTS.
TERRY WASN'T A REAL FISH, HE WAS A MECHANICAL ONE. I GOT HIM FROM A TOY SHOP. HE WAS REAL CUTE, BEFORE YOU TWO EXPLODED HIM.
MECHANICAL? MY BEST FRIEND WAS AN AUTOMATON?
I SUPPOSE I'LL HAVE TO GET ANOTHER ONE NOW. THE LAST ONE WAS MEANT TO KEEP YOU BOTH BUSY ENOUGH THAT YOU DIDN'T BITCH AT ME.
a nice outdoor scene drawn by a professional
La La La
MICROWAVE.
OH YEAH, AND A NEW MICROWAVE.
RIGHT, ONE NEW MICROWAVE. DON'T BLOW THIS ONE UP, OKAY? I MAY NOT HAVE PAID FOR IT YET.
wigga!!
AND HERE YOU GO, A NEW BEST FRIEND!! DON'T BREAK THIS ONE.
I'M NOT SURE I WANT ANOTHER ONE. I DON'T KNOW WHERE MY EMOTIONS ARE AT.
WELL WHATEVER, JUST D...
LOOSHKIN!!
ROWRR!! RUH BEE!!
GET OFF LOOSHKIN!! THAT'S NOT FOR YOU!!
RUH BEEE!! RRGHHHH!!
SWINGGGGGG..
LOOSH THERE IS NO BEE!!
YOU'RE JUST STUPID!!
UP YER BUMS. THE BEE GOT ME FISH!!
CRUNCH CRUNCHH CRUNCHHH
SIGHH, YOU TIT. FINE. WHATEVER. I DIDN'T WANT HIM ANYWAY.
HEY AUGHH PUT ME DOWN!! YOU'RE SQUEEZING MY EYE!!
EEEEE HEE HEE HEE! BEE BEE BEE BEE!!
SLAM!!
BEE!!
EEEEEEEE IT'S HOT!! OH!! SHIT!! AND RADIOACTIVE!!
IT'S OKAY, YOU DON'T HAVE ANY METAL PARTS.
AWW.
DING!!
THAT WAS QUICK. WAS I ON DEFROST?
AUGHHH I FEEL LIKE I'M BURNING!! BURNING!! IN THE HEAD!!
YAY!! THANK YOU!!

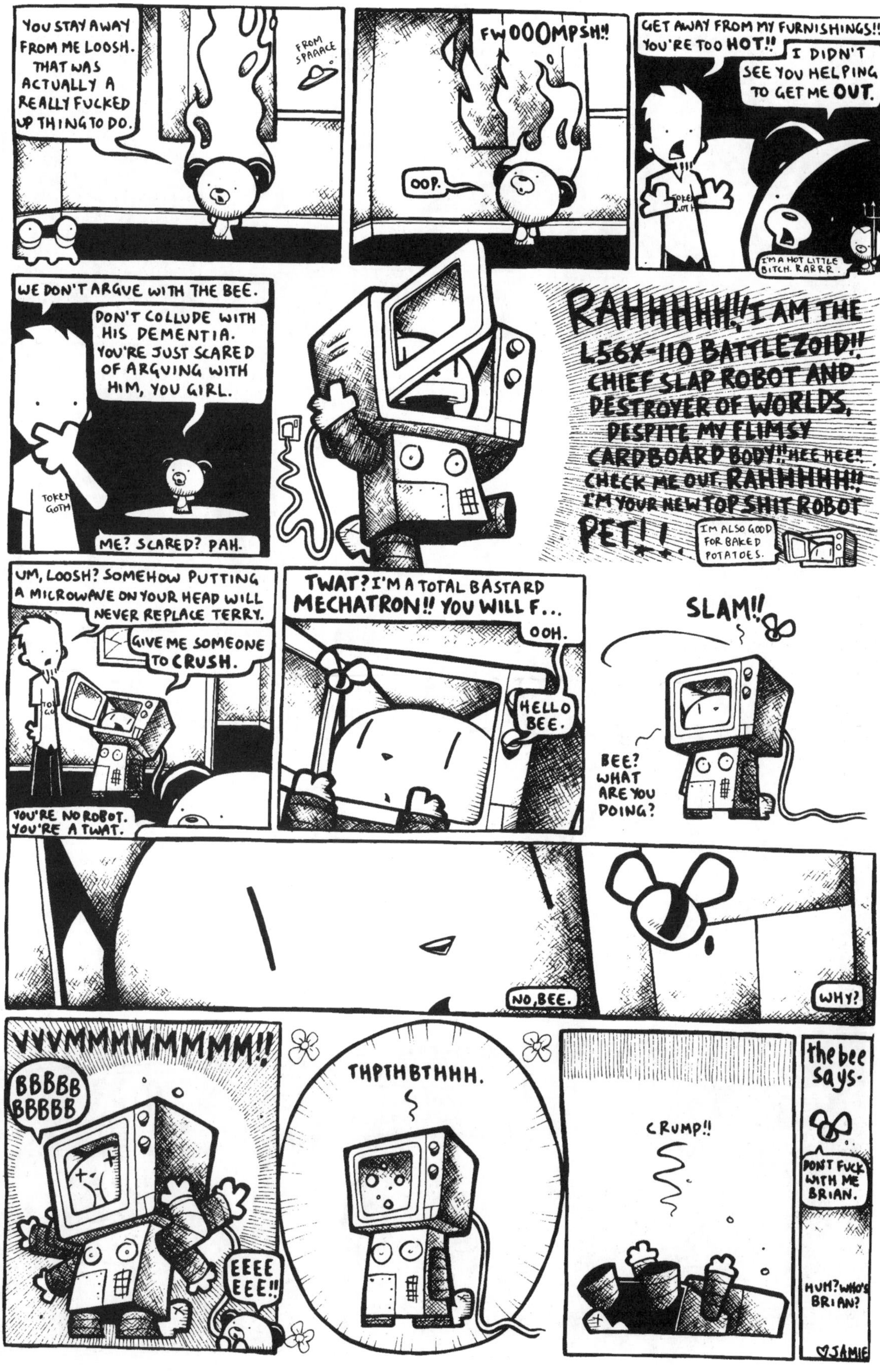
YOU STAY AWAY FROM ME LOOSH. THAT WAS ACTUALLY A REALLY FUCKED UP THING TO DO.
FROM SPAAACE
FWOOOMPSH!!
OOP.
GET AWAY FROM MY FURNISHINGS!! YOU'RE TOO HOT!!
I DIDN'T SEE YOU HELPING TO GET ME OUT.
I'M A HOT LITTLE BITCH. RARRR.
TOKEN GOTH
WE DON'T ARGUE WITH THE BEE.
DON'T COLLUDE WITH HIS DEMENTIA. YOU'RE JUST SCARED OF ARGUING WITH HIM, YOU GIRL.
ME? SCARED? PAH.
RAHHHHH!! I AM THE L56X-110 BATTLEZOID!! CHIEF SLAP ROBOT AND DESTROYER OF WORLDS, DESPITE MY FLIMSY CARDBOARD BODY!! HEE HEE!! CHECK ME OUT. RAHHHHH!! I'M YOUR NEW TOP SHIT ROBOT PET!!
I'M ALSO GOOD FOR BAKED POTATOES.
UM, LOOSH? SOMEHOW PUTTING A MICROWAVE ON YOUR HEAD WILL NEVER REPLACE TERRY.
GIVE ME SOMEONE TO CRUSH.
YOU'RE NO ROBOT. YOU'RE A TWAT.
TWAT? I'M A TOTAL BASTARD MECHATRON!! YOU WILL F...
OOH.
HELLO BEE.
SLAM!!
BEE? WHAT ARE YOU DOING?
NO, BEE.
WHY?
VVVMMMMMMMM!!
BBBBB BBBBB
EEEE EEE!!
THPTHBTHHH.
CRUMP!!
the bee says-
DON'T FUCK WITH ME BRIAN.
HUM? WHO'S BRIAN?
♡JAMIE

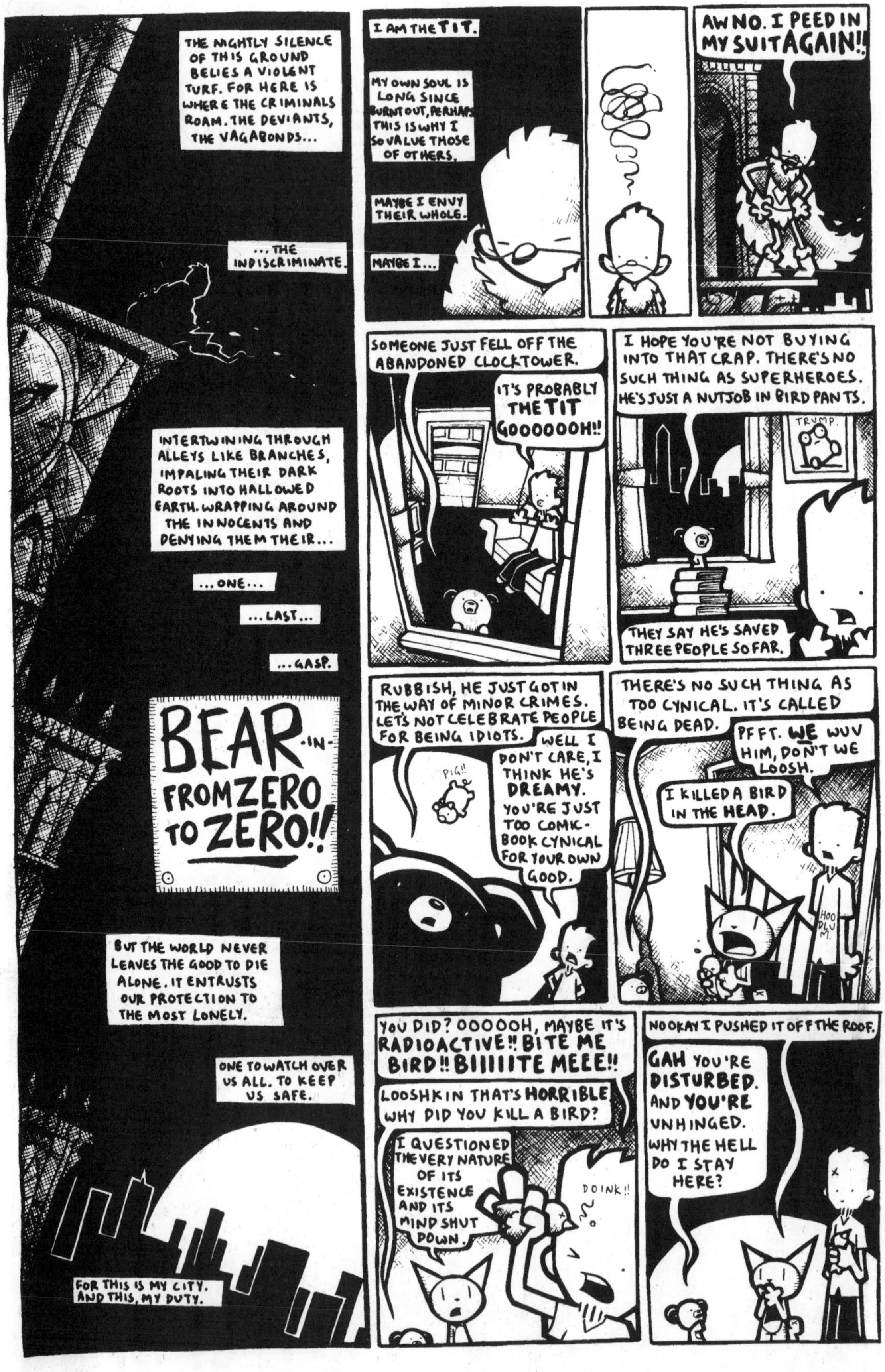
THE NIGHTLY SILENCE OF THIS GROUND BELIES A VIOLENT TURF. FOR HERE IS WHERE THE CRIMINALS ROAM. THE DEVIANTS, THE VAGABONDS...
... THE INDISCRIMINATE.
INTERTWINING THROUGH ALLEYS LIKE BRANCHES, IMPALING THEIR DARK ROOTS INTO HALLOWED EARTH. WRAPPING AROUND THE INNOCENTS AND DENYING THEM THEIR...
...ONE...
...LAST...
...GASP.
BEAR-IN- FROM ZERO TO ZERO!!
BUT THE WORLD NEVER LEAVES THE GOOD TO DIE ALONE. IT ENTRUSTS OUR PROTECTION TO THE MOST LONELY.
ONE TO WATCH OVER US ALL. TO KEEP US SAFE.
FOR THIS IS MY CITY. AND THIS, MY DUTY.
I AM THE TIT.
MY OWN SOUL IS LONG SINCE BURNT OUT, PERHAPS THIS IS WHY I SO VALUE THOSE OF OTHERS.
MAYBE I ENVY THEIR WHOLE.
MAYBE I...
AW NO. I PEED IN MY SUIT AGAIN!!
SOMEONE JUST FELL OFF THE ABANDONED CLOCKTOWER.
IT'S PROBABLY THE TIT GOOOOOOH!!
I HOPE YOU'RE NOT BUYING INTO THAT CRAP. THERE'S NO SUCH THING AS SUPERHEROES. HE'S JUST A NUTJOB IN BIRD PANTS.
TRUMP.
THEY SAY HE'S SAVED THREE PEOPLE SO FAR.
RUBBISH, HE JUST GOT IN THE WAY OF MINOR CRIMES. LET'S NOT CELEBRATE PEOPLE FOR BEING IDIOTS.
PIG!!
WELL I DON'T CARE, I THINK HE'S DREAMY. YOU'RE JUST TOO COMIC-BOOK CYNICAL FOR YOUR OWN GOOD.
THERE'S NO SUCH THING AS TOO CYNICAL. IT'S CALLED BEING DEAD.
PFFT. WE WUV HIM, DON'T WE LOOSH.
I KILLED A BIRD IN THE HEAD.
HOODLUM.
YOU DID? OOOOOH, MAYBE IT'S RADIOACTIVE!! BITE ME BIRD!! BIIIIITE MEEE!!
LOOSHKIN THAT'S HORRIBLE WHY DID YOU KILL A BIRD?
I QUESTIONED THE VERY NATURE OF ITS EXISTENCE AND ITS MIND SHUT DOWN.
DOINK!!
NO OKAY I PUSHED IT OFF THE ROOF.
GAH YOU'RE DISTURBED. AND YOU'RE UNHINGED. WHY THE HELL DO I STAY HERE?

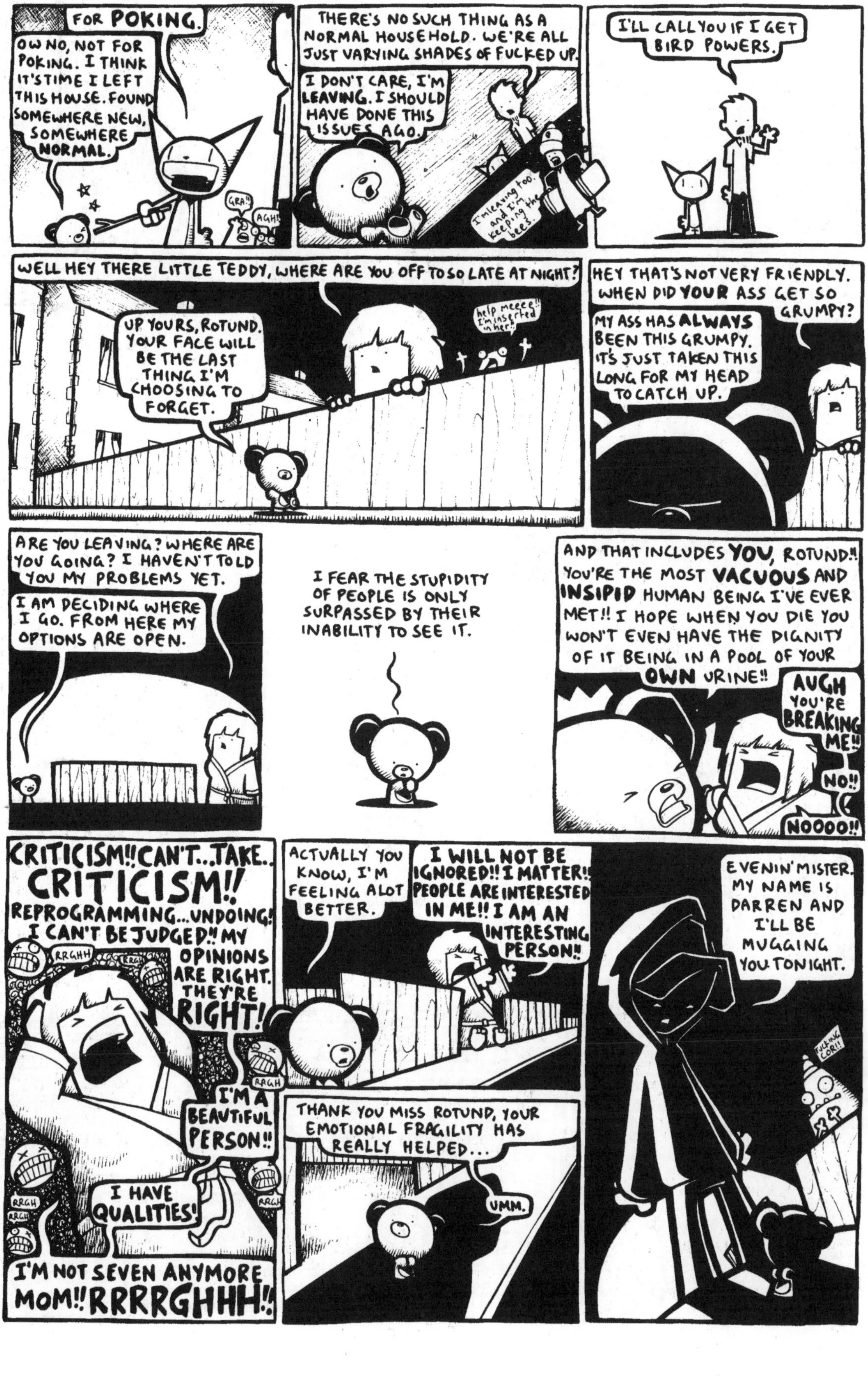
FOR POKING.
OW NO, NOT FOR POKING. I THINK IT'S TIME I LEFT THIS HOUSE. FOUND SOMEWHERE NEW, SOMEWHERE NORMAL.
GRA!!
AGH!
THERE'S NO SUCH THING AS A NORMAL HOUSEHOLD. WE'RE ALL JUST VARYING SHADES OF FUCKED UP.
I DON'T CARE, I'M LEAVING. I SHOULD HAVE DONE THIS ISSUES AGO.
I'm leaving too. and I'm keeping the bees.
I'LL CALL YOU IF I GET BIRD POWERS.
WELL HEY THERE LITTLE TEDDY, WHERE ARE YOU OFF TO SO LATE AT NIGHT?
UP YOURS, ROTUND. YOUR FACE WILL BE THE LAST THING I'M CHOOSING TO FORGET.
help meeee!! I'm inserted in her!!
HEY THAT'S NOT VERY FRIENDLY. WHEN DID YOUR ASS GET SO GRUMPY?
MY ASS HAS ALWAYS BEEN THIS GRUMPY. IT'S JUST TAKEN THIS LONG FOR MY HEAD TO CATCH UP.
ARE YOU LEAVING? WHERE ARE YOU GOING? I HAVEN'T TOLD YOU MY PROBLEMS YET.
I AM DECIDING WHERE I GO. FROM HERE MY OPTIONS ARE OPEN.
I FEAR THE STUPIDITY OF PEOPLE IS ONLY SURPASSED BY THEIR INABILITY TO SEE IT.
AND THAT INCLUDES YOU, ROTUND!! YOU'RE THE MOST VACUOUS AND INSIPID HUMAN BEING I'VE EVER MET!! I HOPE WHEN YOU DIE YOU WON'T EVEN HAVE THE DIGNITY OF IT BEING IN A POOL OF YOUR OWN URINE!!
AUGH YOU'RE BREAKING ME!!
NO!!
NOOOO!!
CRITICISM!! CAN'T...TAKE.. CRITICISM!! REPROGRAMMING...UNDOING! I CAN'T BE JUDGED!! MY OPINIONS ARE RIGHT. THEY'RE RIGHT!
RRGHH
RRGH
RRGH
I'M A BEAUTIFUL PERSON!!
I HAVE QUALITIES!
RRGH
RRGH
RRGH
I'M NOT SEVEN ANYMORE MOM!! RRRRGHHH!!
ACTUALLY YOU KNOW, I'M FEELING ALOT BETTER.
I WILL NOT BE IGNORED!! I MATTER!! PEOPLE ARE INTERESTED IN ME!! I AM AN INTERESTING PERSON!!
THANK YOU MISS ROTUND, YOUR EMOTIONAL FRAGILITY HAS REALLY HELPED...
UMM.
EVENIN' MISTER. MY NAME IS DARREN AND I'LL BE MUGGING YOU TONIGHT.
FUCKING COR!!

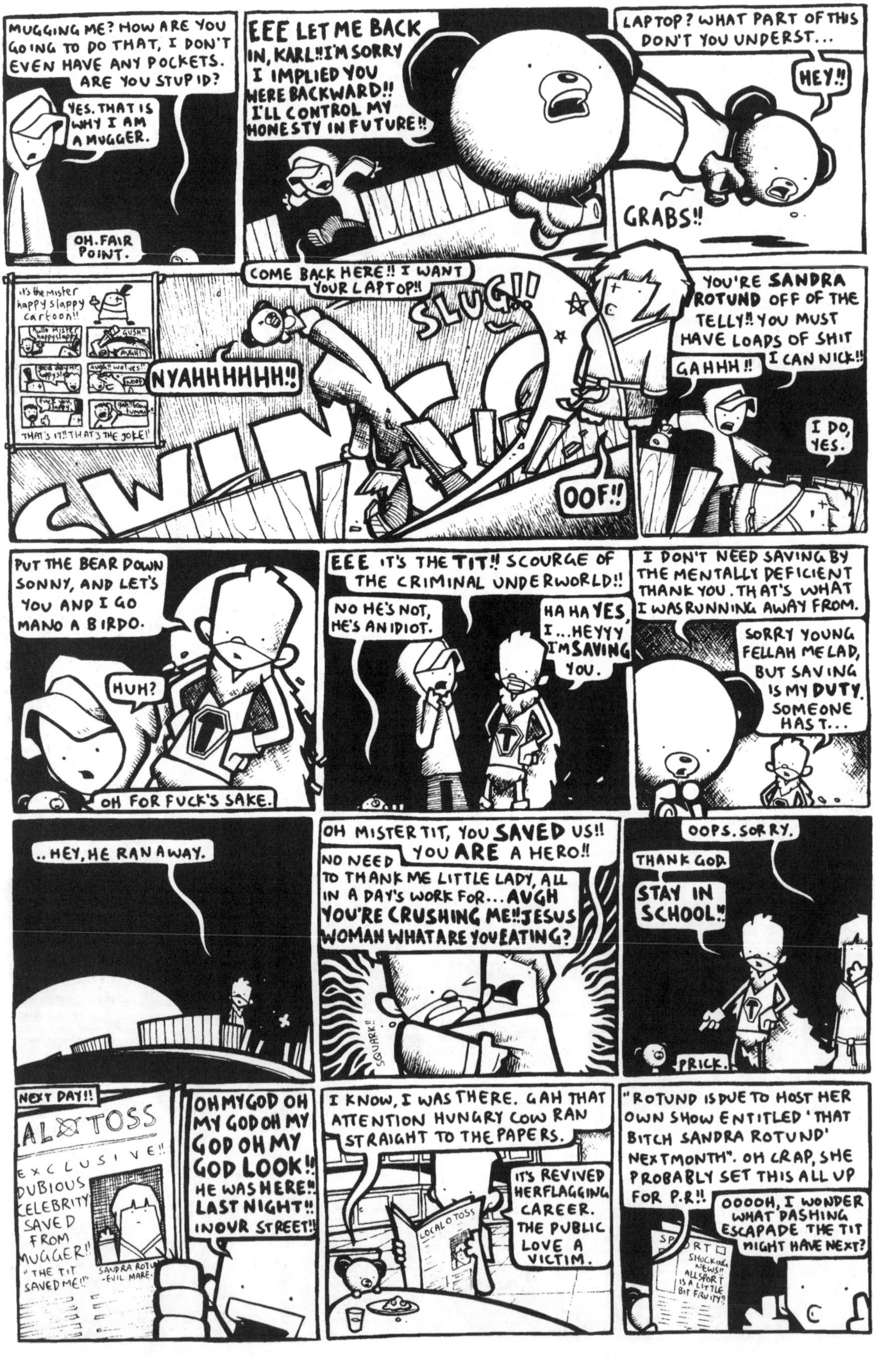
MUGGING ME? HOW ARE YOU GOING TO DO THAT, I DON'T EVEN HAVE ANY POCKETS. ARE YOU STUPID?
YES. THAT IS WHY I AM A MUGGER.
OH. FAIR POINT.
EEE LET ME BACK IN, KARL!! I'M SORRY I IMPLIED YOU WERE BACKWARD!! I'LL CONTROL MY HONESTY IN FUTURE!!
LAPTOP? WHAT PART OF THIS DON'T YOU UNDERST...
HEY!!
GRABS!!
it's the mister happy slappy cartoon!!
THAT'S IT!! THAT'S THE JOKE!
COME BACK HERE!! I WANT YOUR LAPTOP!!
SLUG!!
NYAHHHHHH!!
OOF!!
YOU'RE SANDRA ROTUND OFF OF THE TELLY!! YOU MUST HAVE LOADS OF SHIT I CAN NICK!!
GAHHH!!
I DO, YES.
PUT THE BEAR DOWN SONNY, AND LET'S YOU AND I GO MANO A BIRDO.
HUH?
OH FOR FUCK'S SAKE.
EEE IT'S THE TIT!! SCOURGE OF THE CRIMINAL UNDERWORLD!!
NO HE'S NOT, HE'S AN IDIOT.
HA HA YES, I...HEYYY I'M SAVING YOU.
I DON'T NEED SAVING BY THE MENTALLY DEFICIENT THANK YOU. THAT'S WHAT I WAS RUNNING AWAY FROM.
SORRY YOUNG FELLAH ME LAD, BUT SAVING IS MY DUTY. SOMEONE HAS T...
..HEY, HE RAN AWAY.
OH MISTER TIT, YOU SAVED US!! YOU ARE A HERO!!
NO NEED TO THANK ME LITTLE LADY, ALL IN A DAY'S WORK FOR... AUGH YOU'RE CRUSHING ME!! JESUS WOMAN WHAT ARE YOU EATING?
SQUARK!!
OOPS. SORRY.
THANK GOD.
STAY IN SCHOOL!!
PRICK.
NEXT DAY!!
AL TOSS
EXCLUSIVE!!
DUBIOUS CELEBRITY SAVED FROM MUGGER!!
"THE TIT SAVED ME!!"
SANDRA ROTU -EVIL MARE-
OH MY GOD OH MY GOD OH MY GOD OH MY GOD LOOK!! HE WAS HERE!! LAST NIGHT!! IN OUR STREET!!
I KNOW, I WAS THERE. GAH THAT ATTENTION HUNGRY COW RAN STRAIGHT TO THE PAPERS.
IT'S REVIVED HER FLAGGING CAREER. THE PUBLIC LOVE A VICTIM.
LOCAL TOSS
"ROTUND IS DUE TO HOST HER OWN SHOW ENTITLED 'THAT BITCH SANDRA ROTUND' NEXT MONTH". OH CRAP, SHE PROBABLY SET THIS ALL UP FOR P.R!!
OOOOH, I WONDER WHAT DASHING ESCAPADE THE TIT MIGHT HAVE NEXT?
SPORT
SHOCKING NEWS!! ALLSPORT IS A LITTLE BIT FRUITY!!

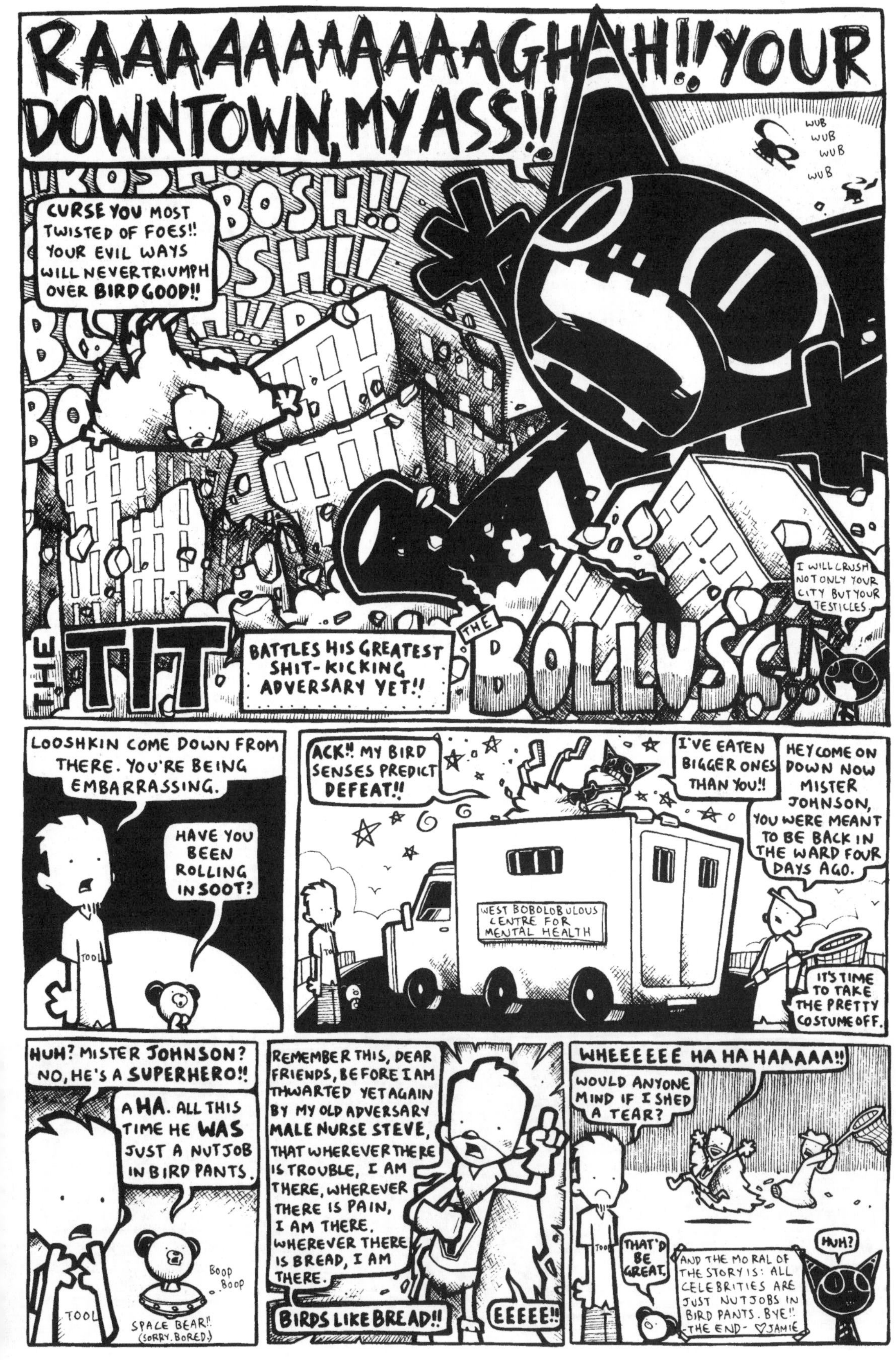
RAAAAAAAAAAAGHAH!! YOUR DOWNTOWN, MY ASS!!
WUB WUB WUB WUB
BOSH!! BOSH!! BOSH!!
CURSE YOU MOST TWISTED OF FOES!! YOUR EVIL WAYS WILL NEVER TRIUMPH OVER BIRD GOOD!!
I WILL CRUSH NOT ONLY YOUR CITY BUT YOUR TESTICLES.
THE TIT
BATTLES HIS GREATEST SHIT-KICKING ADVERSARY YET!!
THE BOLLUSC!!
LOOSHKIN COME DOWN FROM THERE. YOU'RE BEING EMBARRASSING.
HAVE YOU BEEN ROLLING IN SOOT?
TOOL
ACK!! MY BIRD SENSES PREDICT DEFEAT!!
I'VE EATEN BIGGER ONES THAN YOU!!
HEY COME ON DOWN NOW MISTER JOHNSON, YOU WERE MEANT TO BE BACK IN THE WARD FOUR DAYS AGO.
WEST BOBOLOBULOUS CENTRE FOR MENTAL HEALTH
IT'S TIME TO TAKE THE PRETTY COSTUME OFF.
HUH? MISTER JOHNSON? NO, HE'S A SUPERHERO!!
A HA. ALL THIS TIME HE WAS JUST A NUTJOB IN BIRD PANTS.
TOOL
BOOP BOOP
SPACE BEAR!! (SORRY. BORED.)
REMEMBER THIS, DEAR FRIENDS, BEFORE I AM THWARTED YET AGAIN BY MY OLD ADVERSARY MALE NURSE STEVE, THAT WHEREVER THERE IS TROUBLE, I AM THERE, WHEREVER THERE IS PAIN, I AM THERE. WHEREVER THERE IS BREAD, I AM THERE.
BIRDS LIKE BREAD!!
EEEEE!!
WHEEEEEE HA HA HAAAAA!!
WOULD ANYONE MIND IF I SHED A TEAR?
THAT'D BE GREAT.
AND THE MORAL OF THE STORY IS: ALL CELEBRITIES ARE JUST NUTJOBS IN BIRD PANTS. BYE!! -THE END- ♡JAMIE
HUH?

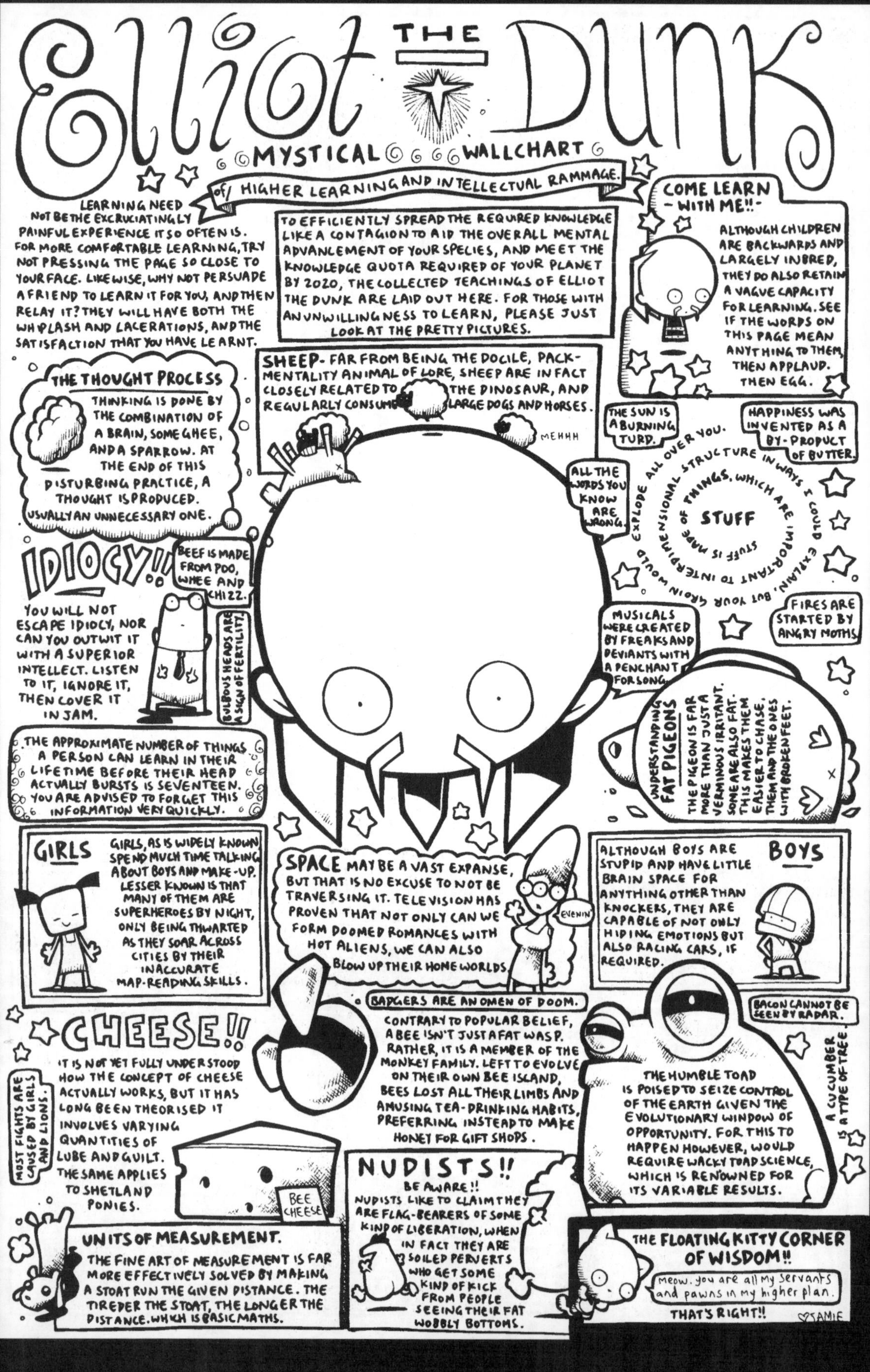

ELLIOT THE DUNK
MYSTICAL WALLCHART
OF HIGHER LEARNING AND INTELLECTUAL RAMMAGE.
LEARNING NEED NOT BE THE EXCRUCIATINGLY PAINFUL EXPERIENCE IT SO OFTEN IS. FOR MORE COMFORTABLE LEARNING, TRY NOT PRESSING THE PAGE SO CLOSE TO YOUR FACE. LIKEWISE, WHY NOT PERSUADE A FRIEND TO LEARN IT FOR YOU, AND THEN RELAY IT? THEY WILL HAVE BOTH THE WHIPLASH AND LACERATIONS, AND THE SATISFACTION THAT YOU HAVE LEARNT.
TO EFFICIENTLY SPREAD THE REQUIRED KNOWLEDGE LIKE A CONTAGION TO AID THE OVERALL MENTAL ADVANCEMENT OF YOUR SPECIES, AND MEET THE KNOWLEDGE QUOTA REQUIRED OF YOUR PLANET BY 2020, THE COLLECTED TEACHINGS OF ELLIOT THE DUNK ARE LAID OUT HERE. FOR THOSE WITH AN UNWILLINGNESS TO LEARN, PLEASE JUST LOOK AT THE PRETTY PICTURES.
COME LEARN - WITH ME!! -
ALTHOUGH CHILDREN ARE BACKWARDS AND LARGELY INBRED, THEY DO ALSO RETAIN A VAGUE CAPACITY FOR LEARNING. SEE IF THE WORDS ON THIS PAGE MEAN ANYTHING TO THEM, THEN APPLAUD. THEN EGG.
THE THOUGHT PROCESS
THINKING IS DONE BY THE COMBINATION OF A BRAIN, SOME GHEE, AND A SPARROW. AT THE END OF THIS DISTURBING PRACTICE, A THOUGHT IS PRODUCED. USUALLY AN UNNECESSARY ONE.
SHEEP - FAR FROM BEING THE DOCILE, PACK-MENTALITY ANIMAL OF LORE, SHEEP ARE IN FACT CLOSELY RELATED TO THE DINOSAUR, AND REGULARLY CONSUME LARGE DOGS AND HORSES.
MEHHH
THE SUN IS A BURNING TURD.
HAPPINESS WAS INVENTED AS A BY-PRODUCT OF BUTTER.
ALL THE WORDS YOU KNOW ARE WRONG.
STUFF
STUFF IS MADE OF THINGS, WHICH ARE IMPORTANT TO INTERDIMENSIONAL STRUCTURE IN WAYS I COULD EXPLAIN, BUT YOUR GROIN WOULD EXPLODE ALL OVER YOU.
IDIOCY!!
BEEF IS MADE FROM POO, WHEE AND CHIZZ.
YOU WILL NOT ESCAPE IDIOCY, NOR CAN YOU OUTWIT IT WITH A SUPERIOR INTELLECT. LISTEN TO IT, IGNORE IT, THEN COVER IT IN JAM.
BULBOUS HEADS ARE A SIGN OF FERTILITY.
MUSICALS WERE CREATED BY FREAKS AND DEVIANTS WITH A PENCHANT FOR SONG.
FIRES ARE STARTED BY ANGRY MOTHS.
UNDERSTANDING FAT PIGEONS
THE PIGEON IS FAR MORE THAN JUST A VERMINOUS IRRITANT. SOME ARE ALSO FAT. THIS MAKES THEM EASIER TO CHASE. THEM AND THE ONES WITH BROKEN FEET.
THE APPROXIMATE NUMBER OF THINGS A PERSON CAN LEARN IN THEIR LIFETIME BEFORE THEIR HEAD ACTUALLY BURSTS IS SEVENTEEN. YOU ARE ADVISED TO FORGET THIS INFORMATION VERY QUICKLY.
GIRLS
GIRLS, AS IS WIDELY KNOWN SPEND MUCH TIME TALKING ABOUT BOYS AND MAKE-UP. LESSER KNOWN IS THAT MANY OF THEM ARE SUPERHEROES BY NIGHT, ONLY BEING THWARTED AS THEY SOAR ACROSS CITIES BY THEIR INACCURATE MAP-READING SKILLS.
SPACE MAY BE A VAST EXPANSE, BUT THAT IS NO EXCUSE TO NOT BE TRAVERSING IT. TELEVISION HAS PROVEN THAT NOT ONLY CAN WE FORM DOOMED ROMANCES WITH HOT ALIENS, WE CAN ALSO BLOW UP THEIR HOME WORLDS.
EVENIN'
BOYS
ALTHOUGH BOYS ARE STUPID AND HAVE LITTLE BRAIN SPACE FOR ANYTHING OTHER THAN KNOCKERS, THEY ARE CAPABLE OF NOT ONLY HIDING EMOTIONS BUT ALSO RACING CARS, IF REQUIRED.
BADGERS ARE AN OMEN OF DOOM.
BACON CANNOT BE SEEN BY RADAR.
CHEESE!!
IT IS NOT YET FULLY UNDERSTOOD HOW THE CONCEPT OF CHEESE ACTUALLY WORKS, BUT IT HAS LONG BEEN THEORISED IT INVOLVES VARYING QUANTITIES OF LUBE AND GUILT. THE SAME APPLIES TO SHETLAND PONIES.
MOST FIGHTS ARE CAUSED BY GIRLS AND LIONS.
BEE CHEESE
CONTRARY TO POPULAR BELIEF, A BEE ISN'T JUST A FAT WASP. RATHER, IT IS A MEMBER OF THE MONKEY FAMILY. LEFT TO EVOLVE ON THEIR OWN BEE ISLAND, BEES LOST ALL THEIR LIMBS AND AMUSING TEA-DRINKING HABITS, PREFERRING INSTEAD TO MAKE HONEY FOR GIFT SHOPS.
A CUCUMBER IS A TYPE OF TREE.
THE HUMBLE TOAD IS POISED TO SEIZE CONTROL OF THE EARTH GIVEN THE EVOLUTIONARY WINDOW OF OPPORTUNITY. FOR THIS TO HAPPEN HOWEVER, WOULD REQUIRE WACKY TOAD SCIENCE, WHICH IS RENOWNED FOR ITS VARIABLE RESULTS.
NUDISTS!!
BE AWARE!!
NUDISTS LIKE TO CLAIM THEY ARE FLAG-BEARERS OF SOME KIND OF LIBERATION, WHEN IN FACT THEY ARE SOILED PERVERTS WHO GET SOME KIND OF KICK FROM PEOPLE SEEING THEIR FAT WOBBLY BOTTOMS.
UNITS OF MEASUREMENT.
THE FINE ART OF MEASUREMENT IS FAR MORE EFFECTIVELY SOLVED BY MAKING A STOAT RUN THE GIVEN DISTANCE. THE TIREDER THE STOAT, THE LONGER THE DISTANCE. WHICH IS BASIC MATHS.
THE FLOATING KITTY CORNER OF WISDOM!!
Meow. you are all my servants and pawns in my higher plan.
THAT'S RIGHT!!
JAMIE

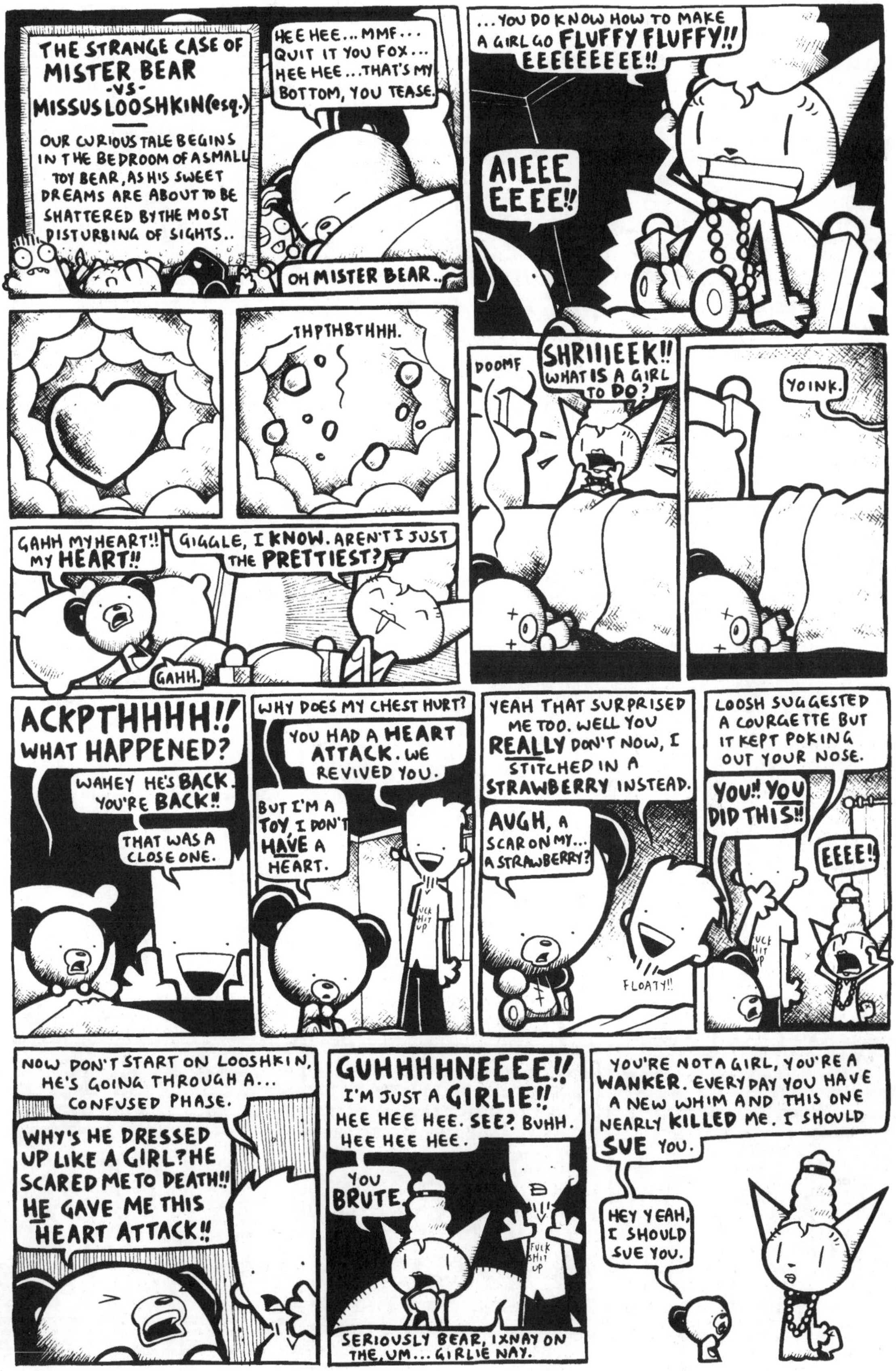
THE STRANGE CASE OF MISTER BEAR -VS- MISSUS LOOSHKIN (esq.)
OUR CURIOUS TALE BEGINS IN THE BEDROOM OF A SMALL TOY BEAR, AS HIS SWEET DREAMS ARE ABOUT TO BE SHATTERED BY THE MOST DISTURBING OF SIGHTS..
HEE HEE... MMF... QUIT IT YOU FOX... HEE HEE... THAT'S MY BOTTOM, YOU TEASE.
OH MISTER BEAR..
...YOU DO KNOW HOW TO MAKE A GIRL GO FLUFFY FLUFFY!! EEEEEEEEE!!
AIEEE EEEE!!
THPTHBTHHH.
DOOMF
SHRIIIEEK!! WHAT IS A GIRL TO DO?
YOINK.
GAHH MY HEART!! MY HEART!!
GIGGLE, I KNOW. AREN'T I JUST THE PRETTIEST?
GAHH.
ACKPTHHHH!! WHAT HAPPENED?
WAHEY HE'S BACK. YOU'RE BACK!!
THAT WAS A CLOSE ONE.
WHY DOES MY CHEST HURT?
YOU HAD A HEART ATTACK. WE REVIVED YOU.
BUT I'M A TOY, I DON'T HAVE A HEART.
YEAH THAT SURPRISED ME TOO. WELL YOU REALLY DON'T NOW, I STITCHED IN A STRAWBERRY INSTEAD.
AUGH, A SCAR ON MY... A STRAWBERRY?
FLOATY!!
LOOSH SUGGESTED A COURGETTE BUT IT KEPT POKING OUT YOUR NOSE.
YOU!! YOU DID THIS!!
EEEE!!
NOW DON'T START ON LOOSHKIN, HE'S GOING THROUGH A... CONFUSED PHASE.
WHY'S HE DRESSED UP LIKE A GIRL? HE SCARED ME TO DEATH!! HE GAVE ME THIS HEART ATTACK!!
GUHHHHNEEEE!! I'M JUST A GIRLIE!! HEE HEE HEE. SEE? BUHH. HEE HEE HEE.
YOU BRUTE.
SERIOUSLY BEAR, IXNAY ON THE, UM... GIRLIE NAY.
YOU'RE NOT A GIRL, YOU'RE A WANKER. EVERY DAY YOU HAVE A NEW WHIM AND THIS ONE NEARLY KILLED ME. I SHOULD SUE YOU.
HEY YEAH, I SHOULD SUE YOU.

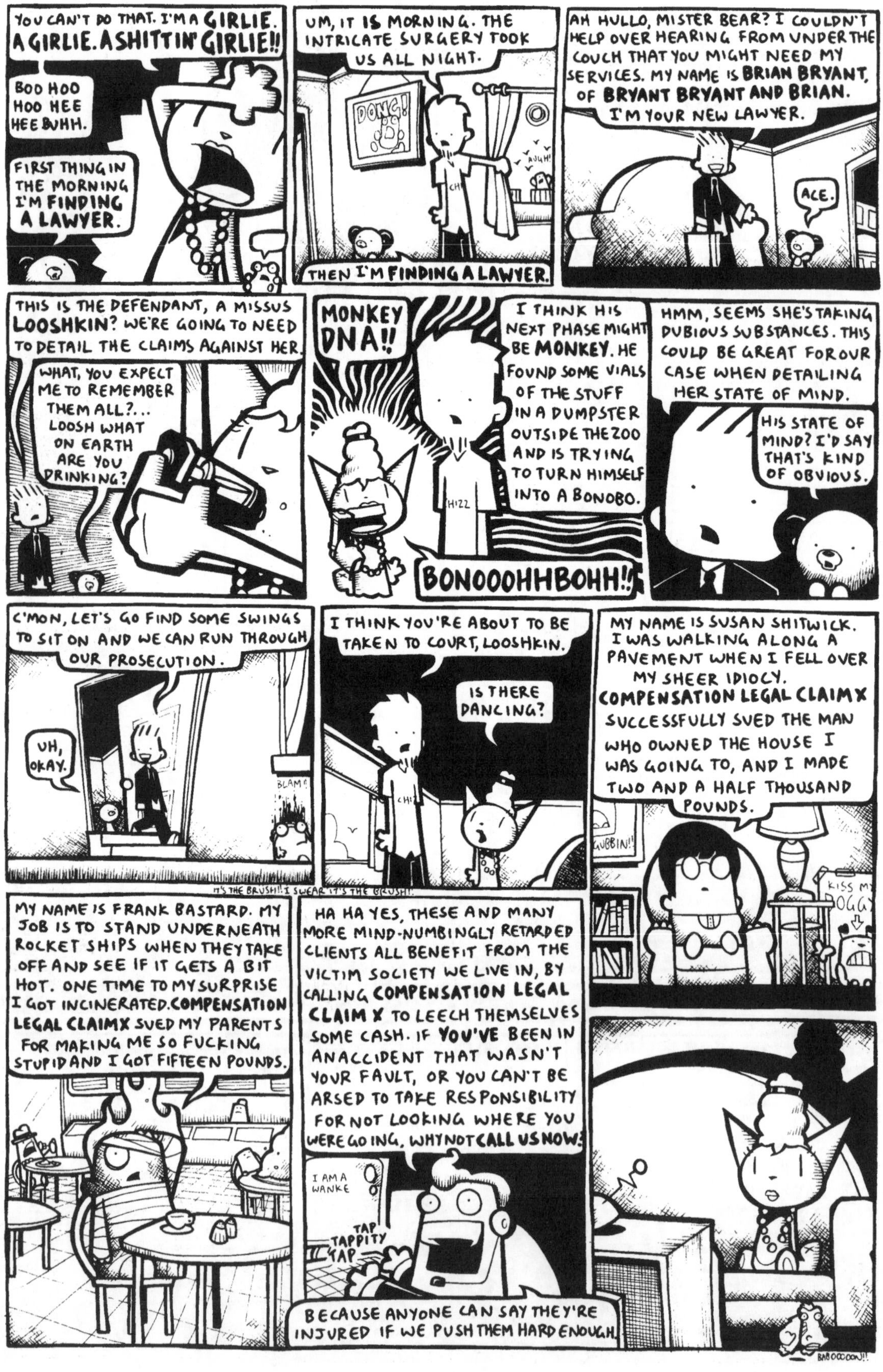

YOU CAN'T DO THAT. I'M A GIRLIE. A GIRLIE. A SHITTIN' GIRLIE!!
BOO HOO HOO HEE HEE BUHH.
FIRST THING IN THE MORNING I'M FINDING A LAWYER.
UM, IT IS MORNING. THE INTRICATE SURGERY TOOK US ALL NIGHT.
DONG!
AAUGH!
CHI
THEN I'M FINDING A LAWYER.
AH HULLO, MISTER BEAR? I COULDN'T HELP OVER HEARING FROM UNDER THE COUCH THAT YOU MIGHT NEED MY SERVICES. MY NAME IS BRIAN BRYANT, OF BRYANT BRYANT AND BRIAN. I'M YOUR NEW LAWYER.
ACE.
THIS IS THE DEFENDANT, A MISSUS LOOSHKIN? WE'RE GOING TO NEED TO DETAIL THE CLAIMS AGAINST HER.
WHAT, YOU EXPECT ME TO REMEMBER THEM ALL?... LOOSH WHAT ON EARTH ARE YOU DRINKING?
MONKEY DNA!!
I THINK HIS NEXT PHASE MIGHT BE MONKEY. HE FOUND SOME VIALS OF THE STUFF IN A DUMPSTER OUTSIDE THE ZOO AND IS TRYING TO TURN HIMSELF INTO A BONOBO.
HIZZ
BONOOOHHBOHH!!
HMM, SEEMS SHE'S TAKING DUBIOUS SUBSTANCES. THIS COULD BE GREAT FOR OUR CASE WHEN DETAILING HER STATE OF MIND.
HIS STATE OF MIND? I'D SAY THAT'S KIND OF OBVIOUS.
C'MON, LET'S GO FIND SOME SWINGS TO SIT ON AND WE CAN RUN THROUGH OUR PROSECUTION.
UH, OKAY.
BLAM!
IT'S THE BRUSH!! I SWEAR IT'S THE BRUSH!!
I THINK YOU'RE ABOUT TO BE TAKEN TO COURT, LOOSHKIN.
IS THERE DANCING?
CHI
MY NAME IS SUSAN SHITWICK. I WAS WALKING ALONG A PAVEMENT WHEN I FELL OVER MY SHEER IDIOCY. COMPENSATION LEGAL CLAIM X SUCCESSFULLY SUED THE MAN WHO OWNED THE HOUSE I WAS GOING TO, AND I MADE TWO AND A HALF THOUSAND POUNDS.
GUBBIN!!
KISS MY DOGGY
MY NAME IS FRANK BASTARD. MY JOB IS TO STAND UNDERNEATH ROCKET SHIPS WHEN THEY TAKE OFF AND SEE IF IT GETS A BIT HOT. ONE TIME TO MY SURPRISE I GOT INCINERATED. COMPENSATION LEGAL CLAIM X SUED MY PARENTS FOR MAKING ME SO FUCKING STUPID AND I GOT FIFTEEN POUNDS.
HA HA YES, THESE AND MANY MORE MIND-NUMBINGLY RETARDED CLIENTS ALL BENEFIT FROM THE VICTIM SOCIETY WE LIVE IN, BY CALLING COMPENSATION LEGAL CLAIM X TO LEECH THEMSELVES SOME CASH. IF YOU'VE BEEN IN AN ACCIDENT THAT WASN'T YOUR FAULT, OR YOU CAN'T BE ARSED TO TAKE RESPONSIBILITY FOR NOT LOOKING WHERE YOU WERE GOING, WHY NOT CALL US NOW!
I AM A WANKE
TAP TAPPITY TAP
BECAUSE ANYONE CAN SAY THEY'RE INJURED IF WE PUSH THEM HARD ENOUGH.
BABOOOOON!!

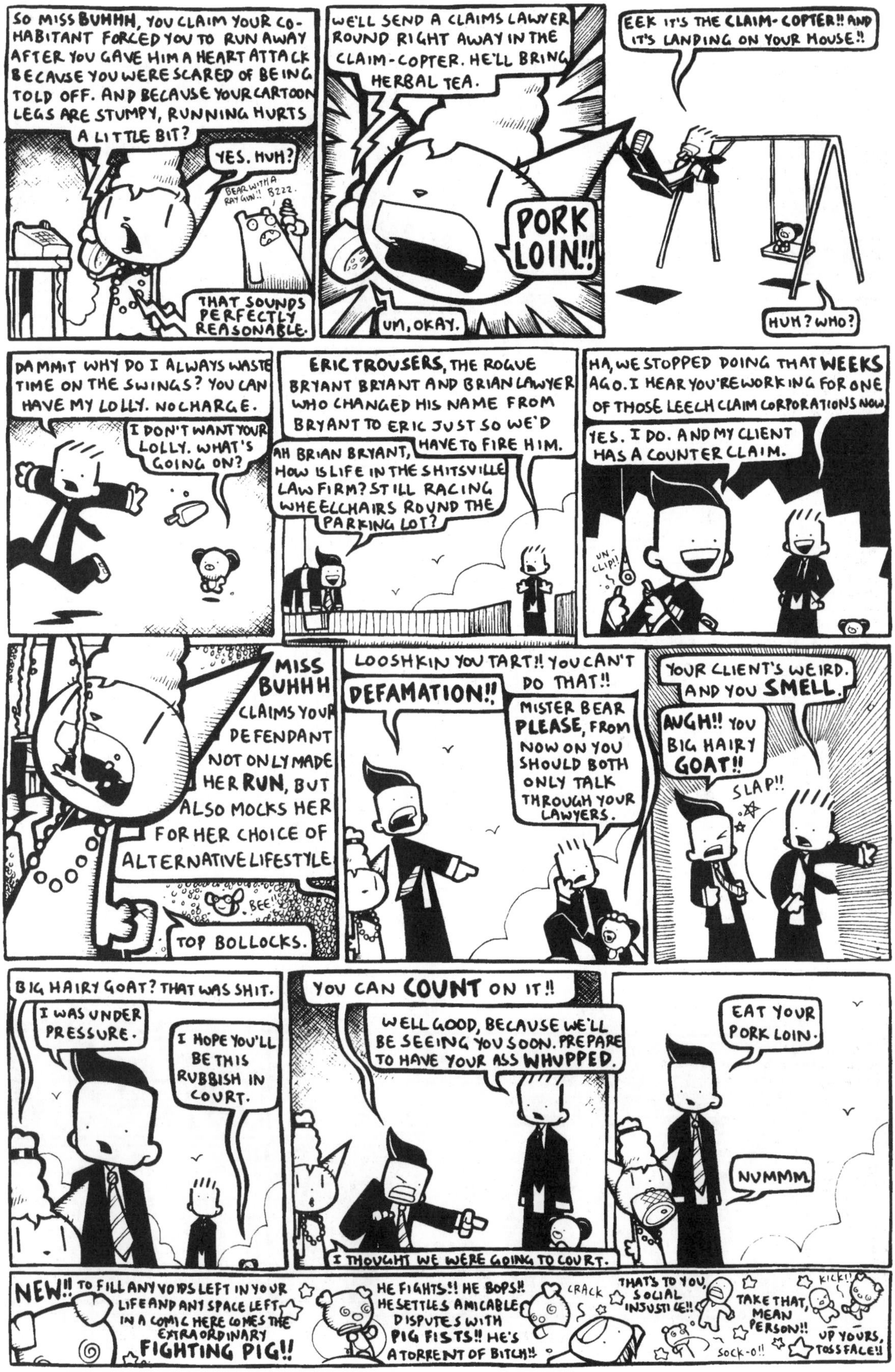

SO MISS BUHHH, YOU CLAIM YOUR CO-HABITANT FORCED YOU TO RUN AWAY AFTER YOU GAVE HIM A HEART ATTACK BECAUSE YOU WERE SCARED OF BEING TOLD OFF. AND BECAUSE YOUR CARTOON LEGS ARE STUMPY, RUNNING HURTS A LITTLE BIT?
YES. HUH?
BEAR WITH A RAY GUN!! BZZZ.
THAT SOUNDS PERFECTLY REASONABLE.
WE'LL SEND A CLAIMS LAWYER ROUND RIGHT AWAY IN THE CLAIM-COPTER. HE'LL BRING HERBAL TEA.
PORK LOIN!!
UM, OKAY.
EEK IT'S THE CLAIM-COPTER!! AND IT'S LANDING ON YOUR HOUSE!!
HUH? WHO?
DAMMIT WHY DO I ALWAYS WASTE TIME ON THE SWINGS? YOU CAN HAVE MY LOLLY. NO CHARGE.
I DON'T WANT YOUR LOLLY. WHAT'S GOING ON?
ERIC TROUSERS, THE ROGUE BRYANT BRYANT AND BRIAN LAWYER WHO CHANGED HIS NAME FROM BRYANT TO ERIC JUST SO WE'D HAVE TO FIRE HIM.
AH BRIAN BRYANT, HOW IS LIFE IN THE SHITSVILLE LAW FIRM? STILL RACING WHEELCHAIRS ROUND THE PARKING LOT?
HA, WE STOPPED DOING THAT WEEKS AGO. I HEAR YOU'RE WORKING FOR ONE OF THOSE LEECH CLAIM CORPORATIONS NOW.
YES. I DO. AND MY CLIENT HAS A COUNTER CLAIM.
UN-CLIP!!
MISS BUHHH CLAIMS YOUR DEFENDANT NOT ONLY MADE HER RUN, BUT ALSO MOCKS HER FOR HER CHOICE OF ALTERNATIVE LIFESTYLE.
BEE!!
TOP BOLLOCKS.
LOOSHKIN YOU TART!! YOU CAN'T DO THAT!!
DEFAMATION!!
MISTER BEAR PLEASE, FROM NOW ON YOU SHOULD BOTH ONLY TALK THROUGH YOUR LAWYERS.
YOUR CLIENT'S WEIRD. AND YOU SMELL.
AUGH!! YOU BIG HAIRY GOAT!!
SLAP!!
BIG HAIRY GOAT? THAT WAS SHIT.
I WAS UNDER PRESSURE.
I HOPE YOU'LL BE THIS RUBBISH IN COURT.
YOU CAN COUNT ON IT!!
WELL GOOD, BECAUSE WE'LL BE SEEING YOU SOON. PREPARE TO HAVE YOUR ASS WHUPPED.
I THOUGHT WE WERE GOING TO COURT.
EAT YOUR PORK LOIN.
NUMMM.
NEW!! TO FILL ANY VOIDS LEFT IN YOUR LIFE AND ANY SPACE LEFT IN A COMIC HERE COMES THE EXTRAORDINARY FIGHTING PIG!!
HE FIGHTS!! HE BOPS!! HE SETTLES AMICABLE DISPUTES WITH PIG FISTS!! HE'S A TORRENT OF BITCH!!
CRACK
THAT'S TO YOU, SOCIAL INJUSTICE!!
TAKE THAT, MEAN PERSON!!
KICK!!
SOCK-O!!
UP YOURS, TOSSFACE!!

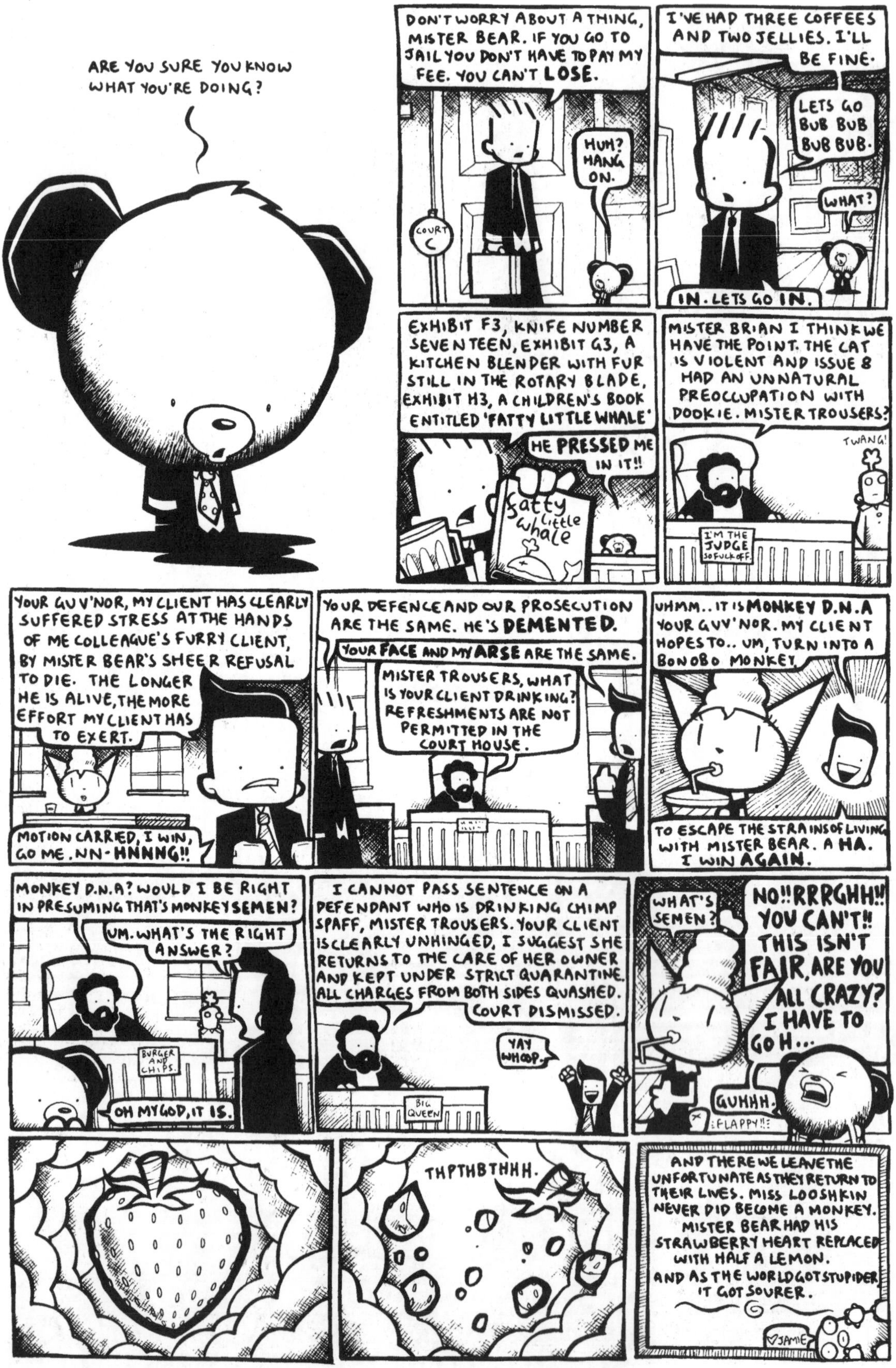
ARE YOU SURE YOU KNOW WHAT YOU'RE DOING?
DON'T WORRY ABOUT A THING, MISTER BEAR. IF YOU GO TO JAIL YOU DON'T HAVE TO PAY MY FEE. YOU CAN'T LOSE.
HUH? HANG ON.
COURT C
I'VE HAD THREE COFFEES AND TWO JELLIES. I'LL BE FINE.
LETS GO BUB BUB BUB BUB.
WHAT?
IN. LETS GO IN.
EXHIBIT F3, KNIFE NUMBER SEVENTEEN, EXHIBIT G3, A KITCHEN BLENDER WITH FUR STILL IN THE ROTARY BLADE, EXHIBIT H3, A CHILDREN'S BOOK ENTITLED 'FATTY LITTLE WHALE'
HE PRESSED ME IN IT!!
fatty little whale
MISTER BRIAN I THINK WE HAVE THE POINT. THE CAT IS VIOLENT AND ISSUE 8 HAD AN UNNATURAL PREOCCUPATION WITH DOOKIE. MISTER TROUSERS?
TWANG!
I'M THE JUDGE SO FUCK OFF.
YOUR GUV'NOR, MY CLIENT HAS CLEARLY SUFFERED STRESS AT THE HANDS OF ME COLLEAGUE'S FURRY CLIENT, BY MISTER BEAR'S SHEER REFUSAL TO DIE. THE LONGER HE IS ALIVE, THE MORE EFFORT MY CLIENT HAS TO EXERT.
MOTION CARRIED, I WIN, GO ME. NN-HNNNG!!
YOUR DEFENCE AND OUR PROSECUTION ARE THE SAME. HE'S DEMENTED.
YOUR FACE AND MY ARSE ARE THE SAME.
MISTER TROUSERS, WHAT IS YOUR CLIENT DRINKING? REFRESHMENTS ARE NOT PERMITTED IN THE COURT HOUSE.
UHMM.. IT IS MONKEY D.N.A YOUR GUV'NOR. MY CLIENT HOPES TO.. UM, TURN INTO A BONOBO MONKEY,
TO ESCAPE THE STRAINS OF LIVING WITH MISTER BEAR. A HA. I WIN AGAIN.
MONKEY D.N.A? WOULD I BE RIGHT IN PRESUMING THAT'S MONKEY SEMEN?
UM. WHAT'S THE RIGHT ANSWER?
BURGER AND CHIPS.
OH MY GOD, IT IS.
I CANNOT PASS SENTENCE ON A DEFENDANT WHO IS DRINKING CHIMP SPAFF, MISTER TROUSERS. YOUR CLIENT IS CLEARLY UNHINGED, I SUGGEST SHE RETURNS TO THE CARE OF HER OWNER AND KEPT UNDER STRICT QUARANTINE. ALL CHARGES FROM BOTH SIDES QUASHED. COURT DISMISSED.
YAY WHOOP.
BIG QUEEN
WHAT'S SEMEN?
NO!! RRRGHH!! YOU CAN'T!! THIS ISN'T FAIR, ARE YOU ALL CRAZY? I HAVE TO GO H...
GUHHH.
FLAPPY!!
THPTHBTHHH.
AND THERE WE LEAVE THE UNFORTUNATE AS THEY RETURN TO THEIR LIVES. MISS LOOSHKIN NEVER DID BECOME A MONKEY. MISTER BEAR HAD HIS STRAWBERRY HEART REPLACED WITH HALF A LEMON.
AND AS THE WORLD GOT STUPIDER IT GOT SOURER.
JAMIE

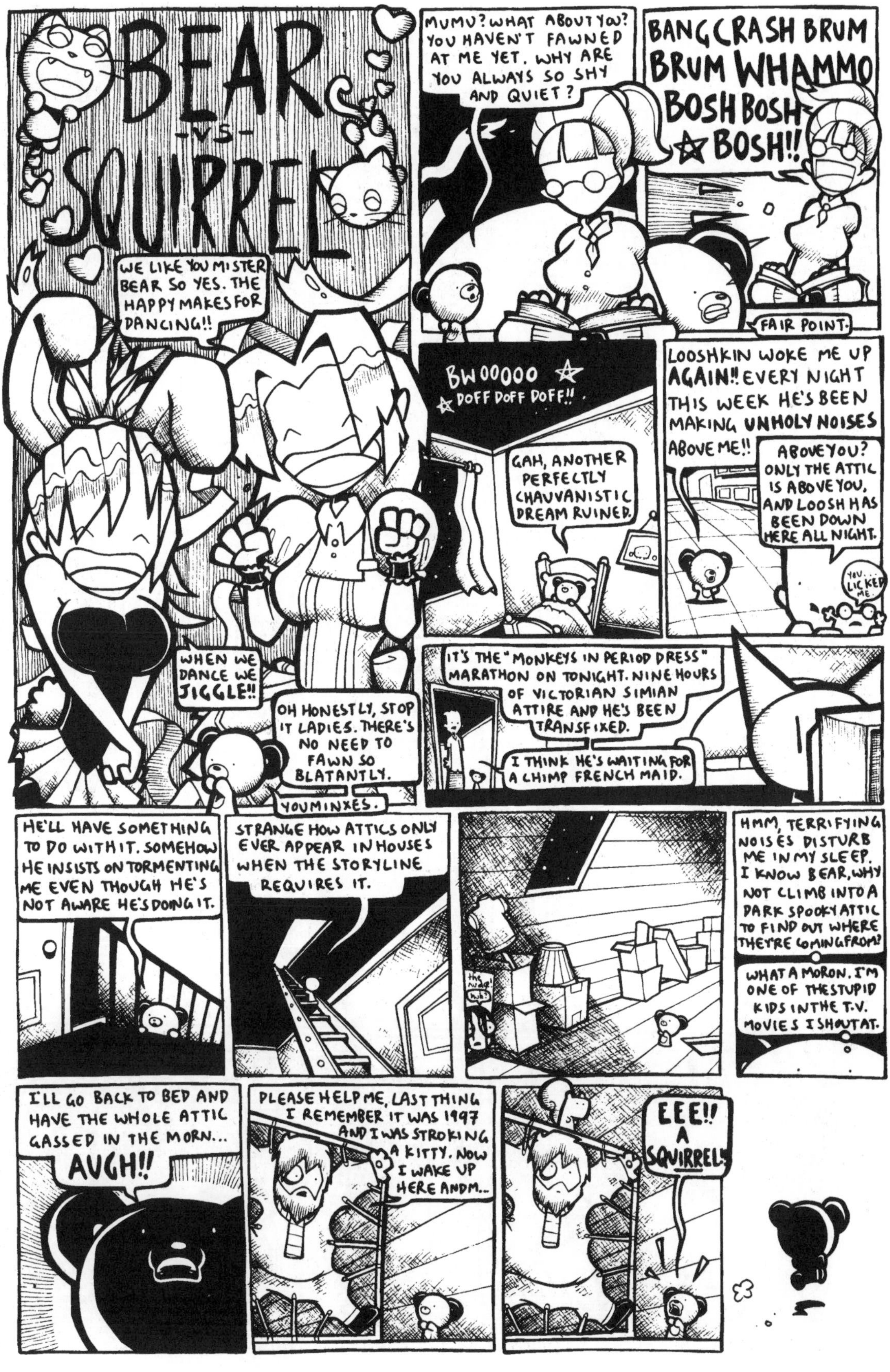
BEAR -VS- SQUIRREL
WE LIKE YOU MISTER BEAR SO YES. THE HAPPY MAKES FOR DANCING!!
WHEN WE DANCE WE JIGGLE!!
OH HONESTLY, STOP IT LADIES. THERE'S NO NEED TO FAWN SO BLATANTLY.
YOU MINXES.
MUMU? WHAT ABOUT YOU? YOU HAVEN'T FAWNED AT ME YET. WHY ARE YOU ALWAYS SO SHY AND QUIET?
BANG CRASH BRUM BRUM WHAMMO BOSH BOSH BOSH!!
FAIR POINT.
BWOOOOO DOFF DOFF DOFF!!
GAH, ANOTHER PERFECTLY CHAUVANISTIC DREAM RUINED.
LOOSHKIN WOKE ME UP AGAIN!! EVERY NIGHT THIS WEEK HE'S BEEN MAKING UNHOLY NOISES ABOVE ME!!
ABOVE YOU? ONLY THE ATTIC IS ABOVE YOU, AND LOOSH HAS BEEN DOWN HERE ALL NIGHT.
YOU... LICKED ME.
IT'S THE "MONKEYS IN PERIOD DRESS" MARATHON ON TONIGHT. NINE HOURS OF VICTORIAN SIMIAN ATTIRE AND HE'S BEEN TRANSFIXED.
I THINK HE'S WAITING FOR A CHIMP FRENCH MAID.
HE'LL HAVE SOMETHING TO DO WITH IT. SOMEHOW HE INSISTS ON TORMENTING ME EVEN THOUGH HE'S NOT AWARE HE'S DOING IT.
STRANGE HOW ATTICS ONLY EVER APPEAR IN HOUSES WHEN THE STORYLINE REQUIRES IT.
the nudge!
huh?
HMM, TERRIFYING NOISES DISTURB ME IN MY SLEEP. I KNOW BEAR, WHY NOT CLIMB INTO A DARK SPOOKY ATTIC TO FIND OUT WHERE THEY'RE COMING FROM?
WHAT A MORON. I'M ONE OF THE STUPID KIDS IN THE T.V. MOVIES I SHOUT AT.
I'LL GO BACK TO BED AND HAVE THE WHOLE ATTIC GASSED IN THE MORN...
AUGH!!
PLEASE HELP ME, LAST THING I REMEMBER IT WAS 1997 AND I WAS STROKING A KITTY. NOW I WAKE UP HERE AND M...
EEE!! A SQUIRREL!!

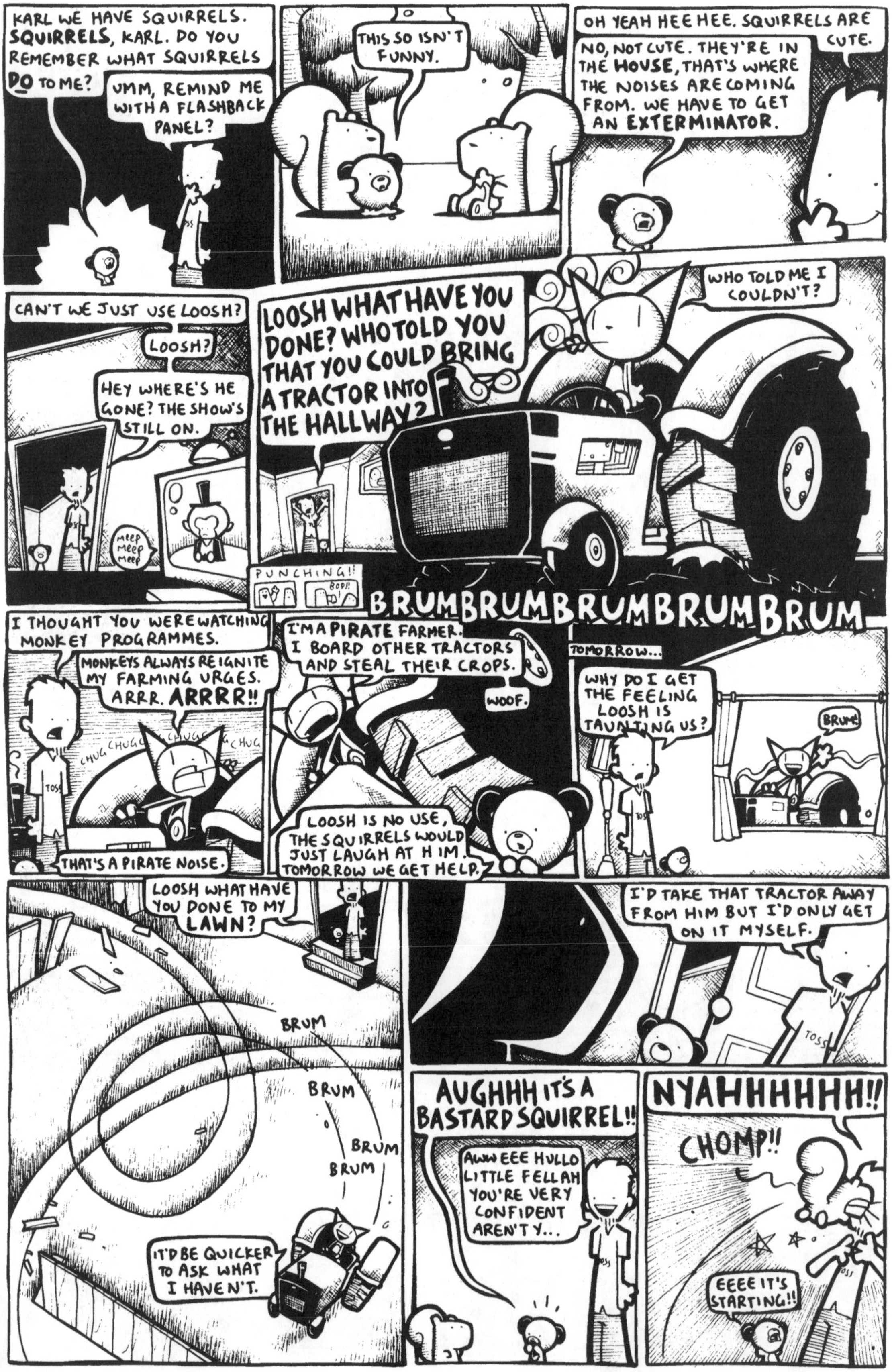
KARL WE HAVE SQUIRRELS. SQUIRRELS, KARL. DO YOU REMEMBER WHAT SQUIRRELS DO TO ME?
UMM, REMIND ME WITH A FLASHBACK PANEL?
THIS SO ISN'T FUNNY.
OH YEAH HEE HEE. SQUIRRELS ARE CUTE.
NO, NOT CUTE. THEY'RE IN THE HOUSE, THAT'S WHERE THE NOISES ARE COMING FROM. WE HAVE TO GET AN EXTERMINATOR.
CAN'T WE JUST USE LOOSH?
LOOSH?
HEY WHERE'S HE GONE? THE SHOW'S STILL ON.
MEEP MEEP MEEP
LOOSH WHAT HAVE YOU DONE? WHO TOLD YOU THAT YOU COULD BRING A TRACTOR INTO THE HALLWAY?
WHO TOLD ME I COULDN'T?
PUNCHING!!
BOP!!
BRUMBRUMBRUMBRUMBRUM
I THOUGHT YOU WERE WATCHING MONKEY PROGRAMMES.
MONKEYS ALWAYS REIGNITE MY FARMING URGES. ARRR. ARRRR!!
CHUG CHUG CHUG CHUG CHUG
THAT'S A PIRATE NOISE.
I'M A PIRATE FARMER. I BOARD OTHER TRACTORS AND STEAL THEIR CROPS.
WOOF.
LOOSH IS NO USE, THE SQUIRRELS WOULD JUST LAUGH AT HIM. TOMORROW WE GET HELP.
TOMORROW...
WHY DO I GET THE FEELING LOOSH IS TAUNTING US?
BRUM!
LOOSH WHAT HAVE YOU DONE TO MY LAWN?
BRUM
BRUM
BRUM
BRUM
IT'D BE QUICKER TO ASK WHAT I HAVEN'T.
I'D TAKE THAT TRACTOR AWAY FROM HIM BUT I'D ONLY GET ON IT MYSELF.
AUGHHH IT'S A BASTARD SQUIRREL!!
AWW EEE HULLO LITTLE FELLAH YOU'RE VERY CONFIDENT AREN'T Y...
NYAHHHHHH!!
CHOMP!!
EEEE IT'S STARTING!!

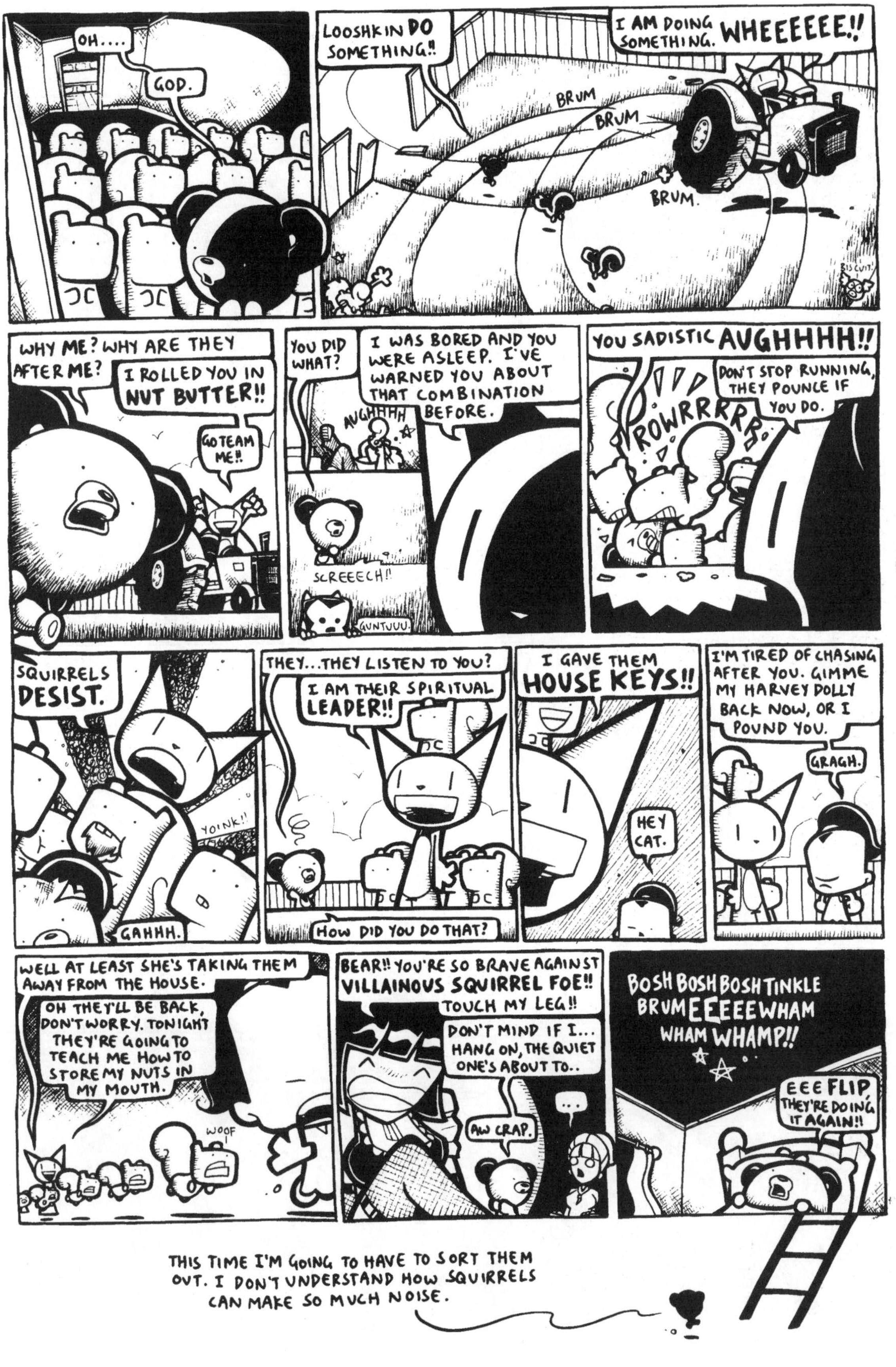
OH....
GOD.
LOOSHKIN DO SOMETHING!!
I AM DOING SOMETHING. WHEEEEEE!!
BRUM
BRUM
BRUM.
BISCUIT!
WHY ME? WHY ARE THEY AFTER ME?
I ROLLED YOU IN NUT BUTTER!!
GO TEAM ME!!
YOU DID WHAT?
I WAS BORED AND YOU WERE ASLEEP. I'VE WARNED YOU ABOUT THAT COMBINATION BEFORE.
AUGHHHH
SCREEECH!!
GUNTUUU.
YOU SADISTIC AUGHHHH!!
DON'T STOP RUNNING, THEY POUNCE IF YOU DO.
ROWRRRRRR.
SQUIRRELS DESIST.
YOINK!!
GAHHH.
THEY...THEY LISTEN TO YOU?
I AM THEIR SPIRITUAL LEADER!!
HOW DID YOU DO THAT?
I GAVE THEM HOUSE KEYS!!
HEY CAT.
I'M TIRED OF CHASING AFTER YOU. GIMME MY HARVEY DOLLY BACK NOW, OR I POUND YOU.
GRAGH.
WELL AT LEAST SHE'S TAKING THEM AWAY FROM THE HOUSE.
OH THEY'LL BE BACK, DON'T WORRY. TONIGHT THEY'RE GOING TO TEACH ME HOW TO STORE MY NUTS IN MY MOUTH.
WOOF!
BEAR!! YOU'RE SO BRAVE AGAINST VILLAINOUS SQUIRREL FOE!! TOUCH MY LEG!!
DON'T MIND IF I... HANG ON, THE QUIET ONE'S ABOUT TO..
AW CRAP.
...
BOSH BOSH BOSH TINKLE BRUM EEEEE WHAM WHAM WHAMP!!
EEE FLIP, THEY'RE DOING IT AGAIN!!
THIS TIME I'M GOING TO HAVE TO SORT THEM OUT. I DON'T UNDERSTAND HOW SQUIRRELS CAN MAKE SO MUCH NOISE.

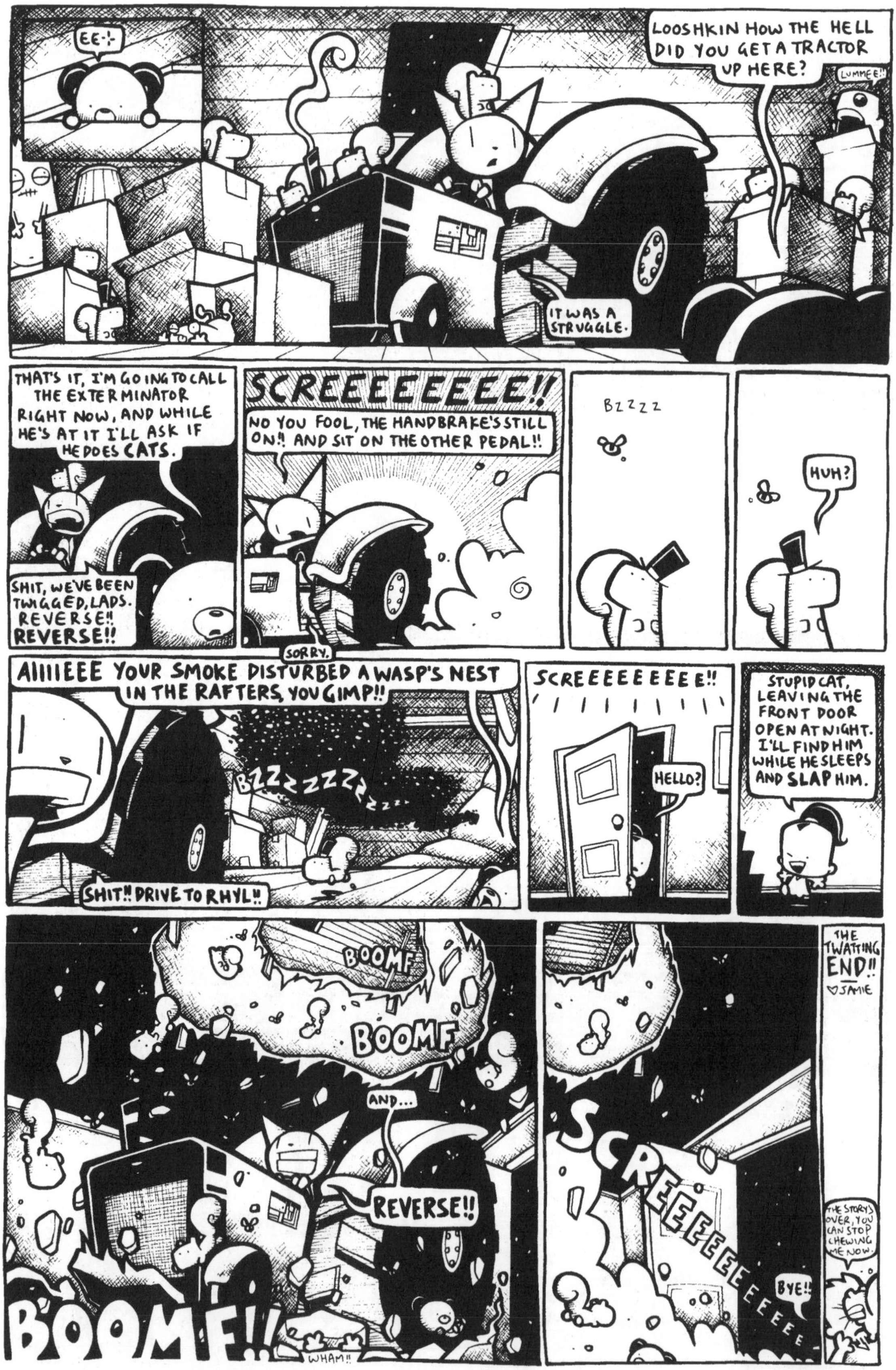
EE-!-
LOOSHKIN HOW THE HELL DID YOU GET A TRACTOR UP HERE?
LUMMEE!!
IT WAS A STRUGGLE.
THAT'S IT, I'M GOING TO CALL THE EXTERMINATOR RIGHT NOW, AND WHILE HE'S AT IT I'LL ASK IF HE DOES CATS.
SHIT, WE'VE BEEN TWIGGED, LADS. REVERSE!! REVERSE!!
SCREEEEEEEEEE!!
NO YOU FOOL, THE HANDBRAKE'S STILL ON!! AND SIT ON THE OTHER PEDAL!!
BZZZZ
HUH?
SORRY.
AIIIIEEE YOUR SMOKE DISTURBED A WASP'S NEST IN THE RAFTERS, YOU GIMP!!
BZZZZZZZZZ...
SHIT!! DRIVE TO RHYL!!
SCREEEEEEEEEE!!
HELLO?
STUPID CAT, LEAVING THE FRONT DOOR OPEN AT NIGHT. I'LL FIND HIM WHILE HE SLEEPS AND SLAP HIM.
BOOMF
BOOMF
AND...
REVERSE!!
BOOMF!!
WHAM!!
SCREEEEEEEEEEEEE
BYE!!
THE TWATTING END!!
♡ JAMIE
THE STORY'S OVER, YOU CAN STOP CHEWING ME NOW.

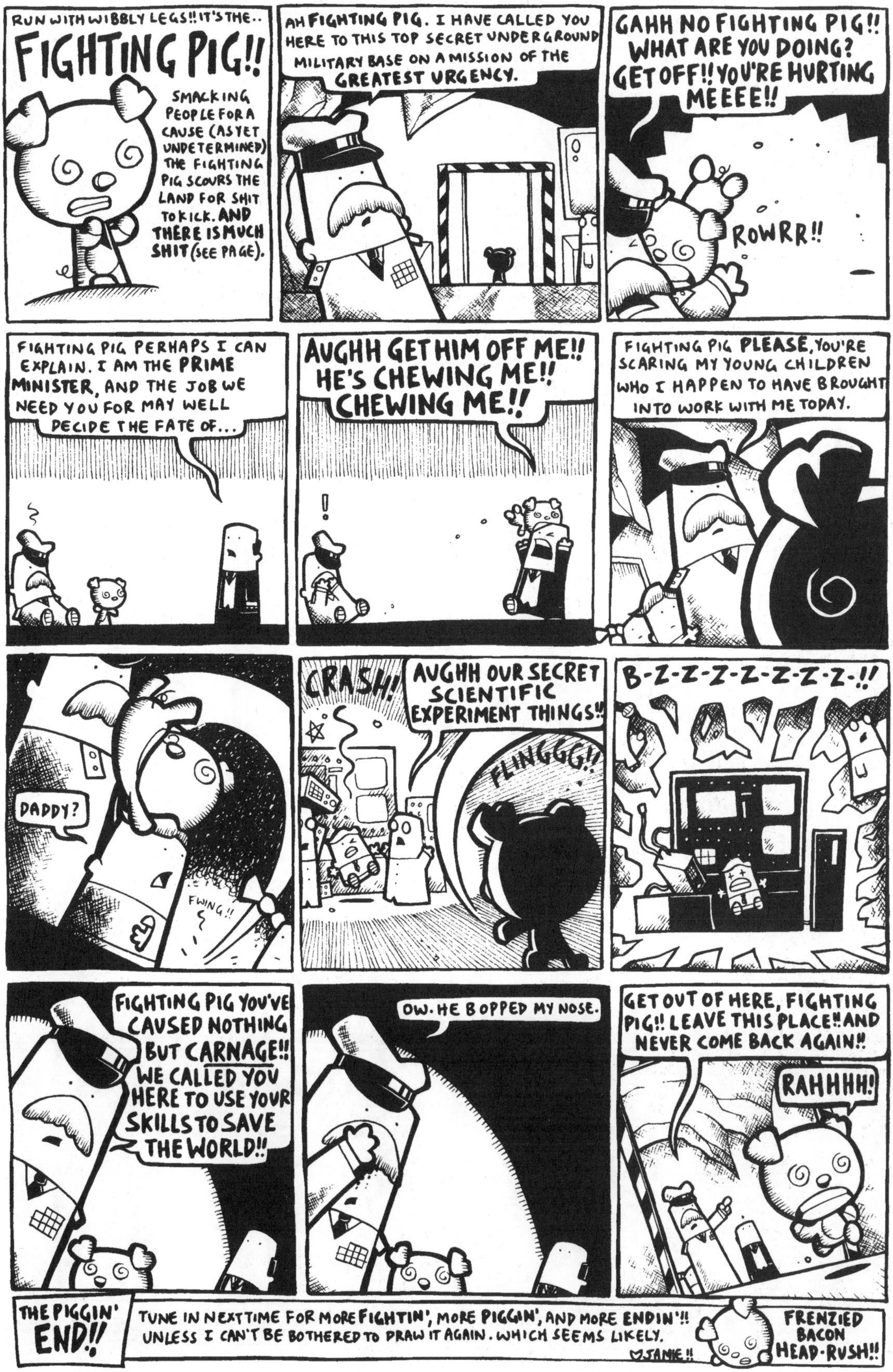
RUN WITH WIBBLY LEGS!! IT'S THE..
FIGHTING PIG!!
SMACKING PEOPLE FOR A CAUSE (AS YET UNDETERMINED) THE FIGHTING PIG SCOURS THE LAND FOR SHIT TO KICK. AND THERE IS MUCH SHIT (SEE PAGE).
AH FIGHTING PIG. I HAVE CALLED YOU HERE TO THIS TOP SECRET UNDERGROUND MILITARY BASE ON A MISSION OF THE GREATEST URGENCY.
GAHH NO FIGHTING PIG!! WHAT ARE YOU DOING? GET OFF!! YOU'RE HURTING MEEEE!!
ROWRR!!
FIGHTING PIG PERHAPS I CAN EXPLAIN. I AM THE PRIME MINISTER, AND THE JOB WE NEED YOU FOR MAY WELL DECIDE THE FATE OF...
AUGHH GET HIM OFF ME!! HE'S CHEWING ME!! CHEWING ME!!
FIGHTING PIG PLEASE, YOU'RE SCARING MY YOUNG CHILDREN WHO I HAPPEN TO HAVE BROUGHT INTO WORK WITH ME TODAY.
DADDY?
FWING!!
CRASH!
AUGHH OUR SECRET SCIENTIFIC EXPERIMENT THINGS!!
FLINGGG!!
B-Z-Z-Z-Z-Z-Z-Z-!!
FIGHTING PIG YOU'VE CAUSED NOTHING BUT CARNAGE!! WE CALLED YOU HERE TO USE YOUR SKILLS TO SAVE THE WORLD!!
OW. HE BOPPED MY NOSE.
GET OUT OF HERE, FIGHTING PIG!! LEAVE THIS PLACE!! AND NEVER COME BACK AGAIN!!
RAHHHH!
THE PIGGIN' END!!
TUNE IN NEXT TIME FOR MORE FIGHTIN', MORE PIGGIN', AND MORE ENDIN'!! UNLESS I CAN'T BE BOTHERED TO DRAW IT AGAIN. WHICH SEEMS LIKELY.
♡JAMIE!!
FRENZIED BACON HEAD-RUSH!!

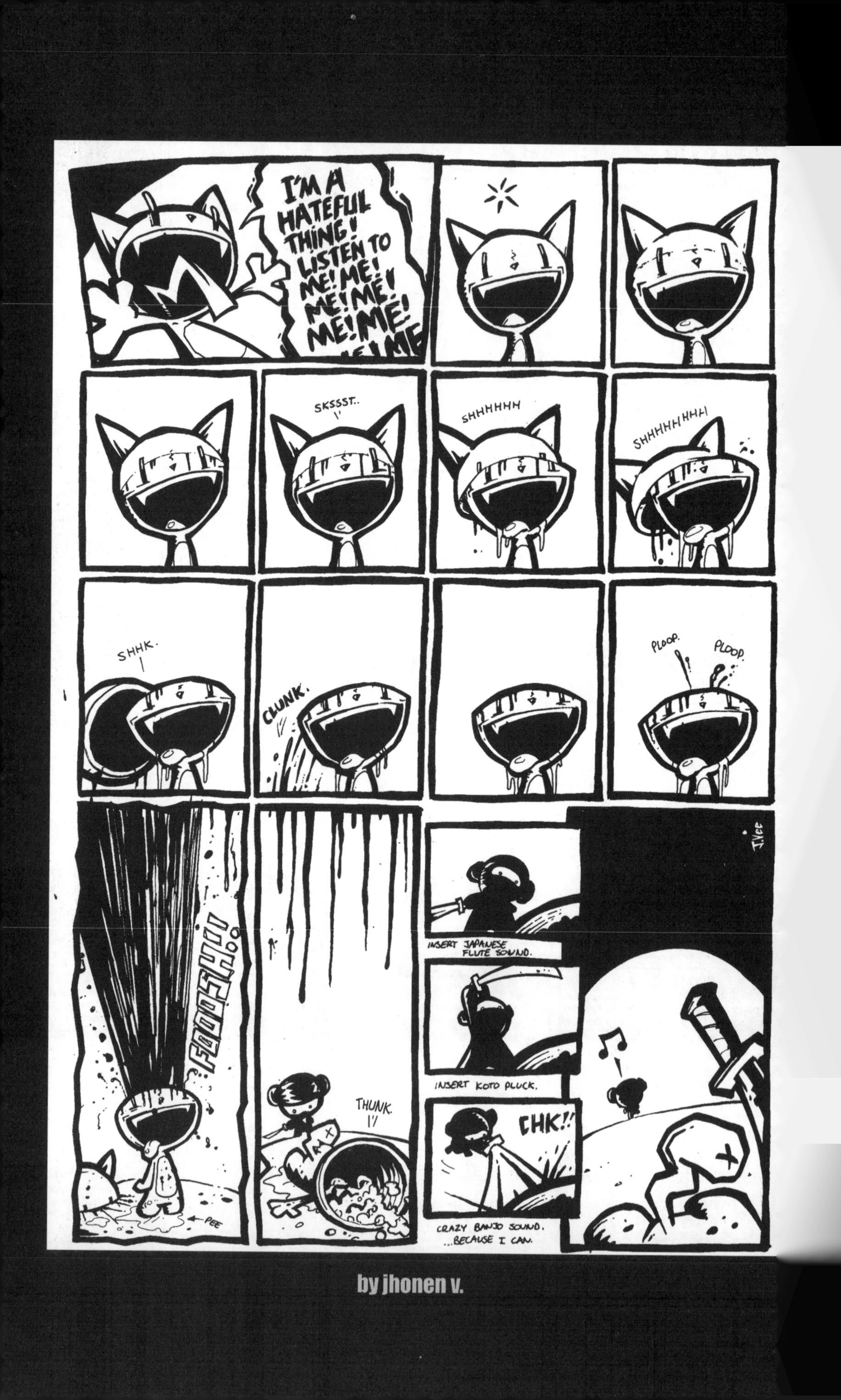
I'M A HATEFUL THING! LISTEN TO ME! ME! ME! ME! ME! ME! ME
SKSSST..
SHHHHHH
SHHHHHHHH
SHHK.
CLUNK.
PLOOP.
PLOOP.
FOOOSHH!!
PEE
THUNK.
INSERT JAPANESE FLUTE SOUND.
INSERT KOTO PLUCK.
CHK!!
CRAZY BANJO SOUND. ...BECAUSE I CAN.

by jhonen v.

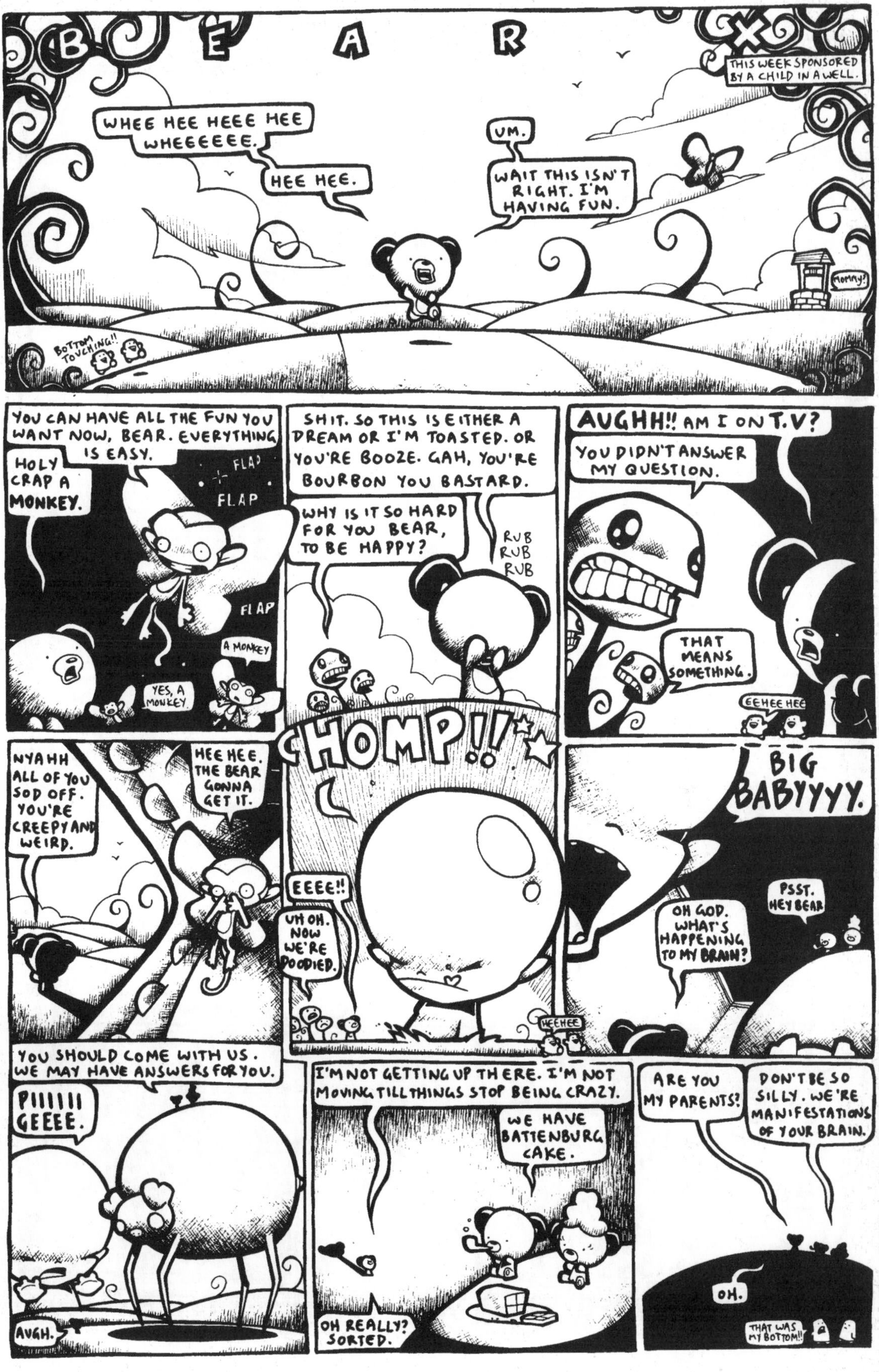
B E A R X
THIS WEEK SPONSORED BY A CHILD IN A WELL.
WHEE HEE HEEE HEE WHEEEEEE.
HEE HEE.
UM.
WAIT THIS ISN'T RIGHT. I'M HAVING FUN.
MOMMY!
BOTTOM TOUCHING!!
YOU CAN HAVE ALL THE FUN YOU WANT NOW, BEAR. EVERYTHING IS EASY.
HOLY CRAP A MONKEY.
FLAP
FLAP
FLAP
A MONKEY
YES, A MONKEY.
SHIT. SO THIS IS EITHER A DREAM OR I'M TOASTED. OR YOU'RE BOOZE. GAH, YOU'RE BOURBON YOU BASTARD.
WHY IS IT SO HARD FOR YOU BEAR, TO BE HAPPY?
RUB RUB RUB
AUGHH!! AM I ON T.V?
YOU DIDN'T ANSWER MY QUESTION.
THAT MEANS SOMETHING.
EEHEE HEE
NYAHH ALL OF YOU SOD OFF. YOU'RE CREEPY AND WEIRD.
HEE HEE. THE BEAR GONNA GET IT.
CHOMP!!
EEEE!!
UH OH. NOW WE'RE DOODIED.
HEEHEE
BIG BABYYYY.
PSST. HEY BEAR
OH GOD. WHAT'S HAPPENING TO MY BRAIN?
YOU SHOULD COME WITH US. WE MAY HAVE ANSWERS FOR YOU.
PIIIIII GEEEE.
AUGH.
I'M NOT GETTING UP THERE. I'M NOT MOVING TILL THINGS STOP BEING CRAZY.
WE HAVE BATTENBURG CAKE.
OH REALLY? SORTED.
ARE YOU MY PARENTS?
DON'T BE SO SILLY. WE'RE MANIFESTATIONS OF YOUR BRAIN.
OH.
THAT WAS MY BOTTOM!!

BEAR?

HEY, BEAR?

IT'S NO USE, HE'S NOT MOVING.

POKE HIM WITH SOMETHING.

GAH!! BEE!!

HEY BEAR, YOU OKAY? STOP FOOLING AROUND.

JAB!!

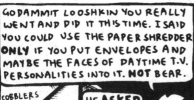
GODAMMIT LOOSHKIN YOU REALLY WENT AND DID IT THIS TIME. I SAID YOU COULD USE THE PAPER SHREDDER **ONLY** IF YOU PUT ENVELOPES AND MAYBE THE FACES OF DAYTIME T.V. PERSONALITIES INTO IT. **NOT BEAR.**

COBBLERS

HE ASKED TO GO IN IT.

NO HE DIDN'T.

YOU GET THAT FUCKING THING AWAY FROM ME.

THAT'S NOT WHAT I HEARD.

IT WAS A MISTAKE EVER LETTING YOU USE INTERNET BIDDING. THE ONLY THINGS YOU'VE GOT HAVE BEEN CRAP OR DANGEROUS.

do the robot!

WHAT ABOUT THE **SWAN PEN-KNIFE?** CRAP <u>AND</u> DANGEROUS.

I WIN. GO ME.

LOOSH YOU'RE BANNED FROM THE INTERNET. AND NO MORE CREDIT CARDS.

THAT'S NOT FAIR!! THERE'S STILL PORN I DON'T HAVE!!

LOOK WHAT YOU DID TO BEAR!! YOU'RE IN TROUBLE, MISTER.

DOG SHIT

FLUMP

GNUHHH YOU'RE SO UNFAIR!! I'M GOING TO PUSH MY THUMBS INTO MY EYES!!

HRRNNGGG!

HOW'S THAT GOING TO HELP?

THPTHBTHH!!

USUALLY BEAR HAS COME ROUND BY NOW. SWEARING A BIT AND GOING 'AUGH' AT ME.

OOP.

GO 'AUGH' BEAR.

PLEASE?

SAY SOMETHING, STUFFING?

AUGH!! BOLLOCKS!!

SORRY, DIDN'T MEAN TO STARTLE YOU.

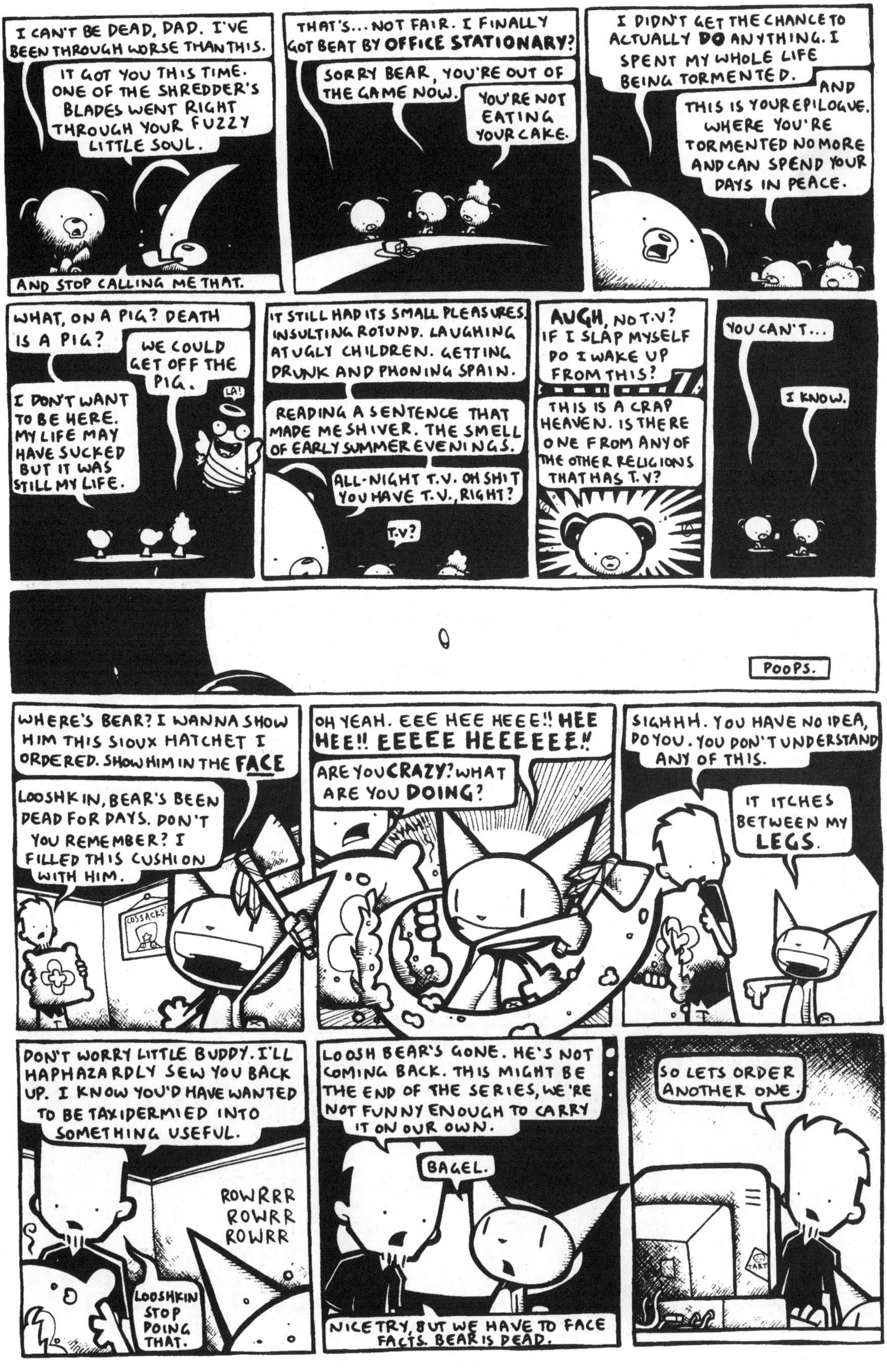
I CAN'T BE DEAD, DAD. I'VE BEEN THROUGH WORSE THAN THIS.
IT GOT YOU THIS TIME. ONE OF THE SHREDDER'S BLADES WENT RIGHT THROUGH YOUR FUZZY LITTLE SOUL.
AND STOP CALLING ME THAT.
THAT'S... NOT FAIR. I FINALLY GOT BEAT BY OFFICE STATIONARY?
SORRY BEAR, YOU'RE OUT OF THE GAME NOW.
YOU'RE NOT EATING YOUR CAKE.
I DIDN'T GET THE CHANCE TO ACTUALLY DO ANYTHING. I SPENT MY WHOLE LIFE BEING TORMENTED.
AND THIS IS YOUR EPILOGUE. WHERE YOU'RE TORMENTED NO MORE AND CAN SPEND YOUR DAYS IN PEACE.
WHAT, ON A PIG? DEATH IS A PIG?
WE COULD GET OFF THE PIG.
I DON'T WANT TO BE HERE. MY LIFE MAY HAVE SUCKED BUT IT WAS STILL MY LIFE.
LA!
IT STILL HAD ITS SMALL PLEASURES. INSULTING ROTUND. LAUGHING AT UGLY CHILDREN. GETTING DRUNK AND PHONING SPAIN.
READING A SENTENCE THAT MADE ME SHIVER. THE SMELL OF EARLY SUMMER EVENINGS.
ALL-NIGHT T.V. OH SHIT YOU HAVE T.V., RIGHT?
T.V?
AUGH, NO T.V? IF I SLAP MYSELF DO I WAKE UP FROM THIS?
THIS IS A CRAP HEAVEN. IS THERE ONE FROM ANY OF THE OTHER RELIGIONS THAT HAS T.V?
YOU CAN'T...
I KNOW.
POOPS.
WHERE'S BEAR? I WANNA SHOW HIM THIS SIOUX HATCHET I ORDERED. SHOW HIM IN THE FACE
LOOSHKIN, BEAR'S BEEN DEAD FOR DAYS. DON'T YOU REMEMBER? I FILLED THIS CUSHION WITH HIM.
COSSACKS!
OH YEAH. EEE HEE HEEE!! HEE HEE!! EEEEE HEEEEEE!!
ARE YOU CRAZY? WHAT ARE YOU DOING?
SIGHHH. YOU HAVE NO IDEA, DO YOU. YOU DON'T UNDERSTAND ANY OF THIS.
IT ITCHES BETWEEN MY LEGS.
DON'T WORRY LITTLE BUDDY. I'LL HAPHAZARDLY SEW YOU BACK UP. I KNOW YOU'D HAVE WANTED TO BE TAXIDERMIED INTO SOMETHING USEFUL.
ROWRRR ROWRR ROWRR
LOOSHKIN STOP DOING THAT.
LOOSH BEAR'S GONE. HE'S NOT COMING BACK. THIS MIGHT BE THE END OF THE SERIES, WE'RE NOT FUNNY ENOUGH TO CARRY IT ON OUR OWN.
BAGEL.
NICE TRY, BUT WE HAVE TO FACE FACTS. BEAR IS DEAD.
SO LETS ORDER ANOTHER ONE.
TART

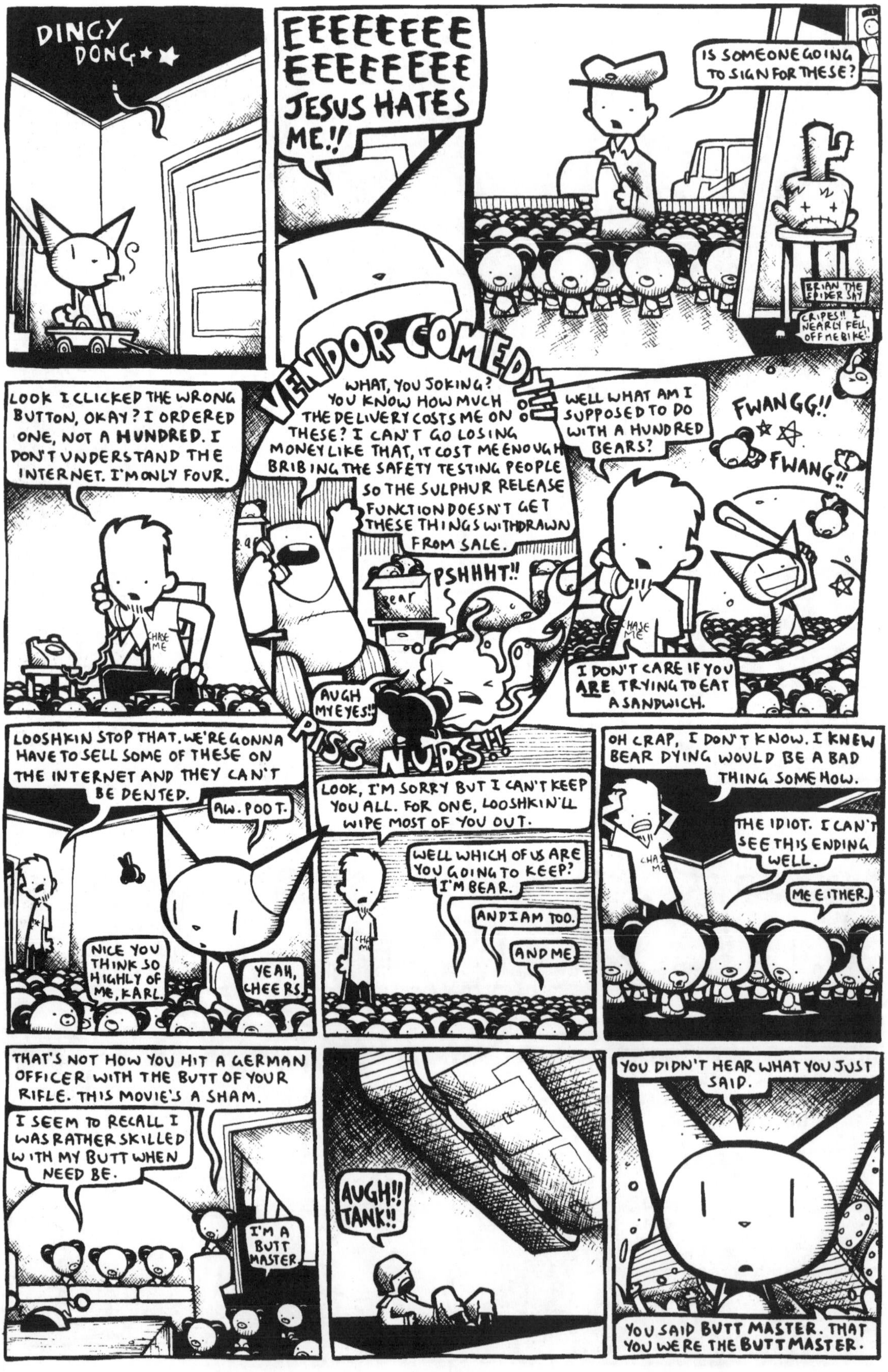
DINGY DONG
EEEEEEEE EEEEEEEE JESUS HATES ME.!!
IS SOMEONE GOING TO SIGN FOR THESE?
BRIAN THE SPIDER SAY
CRIPES!! I NEARLY FELL OFF ME BIKE!!
VENDOR COMEDY!!!
LOOK I CLICKED THE WRONG BUTTON, OKAY? I ORDERED ONE, NOT A HUNDRED. I DON'T UNDERSTAND THE INTERNET. I'M ONLY FOUR.
WHAT, YOU JOKING? YOU KNOW HOW MUCH THE DELIVERY COSTS ME ON THESE? I CAN'T GO LOSING MONEY LIKE THAT, IT COST ME ENOUGH BRIBING THE SAFETY TESTING PEOPLE SO THE SULPHUR RELEASE FUNCTION DOESN'T GET THESE THINGS WITHDRAWN FROM SALE.
BEAR
PSHHHT!!
AUGH MY EYES!!
PISS NUBS!!
WELL WHAT AM I SUPPOSED TO DO WITH A HUNDRED BEARS?
FWANGG!!
FWANG!!
I DON'T CARE IF YOU ARE TRYING TO EAT A SANDWICH.
LOOSHKIN STOP THAT. WE'RE GONNA HAVE TO SELL SOME OF THESE ON THE INTERNET AND THEY CAN'T BE DENTED.
AW. POOT.
NICE YOU THINK SO HIGHLY OF ME, KARL.
YEAH, CHEERS.
LOOK, I'M SORRY BUT I CAN'T KEEP YOU ALL. FOR ONE, LOOSHKIN'LL WIPE MOST OF YOU OUT.
WELL WHICH OF US ARE YOU GOING TO KEEP? I'M BEAR.
AND I AM TOO.
AND ME.
OH CRAP, I DON'T KNOW. I KNEW BEAR DYING WOULD BE A BAD THING SOMEHOW.
THE IDIOT. I CAN'T SEE THIS ENDING WELL.
ME EITHER.
THAT'S NOT HOW YOU HIT A GERMAN OFFICER WITH THE BUTT OF YOUR RIFLE. THIS MOVIE'S A SHAM.
I SEEM TO RECALL I WAS RATHER SKILLED WITH MY BUTT WHEN NEED BE.
I'M A BUTT MASTER.
AUGH!! TANK!!
YOU DIDN'T HEAR WHAT YOU JUST SAID.
YOU SAID BUTT MASTER. THAT YOU WERE THE BUTT MASTER.

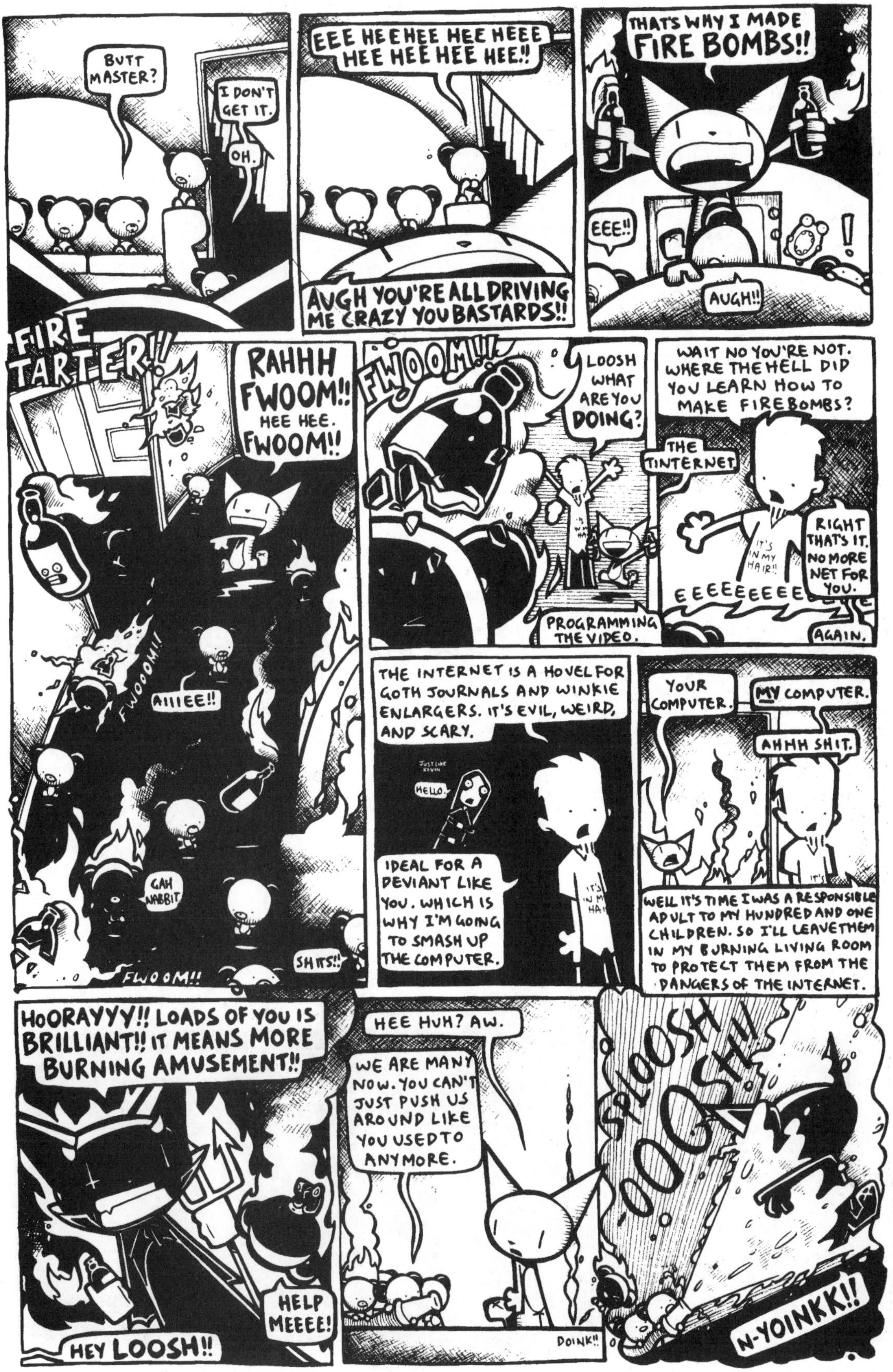
BUTT MASTER?
I DON'T GET IT.
OH.
EEE HEEHEE HEE HEEE HEE HEE HEE HEE.!!
AUGH YOU'RE ALL DRIVING ME CRAZY YOU BASTARDS!!
THAT'S WHY I MADE FIRE BOMBS!!
EEE!!
AUGH!!
!
FIRE STARTER!!
RAHHH FWOOM!! HEE HEE. FWOOM!!
FWOOOM!!
AIIIEE!!
GAH NABBIT.
SHITS!!
FWOOM!!
FWOOM!!
LOOSH WHAT ARE YOU DOING?
PROGRAMMING THE VIDEO.
WAIT NO YOU'RE NOT. WHERE THE HELL DID YOU LEARN HOW TO MAKE FIREBOMBS?
THE TINTERNET.
IT'S IN MY HAIR!!
RIGHT THAT'S IT. NO MORE NET FOR YOU.
EEEEEEEEEE
AGAIN.
THE INTERNET IS A HOVEL FOR GOTH JOURNALS AND WINKIE ENLARGERS. IT'S EVIL, WEIRD, AND SCARY.
HELLO.
IDEAL FOR A DEVIANT LIKE YOU. WHICH IS WHY I'M GOING TO SMASH UP THE COMPUTER.
IT'S IN MY HAIR
YOUR COMPUTER.
MY COMPUTER.
AHHH SHIT.
WELL IT'S TIME I WAS A RESPONSIBLE ADULT TO MY HUNDRED AND ONE CHILDREN. SO I'LL LEAVE THEM IN MY BURNING LIVING ROOM TO PROTECT THEM FROM THE DANGERS OF THE INTERNET.
HOORAYYY!! LOADS OF YOU IS BRILLIANT!! IT MEANS MORE BURNING AMUSEMENT!!
HELP MEEEE!
HEY LOOSH!!
HEE HUH? AW.
WE ARE MANY NOW. YOU CAN'T JUST PUSH US AROUND LIKE YOU USED TO ANYMORE.
DOINK!!
SPLOOSH
OOOOSH!!
N-YOINKK!!

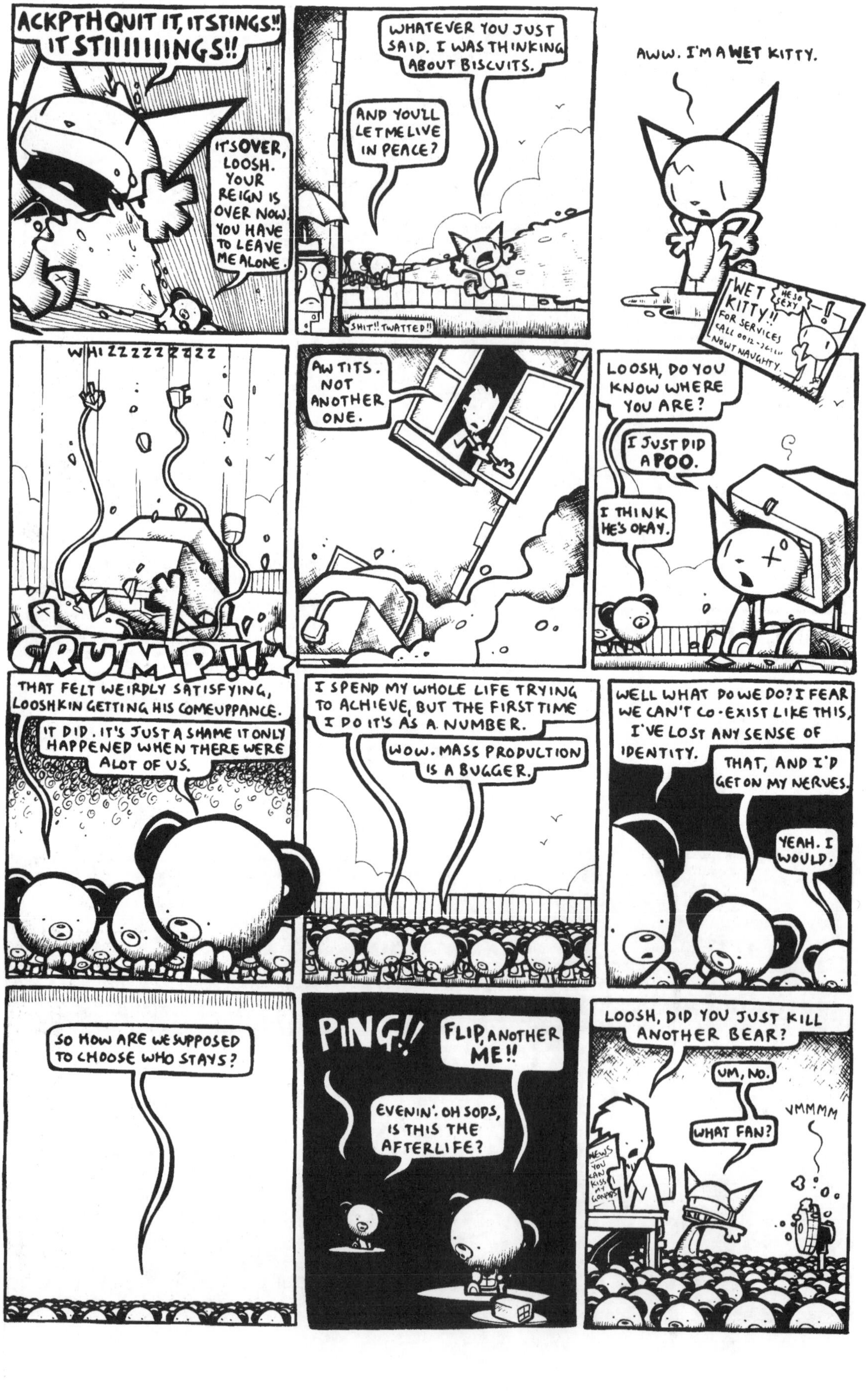
ACKPTH QUIT IT, IT STINGS!! IT STIIIIIIINGS!!
IT'S OVER, LOOSH. YOUR REIGN IS OVER NOW. YOU HAVE TO LEAVE ME ALONE.
AND YOU'LL LET ME LIVE IN PEACE?
WHATEVER YOU JUST SAID. I WAS THINKING ABOUT BISCUITS.
SHIT!! TWATTED!!
AWW. I'M A WET KITTY.
WET KITTY!!
HE SO SEXY
FOR SERVICES
NOWT NAUGHTY.
WHIZZZZZZZZZZ
CRUMP!!
AW TITS. NOT ANOTHER ONE.
LOOSH, DO YOU KNOW WHERE YOU ARE?
I JUST DID A POO.
I THINK HE'S OKAY.
THAT FELT WEIRDLY SATISFYING, LOOSHKIN GETTING HIS COMEUPPANCE.
IT DID. IT'S JUST A SHAME IT ONLY HAPPENED WHEN THERE WERE ALOT OF US.
I SPEND MY WHOLE LIFE TRYING TO ACHIEVE, BUT THE FIRST TIME I DO IT'S AS A NUMBER.
WOW. MASS PRODUCTION IS A BUGGER.
WELL WHAT DO WE DO? I FEAR WE CAN'T CO-EXIST LIKE THIS, I'VE LOST ANY SENSE OF IDENTITY.
THAT, AND I'D GET ON MY NERVES.
YEAH. I WOULD.
SO HOW ARE WE SUPPOSED TO CHOOSE WHO STAYS?
PING!!
FLIP, ANOTHER ME!!
EVENIN'. OH SODS, IS THIS THE AFTERLIFE?
LOOSH, DID YOU JUST KILL ANOTHER BEAR?
UM, NO.
WHAT FAN?
VMMMM

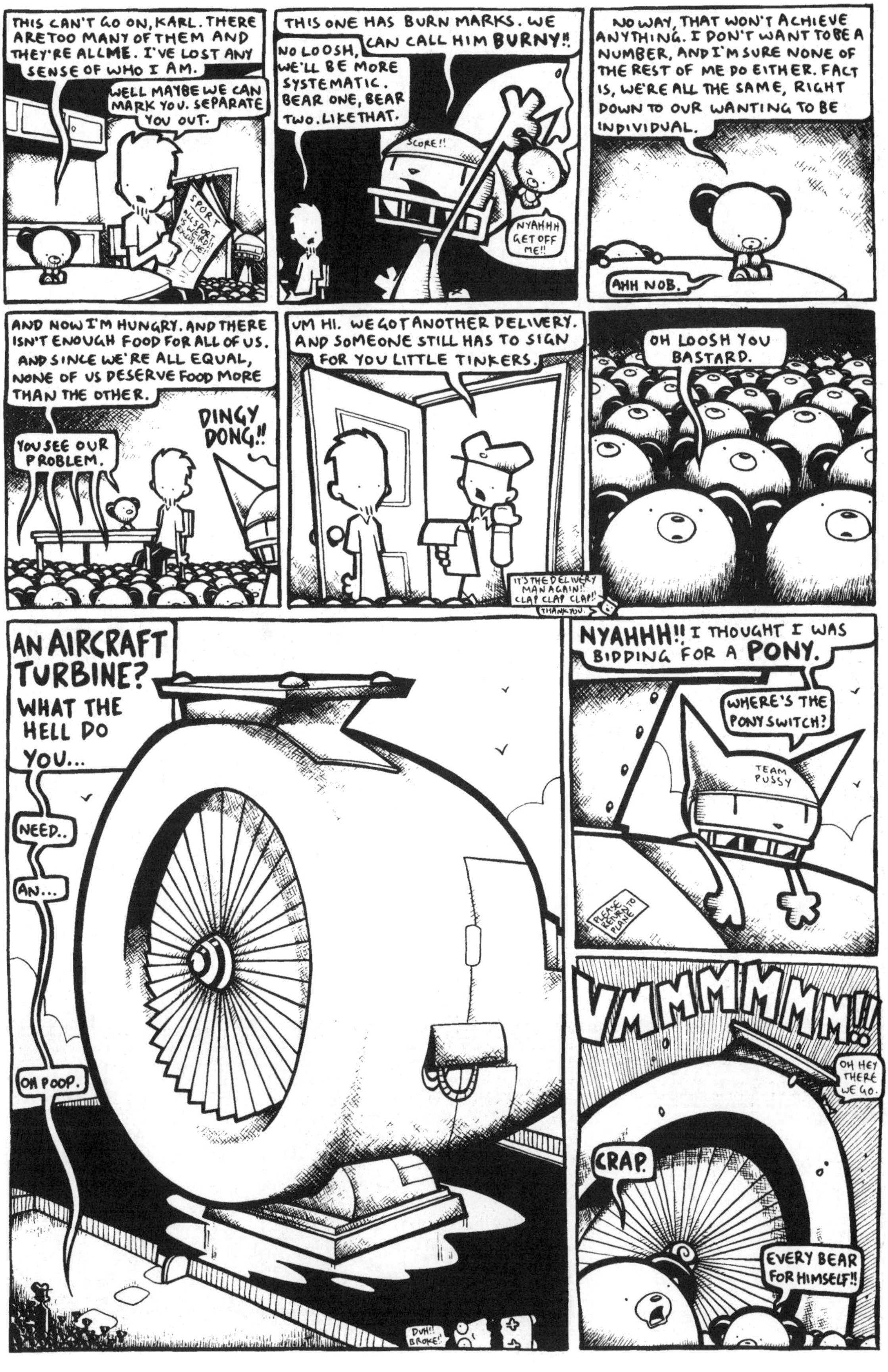
THIS CAN'T GO ON, KARL. THERE ARE TOO MANY OF THEM AND THEY'RE ALL ME. I'VE LOST ANY SENSE OF WHO I AM.
WELL MAYBE WE CAN MARK YOU. SEPARATE YOU OUT.
SPORT
ALL SPORT IS WEIRD!! EXCLUSIVE!!
THIS ONE HAS BURN MARKS. WE CAN CALL HIM BURNY!!
NO LOOSH, WE'LL BE MORE SYSTEMATIC. BEAR ONE, BEAR TWO. LIKE THAT.
SCORE!!
NYAHHH GET OFF ME!!
NO WAY, THAT WON'T ACHIEVE ANYTHING. I DON'T WANT TO BE A NUMBER, AND I'M SURE NONE OF THE REST OF ME DO EITHER. FACT IS, WE'RE ALL THE SAME, RIGHT DOWN TO OUR WANTING TO BE INDIVIDUAL.
AHH NOB.
AND NOW I'M HUNGRY. AND THERE ISN'T ENOUGH FOOD FOR ALL OF US. AND SINCE WE'RE ALL EQUAL, NONE OF US DESERVE FOOD MORE THAN THE OTHER.
YOU SEE OUR PROBLEM.
DINGY DONG!!
UM HI. WE GOT ANOTHER DELIVERY. AND SOMEONE STILL HAS TO SIGN FOR YOU LITTLE TINKERS.
IT'S THE DELIVERY MAN AGAIN!! CLAP CLAP CLAP!!
THANK YOU.
OH LOOSH YOU BASTARD.
AN AIRCRAFT TURBINE? WHAT THE HELL DO YOU...
NEED..
AN...
OH POOP.
DUH!! BROKE!
NYAHHH!! I THOUGHT I WAS BIDDING FOR A PONY.
WHERE'S THE PONY SWITCH?
TEAM PUSSY
PLEASE RETURN TO PLANE
VMMMMMMM!!
OH HEY THERE WE GO.
CRAP.
EVERY BEAR FOR HIMSELF!!

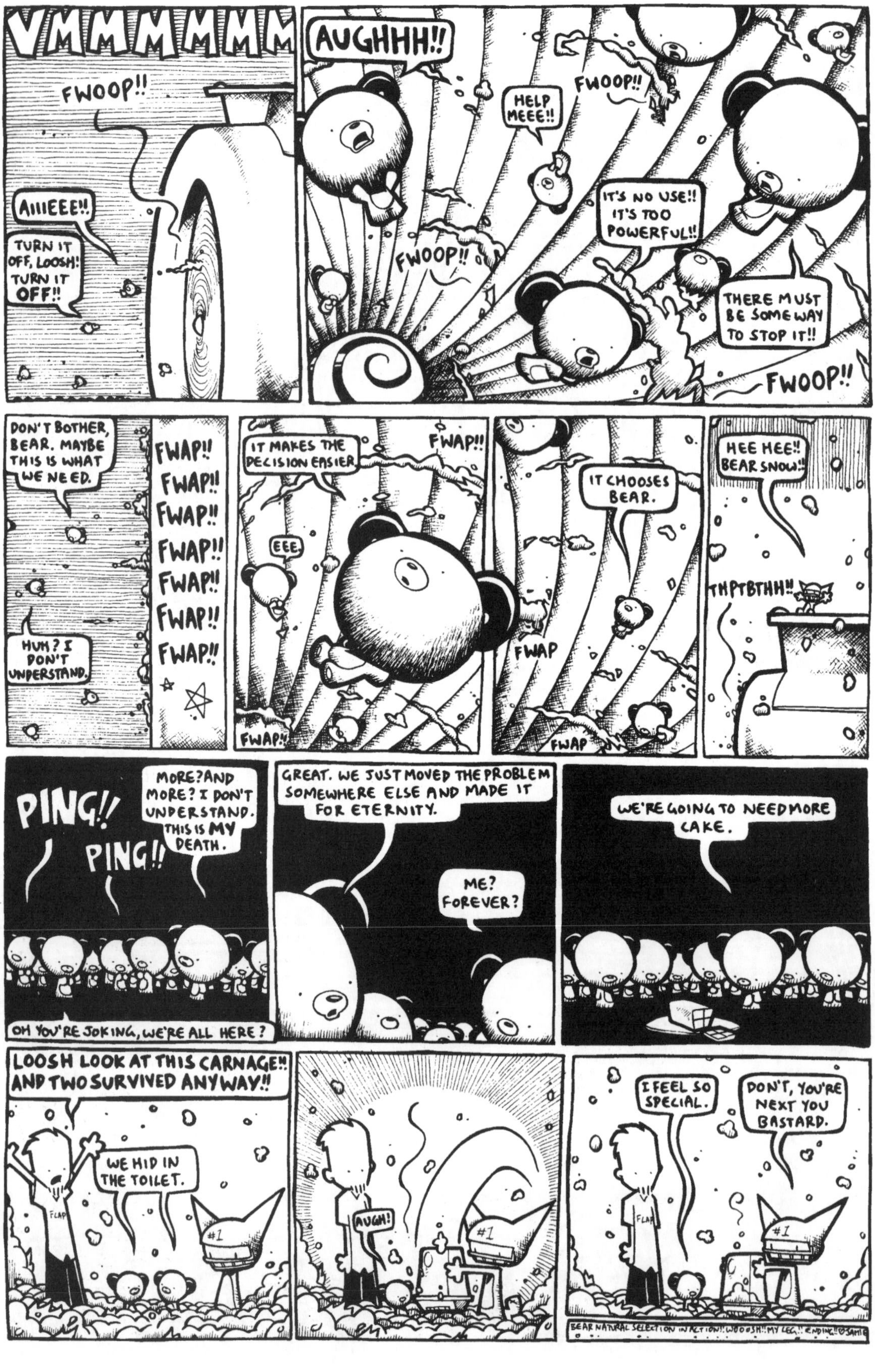
VMMMMMMM
FWOOP!!
AIIIEEE!!
TURN IT OFF, LOOSH! TURN IT OFF!!
AUGHHH!!
HELP MEEE!!
FWOOP!!
FWOOP!!
IT'S NO USE!! IT'S TOO POWERFUL!!
THERE MUST BE SOME WAY TO STOP IT!!
FWOOP!!
DON'T BOTHER, BEAR. MAYBE THIS IS WHAT WE NEED.
HUH? I DON'T UNDERSTAND.
FWAP!! FWAP!! FWAP!! FWAP!! FWAP!! FWAP!! FWAP!!
IT MAKES THE DECISION EASIER.
FWAP!!
EEE.
FWAP!!
IT CHOOSES BEAR.
FWAP
FWAP
HEE HEE!! BEAR SNOW!!
THPTBTHH!!
PING!!
PING!!
MORE? AND MORE? I DON'T UNDERSTAND. THIS IS MY DEATH.
OH YOU'RE JOKING, WE'RE ALL HERE?
GREAT. WE JUST MOVED THE PROBLEM SOMEWHERE ELSE AND MADE IT FOR ETERNITY.
ME? FOREVER?
WE'RE GOING TO NEED MORE CAKE.
LOOSH LOOK AT THIS CARNAGE!! AND TWO SURVIVED ANYWAY!!
WE HID IN THE TOILET.
FLAP
#1
AUGH!
#1
I FEEL SO SPECIAL.
DON'T, YOU'RE NEXT YOU BASTARD.
FLAP
#1
BEAR NATURAL SELECTION IN ACTION!! WOOOSH!! MY LEG!! ENDING!! ©JAMIE

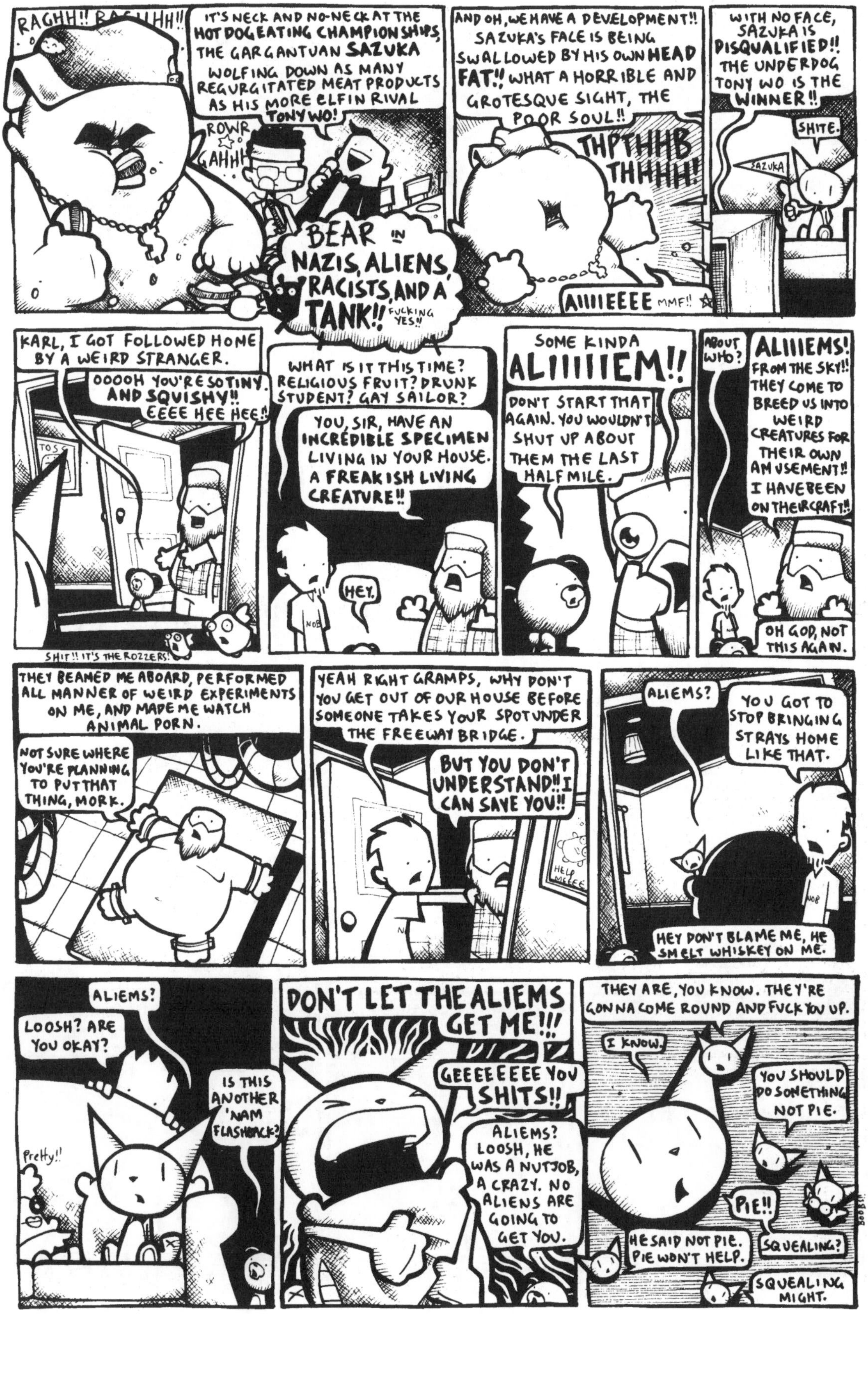
RAGHH!! RAGHHH!!
IT'S NECK AND NO-NECK AT THE HOT DOG EATING CHAMPIONSHIPS, THE GARGANTUAN SAZUKA WOLFING DOWN AS MANY REGURGITATED MEAT PRODUCTS AS HIS MORE ELFIN RIVAL TONY WO!
ROWR GAHH!
AND OH, WE HAVE A DEVELOPMENT!! SAZUKA'S FACE IS BEING SWALLOWED BY HIS OWN HEAD FAT!! WHAT A HORRIBLE AND GROTESQUE SIGHT, THE POOR SOUL!!
THPTHHB THHHH!
AIIIIEEEE
MMF!!
WITH NO FACE, SAZUKA IS DISQUALIFIED!! THE UNDERDOG TONY WO IS THE WINNER!!
SHITE.
SAZUKA
BEAR IN NAZIS, ALIENS, RACISTS, AND A TANK!!
FUCKING YES!!
KARL, I GOT FOLLOWED HOME BY A WEIRD STRANGER.
OOOOH YOU'RE SO TINY. AND SQUISHY!! EEEE HEE HEE!!
SHIT!! IT'S THE ROZZERS!
WHAT IS IT THIS TIME? RELIGIOUS FRUIT? DRUNK STUDENT? GAY SAILOR?
YOU, SIR, HAVE AN INCREDIBLE SPECIMEN LIVING IN YOUR HOUSE. A FREAKISH LIVING CREATURE!!
HEY.
SOME KINDA ALIIIIIEM!!
DON'T START THAT AGAIN. YOU WOULDN'T SHUT UP ABOUT THEM THE LAST HALF MILE.
ABOUT WHO?
ALIIIEMS! FROM THE SKY!! THEY COME TO BREED US INTO WEIRD CREATURES FOR THEIR OWN AMUSEMENT!! I HAVE BEEN ON THEIR CRAFT!!
OH GOD, NOT THIS AGAIN.
THEY BEAMED ME ABOARD, PERFORMED ALL MANNER OF WEIRD EXPERIMENTS ON ME, AND MADE ME WATCH ANIMAL PORN.
NOT SURE WHERE YOU'RE PLANNING TO PUT THAT THING, MORK.
YEAH RIGHT GRAMPS, WHY DON'T YOU GET OUT OF OUR HOUSE BEFORE SOMEONE TAKES YOUR SPOT UNDER THE FREEWAY BRIDGE.
BUT YOU DON'T UNDERSTAND!! I CAN SAVE YOU!!
HELP MEEEE
ALIEMS?
YOU GOT TO STOP BRINGING STRAYS HOME LIKE THAT.
HEY DON'T BLAME ME, HE SMELT WHISKEY ON ME.
ALIEMS?
LOOSH? ARE YOU OKAY?
IS THIS ANOTHER 'NAM FLASHBACK?
Pretty!!
DON'T LET THE ALIEMS GET ME!!!
GEEEEEEEE YOU SHITS!!
ALIEMS? LOOSH, HE WAS A NUTJOB, A CRAZY. NO ALIENS ARE GOING TO GET YOU.
THEY ARE, YOU KNOW. THEY'RE GONNA COME ROUND AND FUCK YOU UP.
I KNOW.
YOU SHOULD DO SOMETHING NOT PIE.
PIE!!
HE SAID NOT PIE. PIE WON'T HELP.
SQUEALING?
SQUEALING MIGHT.

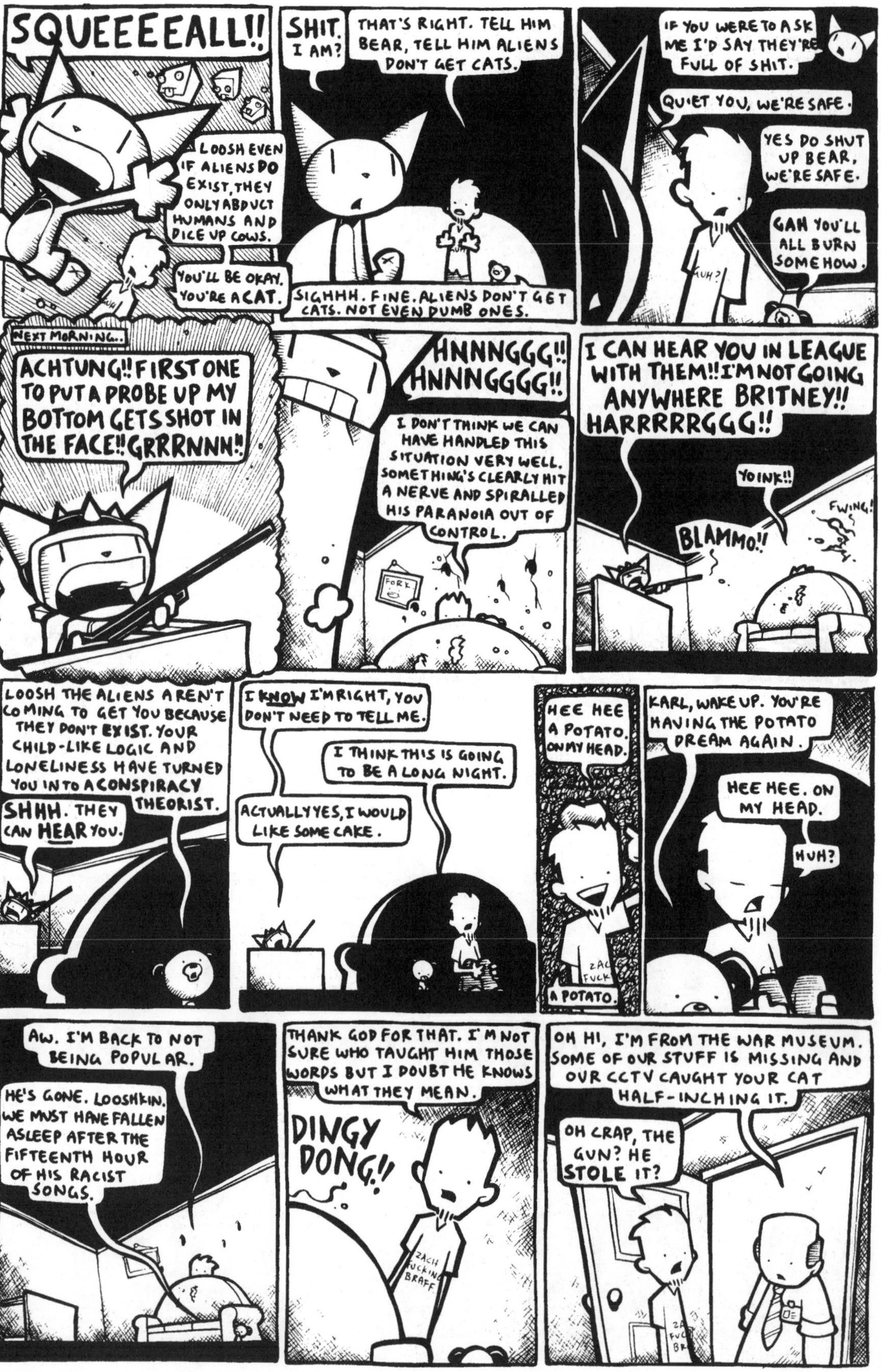

SQUEEEEALL!!
LOOSH EVEN IF ALIENS DO EXIST, THEY ONLY ABDUCT HUMANS AND DICE UP COWS.
YOU'LL BE OKAY. YOU'RE A CAT.
SHIT. I AM?
THAT'S RIGHT. TELL HIM BEAR, TELL HIM ALIENS DON'T GET CATS.
SIGHHH. FINE. ALIENS DON'T GET CATS. NOT EVEN DUMB ONES.
IF YOU WERE TO ASK ME I'D SAY THEY'RE FULL OF SHIT.
QUIET YOU, WE'RE SAFE.
YES DO SHUT UP BEAR, WE'RE SAFE.
GAH YOU'LL ALL BURN SOMEHOW.
HUH?
NEXT MORNING..
ACHTUNG!! FIRST ONE TO PUT A PROBE UP MY BOTTOM GETS SHOT IN THE FACE!! GRRRNNN!!
HNNNGGG!! HNNNGGGG!!
I DON'T THINK WE CAN HAVE HANDLED THIS SITUATION VERY WELL. SOMETHING'S CLEARLY HIT A NERVE AND SPIRALLED HIS PARANOIA OUT OF CONTROL.
FORK
I CAN HEAR YOU IN LEAGUE WITH THEM!! I'M NOT GOING ANYWHERE BRITNEY!! HARRRRRGGG!!
YOINK!!
FWING!
BLAMMO!!
LOOSH THE ALIENS AREN'T COMING TO GET YOU BECAUSE THEY DON'T EXIST. YOUR CHILD-LIKE LOGIC AND LONELINESS HAVE TURNED YOU INTO A CONSPIRACY THEORIST.
SHHH. THEY CAN HEAR YOU.
I KNOW I'M RIGHT, YOU DON'T NEED TO TELL ME.
I THINK THIS IS GOING TO BE A LONG NIGHT.
ACTUALLY YES, I WOULD LIKE SOME CAKE.
HEE HEE A POTATO. ON MY HEAD.
ZACH FUCK
A POTATO.
KARL, WAKE UP. YOU'RE HAVING THE POTATO DREAM AGAIN.
HEE HEE. ON MY HEAD.
HUH?
AW. I'M BACK TO NOT BEING POPULAR.
HE'S GONE. LOOSHKIN. WE MUST HAVE FALLEN ASLEEP AFTER THE FIFTEENTH HOUR OF HIS RACIST SONGS.
THANK GOD FOR THAT. I'M NOT SURE WHO TAUGHT HIM THOSE WORDS BUT I DOUBT HE KNOWS WHAT THEY MEAN.
DINGY DONG!!
ZACH FUCKING BRAFF
OH HI, I'M FROM THE WAR MUSEUM. SOME OF OUR STUFF IS MISSING AND OUR CCTV CAUGHT YOUR CAT HALF-INCHING IT.
OH CRAP, THE GUN? HE STOLE IT?

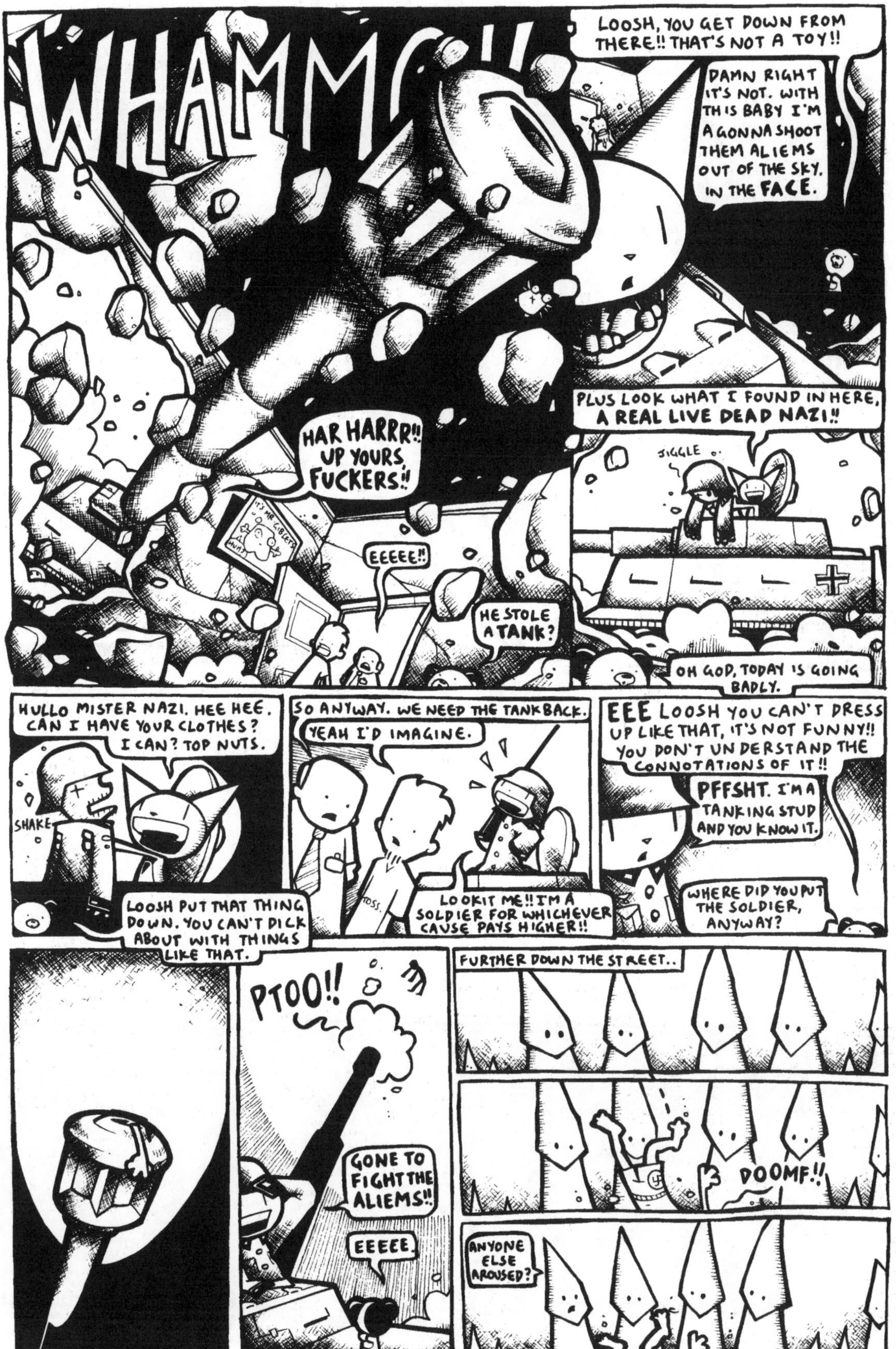
WHAMMO!!
LOOSH, YOU GET DOWN FROM THERE!! THAT'S NOT A TOY!!
DAMN RIGHT IT'S NOT. WITH THIS BABY I'M A GONNA SHOOT THEM ALIEMS OUT OF THE SKY. IN THE FACE.
HAR HARRR!! UP YOURS, FUCKERS!!
IT'S MR. GIBLETS
EEEEE!!
HE STOLE A TANK?
PLUS LOOK WHAT I FOUND IN HERE, A REAL LIVE DEAD NAZI!!
JIGGLE
OH GOD, TODAY IS GOING BADLY.
HULLO MISTER NAZI. HEE HEE. CAN I HAVE YOUR CLOTHES? I CAN? TOP NUTS.
SHAKE
LOOSH PUT THAT THING DOWN. YOU CAN'T DICK ABOUT WITH THINGS LIKE THAT.
SO ANYWAY. WE NEED THE TANK BACK.
YEAH I'D IMAGINE.
LOOKIT ME!! I'M A SOLDIER FOR WHICHEVER CAUSE PAYS HIGHER!!
TOSS.
EEE LOOSH YOU CAN'T DRESS UP LIKE THAT, IT'S NOT FUNNY!! YOU DON'T UNDERSTAND THE CONNOTATIONS OF IT!!
PFFSHT. I'M A TANKING STUD AND YOU KNOW IT.
WHERE DID YOU PUT THE SOLDIER, ANYWAY?
PTOO!!
GONE TO FIGHT THE ALIEMS!!
EEEEE.
FURTHER DOWN THE STREET..
DOOMF!!
ANYONE ELSE AROUSED?

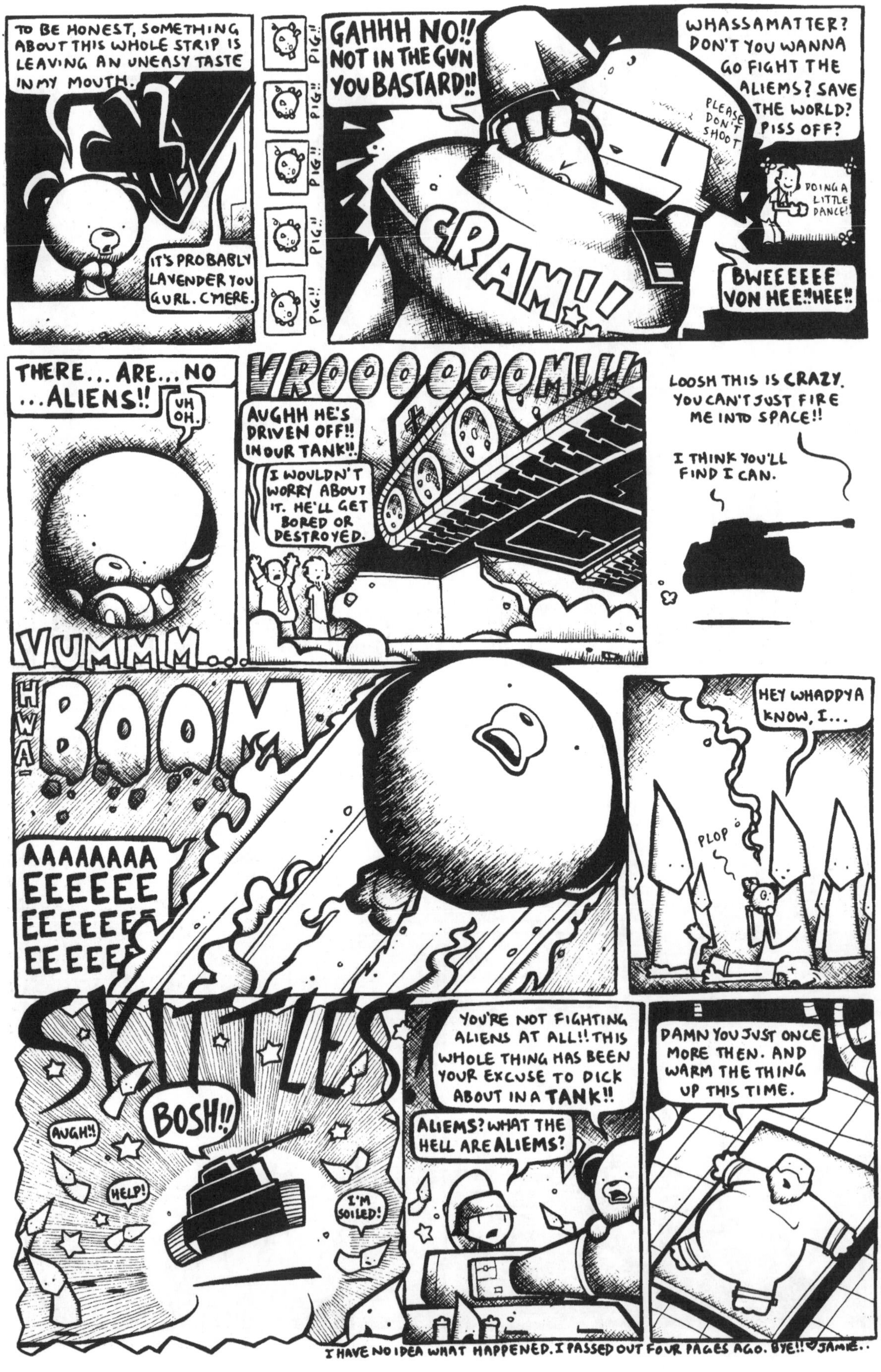
TO BE HONEST, SOMETHING ABOUT THIS WHOLE STRIP IS LEAVING AN UNEASY TASTE IN MY MOUTH.
IT'S PROBABLY LAVENDER YOU GURL. C'MERE.
PIG!!
PIG!!
PIG!!
PIG!!
PIG!!
GAHHH NO!! NOT IN THE GUN YOU BASTARD!!
CRAM!!
PLEASE DON'T SHOOT
WHASSAMATTER? DON'T YOU WANNA GO FIGHT THE ALIEMS? SAVE THE WORLD? PISS OFF?
DOING A LITTLE DANCE!!
BWEEEEEE VON HEE!!HEE!!
THERE... ARE... NO ...ALIENS!!
UH OH.
VUMMM...
VROOOOOOOM!!!!
AUGHH HE'S DRIVEN OFF!! IN OUR TANK!!
I WOULDN'T WORRY ABOUT IT. HE'LL GET BORED OR DESTROYED.
LOOSH THIS IS CRAZY. YOU CAN'T JUST FIRE ME INTO SPACE!!
I THINK YOU'LL FIND I CAN.
HWA-BOOM
AAAAAAAA EEEEEE EEEEEE EEEEE
HEY WHADDYA KNOW, I...
PLOP
SKITTLES!
BOSH!!
AUGH!!
HELP!
I'M SOILED!
YOU'RE NOT FIGHTING ALIENS AT ALL!! THIS WHOLE THING HAS BEEN YOUR EXCUSE TO DICK ABOUT IN A TANK!!
ALIEMS? WHAT THE HELL ARE ALIEMS?
DAMN YOU JUST ONCE MORE THEN. AND WARM THE THING UP THIS TIME.

I HAVE NO IDEA WHAT HAPPENED. I PASSED OUT FOUR PAGES AGO. BYE!! ♡ JAMIE..

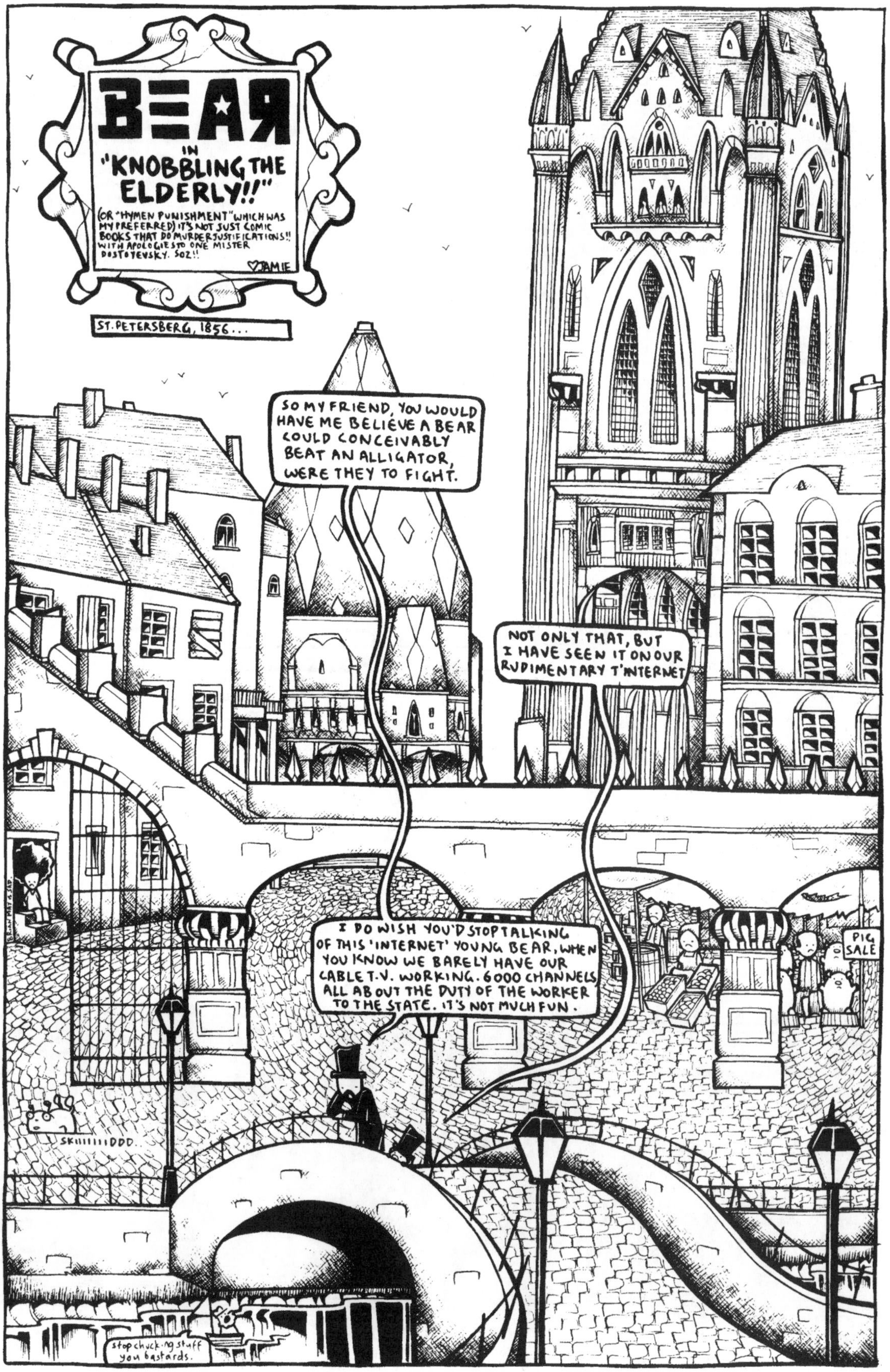
BEAR
IN
"KNOBBLING THE ELDERLY!!"
(OR "HYMEN PUNISHMENT" WHICH WAS MY PREFERRED) IT'S NOT JUST COMIC BOOKS THAT DO MURDER JUSTIFICATIONS!! WITH APOLOGIES TO ONE MISTER DOSTOYEVSKY. SOZ!!
♡JAMIE
ST. PETERSBERG, 1856...
SO MY FRIEND, YOU WOULD HAVE ME BELIEVE A BEAR COULD CONCEIVABLY BEAT AN ALLIGATOR, WERE THEY TO FIGHT.
NOT ONLY THAT, BUT I HAVE SEEN IT ON OUR RUDIMENTARY T'INTERNET
I DO WISH YOU'D STOP TALKING OF THIS 'INTERNET' YOUNG BEAR, WHEN YOU KNOW WE BARELY HAVE OUR CABLE T.V. WORKING. 6000 CHANNELS ALL ABOUT THE DUTY OF THE WORKER TO THE STATE. IT'S NOT MUCH FUN.
PIG SALE
SKIIIIIIIDDD..
stop chucking stuff you bastards.

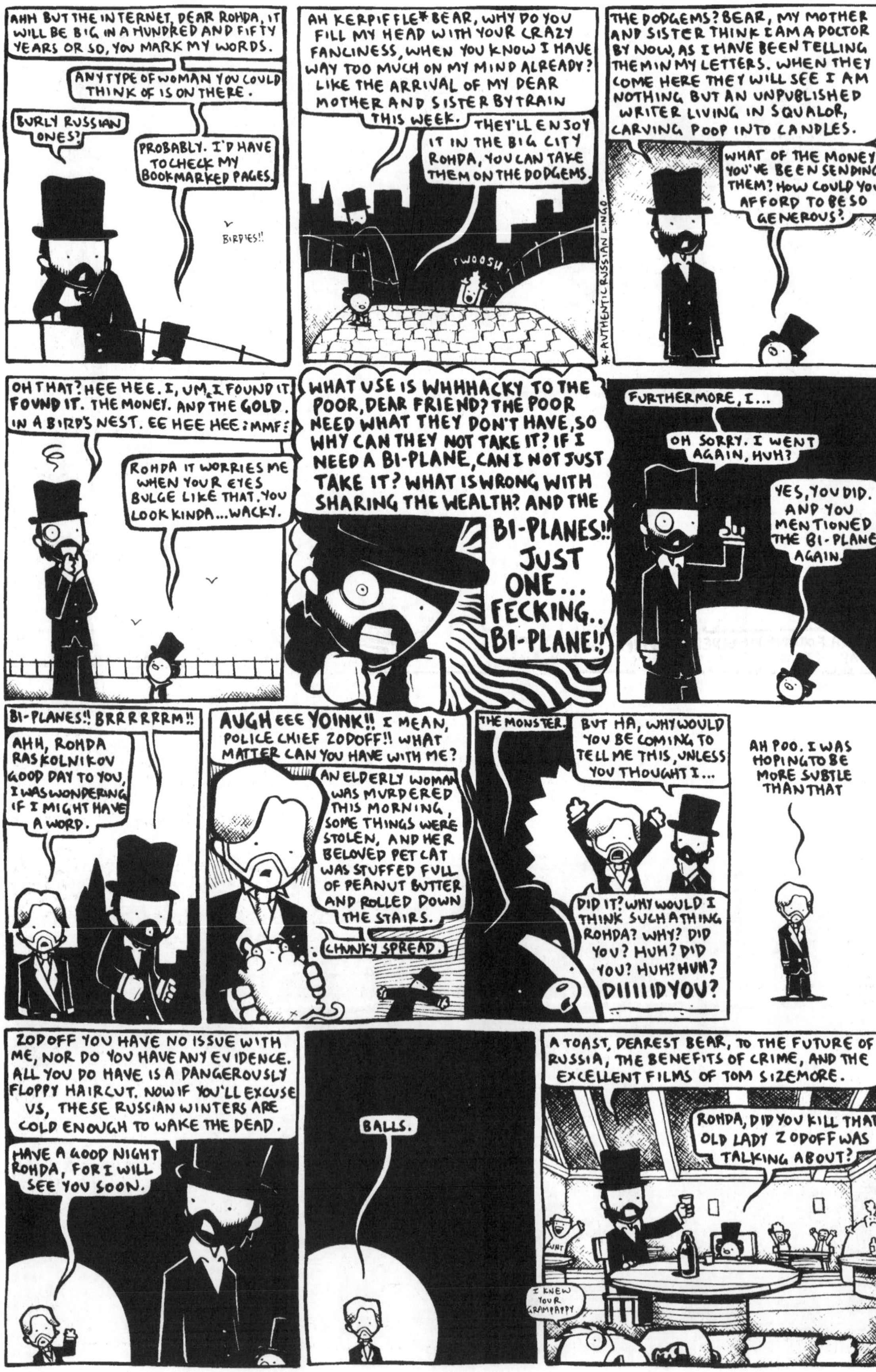
AHH BUT THE INTERNET, DEAR ROHDA, IT WILL BE BIG IN A HUNDRED AND FIFTY YEARS OR SO, YOU MARK MY WORDS.
ANY TYPE OF WOMAN YOU COULD THINK OF IS ON THERE.
BURLY RUSSIAN ONES?
PROBABLY. I'D HAVE TO CHECK MY BOOKMARKED PAGES.
BIRDIES!!
AH KERPIFFLE* BEAR, WHY DO YOU FILL MY HEAD WITH YOUR CRAZY FANCINESS, WHEN YOU KNOW I HAVE WAY TOO MUCH ON MY MIND ALREADY? LIKE THE ARRIVAL OF MY DEAR MOTHER AND SISTER BY TRAIN THIS WEEK.
THEY'LL ENJOY IT IN THE BIG CITY ROHDA, YOU CAN TAKE THEM ON THE DODGEMS.
FWOOSH
*- AUTHENTIC RUSSIAN LINGO.
THE DODGEMS? BEAR, MY MOTHER AND SISTER THINK I AM A DOCTOR BY NOW, AS I HAVE BEEN TELLING THEM IN MY LETTERS. WHEN THEY COME HERE THEY WILL SEE I AM NOTHING BUT AN UNPUBLISHED WRITER LIVING IN SQUALOR, CARVING POOP INTO CANDLES.
WHAT OF THE MONEY YOU'VE BEEN SENDING THEM? HOW COULD YOU AFFORD TO BE SO GENEROUS?
OH THAT? HEE HEE. I, UM, I FOUND IT. FOUND IT. THE MONEY. AND THE GOLD. IN A BIRD'S NEST. EE HEE HEE: MMF:
ROHDA IT WORRIES ME WHEN YOUR EYES BULGE LIKE THAT. YOU LOOK KINDA... WACKY.
WHAT USE IS WHHHACKY TO THE POOR, DEAR FRIEND? THE POOR NEED WHAT THEY DON'T HAVE, SO WHY CAN THEY NOT TAKE IT? IF I NEED A BI-PLANE, CAN I NOT JUST TAKE IT? WHAT IS WRONG WITH SHARING THE WEALTH? AND THE
BI-PLANES!! JUST ONE... FECKING.. BI-PLANE!!
FURTHERMORE, I...
OH SORRY. I WENT AGAIN, HUH?
YES, YOU DID. AND YOU MENTIONED THE BI-PLANE AGAIN.
BI-PLANES!! BRRRRRRM!!
AHH, ROHDA RASKOLNIKOV GOOD DAY TO YOU, I WAS WONDERING IF I MIGHT HAVE A WORD.
AUGH EEE YOINK!! I MEAN, POLICE CHIEF ZODOFF!! WHAT MATTER CAN YOU HAVE WITH ME?
AN ELDERLY WOMAN WAS MURDERED THIS MORNING, SOME THINGS WERE STOLEN, AND HER BELOVED PET CAT WAS STUFFED FULL OF PEANUT BUTTER AND ROLLED DOWN THE STAIRS.
CHUNKY SPREAD.
THE MONSTER.
BUT HA, WHY WOULD YOU BE COMING TO TELL ME THIS, UNLESS YOU THOUGHT I...
DID IT? WHY WOULD I THINK SUCH A THING ROHDA? WHY? DID YOU? HUH? DID YOU? HUH? HUH? DIIIIID YOU?
AH POO. I WAS HOPING TO BE MORE SUBTLE THAN THAT
ZODOFF YOU HAVE NO ISSUE WITH ME, NOR DO YOU HAVE ANY EVIDENCE. ALL YOU DO HAVE IS A DANGEROUSLY FLOPPY HAIRCUT. NOW IF YOU'LL EXCUSE US, THESE RUSSIAN WINTERS ARE COLD ENOUGH TO WAKE THE DEAD.
HAVE A GOOD NIGHT ROHDA, FOR I WILL SEE YOU SOON.
BALLS.
A TOAST, DEAREST BEAR, TO THE FUTURE OF RUSSIA, THE BENEFITS OF CRIME, AND THE EXCELLENT FILMS OF TOM SIZEMORE.
ROHDA, DID YOU KILL THAT OLD LADY ZODOFF WAS TALKING ABOUT?
GRUNT
I KNEW YOUR GRAMPAPPY.

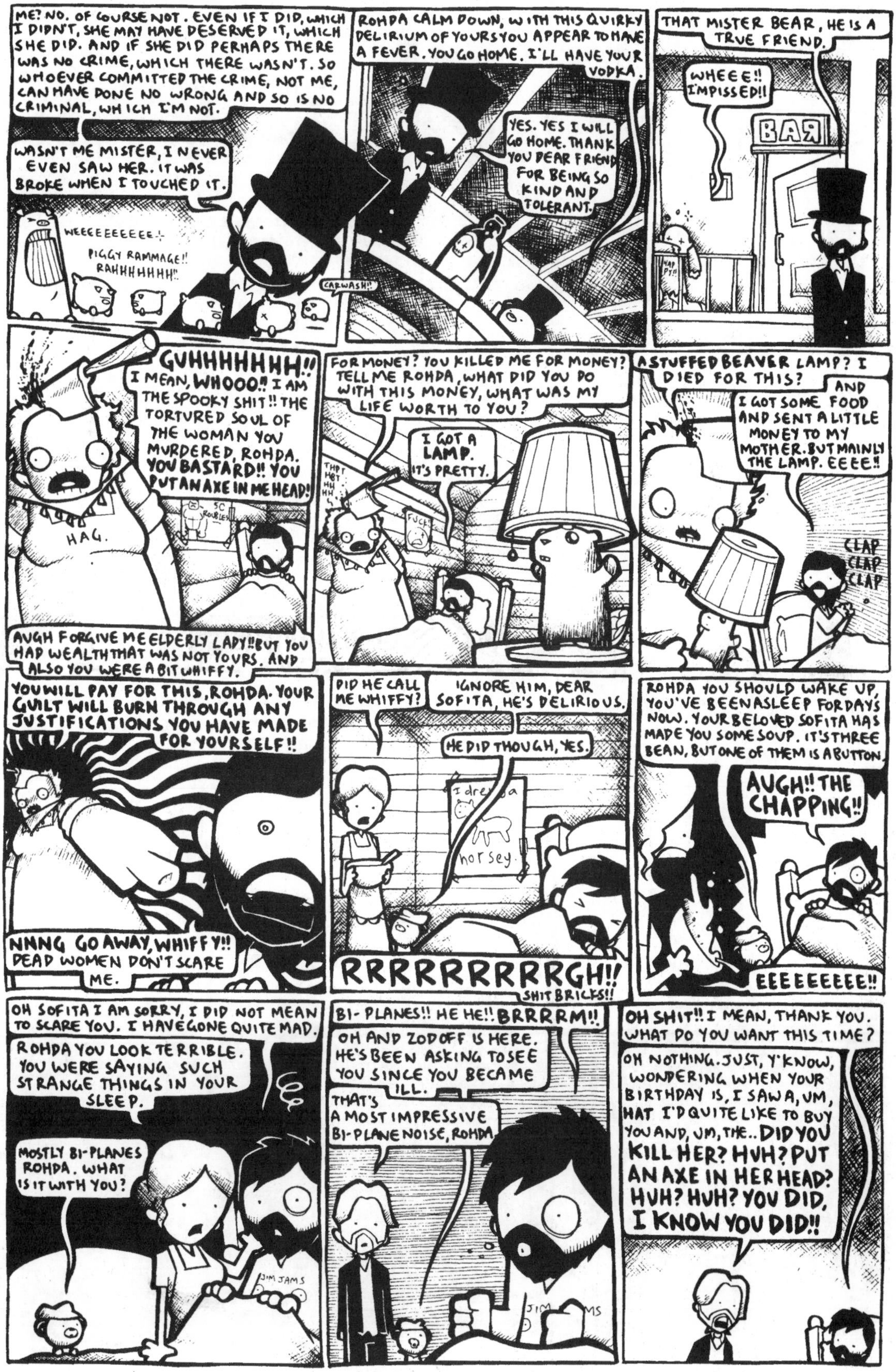

ME? NO. OF COURSE NOT. EVEN IF I DID, WHICH I DIDN'T, SHE MAY HAVE DESERVED IT, WHICH SHE DID. AND IF SHE DID PERHAPS THERE WAS NO CRIME, WHICH THERE WASN'T. SO WHOEVER COMMITTED THE CRIME, NOT ME, CAN HAVE DONE NO WRONG AND SO IS NO CRIMINAL, WHICH I'M NOT.
WASN'T ME MISTER, I NEVER EVEN SAW HER. IT WAS BROKE WHEN I TOUCHED IT.
WEEEEEEEEEE!
PIGGY RAMMAGE!! RAHHHHHHH!!
ROHDA CALM DOWN, WITH THIS QUIRKY DELIRIUM OF YOURS YOU APPEAR TO HAVE A FEVER. YOU GO HOME. I'LL HAVE YOUR VODKA.
YES. YES I WILL GO HOME. THANK YOU DEAR FRIEND FOR BEING SO KIND AND TOLERANT.
CARWASH!!
THAT MISTER BEAR, HE IS A TRUE FRIEND.
WHEEE!! IMPISSED!!
BAR
GUHHHHHHH!! I MEAN, WHOOO!! I AM THE SPOOKY SHIT!! THE TORTURED SOUL OF THE WOMAN YOU MURDERED, ROHDA. YOU BASTARD!! YOU PUT AN AXE IN ME HEAD!
HAG.
AUGH FORGIVE ME ELDERLY LADY!! BUT YOU HAD WEALTH THAT WAS NOT YOURS. AND ALSO YOU WERE A BIT WHIFFY.
FOR MONEY? YOU KILLED ME FOR MONEY? TELL ME ROHDA, WHAT DID YOU DO WITH THIS MONEY, WHAT WAS MY LIFE WORTH TO YOU?
I GOT A LAMP. IT'S PRETTY.
FUCK!
A STUFFED BEAVER LAMP? I DIED FOR THIS?
AND I GOT SOME FOOD AND SENT A LITTLE MONEY TO MY MOTHER. BUT MAINLY THE LAMP. EEEE!!
CLAP CLAP CLAP
YOU WILL PAY FOR THIS, ROHDA. YOUR GUILT WILL BURN THROUGH ANY JUSTIFICATIONS YOU HAVE MADE FOR YOURSELF!!
NNNG GO AWAY, WHIFFY!! DEAD WOMEN DON'T SCARE ME.
DID HE CALL ME WHIFFY?
IGNORE HIM, DEAR SOFITA, HE'S DELIRIOUS.
HE DID THOUGH, YES.
I drew a horsey
RRRRRRRRRRGH!!
SHIT BRICKS!!
ROHDA YOU SHOULD WAKE UP, YOU'VE BEEN ASLEEP FOR DAYS NOW. YOUR BELOVED SOFITA HAS MADE YOU SOME SOUP. IT'S THREE BEAN, BUT ONE OF THEM IS A BUTTON.
AUGH!! THE CHAPPING!!
EEEEEEEEE!!
OH SOFITA I AM SORRY, I DID NOT MEAN TO SCARE YOU. I HAVE GONE QUITE MAD.
ROHDA YOU LOOK TERRIBLE. YOU WERE SAYING SUCH STRANGE THINGS IN YOUR SLEEP.
MOSTLY BI-PLANES ROHDA. WHAT IS IT WITH YOU?
JIM JAMS
BI-PLANES!! HE HE!! BRRRRM!!
OH AND ZODOFF IS HERE. HE'S BEEN ASKING TO SEE YOU SINCE YOU BECAME ILL.
THAT'S A MOST IMPRESSIVE BI-PLANE NOISE, ROHDA.
JIM JAMS
OH SHIT!! I MEAN, THANK YOU. WHAT DO YOU WANT THIS TIME?
OH NOTHING. JUST, Y'KNOW, WONDERING WHEN YOUR BIRTHDAY IS, I SAW A, UM, HAT I'D QUITE LIKE TO BUY YOU AND, UM, THE.. DID YOU KILL HER? HUH? PUT AN AXE IN HER HEAD? HUH? HUH? YOU DID, I KNOW YOU DID!!

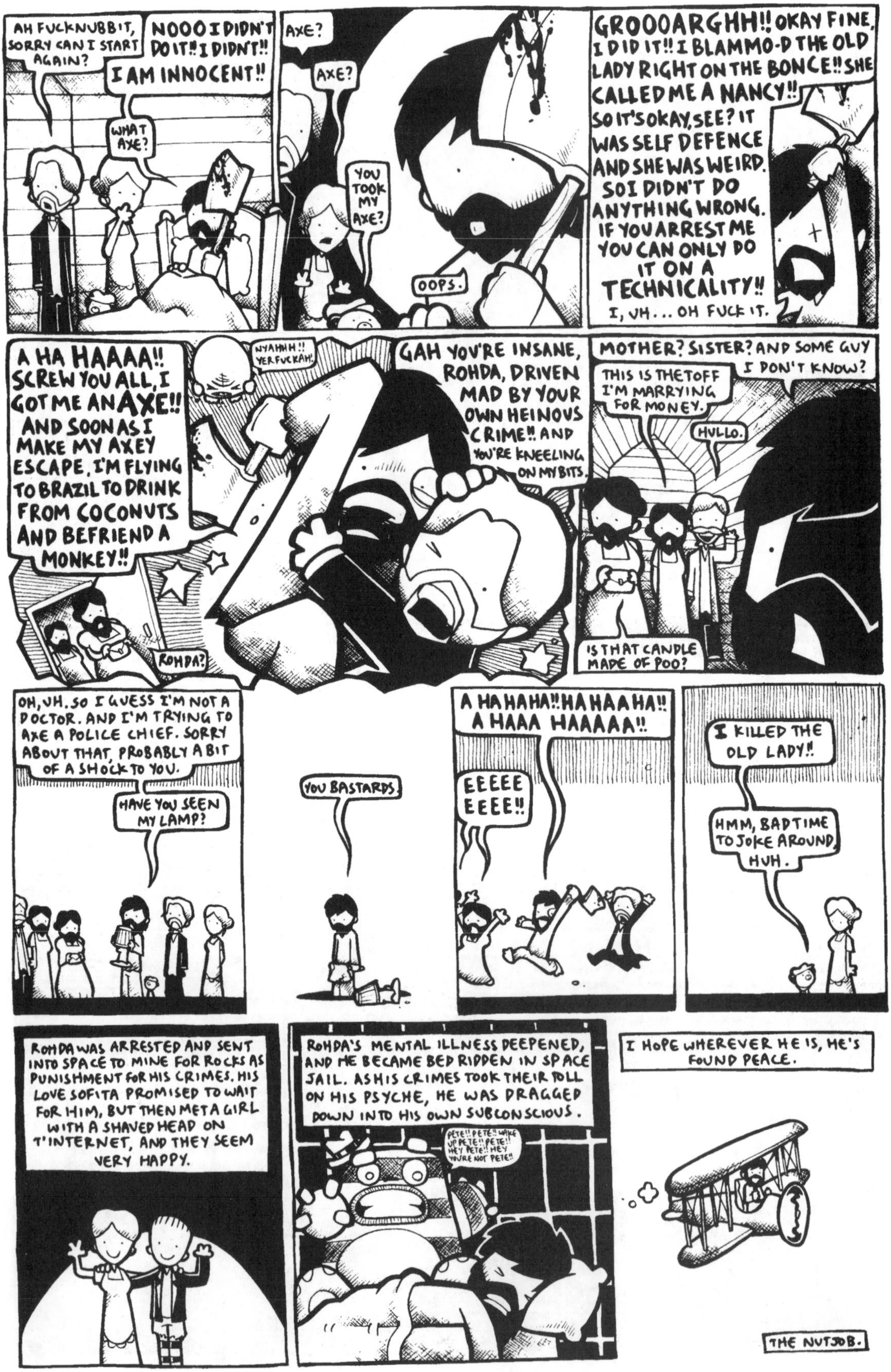

AH FUCKNUBBIT, SORRY CAN I START AGAIN?
NOOO I DIDN'T DO IT!! I DIDN'T!!
I AM INNOCENT!!
WHAT AXE?
AXE?
AXE?
YOU TOOK MY AXE?
OOPS.
GROOOARGHH!! OKAY FINE, I DID IT!! I BLAMMO-D THE OLD LADY RIGHT ON THE BONCE!! SHE CALLED ME A NANCY!!
SO IT'S OKAY, SEE? IT WAS SELF DEFENCE AND SHE WAS WEIRD. SO I DIDN'T DO ANYTHING WRONG. IF YOU ARREST ME YOU CAN ONLY DO IT ON A TECHNICALITY!!
I, UH... OH FUCK IT.
A HA HAAAA!! SCREW YOU ALL, I GOT ME AN AXE!! AND SOON AS I MAKE MY AXEY ESCAPE, I'M FLYING TO BRAZIL TO DRINK FROM COCONUTS AND BEFRIEND A MONKEY!!
NYAHHH!! YER FUCKAH!
ROHDA?
GAH YOU'RE INSANE, ROHDA, DRIVEN MAD BY YOUR OWN HEINOUS CRIME!! AND YOU'RE KNEELING ON MY BITS.
MOTHER? SISTER? AND SOME GUY I DON'T KNOW?
THIS IS THE TOFF I'M MARRYING FOR MONEY.
HULLO.
IS THAT CANDLE MADE OF POO?
OH, UH. SO I GUESS I'M NOT A DOCTOR. AND I'M TRYING TO AXE A POLICE CHIEF. SORRY ABOUT THAT, PROBABLY A BIT OF A SHOCK TO YOU.
HAVE YOU SEEN MY LAMP?
YOU BASTARDS.
A HAHAHA!! HA HAAHA!! A HAAA HAAAAA!!
EEEEE EEEE!!
I KILLED THE OLD LADY!!
HMM, BAD TIME TO JOKE AROUND, HUH.
ROHDA WAS ARRESTED AND SENT INTO SPACE TO MINE FOR ROCKS AS PUNISHMENT FOR HIS CRIMES. HIS LOVE SOFITA PROMISED TO WAIT FOR HIM, BUT THEN MET A GIRL WITH A SHAVED HEAD ON T'INTERNET, AND THEY SEEM VERY HAPPY.
ROHDA'S MENTAL ILLNESS DEEPENED, AND HE BECAME BED RIDDEN IN SPACE JAIL. AS HIS CRIMES TOOK THEIR TOLL ON HIS PSYCHE, HE WAS DRAGGED DOWN INTO HIS OWN SUBCONSCIOUS.
PETE!! PETE!! WAKE UP PETE!! PETE!! HEY PETE!! HEY YOU'RE NOT PETE!!
I HOPE WHEREVER HE IS, HE'S FOUND PEACE.
THE NUTJOB.

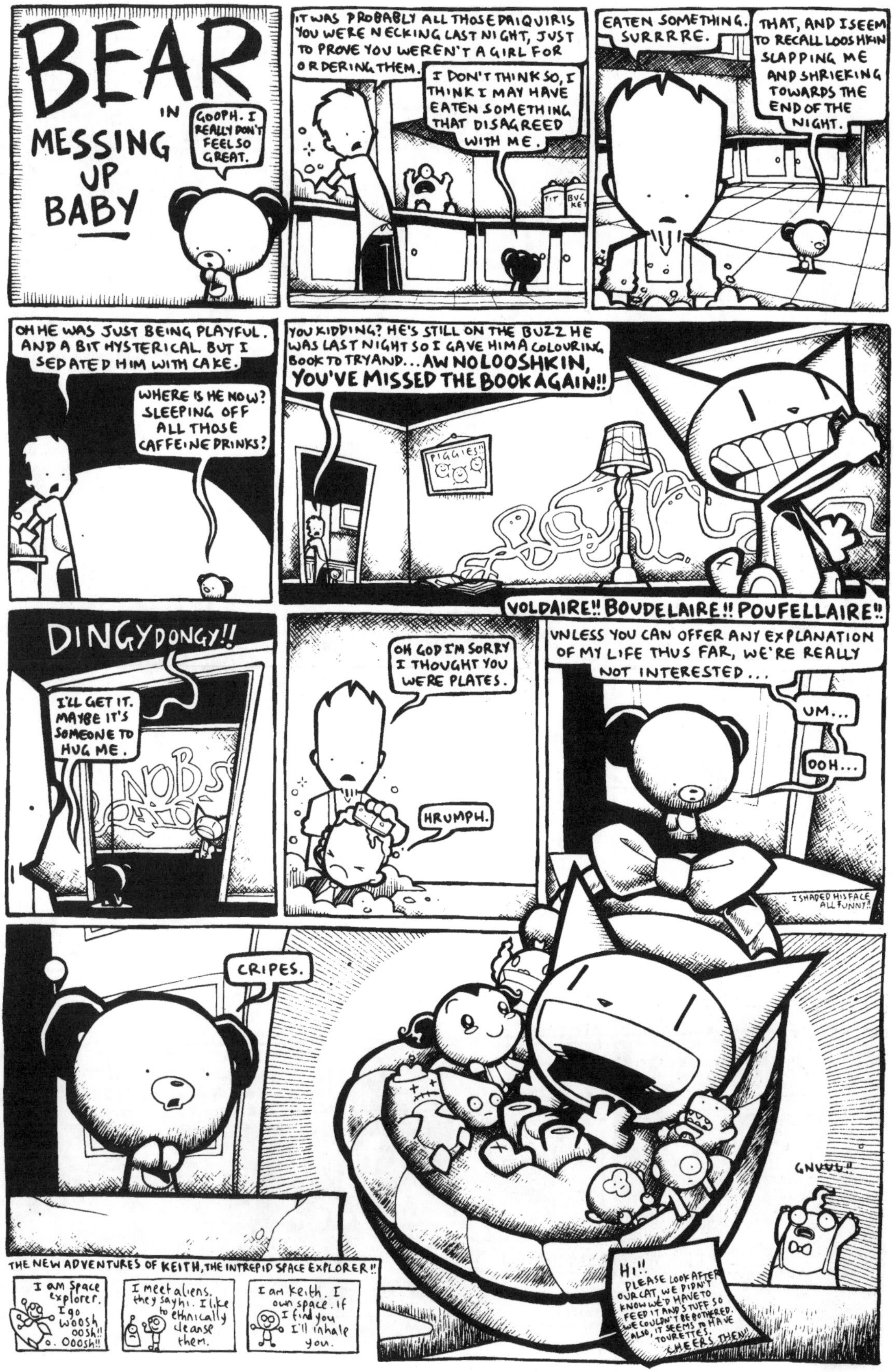
BEAR
IN
MESSING UP BABY
GOOPH. I REALLY DON'T FEEL SO GREAT.
IT WAS PROBABLY ALL THOSE DAIQUIRIS YOU WERE NECKING LAST NIGHT, JUST TO PROVE YOU WEREN'T A GIRL FOR ORDERING THEM.
I DON'T THINK SO, I THINK I MAY HAVE EATEN SOMETHING THAT DISAGREED WITH ME.
TIT
BUC KET
EATEN SOMETHING. SURRRRE.
THAT, AND I SEEM TO RECALL LOOSHKIN SLAPPING ME AND SHRIEKING TOWARDS THE END OF THE NIGHT.
OH HE WAS JUST BEING PLAYFUL. AND A BIT HYSTERICAL. BUT I SEDATED HIM WITH CAKE.
WHERE IS HE NOW? SLEEPING OFF ALL THOSE CAFFEINE DRINKS?
YOU KIDDING? HE'S STILL ON THE BUZZ HE WAS LAST NIGHT SO I GAVE HIM A COLOURING BOOK TO TRY AND... AW NO LOOSHKIN, YOU'VE MISSED THE BOOK AGAIN!!
PIGGIES!!
VOLDAIRE!! BOUDELAIRE!! POUFELLAIRE!!
DINGY DONGY!!
I'LL GET IT. MAYBE IT'S SOMEONE TO HUG ME.
OH GOD I'M SORRY I THOUGHT YOU WERE PLATES.
HRUMPH.
UNLESS YOU CAN OFFER ANY EXPLANATION OF MY LIFE THUS FAR, WE'RE REALLY NOT INTERESTED...
UM...
OOH...
I SHADED HIS FACE ALL FUNNY!!
CRIPES.
GNUUU!!
HI!! PLEASE LOOK AFTER OUR CAT, WE DIDN'T KNOW WE'D HAVE TO FEED IT AND STUFF SO WE COULDN'T BE BOTHERED. ALSO, IT SEEMS TO HAVE TOURETTES. CHEERS THEN!!
THE NEW ADVENTURES OF KEITH, THE INTREPID SPACE EXPLORER!!
I am Space explorer. I go woosh oosh!! o. Ooosh!!
I meet aliens. they say hi. I like to ethnically cleanse them.
I am keith. I own space. If I find you I'll inhale you.

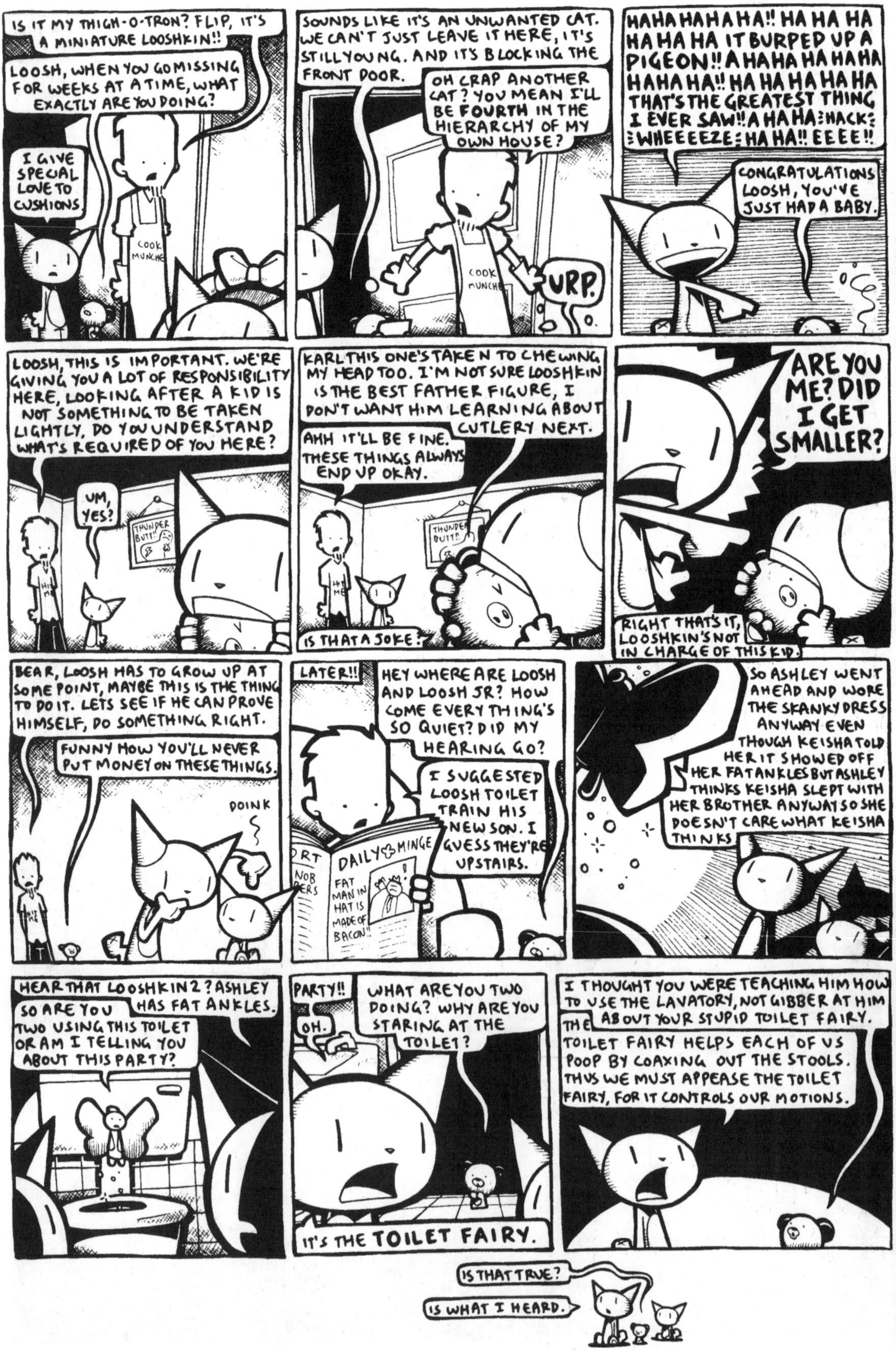
IS IT MY THIGH-O-TRON? FLIP, IT'S A MINIATURE LOOSHKIN!!
LOOSH, WHEN YOU GO MISSING FOR WEEKS AT A TIME, WHAT EXACTLY ARE YOU DOING?
I GIVE SPECIAL LOVE TO CUSHIONS
COOK MUNCHE
SOUNDS LIKE IT'S AN UNWANTED CAT. WE CAN'T JUST LEAVE IT HERE, IT'S STILL YOUNG. AND IT'S BLOCKING THE FRONT DOOR.
OH CRAP ANOTHER CAT? YOU MEAN I'LL BE FOURTH IN THE HIERARCHY OF MY OWN HOUSE?
COOK MUNCHE
URP.
HAHAHAHAHA!! HA HA HA HA HA HA IT BURPED UP A PIGEON!! A HAHA HA HA HA HAHAHA!! HA HA HA HA HA THAT'S THE GREATEST THING I EVER SAW!! A HA HA: HACK: WHEEEEZE: HA HA!! EEEE!!
CONGRATULATIONS LOOSH, YOU'VE JUST HAD A BABY.
LOOSH, THIS IS IMPORTANT. WE'RE GIVING YOU A LOT OF RESPONSIBILITY HERE, LOOKING AFTER A KID IS NOT SOMETHING TO BE TAKEN LIGHTLY, DO YOU UNDERSTAND WHAT'S REQUIRED OF YOU HERE?
UM, YES?
THUNDER BUTT!!
KARL THIS ONE'S TAKEN TO CHEWING MY HEAD TOO. I'M NOT SURE LOOSHKIN IS THE BEST FATHER FIGURE, I DON'T WANT HIM LEARNING ABOUT CUTLERY NEXT.
AHH IT'LL BE FINE. THESE THINGS ALWAYS END UP OKAY.
THUNDER BUTT!!
IS THAT A JOKE?
ARE YOU ME? DID I GET SMALLER?
RIGHT THAT'S IT, LOOSHKIN'S NOT IN CHARGE OF THIS KID.
BEAR, LOOSH HAS TO GROW UP AT SOME POINT, MAYBE THIS IS THE THING TO DO IT. LETS SEE IF HE CAN PROVE HIMSELF, DO SOMETHING RIGHT.
FUNNY HOW YOU'LL NEVER PUT MONEY ON THESE THINGS.
DOINK
LATER!!
HEY WHERE ARE LOOSH AND LOOSH JR? HOW COME EVERYTHING'S SO QUIET? DID MY HEARING GO?
I SUGGESTED LOOSH TOILET TRAIN HIS NEW SON. I GUESS THEY'RE UPSTAIRS.
DAILY MINGE
FAT MAN IN HAT IS MADE OF BACON!!
SO ASHLEY WENT AHEAD AND WORE THE SKANKY DRESS ANYWAY EVEN THOUGH KEISHA TOLD HER IT SHOWED OFF HER FAT ANKLES BUT ASHLEY THINKS KEISHA SLEPT WITH HER BROTHER ANYWAY SO SHE DOESN'T CARE WHAT KEISHA THINKS
HEAR THAT LOOSHKIN 2? ASHLEY HAS FAT ANKLES.
SO ARE YOU TWO USING THIS TOILET OR AM I TELLING YOU ABOUT THIS PARTY?
PARTY!!
OH.
WHAT ARE YOU TWO DOING? WHY ARE YOU STARING AT THE TOILET?
IT'S THE TOILET FAIRY.
I THOUGHT YOU WERE TEACHING HIM HOW TO USE THE LAVATORY, NOT GIBBER AT HIM ABOUT YOUR STUPID TOILET FAIRY.
THE TOILET FAIRY HELPS EACH OF US POOP BY COAXING OUT THE STOOLS. THUS WE MUST APPEASE THE TOILET FAIRY, FOR IT CONTROLS OUR MOTIONS.
IS THAT TRUE?
IS WHAT I HEARD.

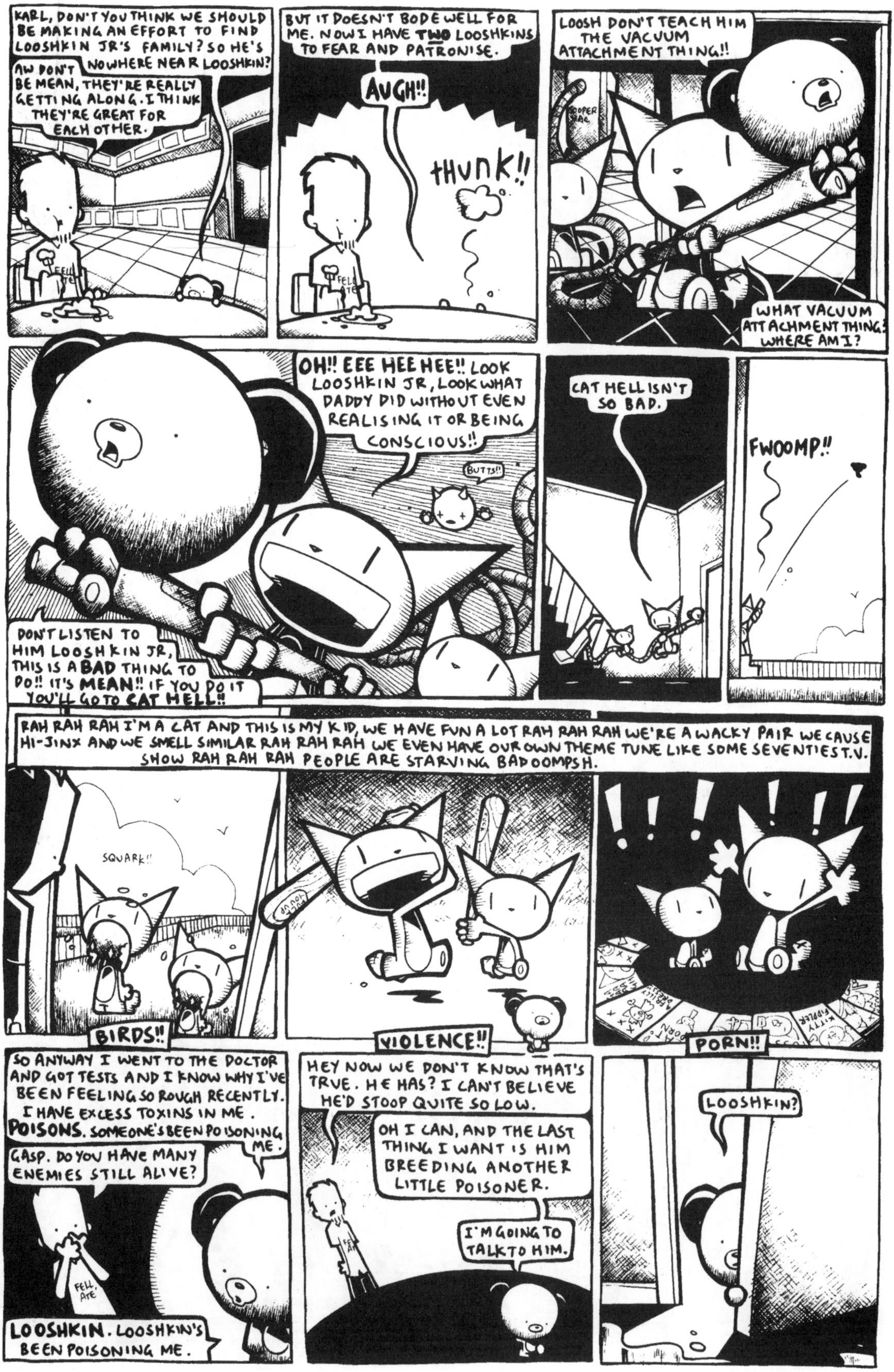
KARL, DON'T YOU THINK WE SHOULD BE MAKING AN EFFORT TO FIND LOOSHKIN JR'S FAMILY? SO HE'S NOWHERE NEAR LOOSHKIN?
AW DON'T BE MEAN, THEY'RE REALLY GETTING ALONG. I THINK THEY'RE GREAT FOR EACH OTHER.
BUT IT DOESN'T BODE WELL FOR ME. NOW I HAVE TWO LOOSHKINS TO FEAR AND PATRONISE.
AUGH!!
THUNK!!
LOOSH DON'T TEACH HIM THE VACUUM ATTACHMENT THING!!
WHAT VACUUM ATTACHMENT THING? WHERE AM I?
OH!! EEE HEE HEE!! LOOK LOOSHKIN JR, LOOK WHAT DADDY DID WITHOUT EVEN REALISING IT OR BEING CONSCIOUS!!
BUTTS!!
DON'T LISTEN TO HIM LOOSHKIN JR, THIS IS A BAD THING TO DO!! IT'S MEAN!! IF YOU DO IT YOU'LL GO TO CAT HELL!!
CAT HELL ISN'T SO BAD.
FWOOMP!!
RAH RAH RAH I'M A CAT AND THIS IS MY KID, WE HAVE FUN A LOT RAH RAH RAH WE'RE A WACKY PAIR WE CAUSE HI-JINX AND WE SMELL SIMILAR RAH RAH RAH WE EVEN HAVE OUR OWN THEME TUNE LIKE SOME SEVENTIES T.V. SHOW RAH RAH RAH PEOPLE ARE STARVING BADOOMPSH.
SQUARK!!
BIRDS!!
VIOLENCE!!
PORN!!
SO ANYWAY I WENT TO THE DOCTOR AND GOT TESTS AND I KNOW WHY I'VE BEEN FEELING SO ROUGH RECENTLY. I HAVE EXCESS TOXINS IN ME. POISONS. SOMEONE'S BEEN POISONING ME.
GASP. DO YOU HAVE MANY ENEMIES STILL ALIVE?
LOOSHKIN. LOOSHKIN'S BEEN POISONING ME.
HEY NOW WE DON'T KNOW THAT'S TRUE. HE HAS? I CAN'T BELIEVE HE'D STOOP QUITE SO LOW.
OH I CAN, AND THE LAST THING I WANT IS HIM BREEDING ANOTHER LITTLE POISONER.
I'M GOING TO TALK TO HIM.
LOOSHKIN?

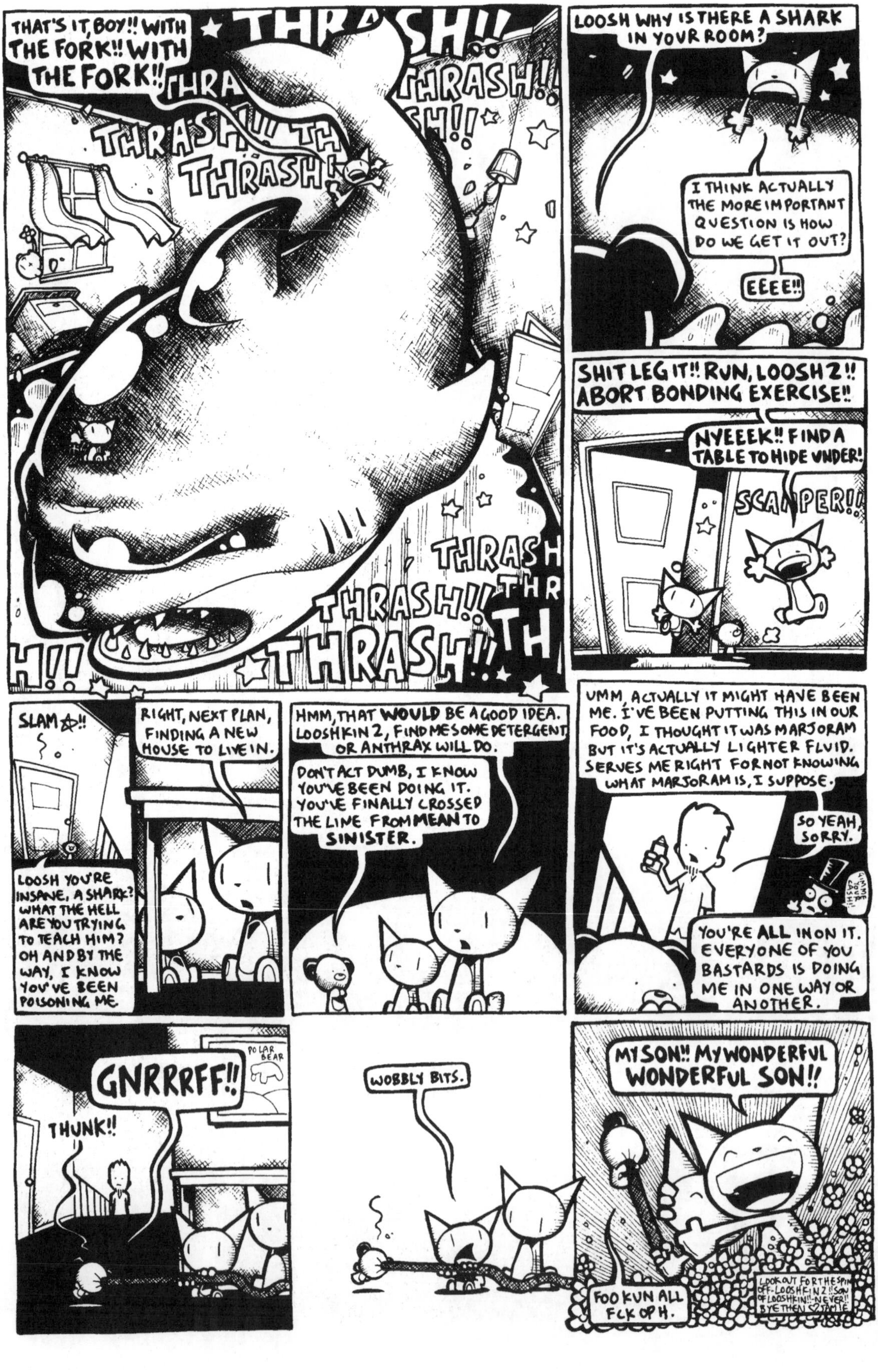
THAT'S IT, BOY!! WITH THE FORK!! WITH THE FORK!!
THRASH!!
THRASH!!
THRASH!!
THRASH!!
THRASH!!
THRASH!!
THRASH!!
LOOSH WHY IS THERE A SHARK IN YOUR ROOM?
I THINK ACTUALLY THE MORE IMPORTANT QUESTION IS HOW DO WE GET IT OUT?
EEEE!!
SHIT LEG IT!! RUN, LOOSH 2!! ABORT BONDING EXERCISE!!
NYEEEK!! FIND A TABLE TO HIDE UNDER!
SCAMPER!!
SLAM!!
LOOSH YOU'RE INSANE, A SHARK? WHAT THE HELL ARE YOU TRYING TO TEACH HIM? OH AND BY THE WAY, I KNOW YOU'VE BEEN POISONING ME.
RIGHT, NEXT PLAN, FINDING A NEW HOUSE TO LIVE IN.
HMM, THAT WOULD BE A GOOD IDEA. LOOSHKIN 2, FIND ME SOME DETERGENT OR ANTHRAX WILL DO.
DON'T ACT DUMB, I KNOW YOU'VE BEEN DOING IT. YOU'VE FINALLY CROSSED THE LINE FROM MEAN TO SINISTER.
UMM, ACTUALLY IT MIGHT HAVE BEEN ME. I'VE BEEN PUTTING THIS IN OUR FOOD, I THOUGHT IT WAS MARJORAM BUT IT'S ACTUALLY LIGHTER FLUID. SERVES ME RIGHT FOR NOT KNOWING WHAT MARJORAM IS, I SUPPOSE.
SO YEAH, SORRY.
GIMME YOUR CASH!!
YOU'RE ALL IN ON IT. EVERYONE OF YOU BASTARDS IS DOING ME IN ONE WAY OR ANOTHER.
POLAR BEAR
GNRRRFF!!
THUNK!!
WOBBLY BITS.
MY SON!! MY WONDERFUL WONDERFUL SON!!
FOO KUN ALL FCK OP H.
LOOK OUT FOR THE SPIN OFF-LOOSHKIN 2!! SON OF LOOSHKIN!!-NEVER!! BYE THEN ♡ JAMIE

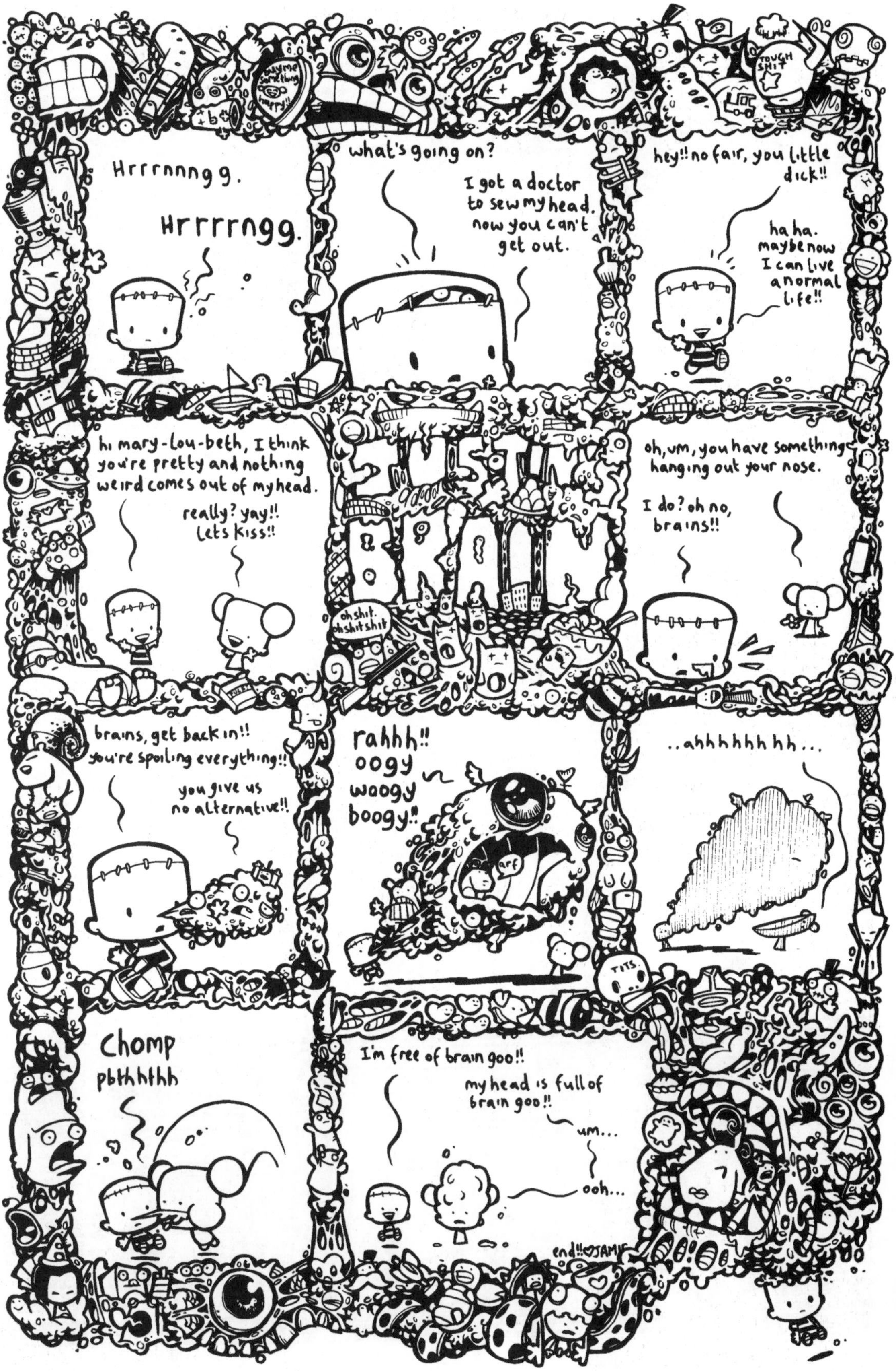
Hrrrnnngg.
Hrrrrngg.
what's going on?
I got a doctor to sew my head. now you can't get out.
hey!! no fair, you little dick!!
ha ha. maybe now I can live a normal life!!
hi mary-lou-beth, I think you're pretty and nothing weird comes out of my head.
really? yay!! lets kiss!!
oh shit. oh shit shit
oh, um, you have something hanging out your nose.
I do? oh no, brains!!
brains, get back in!! you're spoiling everything!!
you give us no alternative!!
rahhh!! oogy woogy boogy!!
arf
..ahhhhhhhh...
Chomp
pbthhthh
I'm free of brain goo!!
my head is full of brain goo!!
um...
ooh...
end!! ♥ JAMIE

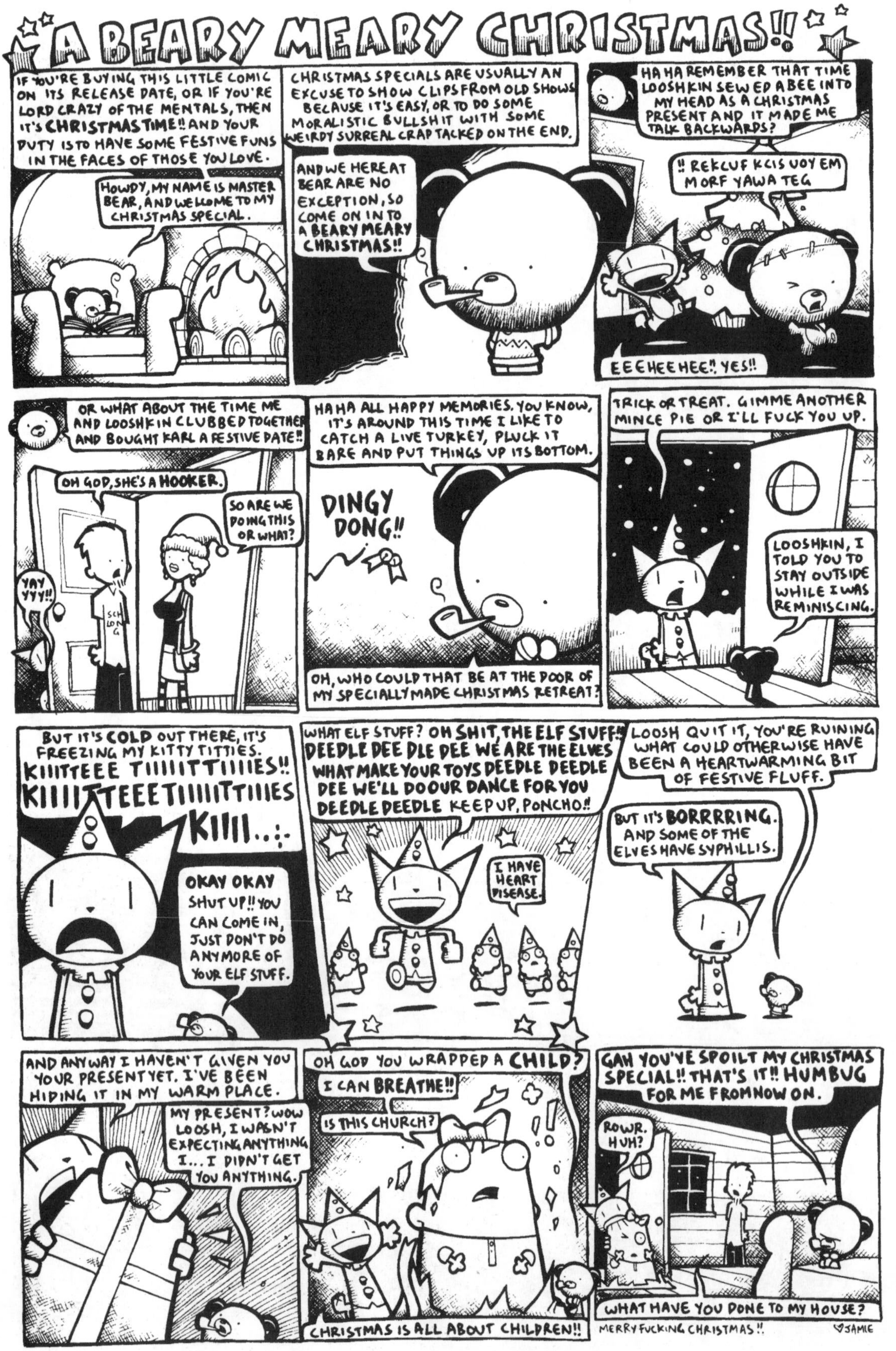
A BEARY MEARY CHRISTMAS!!
IF YOU'RE BUYING THIS LITTLE COMIC ON ITS RELEASE DATE, OR IF YOU'RE LORD CRAZY OF THE MENTALS, THEN IT'S CHRISTMAS TIME!! AND YOUR DUTY IS TO HAVE SOME FESTIVE FUNS IN THE FACES OF THOSE YOU LOVE.
HOWDY, MY NAME IS MASTER BEAR, AND WELCOME TO MY CHRISTMAS SPECIAL.
CHRISTMAS SPECIALS ARE USUALLY AN EXCUSE TO SHOW CLIPS FROM OLD SHOWS BECAUSE IT'S EASY, OR TO DO SOME MORALISTIC BULLSHIT WITH SOME WEIRDY SURREAL CRAP TACKED ON THE END.
AND WE HERE AT BEAR ARE NO EXCEPTION, SO COME ON IN TO A BEARY MEARY CHRISTMAS!!
HA HA REMEMBER THAT TIME LOOSHKIN SEWED A BEE INTO MY HEAD AS A CHRISTMAS PRESENT AND IT MADE ME TALK BACKWARDS?
!! REKCUF KCIS UOY EM MORF YAWA TEG
EEEHEEHEE!! YES!!
OR WHAT ABOUT THE TIME ME AND LOOSHKIN CLUBBED TOGETHER AND BOUGHT KARL A FESTIVE DATE!!
OH GOD, SHE'S A HOOKER.
SO ARE WE DOING THIS OR WHAT?
YAY YYY!!
SCH LON G
HA HA ALL HAPPY MEMORIES. YOU KNOW, IT'S AROUND THIS TIME I LIKE TO CATCH A LIVE TURKEY, PLUCK IT BARE AND PUT THINGS UP ITS BOTTOM.
DINGY DONG!!
OH, WHO COULD THAT BE AT THE DOOR OF MY SPECIALLY MADE CHRISTMAS RETREAT?
TRICK OR TREAT. GIMME ANOTHER MINCE PIE OR I'LL FUCK YOU UP.
LOOSHKIN, I TOLD YOU TO STAY OUTSIDE WHILE I WAS REMINISCING.
BUT IT'S COLD OUT THERE, IT'S FREEZING MY KITTY TITTIES. KIIITTEEE TIIIIITTIIIIES!! KIIIITTEEETIIIIITTIIIES KIIII..:.
OKAY OKAY SHUT UP!! YOU CAN COME IN, JUST DON'T DO ANYMORE OF YOUR ELF STUFF.
WHAT ELF STUFF? OH SHIT, THE ELF STUFF!! DEEDLE DEE DLE DEE WE ARE THE ELVES WHAT MAKE YOUR TOYS DEEDLE DEEDLE DEE WE'LL DO OUR DANCE FOR YOU DEEDLE DEEDLE KEEP UP, PONCHO!!
I HAVE HEART DISEASE.
LOOSH QUIT IT, YOU'RE RUINING WHAT COULD OTHERWISE HAVE BEEN A HEARTWARMING BIT OF FESTIVE FLUFF.
BUT IT'S BORRRRING. AND SOME OF THE ELVES HAVE SYPHILLIS.
AND ANYWAY I HAVEN'T GIVEN YOU YOUR PRESENT YET. I'VE BEEN HIDING IT IN MY WARM PLACE.
MY PRESENT? WOW LOOSH, I WASN'T EXPECTING ANYTHING I... I DIDN'T GET YOU ANYTHING.
OH GOD YOU WRAPPED A CHILD?
I CAN BREATHE!!
IS THIS CHURCH?
CHRISTMAS IS ALL ABOUT CHILDREN!!
GAH YOU'VE SPOILT MY CHRISTMAS SPECIAL!! THAT'S IT!! HUMBUG FOR ME FROM NOW ON.
ROWR. HUH?
WHAT HAVE YOU DONE TO MY HOUSE?
MERRY FUCKING CHRISTMAS!!
♥JAMIE

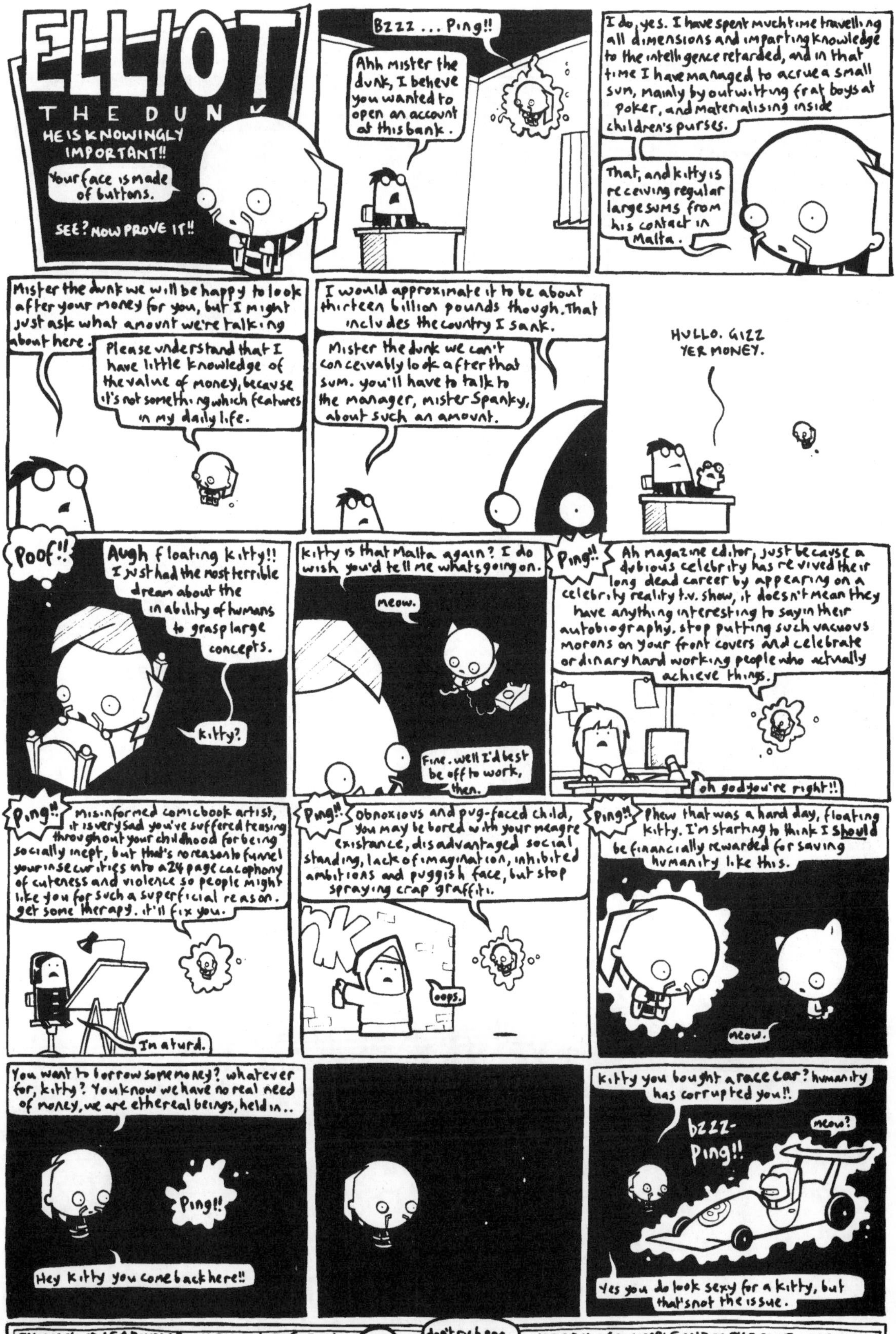
ELLIOT
THE DUNK
HE IS KNOWINGLY IMPORTANT!!
Your face is made of buttons.
SEE? NOW PROVE IT!!
Bzzz ... Ping!!
Ahh mister the dunk, I believe you wanted to open an account at this bank.
I do, yes. I have spent much time travelling all dimensions and imparting knowledge to the intelligence retarded, and in that time I have managed to acrue a small sum, mainly by outwitting frat boys at poker, and materialising inside children's purses.
That, and kitty is receiving regular large sums from his contact in Malta.
Mister the dunk we will be happy to look after your money for you, but I might just ask what amount we're talking about here.
Please understand that I have little knowledge of the value of money, because it's not something which features in my daily life.
I would approximate it to be about thirteen billion pounds though. That includes the country I sank.
Mister the dunk we can't conceivably look after that sum. you'll have to talk to the manager, mister Spanky, about such an amount.
HULLO. GIZZ YER MONEY.
Poof!!
Augh floating kitty!! I just had the most terrible dream about the inability of humans to grasp large concepts.
kitty?
kitty is that Malta again? I do wish you'd tell me whats going on.
meow.
Fine. well I'd best be off to work, then.
Ping!!
Ah magazine editor, just because a dubious celebrity has revived their long dead career by appearing on a celebrity reality t.v. show, it doesn't mean they have anything interesting to say in their autobiography. stop putting such vacuous morons on your front covers and celebrate ordinary hard working people who actually achieve things.
oh god you're right!!
Ping!!
misinformed comicbook artist, it is very sad you've suffered teasing throughout your childhood for being socially inept, but that's no reason to funnel your insecurities into a 24 page cacophony of cuteness and violence so people might like you for such a superficial reason. get some therapy. it'll fix you.
Im a turd.
Ping!!
Obnoxious and pug-faced child, you may be bored with your meagre existance, disadvantaged social standing, lack of imagination, inhibited ambitions and puggish face, but stop spraying crap graffiti.
oops.
Ping!!
Phew that was a hard day, floating kitty. I'm starting to think I should be financially rewarded for saving humanity like this.
meow.
You want to borrow some money? whatever for, kitty? You know we have no real need of money, we are ethereal beings, held in..
Ping!!
Hey kitty you come back here!!
kitty you bought a race car? humanity has corrupted you!!
bzzz-Ping!!
meow?
Yes you do look sexy for a kitty, but that's not the issue.
THIS IS YOUR LEARNING!! IT IS TOO BIG TO FIT IN YOUR HEAD, SO PUT SOME OF IT IN YOUR ASS!!
don't rub poo in your eyes.
THERE YOU GO, SIMPLE AND TO THE POINT. LEARNING NEED NOT BE FRILLY. OR PLEASANT.
♡JAMIE

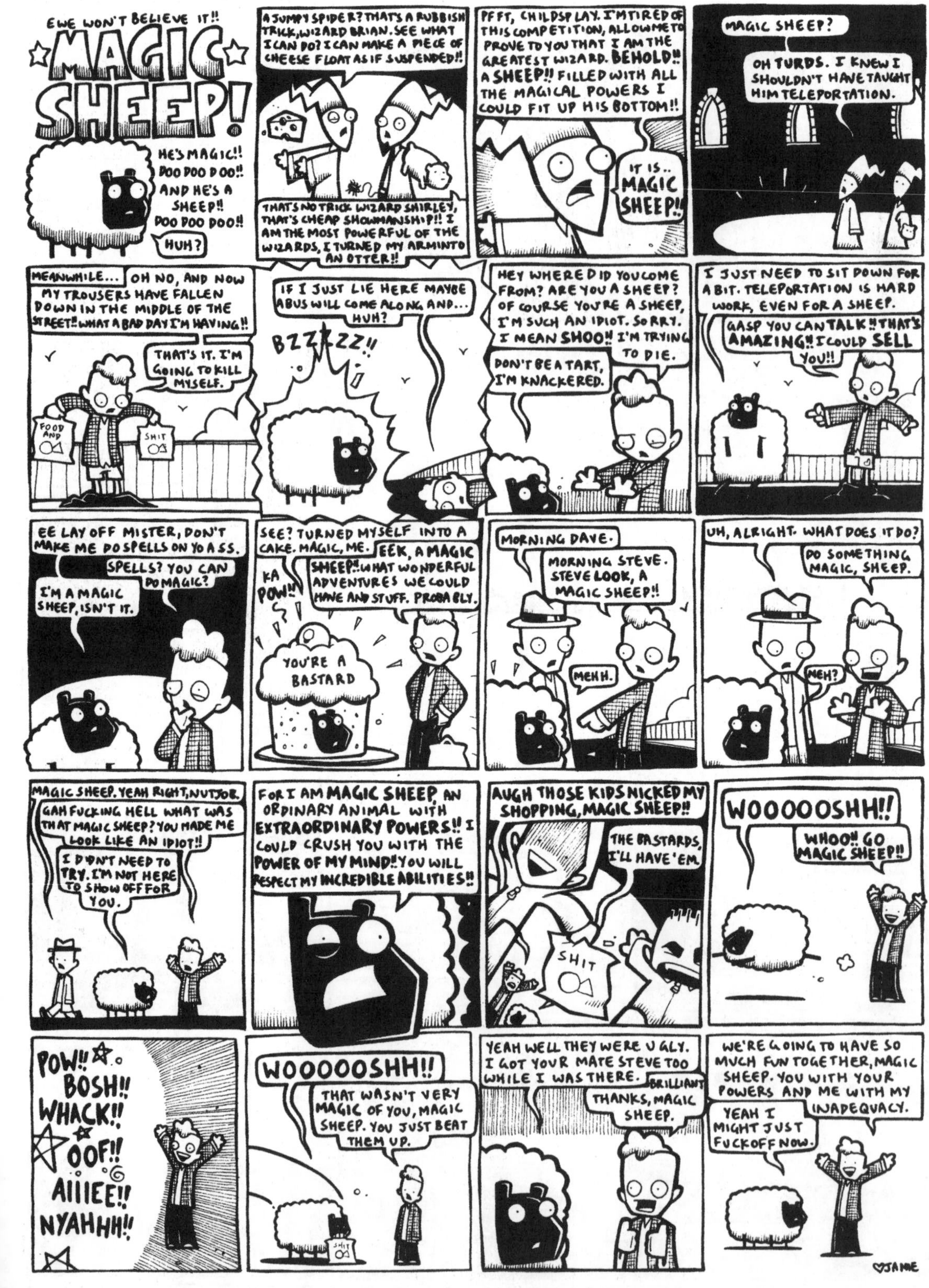
EWE WON'T BELIEVE IT!!
MAGIC SHEEP!
HE'S MAGIC!! DOO DOO DOO!! AND HE'S A SHEEP!! DOO DOO DOO!!
HUH?
A JUMPY SPIDER? THAT'S A RUBBISH TRICK, WIZARD BRIAN. SEE WHAT I CAN DO? I CAN MAKE A PIECE OF CHEESE FLOAT AS IF SUSPENDED!!
THAT'S NO TRICK WIZARD SHIRLEY, THAT'S CHEAP SHOWMANSHIP!! I AM THE MOST POWERFUL OF THE WIZARDS, I TURNED MY ARM INTO AN OTTER!!
PFFT, CHILDSPLAY. I'M TIRED OF THIS COMPETITION, ALLOW ME TO PROVE TO YOU THAT I AM THE GREATEST WIZARD. BEHOLD!! A SHEEP!! FILLED WITH ALL THE MAGICAL POWERS I COULD FIT UP HIS BOTTOM!!
IT IS.. MAGIC SHEEP!!
MAGIC SHEEP?
OH TURDS. I KNEW I SHOULDN'T HAVE TAUGHT HIM TELEPORTATION.
MEANWHILE...
OH NO, AND NOW MY TROUSERS HAVE FALLEN DOWN IN THE MIDDLE OF THE STREET!! WHAT A BAD DAY I'M HAVING!!
THAT'S IT. I'M GOING TO KILL MYSELF.
FOOD AND
SHIT
IF I JUST LIE HERE MAYBE A BUS WILL COME ALONG AND... HUH?
BZZZZZ!!
HEY WHERE DID YOU COME FROM? ARE YOU A SHEEP? OF COURSE YOU'RE A SHEEP, I'M SUCH AN IDIOT. SORRY. I MEAN SHOO!! I'M TRYING TO DIE.
DON'T BE A TART, I'M KNACKERED.
I JUST NEED TO SIT DOWN FOR A BIT. TELEPORTATION IS HARD WORK, EVEN FOR A SHEEP.
GASP YOU CAN TALK!! THAT'S AMAZING!! I COULD SELL YOU!!
EE LAY OFF MISTER, DON'T MAKE ME DO SPELLS ON YO ASS.
SPELLS? YOU CAN DO MAGIC?
I'M A MAGIC SHEEP, ISN'T IT.
SEE? TURNED MYSELF INTO A CAKE. MAGIC, ME.
KA POW!!
EEK, A MAGIC SHEEP!! WHAT WONDERFUL ADVENTURES WE COULD HAVE AND STUFF. PROBABLY.
YOU'RE A BASTARD
MORNING DAVE.
MORNING STEVE. STEVE LOOK, A MAGIC SHEEP!!
MEHH.
UH, ALRIGHT. WHAT DOES IT DO?
DO SOMETHING MAGIC, SHEEP.
MEH?
MAGIC SHEEP. YEAH RIGHT, NUTJOB.
GAH FUCKING HELL WHAT WAS THAT MAGIC SHEEP? YOU MADE ME LOOK LIKE AN IDIOT!!
I DON'T NEED TO TRY. I'M NOT HERE TO SHOW OFF FOR YOU.
FOR I AM MAGIC SHEEP, AN ORDINARY ANIMAL WITH EXTRAORDINARY POWERS!! I COULD CRUSH YOU WITH THE POWER OF MY MIND!! YOU WILL RESPECT MY INCREDIBLE ABILITIES!!
AUGH THOSE KIDS NICKED MY SHOPPING, MAGIC SHEEP!!
THE BASTARDS, I'LL HAVE 'EM.
SHIT
WOOOOOSHH!!
WHOO!! GO MAGIC SHEEP!!
POW!! BOSH!! WHACK!! OOF!! AIIIEE!! NYAHHH!!
WOOOOOSHH!!
THAT WASN'T VERY MAGIC OF YOU, MAGIC SHEEP. YOU JUST BEAT THEM UP.
SHIT
YEAH WELL THEY WERE UGLY. I GOT YOUR MATE STEVE TOO WHILE I WAS THERE.
BRILLIANT THANKS, MAGIC SHEEP.
WE'RE GOING TO HAVE SO MUCH FUN TOGETHER, MAGIC SHEEP. YOU WITH YOUR POWERS AND ME WITH MY INADEQUACY.
YEAH I MIGHT JUST FUCK OFF NOW.
♡JAMIE

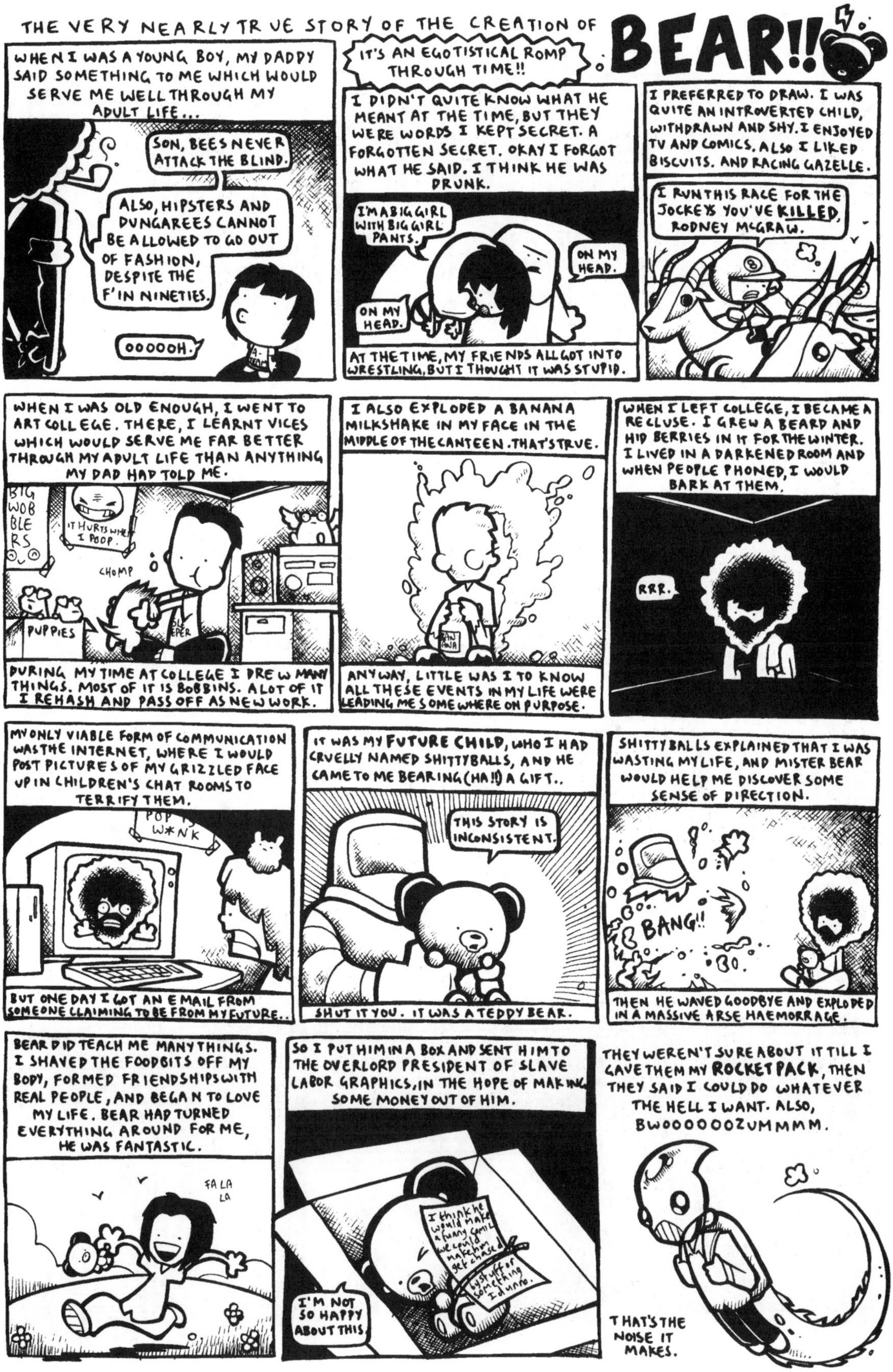
THE VERY NEARLY TRUE STORY OF THE CREATION OF BEAR!!
WHEN I WAS A YOUNG BOY, MY DADDY SAID SOMETHING TO ME WHICH WOULD SERVE ME WELL THROUGH MY ADULT LIFE...
SON, BEES NEVER ATTACK THE BLIND.
ALSO, HIPSTERS AND DUNGAREES CANNOT BE ALLOWED TO GO OUT OF FASHION, DESPITE THE F'IN NINETIES.
OOOOOH.
IT'S AN EGOTISTICAL ROMP THROUGH TIME!!
I DIDN'T QUITE KNOW WHAT HE MEANT AT THE TIME, BUT THEY WERE WORDS I KEPT SECRET. A FORGOTTEN SECRET. OKAY I FORGOT WHAT HE SAID. I THINK HE WAS DRUNK.
I'M A BIG GIRL WITH BIG GIRL PANTS.
ON MY HEAD.
ON MY HEAD.
AT THE TIME, MY FRIENDS ALL GOT INTO WRESTLING, BUT I THOUGHT IT WAS STUPID.
I PREFERRED TO DRAW. I WAS QUITE AN INTROVERTED CHILD, WITHDRAWN AND SHY. I ENJOYED TV AND COMICS. ALSO I LIKED BISCUITS. AND RACING GAZELLE.
I RUN THIS RACE FOR THE JOCKEYS YOU'VE KILLED, RODNEY McGRAW.
WHEN I WAS OLD ENOUGH, I WENT TO ART COLLEGE. THERE, I LEARNT VICES WHICH WOULD SERVE ME FAR BETTER THROUGH MY ADULT LIFE THAN ANYTHING MY DAD HAD TOLD ME.
BIG WOBBLERS
IT HURTS WHEN I POOP.
CHOMP
PUPPIES
DURING MY TIME AT COLLEGE I DREW MANY THINGS. MOST OF IT IS BOBBINS. A LOT OF IT I REHASH AND PASS OFF AS NEW WORK.
I ALSO EXPLODED A BANANA MILKSHAKE IN MY FACE IN THE MIDDLE OF THE CANTEEN. THAT'S TRUE.
ANYWAY, LITTLE WAS I TO KNOW ALL THESE EVENTS IN MY LIFE WERE LEADING ME SOMEWHERE ON PURPOSE.
WHEN I LEFT COLLEGE, I BECAME A RECLUSE. I GREW A BEARD AND HID BERRIES IN IT FOR THE WINTER. I LIVED IN A DARKENED ROOM AND WHEN PEOPLE PHONED, I WOULD BARK AT THEM.
RRR.
MY ONLY VIABLE FORM OF COMMUNICATION WAS THE INTERNET, WHERE I WOULD POST PICTURES OF MY GRIZZLED FACE UP IN CHILDREN'S CHAT ROOMS TO TERRIFY THEM.
POP W*NK
BUT ONE DAY I GOT AN EMAIL FROM SOMEONE CLAIMING TO BE FROM MY FUTURE..
IT WAS MY FUTURE CHILD, WHO I HAD CRUELLY NAMED SHITTYBALLS, AND HE CAME TO ME BEARING (HA!!) A GIFT..
THIS STORY IS INCONSISTENT.
SHUT IT YOU. IT WAS A TEDDY BEAR.
SHITTYBALLS EXPLAINED THAT I WAS WASTING MY LIFE, AND MISTER BEAR WOULD HELP ME DISCOVER SOME SENSE OF DIRECTION.
BANG!!
THEN HE WAVED GOODBYE AND EXPLODED IN A MASSIVE ARSE HAEMORRAGE.
BEAR DID TEACH ME MANY THINGS. I SHAVED THE FOODBITS OFF MY BODY, FORMED FRIENDSHIPS WITH REAL PEOPLE, AND BEGAN TO LOVE MY LIFE. BEAR HAD TURNED EVERYTHING AROUND FOR ME, HE WAS FANTASTIC.
FA LA LA
SO I PUT HIM IN A BOX AND SENT HIM TO THE OVERLORD PRESIDENT OF SLAVE LABOR GRAPHICS, IN THE HOPE OF MAKING SOME MONEY OUT OF HIM.
I think he would make a funny comic we could make him get chased by stuff or something I dunno.
I'M NOT SO HAPPY ABOUT THIS.
THEY WEREN'T SURE ABOUT IT TILL I GAVE THEM MY ROCKET PACK, THEN THEY SAID I COULD DO WHATEVER THE HELL I WANT. ALSO, BWOOOOOOZUMMMM.
THAT'S THE NOISE IT MAKES.

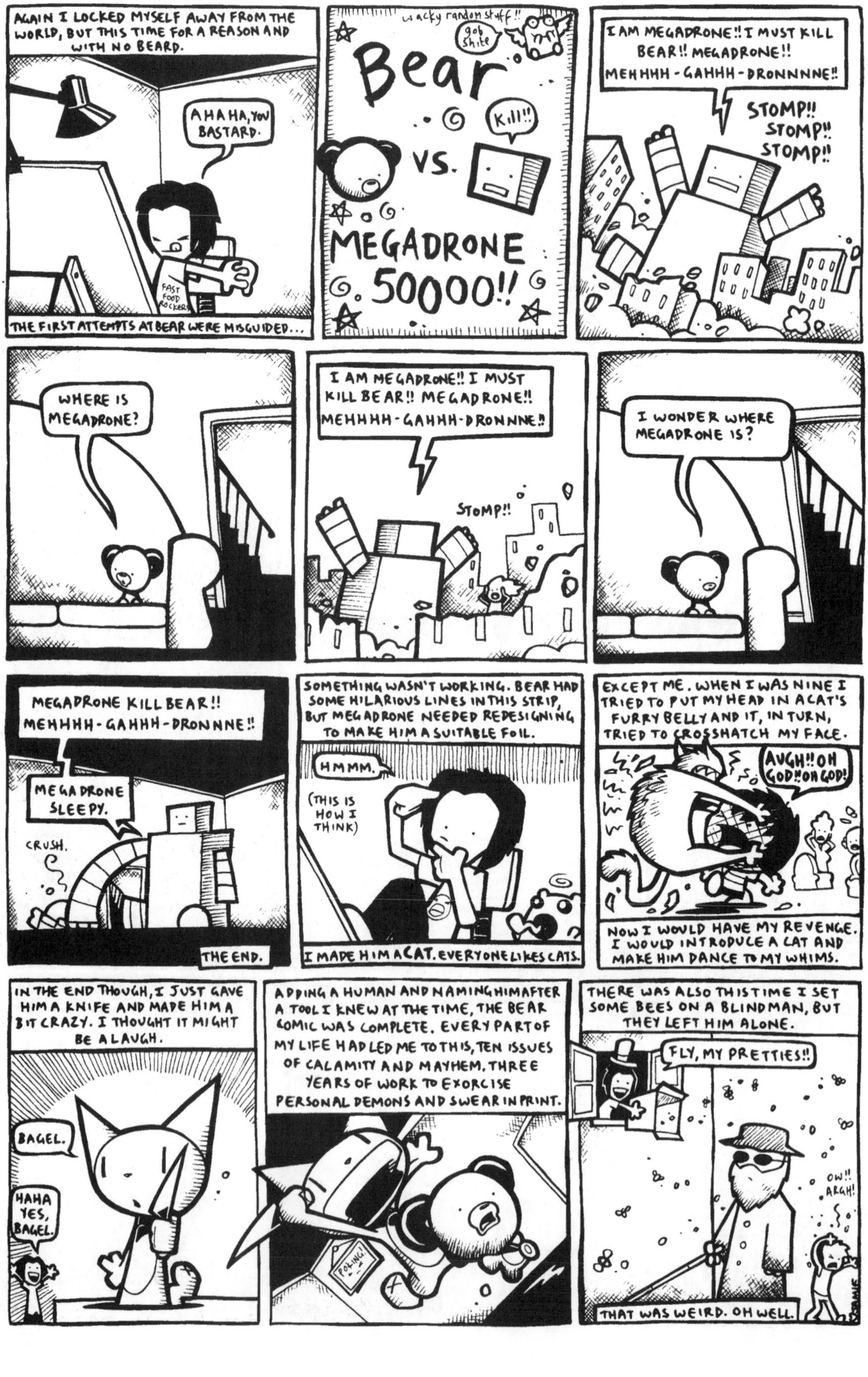
AGAIN I LOCKED MYSELF AWAY FROM THE WORLD, BUT THIS TIME FOR A REASON AND WITH NO BEARD.
AHAHA, YOU BASTARD.
FAST FOOD ROCKERS
THE FIRST ATTEMPTS AT BEAR WERE MISGUIDED...
wacky random stuff!!
gob shite
Bear
Kill!!
VS.
MEGADRONE 50000!!
I AM MEGADRONE!! I MUST KILL BEAR!! MEGADRONE!! MEHHHH-GAHHH-DRONNNNE!!
STOMP!! STOMP!! STOMP!!
WHERE IS MEGADRONE?
I AM MEGADRONE!! I MUST KILL BEAR!! MEGADRONE!! MEHHHH-GAHHH-DRONNNE!!
STOMP!!
I WONDER WHERE MEGADRONE IS?
MEGADRONE KILL BEAR!! MEHHHH-GAHHH-DRONNNE!!
MEGADRONE SLEEPY.
CRUSH.
THE END.
SOMETHING WASN'T WORKING. BEAR HAD SOME HILARIOUS LINES IN THIS STRIP, BUT MEGADRONE NEEDED REDESIGNING TO MAKE HIM A SUITABLE FOIL.
HMMM.
(THIS IS HOW I THINK)
I MADE HIM A CAT. EVERYONE LIKES CATS.
EXCEPT ME. WHEN I WAS NINE I TRIED TO PUT MY HEAD IN A CAT'S FURRY BELLY AND IT, IN TURN, TRIED TO CROSSHATCH MY FACE.
AUGH!! OH GOD!! OH GOD!
NOW I WOULD HAVE MY REVENGE. I WOULD INTRODUCE A CAT AND MAKE HIM DANCE TO MY WHIMS.
IN THE END THOUGH, I JUST GAVE HIM A KNIFE AND MADE HIM A BIT CRAZY. I THOUGHT IT MIGHT BE A LAUGH.
BAGEL.
HAHA YES, BAGEL.
ADDING A HUMAN AND NAMING HIM AFTER A TOOL I KNEW AT THE TIME, THE BEAR COMIC WAS COMPLETE. EVERY PART OF MY LIFE HAD LED ME TO THIS, TEN ISSUES OF CALAMITY AND MAYHEM, THREE YEARS OF WORK TO EXORCISE PERSONAL DEMONS AND SWEAR IN PRINT.
POING!
THERE WAS ALSO THIS TIME I SET SOME BEES ON A BLINDMAN, BUT THEY LEFT HIM ALONE.
FLY, MY PRETTIES!!
OW!! ARGH!
THAT WAS WEIRD. OH WELL.

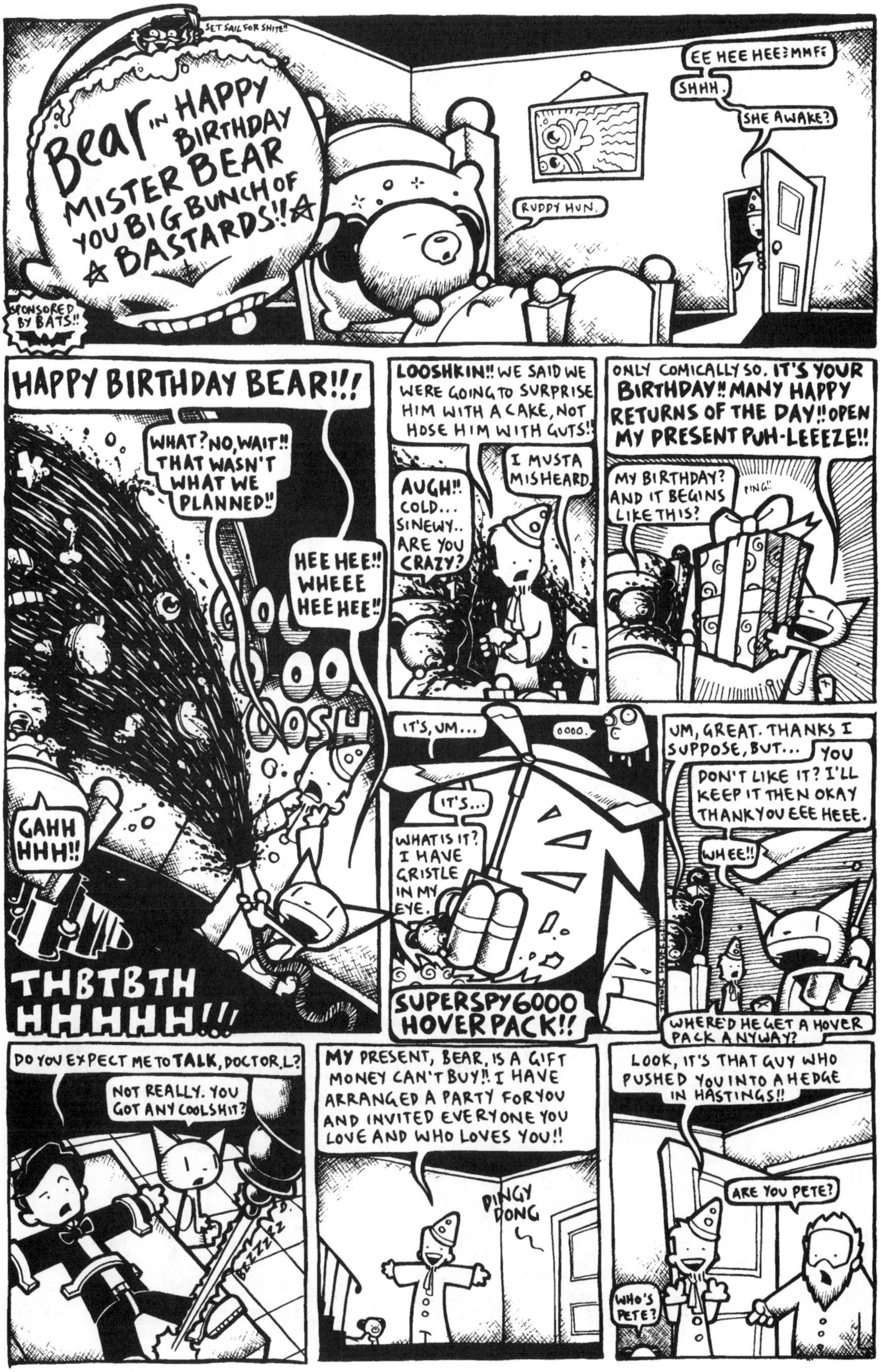

SET SAIL FOR SHITE!!
Bear IN HAPPY BIRTHDAY MISTER BEAR YOU BIG BUNCH OF BASTARDS!!
SPONSORED BY BATS!!
EE HEE HEE: MMF:
SHHH.
SHE AWAKE?
RUDDY HUN.
HAPPY BIRTHDAY BEAR!!!
WHAT? NO, WAIT!! THAT WASN'T WHAT WE PLANNED!!
HEE HEE!! WHEEE HEE HEE!!
GAHH HHH!!
THBTBTH HHHHH!!!
LOOSHKIN!! WE SAID WE WERE GOING TO SURPRISE HIM WITH A CAKE, NOT HOSE HIM WITH GUTS!!
I MUSTA MISHEARD.
AUGH!! COLD... SINEWY.. ARE YOU CRAZY?
ONLY COMICALLY SO. IT'S YOUR BIRTHDAY!! MANY HAPPY RETURNS OF THE DAY!! OPEN MY PRESENT PUH-LEEEZE!!
MY BIRTHDAY? AND IT BEGINS LIKE THIS?
PING!!
IT'S, UM...
OOOO.
IT'S...
WHAT IS IT? I HAVE GRISTLE IN MY EYE.
SUPERSPY 6000 HOVER PACK!!
UM, GREAT. THANKS I SUPPOSE, BUT...
YOU DON'T LIKE IT? I'LL KEEP IT THEN OKAY THANK YOU EEE HEEE.
WHEE!!
WHERE'D HE GET A HOVER PACK ANYWAY?
DO YOU EXPECT ME TO TALK, DOCTOR L?
NOT REALLY. YOU GOT ANY COOL SHIT?
MY PRESENT, BEAR, IS A GIFT MONEY CAN'T BUY!! I HAVE ARRANGED A PARTY FOR YOU AND INVITED EVERYONE YOU LOVE AND WHO LOVES YOU!!
DINGY DONG
LOOK, IT'S THAT GUY WHO PUSHED YOU INTO A HEDGE IN HASTINGS!!
ARE YOU PETE?
WHO'S PETE?

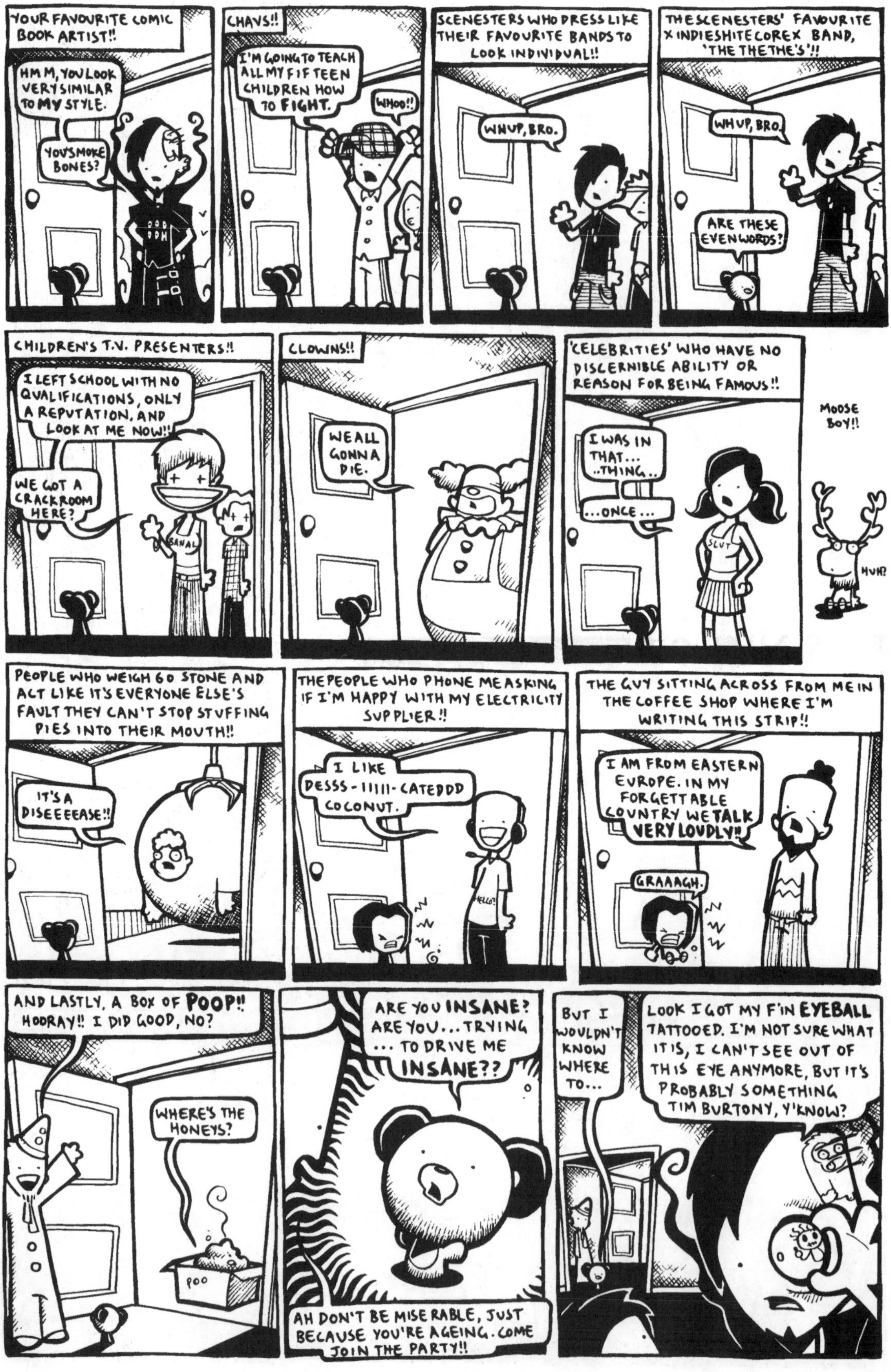
YOUR FAVOURITE COMIC BOOK ARTIST!!
HMM, YOU LOOK VERY SIMILAR TO MY STYLE.
YOU'S MOKE BONES?
CHAVS!!
I'M GOING TO TEACH ALL MY FIFTEEN CHILDREN HOW TO FIGHT.
WHOO!!
SCENESTERS WHO DRESS LIKE THEIR FAVOURITE BANDS TO LOOK INDIVIDUAL!!
WHUP, BRO.
THE SCENESTERS' FAVOURITE X INDIESHITECOREX BAND, 'THE THE THE'S'!!
WHUP, BRO.
ARE THESE EVEN WORDS?
CHILDREN'S T.V. PRESENTERS!!
I LEFT SCHOOL WITH NO QUALIFICATIONS, ONLY A REPUTATION. AND LOOK AT ME NOW!!
WE GOT A CRACKROOM HERE?
BANAL
CLOWNS!!
WE ALL GONNA DIE.
'CELEBRITIES' WHO HAVE NO DISCERNIBLE ABILITY OR REASON FOR BEING FAMOUS!!
I WAS IN THAT... ..THING...
...ONCE...
SLUT
MOOSE BOY!!
HUH?
PEOPLE WHO WEIGH 60 STONE AND ACT LIKE IT'S EVERYONE ELSE'S FAULT THEY CAN'T STOP STUFFING PIES INTO THEIR MOUTH!!
IT'S A DISEEEEASE!!
THE PEOPLE WHO PHONE ME ASKING IF I'M HAPPY WITH MY ELECTRICITY SUPPLIER!!
I LIKE DESSS-IIIII-CATEDDD COCONUT.
HELLO!
THE GUY SITTING ACROSS FROM ME IN THE COFFEE SHOP WHERE I'M WRITING THIS STRIP!!
I AM FROM EASTERN EUROPE. IN MY FORGETTABLE COUNTRY WE TALK VERY LOUDLY!!
GRAAAGH.
AND LASTLY, A BOX OF POOP!! HOORAY!! I DID GOOD, NO?
WHERE'S THE HONEYS?
POO
ARE YOU INSANE? ARE YOU... TRYING ... TO DRIVE ME INSANE??
AH DON'T BE MISERABLE, JUST BECAUSE YOU'RE AGEING. COME JOIN THE PARTY!!
BUT I WOULDN'T KNOW WHERE TO...
LOOK I GOT MY F'IN EYEBALL TATTOOED. I'M NOT SURE WHAT IT IS, I CAN'T SEE OUT OF THIS EYE ANYMORE, BUT IT'S PROBABLY SOMETHING TIM BURTONY, Y'KNOW?

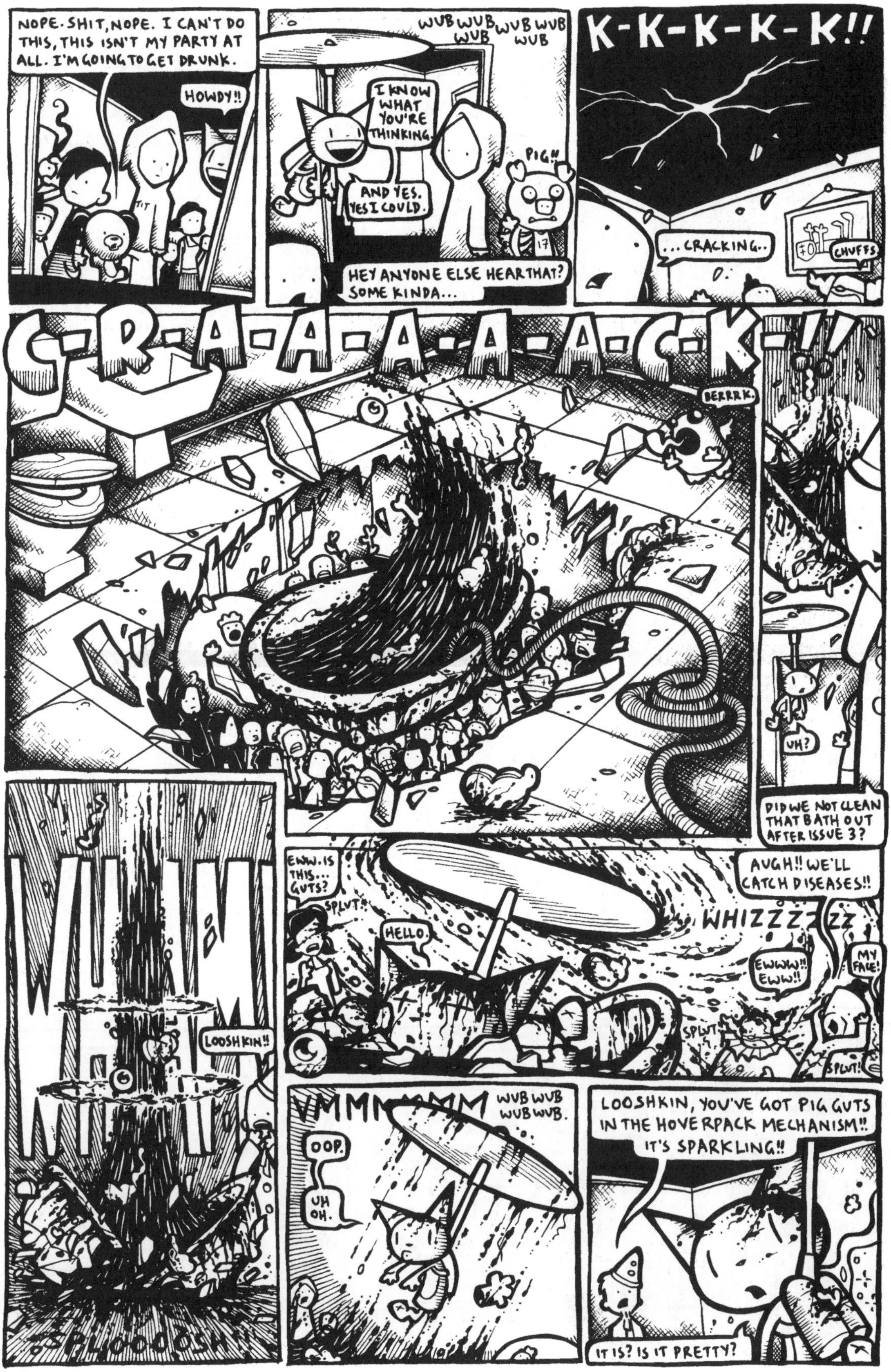

NOPE. SHIT, NOPE. I CAN'T DO THIS, THIS ISN'T MY PARTY AT ALL. I'M GOING TO GET DRUNK.
HOWDY!!
WUB WUB WUB WUB WUB WUB
I KNOW WHAT YOU'RE THINKING.
AND YES. YES I COULD.
PIG!!
HEY ANYONE ELSE HEAR THAT? SOME KINDA...
K-K-K-K-K!!
...CRACKING..
CHUFFS
C-R-A-A-A-A-C-K-!!
BERRRK.
UH?
DID WE NOT CLEAN THAT BATH OUT AFTER ISSUE 3?
LOOSHKIN!!
SPLOOOOSH!!
EWW. IS THIS... GUTS?
SPLUT!
HELLO.
AUGH!! WE'LL CATCH DISEASES!!
WHIZZZZZZ
EWWW!! EWW!!
MY FACE!
SPLUT!
SPLUT!
VMMMMMM
WUB WUB WUB WUB.
OOP.
UH OH.
LOOSHKIN, YOU'VE GOT PIG GUTS IN THE HOVERPACK MECHANISM!! IT'S SPARKLING!!
IT IS? IS IT PRETTY?

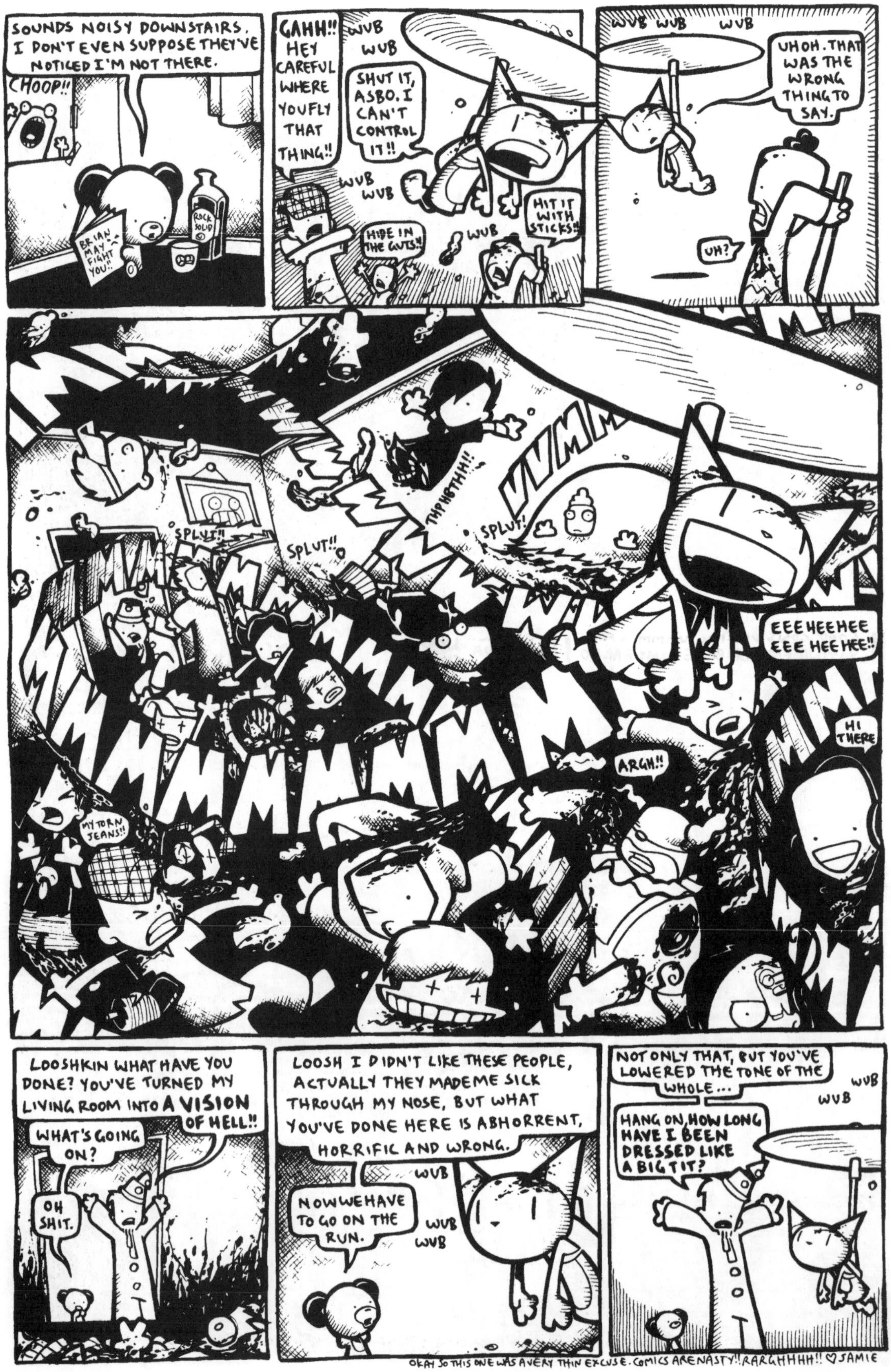
SOUNDS NOISY DOWNSTAIRS. I DON'T EVEN SUPPOSE THEY'VE NOTICED I'M NOT THERE.
CHOOP!!
BRIAN MAY FIGHT YOU!!
ROCK SOLID
GAHH!! HEY CAREFUL WHERE YOU FLY THAT THING!!
WUB WUB
SHUT IT, ASBO. I CAN'T CONTROL IT!!
WUB WUB
HIDE IN THE GUTS!!
WUB
HIT IT WITH STICKS!!
WUB WUB WUB
UH OH. THAT WAS THE WRONG THING TO SAY.
UH?
SPLUT!!
SPLUT!!
THPHBTHH!!
SPLUT!!
VVMMMMMMMMMMMMMMMMMMMMMMMMMMMMMMMMMMMM
EEE HEE HEE EEE HEE HEE!!
HI THERE
ARGH!!
MY TORN JEANS!!
LOOSHKIN WHAT HAVE YOU DONE? YOU'VE TURNED MY LIVING ROOM INTO A VISION OF HELL!!
WHAT'S GOING ON?
OH SHIT.
LOOSH I DIDN'T LIKE THESE PEOPLE, ACTUALLY THEY MADE ME SICK THROUGH MY NOSE, BUT WHAT YOU'VE DONE HERE IS ABHORRENT, HORRIFIC AND WRONG.
WUB
NOW WE HAVE TO GO ON THE RUN.
WUB WUB
NOT ONLY THAT, BUT YOU'VE LOWERED THE TONE OF THE WHOLE...
WUB WUB
HANG ON, HOW LONG HAVE I BEEN DRESSED LIKE A BIG TIT?

OKAY SO THIS ONE WAS A VERY THIN EXCUSE. COMICS ARE NASTY!! RARGHHHH!! ♡ JAMIE

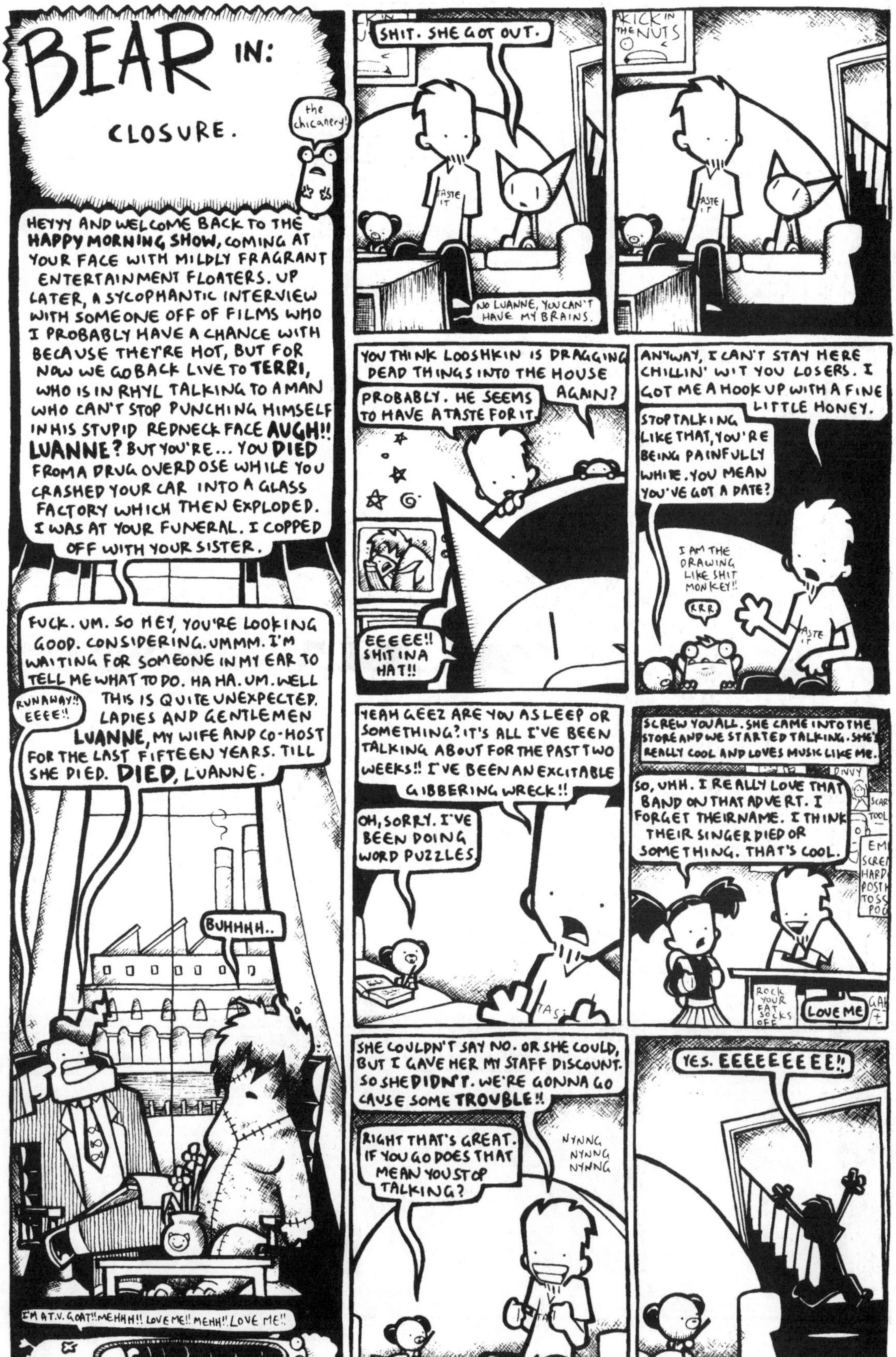
BEAR IN:
CLOSURE.
the chicanery!
HEYYY AND WELCOME BACK TO THE HAPPY MORNING SHOW, COMING AT YOUR FACE WITH MILDLY FRAGRANT ENTERTAINMENT FLOATERS. UP LATER, A SYCOPHANTIC INTERVIEW WITH SOMEONE OFF OF FILMS WHO I PROBABLY HAVE A CHANCE WITH BECAUSE THEY'RE HOT, BUT FOR NOW WE GO BACK LIVE TO TERRI, WHO IS IN RHYL TALKING TO A MAN WHO CAN'T STOP PUNCHING HIMSELF IN HIS STUPID REDNECK FACE AUGH!! LUANNE? BUT YOU'RE... YOU DIED FROM A DRUG OVERDOSE WHILE YOU CRASHED YOUR CAR INTO A GLASS FACTORY WHICH THEN EXPLODED. I WAS AT YOUR FUNERAL. I COPPED OFF WITH YOUR SISTER.
FUCK. UM. SO HEY, YOU'RE LOOKING GOOD. CONSIDERING. UMMM. I'M WAITING FOR SOMEONE IN MY EAR TO TELL ME WHAT TO DO. HA HA. UM. WELL THIS IS QUITE UNEXPECTED. LADIES AND GENTLEMEN LUANNE, MY WIFE AND CO-HOST FOR THE LAST FIFTEEN YEARS. TILL SHE DIED. DIED, LUANNE.
RUNAWAY!! EEEE!!
BUHHHH..
I'M A T.V. GOAT!! MEHHH!! LOVE ME!! MEHH!! LOVE ME!!
SHIT. SHE GOT OUT.
TASTE IT
NO LUANNE, YOU CAN'T HAVE MY BRAINS.
KICK IN THE NUTS
YOU THINK LOOSHKIN IS DRAGGING DEAD THINGS INTO THE HOUSE AGAIN?
PROBABLY. HE SEEMS TO HAVE A TASTE FOR IT.
EEEEE!! SHIT IN A HAT!!
ANYWAY, I CAN'T STAY HERE CHILLIN' WIT YOU LOSERS. I GOT ME A HOOK UP WITH A FINE LITTLE HONEY.
STOP TALKING LIKE THAT, YOU'RE BEING PAINFULLY WHITE. YOU MEAN YOU'VE GOT A DATE?
I AM THE DRAWING LIKE SHIT MONKEY!!
RRR
YEAH GEEZ ARE YOU ASLEEP OR SOMETHING? IT'S ALL I'VE BEEN TALKING ABOUT FOR THE PAST TWO WEEKS!! I'VE BEEN AN EXCITABLE GIBBERING WRECK!!
OH, SORRY. I'VE BEEN DOING WORD PUZZLES.
SCREW YOU ALL. SHE CAME INTO THE STORE AND WE STARTED TALKING. SHE'S REALLY COOL AND LOVES MUSIC LIKE ME.
SO, UHH. I REALLY LOVE THAT BAND ON THAT ADVERT. I FORGET THEIR NAME. I THINK THEIR SINGER DIED OR SOMETHING. THAT'S COOL.
ROCK YOUR FAT SOCKS OFF
LOVE ME
SHE COULDN'T SAY NO. OR SHE COULD, BUT I GAVE HER MY STAFF DISCOUNT. SO SHE DIDN'T. WE'RE GONNA GO CAUSE SOME TROUBLE!!
RIGHT THAT'S GREAT. IF YOU GO DOES THAT MEAN YOU STOP TALKING?
NYNNG NYNNG NYNNG
YES. EEEEEEEEE!!

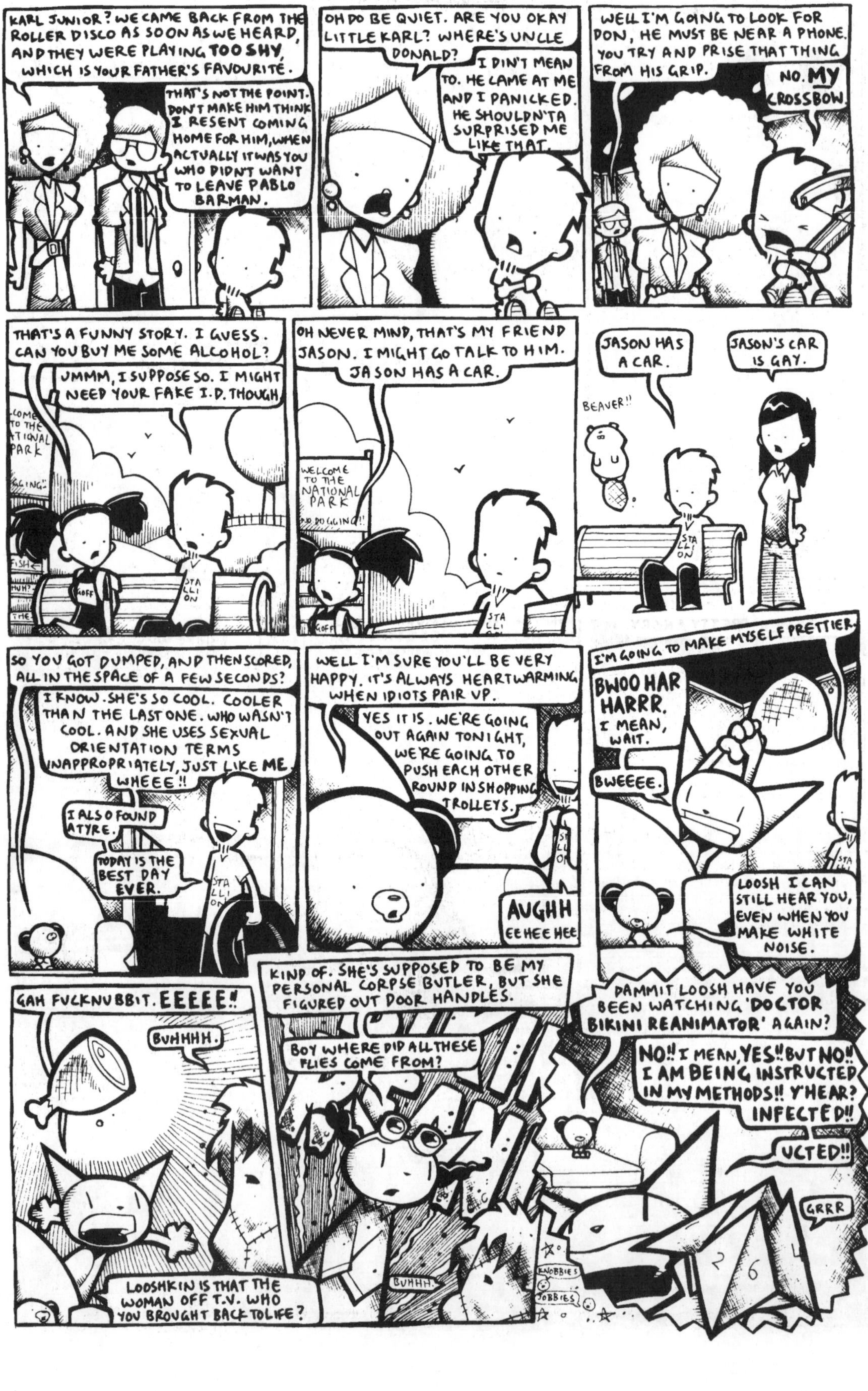
KARL JUNIOR? WE CAME BACK FROM THE ROLLER DISCO AS SOON AS WE HEARD, AND THEY WERE PLAYING TOO SHY, WHICH IS YOUR FATHER'S FAVOURITE.
THAT'S NOT THE POINT. DON'T MAKE HIM THINK I RESENT COMING HOME FOR HIM, WHEN ACTUALLY IT WAS YOU WHO DIDN'T WANT TO LEAVE PABLO BARMAN.
OH DO BE QUIET. ARE YOU OKAY LITTLE KARL? WHERE'S UNCLE DONALD?
I DIN'T MEAN TO. HE CAME AT ME AND I PANICKED. HE SHOULDN'TA SURPRISED ME LIKE THAT.
WELL I'M GOING TO LOOK FOR DON, HE MUST BE NEAR A PHONE. YOU TRY AND PRISE THAT THING FROM HIS GRIP.
NO. MY CROSSBOW.
THAT'S A FUNNY STORY. I GUESS. CAN YOU BUY ME SOME ALCOHOL?
UMMM, I SUPPOSE SO. I MIGHT NEED YOUR FAKE I.D. THOUGH.
GOFF
STALLION
OH NEVER MIND, THAT'S MY FRIEND JASON. I MIGHT GO TALK TO HIM. JASON HAS A CAR.
WELCOME TO THE NATIONAL PARK
NO DOGGING!!
JASON HAS A CAR.
JASON'S CAR IS GAY.
BEAVER!!
SO YOU GOT DUMPED, AND THEN SCORED, ALL IN THE SPACE OF A FEW SECONDS?
I KNOW. SHE'S SO COOL. COOLER THAN THE LAST ONE. WHO WASN'T COOL. AND SHE USES SEXUAL ORIENTATION TERMS INAPPROPRIATELY, JUST LIKE ME. WHEEE!!
I ALSO FOUND A TYRE.
TODAY IS THE BEST DAY EVER.
WELL I'M SURE YOU'LL BE VERY HAPPY. IT'S ALWAYS HEARTWARMING WHEN IDIOTS PAIR UP.
YES IT IS. WE'RE GOING OUT AGAIN TONIGHT, WE'RE GOING TO PUSH EACH OTHER ROUND IN SHOPPING TROLLEYS.
AUGHH
EEHEEHEE
I'M GOING TO MAKE MYSELF PRETTIER.
BWOO HAR HARRR. I MEAN, WAIT.
BWEEEE.
LOOSH I CAN STILL HEAR YOU, EVEN WHEN YOU MAKE WHITE NOISE.
GAH FUCKNUBBIT. EEEEE!!
BUHHHH.
LOOSHKIN IS THAT THE WOMAN OFF T.V. WHO YOU BROUGHT BACK TO LIFE?
KIND OF. SHE'S SUPPOSED TO BE MY PERSONAL CORPSE BUTLER, BUT SHE FIGURED OUT DOOR HANDLES.
BOY WHERE DID ALL THESE FLIES COME FROM?
BUHHH.
DAMMIT LOOSH HAVE YOU BEEN WATCHING 'DOCTOR BIKINI REANIMATOR' AGAIN?
NO!! I MEAN, YES!! BUT NO!! I AM BEING INSTRUCTED IN MY METHODS!! Y'HEAR? INFECTED!!
UCTED!!
GRRR
KNOBBIES
JOBBIES
26

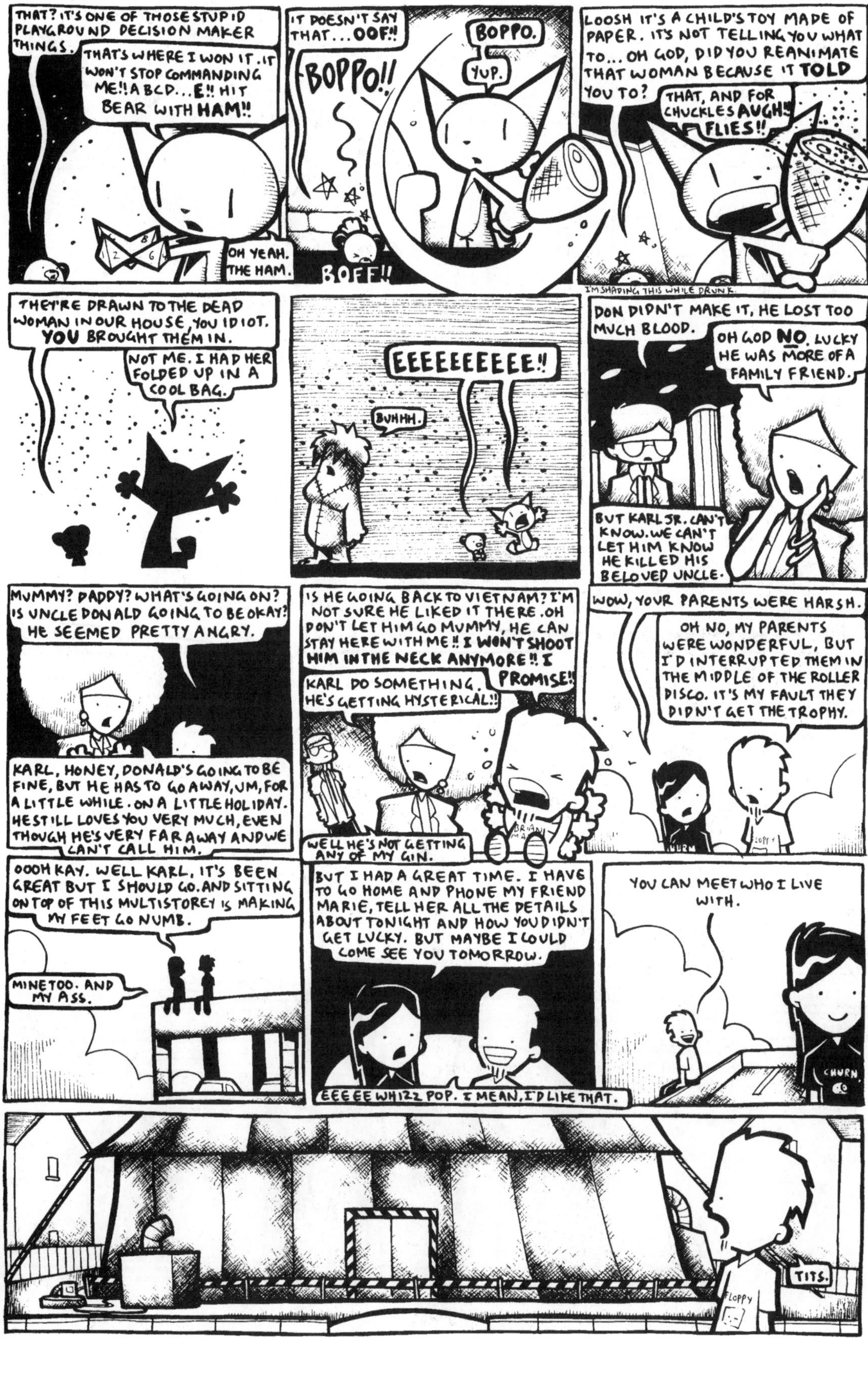

THAT? IT'S ONE OF THOSE STUPID PLAYGROUND DECISION MAKER THINGS.
THAT'S WHERE I WON IT. IT WON'T STOP COMMANDING ME!! A B C D... E!! HIT BEAR WITH HAM!!
OH YEAH. THE HAM.
IT DOESN'T SAY THAT... OOF!!
BOPPO!!
BOPPO.
YUP.
BOFF!!
LOOSH IT'S A CHILD'S TOY MADE OF PAPER. IT'S NOT TELLING YOU WHAT TO... OH GOD, DID YOU REANIMATE THAT WOMAN BECAUSE IT TOLD YOU TO?
THAT, AND FOR CHUCKLES AUGH!! FLIES!!
I'M SHADING THIS WHILE DRUNK.
THEY'RE DRAWN TO THE DEAD WOMAN IN OUR HOUSE, YOU IDIOT. YOU BROUGHT THEM IN.
NOT ME. I HAD HER FOLDED UP IN A COOL BAG.
EEEEEEEEEE!!
BUHHH.
DON DIDN'T MAKE IT, HE LOST TOO MUCH BLOOD.
OH GOD NO. LUCKY HE WAS MORE OF A FAMILY FRIEND.
BUT KARL JR. CAN'T KNOW. WE CAN'T LET HIM KNOW HE KILLED HIS BELOVED UNCLE.
MUMMY? DADDY? WHAT'S GOING ON? IS UNCLE DONALD GOING TO BE OKAY? HE SEEMED PRETTY ANGRY.
KARL, HONEY, DONALD'S GOING TO BE FINE, BUT HE HAS TO GO AWAY, UM, FOR A LITTLE WHILE. ON A LITTLE HOLIDAY. HE STILL LOVES YOU VERY MUCH, EVEN THOUGH HE'S VERY FAR AWAY AND WE CAN'T CALL HIM.
IS HE GOING BACK TO VIETNAM? I'M NOT SURE HE LIKED IT THERE. OH DON'T LET HIM GO MUMMY, HE CAN STAY HERE WITH ME!! I WON'T SHOOT HIM IN THE NECK ANYMORE!! I PROMISE!!
KARL DO SOMETHING. HE'S GETTING HYSTERICAL!!
WELL HE'S NOT GETTING ANY OF MY GIN.
WOW, YOUR PARENTS WERE HARSH.
OH NO, MY PARENTS WERE WONDERFUL, BUT I'D INTERRUPTED THEM IN THE MIDDLE OF THE ROLLER DISCO. IT'S MY FAULT THEY DIDN'T GET THE TROPHY.
OOOH KAY. WELL KARL, IT'S BEEN GREAT BUT I SHOULD GO. AND SITTING ON TOP OF THIS MULTISTOREY IS MAKING MY FEET GO NUMB.
MINE TOO. AND MY ASS.
BUT I HAD A GREAT TIME. I HAVE TO GO HOME AND PHONE MY FRIEND MARIE, TELL HER ALL THE DETAILS ABOUT TONIGHT AND HOW YOU DIDN'T GET LUCKY. BUT MAYBE I COULD COME SEE YOU TOMORROW.
EEEEE WHIZZ POP. I MEAN, I'D LIKE THAT.
YOU CAN MEET WHO I LIVE WITH.
CHURN
TITS.
FLOPPY

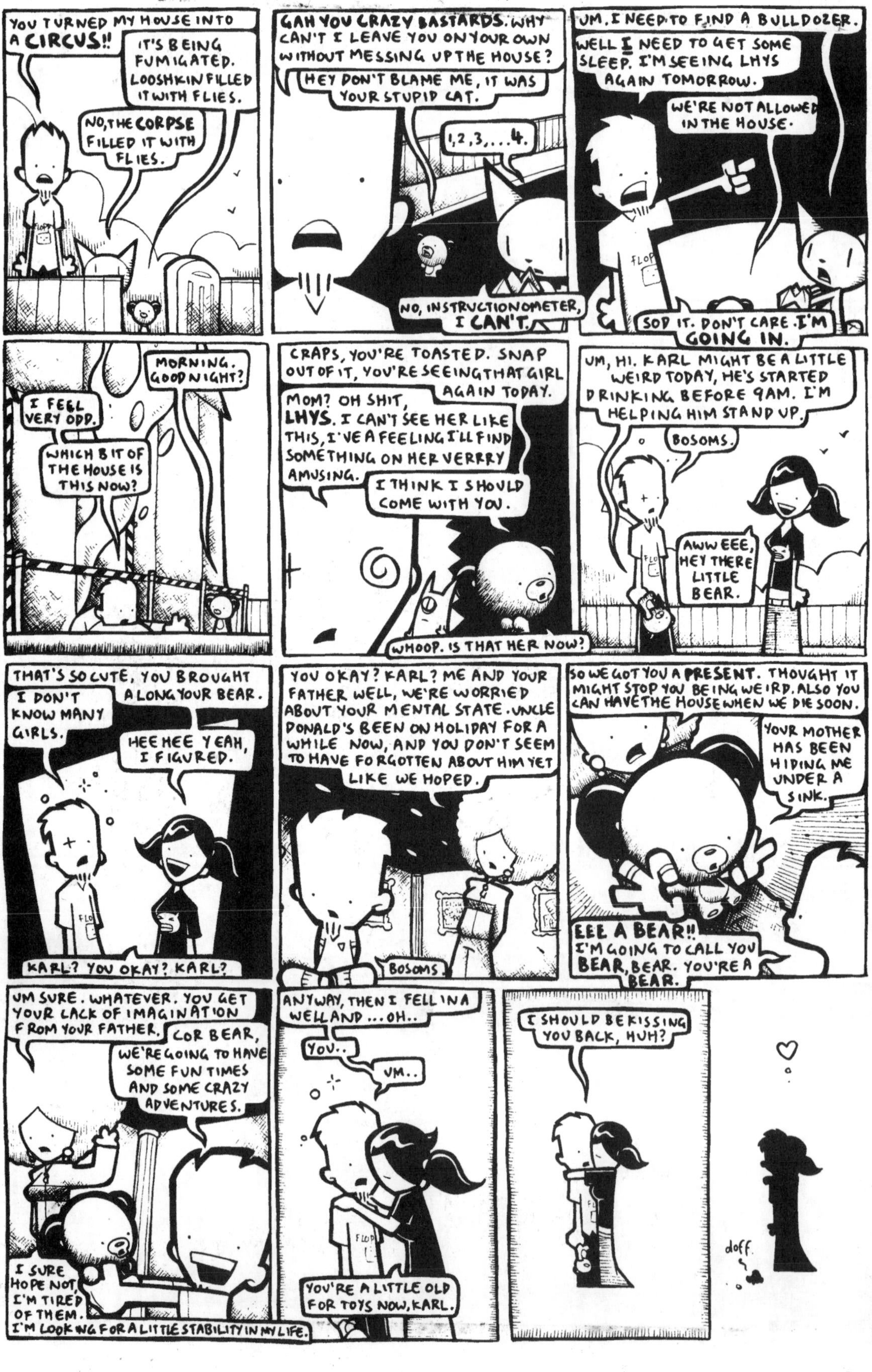
YOU TURNED MY HOUSE INTO A CIRCUS!!
IT'S BEING FUMIGATED. LOOSHKIN FILLED IT WITH FLIES.
NO, THE CORPSE FILLED IT WITH FLIES.
GAH YOU CRAZY BASTARDS. WHY CAN'T I LEAVE YOU ON YOUR OWN WITHOUT MESSING UP THE HOUSE?
HEY DON'T BLAME ME, IT WAS YOUR STUPID CAT.
1,2,3,...4.
NO, INSTRUCTIONOMETER, I CAN'T.
UM. I NEED TO FIND A BULLDOZER.
WELL I NEED TO GET SOME SLEEP. I'M SEEING LHYS AGAIN TOMORROW.
WE'RE NOT ALLOWED IN THE HOUSE.
SOD IT. DON'T CARE. I'M GOING IN.
MORNING. GOOD NIGHT?
I FEEL VERY ODD.
WHICH BIT OF THE HOUSE IS THIS NOW?
CRAPS, YOU'RE TOASTED. SNAP OUT OF IT, YOU'RE SEEING THAT GIRL AGAIN TODAY.
MOM? OH SHIT, LHYS. I CAN'T SEE HER LIKE THIS, I'VE A FEELING I'LL FIND SOMETHING ON HER VERRRY AMUSING.
I THINK I SHOULD COME WITH YOU.
WHOOP. IS THAT HER NOW?
UM, HI. KARL MIGHT BE A LITTLE WEIRD TODAY, HE'S STARTED DRINKING BEFORE 9AM. I'M HELPING HIM STAND UP.
BOSOMS.
AWW EEE, HEY THERE LITTLE BEAR.
THAT'S SO CUTE, YOU BROUGHT ALONG YOUR BEAR.
I DON'T KNOW MANY GIRLS.
HEE HEE YEAH, I FIGURED.
KARL? YOU OKAY? KARL?
YOU OKAY? KARL? ME AND YOUR FATHER WELL, WE'RE WORRIED ABOUT YOUR MENTAL STATE. UNCLE DONALD'S BEEN ON HOLIDAY FOR A WHILE NOW, AND YOU DON'T SEEM TO HAVE FORGOTTEN ABOUT HIM YET LIKE WE HOPED.
BOSOMS.
SO WE GOT YOU A PRESENT. THOUGHT IT MIGHT STOP YOU BEING WEIRD. ALSO YOU CAN HAVE THE HOUSE WHEN WE DIE SOON.
YOUR MOTHER HAS BEEN HIDING ME UNDER A SINK.
EEE A BEAR!! I'M GOING TO CALL YOU BEAR, BEAR. YOU'RE A BEAR.
UM SURE. WHATEVER. YOU GET YOUR LACK OF IMAGINATION FROM YOUR FATHER.
COR BEAR, WE'RE GOING TO HAVE SOME FUN TIMES AND SOME CRAZY ADVENTURES.
I SURE HOPE NOT, I'M TIRED OF THEM. I'M LOOKING FOR A LITTLE STABILITY IN MY LIFE.
ANYWAY, THEN I FELL IN A WELL AND ... OH..
YOU..
UM..
YOU'RE A LITTLE OLD FOR TOYS NOW, KARL.
I SHOULD BE KISSING YOU BACK, HUH?
doff.